Radical Co

Studies in Mathematics Education Series

Series Editor: Paul Ernest, University of Exeter, UK

The Philosophy of Mathematics Education
Paul Ernest

Understanding in Mathematics
Anna Sierpinska

Mathematics Education and Philosophy
Edited by Paul Ernest

Constructing Mathematical Knowledge
Edited by Paul Ernest

Investigating Mathematics Teaching
Barbara Jaworski

Radical Contructivism
Ernst von Glasersfeld

The Sociology of Mathematics Education
Paul Dowling

Counting Girls Out: Girls and Mathematics
Valerie Walkerdine

Writing Mathematically: The Discourse of Investigation
Candia Morgan

Rethinking the Mathematics Curriculum
Edited by Celia Hoyles, Candia Morgan and Geoffrey Woodhouse

International Comparisons in Mathematics Education
Edited by Gabriele Kaiser, Eduardo Luna and Ian Huntley

Mathematics Teacher Education: Critical International Perspectives
Edited by Barbara Jaworski, Terry Wood and A.J. Dawson

Learning Mathematics: From Hierarchies to Networks
Edited by Leone Burton

The Pragmatics of Mathematics Education: Vagueness and Mathematical Discourse
Tim Rowland

Radical Constructivism in Action: Building on the Pioneering Work of Ernst von Glasersfeld
Edited by Leslie P. Steffe and Patrick W. Thompson

Studies in Mathematics Education Series: 15

Radical Constructivism in Action
Building on the Pioneering Work of Ernst von Glasersfeld

edited by

Leslie P. Steffe
and
Patrick W. Thompson

Routledge
Taylor & Francis Group

LONDON AND NEW YORK

First published in 2000 by RoutledgeFalmer

Published 2016 by Routledge
2 Park Square, Milton Park, Abingdon, Oxfordshire OX14 4RN
711 Third Avenue, New York, NY 10017

First issued in paperback 2016

Routledge is an imprint of the Taylor and Francis Group, an informa business

© 2000 Leslie P. Steffe and Patrick W. Thompson

Typeset in 10/12pt Times by Graphicraft Limited, Hong Kong

All rights reserved. No part of this book may be reprinted or reproduced or utilised in any form or by any electronic, mechanical, or other means, now known or hereafter invented, including photocopying and recording, or in any information storage or retrieval system, without permission in writing from the publishers.

British Library Cataloguing in Publication Data
A catalogue record for this book is available from the British Library

Library of Congress Cataloging-in-Publication Data
Radical constructivism in action : building on the pioneering work of Ernst von Glasersfeld / edited by Leslie P. Steffe and Patrick W. Thompson.
    p. cm. — (Studies in mathematics education series)
  Includes bibliographical references and index.
  1. Mathematics—Study and teaching. 2. Mathematics teachers—Training of. 3. Science teachers—Training of. 4. Constructivism (Education) I. Steffe, Leslie P. II. Thompson, Patrick W., 1949– III. Series.

QA11.R33 2000
510'.71—dc21
                                                                         99–055458

ISBN 13: 978-1-138-98447-9 (pbk)
ISBN 13: 978-0-7507-0989-7 (hbk)

Contents

List of Figures		vii
Series Editor's Preface		ix
Preamble Heinz von Foerster		xi
Section One	**Knowledge, Language, and Communication**	1
Chapter 1	Problems of Constructivism Ernst von Glasersfeld	3
Chapter 2	The Topic of Entity as it Relates to Ernst von Glasersfeld's Constructivism Edmond Wright	10
Chapter 3	Ernst von Glasersfeld's Philosophy of Language: Roots, Concepts, Perspectives S.J. Schmidt	23
Section Two	**Construction of the Self, Ethics, and *Paideia***	35
Chapter 4	Constructivism and *Paideia* Philip Lewin	37
Chapter 5	Radical Constructivism: Notes on Viability, Ethics and Other Educational Issues Marie Larochelle	55
Chapter 6	Constraints, *Paideia* and Occasioning: Can Mathematics Teaching be Part of *Paideia*? Thomas E. Kieren	69
Chapter 7	Epistemological Origins of Ethics Hugh Gash	80
Chapter 8	Perspectives on Issues Concerning the Self, *Paideia*, Constraints and Viability, and Ethics Leslie P. Steffe	91
Section Three	**Practice of Mathematics Education**	103
Chapter 9	Students' Constructions: A Necessity for Formalizations in Geometry Jan van den Brink	105

Contents

Chapter 10	Professional Development in Recovery Education Robert J. Wright	134
Chapter 11	Constructivism in Social Context Paul Cobb	152
Chapter 12	Perspectives on Practice in Mathematics Education Leslie P. Steffe	179
Section Four	**Teacher Education in Mathematics and Science**	193
Chapter 13	Science Teacher Preparation: An Attempt at Breaking the Re-Production Cycle of the Traditional Model of Teaching Jacques Désautels	195
Chapter 14	Constructivism, Mathematics Teacher Education, and Research in Mathematics Teacher Development Martin A. Simon	213
Chapter 15	Themes and Issues in Mathematics Teacher Education Robert P. Hunting	231
Chapter 16	Becoming a Teacher-Researcher in a Constructivist Teaching Experiment Despina Potari	248
Chapter 17	Perspectives on Constructivism in Teacher Education Leslie P. Steffe	277
Section Five	**Reflections and Directions**	289
Chapter 18	Radical Constructivism: Reflections and Directions Patrick W. Thompson	291
Notes on Contributors		316
Index		320

List of Figures

Figure 9.1	Mecca-meter at 250	108
Figure 9.2	Havana–Mecca bow	110
Figure 9.3	A world map	111
Figure 9.4	A bunch of circles	112
Figure 9.5	A bunch of circles and a straight line	112
Figure 9.6	Two cross-sections of the earth	113
Figure 9.7	Revolving door with axis AB	114
Figure 9.8	Amsterdam–Atlanta problem	114
Figure 9.9	Three circles on a plastic sphere	115
Figure 9.10	The curve from Havana to Mecca	116
Figure 9.11	Balloon northwards and Amsterdam	124
Figure 9.12	Four drawings	125
Figure 9.13	Central projection	125
Figure 9.14	Line of course and arrow	126
Figure 9.15	Draw the antipoles of points A, B and C	128
Figure 9.16	Construct the centre of the sphere using the antipoles pictured	129
Figure 9.17	Erik's method: M = middle point	129
Figure 9.18	Three lines and two angles	132
Figure 11.1	Aspects of the developmental research cycle	156
Figure 11.2	An interpretive framework for analyzing the classroom microculture perspectives	159
Figure 11.3	Relations between mathematical practices, instructional sequences and social situation of development	171
Figure 11.4	Chain of signification for the sample instructional sequence	173
Figure 13.1	Frequency of positions: relation of theory and observation	201
Figure 13.2	Frequency of positions: relation of classification and nature	202
Figure 14.1	Influence of constructivism on mathematics teacher education	214
Figure 14.2	Mathematics teaching cycle	220
Figure 14.3	Mathematics teaching cycle: expanded	221
Figure 15.1	How would you find the area of this figure?	239
Figure 15.2	Question on an examination in an elementary mathematics methods course	243

vii

List of Figures

Figure 16.1	A staircase of sticks	252
Figure 18.1	A symbolic interactionist view of one moment in human communication	306
Figure 18.2	Joe has $15 more than Fred	310
Figure 18.3	Fred has $15 less than Joe	310

Series Editor's Preface

Mathematics education is established world-wide as a major area of study, with numerous dedicated journals and conferences serving ever-growing national and international communities of scholars. As it develops, research in mathematics education is becoming more theoretically orientated. Although originally rooted in mathematics and psychology, vigorous new perspectives are pervading it from disciplines and fields as diverse as philosophy, logic, sociology, anthropology, history, women's studies, cognitive science, linguistics, semiotics, hermeneutics, post-structuralism and post-modernism. These new research perspectives are providing fresh lenses through which teachers and researchers can view the theory and practice of mathematics teaching and learning.

The series Studies in Mathematics Education aims to encourage the development and dissemination of theoretical perspectives in mathematics education as well as their critical scrutiny. It is a series of research contributions to the field based on disciplined perspectives that link theory with practice. The series is founded on the philosophy that theory is the practitioner's most powerful tool in understanding and changing practice. Whether the practice concerns the teaching and learning of mathematics, teacher education, or educational research, the series offers new perspectives to help clarify issues, pose and solve problems and stimulate debate. It aims to have a major impact on the development of mathematics education as a field of study in the third millennium.

In the past two decades perhaps the most important theoretical perspective to emerge in mathematics education, as well as in several other domains of thought, has been that of constructivism. It features prominently in previous books in this series, most notably in Ernst von Glasersfeld's 1995 masterwork, *Radical Constructivism: A Way of Knowing and Learning.* That work offered two genealogies of knowledge. These veritable genetic epistemologies trace the development of the central ideas of radical constructivism along two tracks. The first is the history of philosophy from the pre-Socratic masters of Ancient Greece to the works of current scholars and masters. The second is Glasersfeld's own intellectual career. In the book Glasersfeld illustrates how a number of lines of thought from cybernetics, linguistics, developmental psychology, cognitive science and philosophy became synthesized into radical constructivism. Working with a number of collaborators, including Leslie P. Steffe, Glasersfeld has steadily developed radical constructivism both in theory and its applications until by now there are literally thousands of constructivist-related publications building on this and parallel perspectives. Even such recent and differently named perspectives as Enactive Theory can be seen as an offshoot of the constructivist insight that all knowing and experiencing are embodied and that all knowledge reflects our physical and social modes of being.

Series Editor's Preface

The present volume, edited by leading constructivist scholars Leslie P. Steffe and Patrick W. Thompson, represents both a celebration of Ernst von Glasersfeld's achievement, and vibrant evidence of the continued vitality of research in the constructivist tradition. The four main sections of the book explore first Glasersfeld's radical constructivism and the epistemological issues and problems it raises, and then associated issues and explorations concerning ethics and the self, educational practices in mathematics, and mathematics and science teacher education. The fifth and last section comprises an extensive and self-critical reflection on the nature, achievements and critics of constructivism by Pat Thompson. However, this represents only the endpoint of a self-reflective strand – very appropriately, given the subject matter – that runs through the book most visibly in the form of Les Steffe's concluding chapters in three of the sections. The individual chapters are written by leading European and North American researchers and include many of the persons best known for extending and developing the constructivist research paradigm. Together, the contributions show constructivism to be a giant presence, with one foot firmly planted in the domain of theory and the other deeply entrenched in practice. Through the work of these scholars we see the epistemological perspective of constructivism debated, contested and clarified, and then applied in a variety of practices and inquiries, perfectly embodying the philosophy of this series.

There is now at least one very extensive website devoted to radical constructivism, currently to be found at <http://www.univie.ac.at/cognition/constructivism/>. This lists six famous masters of constructivism: Heinz von Foerster, Ernst von Glasersfeld, George Kelly, Humberto Maturana, Gordon Pask, and Jakob von Uexküll. Whether or not one agrees with this precise line-up, for example, one could certainly add Jean Piaget, their pre-eminence is undisputed. Therefore it is delightful to note that the first two stars in this pantheon are also the first two contributors to this book.

Paul Ernest
University of Exeter
1999

Preamble

Heinz von Foerster

First of all I would like to express my gratitude to the organizers of this conference for having included me as a participant.[1] I am particularly grateful that you invited me to take part in your professional discussion of various aspects of mathematics and science education, since – at best – I can see myself as an amateur in these matters.

Moreover, I was very happy to have been scheduled as the last speaker at this gathering, for it breaks with a tradition that began a few years ago when I crossed the critical age of four score years, after which organizers now place me as the first speaker because I may not last through their conferences. Apparently, no such fears clouded the perception of the organizers of this festival during which, I can assure you, I enjoyed every moment.

In fact, I feel that this 'Ernst von Glasersfeld Celebration' was the proper anacrusis, the proper *Auftakt*, the proper prelude for a style of thinking that will initiate, and then dominate, the third millennium.

Isn't that an overstatement?

I say: 'No!'

Now, in which way can I justify this contention? I shall try to do this in three ways: I shall talk about disappearance, about essence, and about emergence.

Disappearance

I would like to draw your attention to the current disappearance of certain words and their corresponding concepts from our scientific vocabulary. Of course, this is a process that has been going on for centuries. Who, among today's chemists, would know the meaning of 'phlogiston', a most important agent just a century ago. Or, I venture to say, only historians of science may recall the exact meaning of the notion of 'action at a distance' which, after Faraday, shriveled away to give now the concept of 'field' its prominent position. Or think of the fate of 'ether', the invisible, transparent, and weightless substance that, in the pre-Einstein days, occupied the entire universe. And remember the highly sophisticated apparatus that Michelson and Morley built to determine the movement of spaceship Earth relative to this ubiquitous substance. I can't help thinking of the burghers of Gotham, or of the city of Schilda in Germany, who tried to catch sunlight in bags to carry it into their

Preamble

church, because they forgot to allow for windows. When, after years of experimentation, Michelson and Morley couldn't detect any signs of a movement against the ether, they were finally told by Einstein that there is no such thing.

I can easily imagine a youngster asking his father: 'Daddy, what is an ether?' and, following Gregory Bateson (1972) in one of his Metalogs (1), getting the answer: 'An explanatory principle'. And when further asked: 'What does it explain'?, being told: 'Anything, almost anything at all, anything you want it to explain'.

Today, however, it is not 'phlogiston', 'action at a distance', or 'ether' that are disappearing from our scientific vocabulary. They are already gone. I say, what is evaporating today is the triplet of the mutually supporting concepts of 'ontology', 'reality', and 'truth'. 'Ontology' is, as you may remember, the study of 'how things are'. It would not have been invented without a belief in 'reality'; and if one believes in 'reality', one may pretend to know 'how things are', that is, one knows the 'truth'.

It is usually said that 'truth versus error' is the origin of comedy. In a conciliatory mood I think of truth as the invention of a liar, because without him, truth need not appear at all. But it is also said that 'truth versus thruth' is the origin of tragedy. Thus, in a more critical mood, I think of 'truth' as the invention of the Devil, because of all those myriads who were tortured, maimed and killed in its name.

What fascinated me especially at our celebration here is that during these two days this fateful triplet was surgically removed from our language without protest and without pain, but instead was politely and decisively marched out through these doors.

I can now easily imagine a youngster asking his father: 'Daddy, what is reality'? and now going through the same question and answer cycle as before: 'An explanatory principle' etc., etc.!

Essence

I shall now bring my second argument in favor of my contention that in our gathering here a style of thinking was prevalent that transformed such meetings' usual concern with peripherals into an undivided attention to essentials.

I have chosen two famous conferences in the past as examples for my argument, because the participants in both of these conferences represented perhaps the leading minds on the topics under consideration, where the topics themselves were probably the most urgent and profound problems at that time.

(i) New York, 1956

The first example comes from the research publications of the Association for Research in Nervous and Mental Disease reporting on a conference in 1956

Preamble

entitled 'The Brain and Human Behavior'. Among the about two dozen participants you find Jerome Bruner, Ward Halstaed, Karl Lashley, Wilder Penfield and other trailblazers in neurology. Now listen to the preamble for the program of this conference:

> Our subject 'The brain and human behavior' is an intriguing one, the limits of which are not readily discerned. Philosophers, logicians, psychologists, biochemists and theologians have given their best thoughts to one aspect of the subject, namely the relation of brain and mind.

So far so good. Particularly the observation that a wide spectrum of scholars has *'given their best thoughts'* to 'the relation of brain and mind'. It then goes on to say:

> It seemed to the Program committee that this area could well be omitted from the discussion.

'What'?! I thought when I first read this, 'the *best* thoughts [of these scholars] could *well* be omitted'?? There must be a mistake. I couldn't imagine such a severe case of phobosophy. But a few lines below you find a gleeful reiteration of the previous position: 'Philosophic and psychodynamic considerations were omitted.'

I invite you to project the discussions, considerations and reflections of our two days of meeting here against that background, and you will sense what I was trying to show. Here our concerns were learning and teaching in their broadest sense, whether *'paideia'*, 'neural networks', 'the culture of the mathematics classroom', 'ethics', 'philosophy of language', or other philosophical and psychodynamic notions. Not only were they *not* omitted, they were central to our discussions in which words like 'soul', 'entity', etc. – unthinkable then – proved their generative and creative power.

    (ii)   Abbey de Royaumont, 1975

This breathtaking conference complex to the north of Paris was the location for a formidable conference, organized by brilliant young philosopher Massimo Piattelli-Palmarini, who succeeded in getting Jean Piaget and Noam Chomsky together for a debate on 'Language and Learning'.

Supporting cast for this event were the international *crème da la crème* of philosophical and scientific thinkers like Gregory Bateson, Jerry Fodor, Barbel Inhelder, Jacques Monod, Stephen Toulmin, to name only a few of the twenty-five participants. Clearly, a unique opportunity was given for these giants to open the door to a profound understanding of language and learning. In an impressive publishing venture Piattelli-Palmarini managed to give us a superb report of that meeting.

Preamble

For me, one of the most fascinating results was that although the words language and learning were in the title of that meeting, they were not used to open any door for understanding language or learning.

Why? Because, I think, some of the brilliant speakers were poor listeners. Some, I feel, even refused to listen to somebody else's story. Could arrogance be behind this?

In contrast, for me one of the most fascinating results of our meeting here was the visible joy of all of us listening to each other's stories, thus keeping the dialogue going around and around and around. This was topped by the delightful play on Vygotskiism which, to my ears, transformed itself into a musical!

And then the other joy for me was the fact that ethics were ever present in our dialogue, implicit at all times.

Emergence

I wondered what made our gathering so different from the others I have just mentioned. Why is it that our presentations took on the form of presents, and the mood was not so much that of argumentation as of celebration? My sense is that it has to do with properties of the man we had come together to celebrate. A metaphor, by now perhaps 2,400 years old and told by Chuang Tsu, the master of Tao, may help to tell what I sense.

> The instrument maker Ching created a bell-stand so extraordinarily beautiful that he could not think of selling it to anyone, but only to present it to the emperor. After a journey of a week he reached the emperor's palace, and when he approached the gate, carrying his bell-stand in front of him, the guards, overwhelmed by its beauty, stepped aside and let him pass. And so did the ministers of the empire and then the bodyguards of the emperor when he arrived at the ultimate chamber.
>
> The emperor took the bell-stand, stood up and asked: 'How could you ever create such a wonderful piece of woodwork?' and Ching answered: 'There was nothing to it. I just went into the woods and found it.' 'This cannot be the whole story,' the emperor replied, 'tell me more!'
>
> 'When I began thinking of this bell-stand, I started to collect, so to say, the fibers of my strength and the calmness of my mind. After a week I had forgotten whatever I could earn by selling it, and after two weeks about the fame that would accrue to me. A month went by and I forgot about my family and after two months I forgot even you, my emperor. When I was in this state of mind, I walked into the woods and here in one of the trees was the bell-stand. I carefully removed it from the tree and I knew I had to bring it to you.'

When I think of the instrument maker Ching, Ernst von Glasersfeld comes to my mind.

Note

1   Papers from the International Symposium on Radical Constructivism held in honor of the work of Ernst von Glasersfeld form the core of this volume.

References

BATESON, G. (1972) 'What is an instinct'? in BATESON, G., *Steps to an Ecology of Mind*, New York: Ballantine, pp. 38–58.
PIATTELLI-PALMARINI, M. (ed.) (1980) *On Language and Learning: The Debate Between Jean Piaget and Noam Chomsky*, Cambridge, Mass.: Harvard University Press.
SOLOMON, H. (ed.) (1956) *The Brain and Human Behavior*, Baltimore, Md: Williams & Williams.

Section One
Knowledge, Language, and Communication

1 Problems of Constructivism

Ernst von Glasersfeld

I want to express my profound gratitude to those who organized the Atlanta conference and to all who agreed to contribute to it. As you know, constructivism is a subject that has occupied my thinking over the years and, as you requested it, I shall comment on some problems I see with it. Before I do this, let me remind you how it all came about.

Radical constructivism arose from a variety of disorderly readings. It was an attempt to fit into a coherent model a number of ideas about knowing that had been disregarded by the philosophical mainstream. This effort would not have been successful had it not been for my early acquaintance with the work of Silvio Ceccato and a subsequent decade of assimilating parts of Jean Piaget's inexhaustible heritage.

I never thought that constructing such a model would amount to anything but a private quest. I and my research team were originally brought to the United States to continue the line of work in computational linguistics that we had started in Italy. When the funds for the project dried up, I had the good fortune to be offered a position as psycholinguist in the Department of Psychology at the University of Georgia. Epistemology was of marginal interest in that discipline. Whatever reputation I gained there was due to the adeptness with which the chimpanzee Lana used the language I designed for the communication study at the Yerkes Center. Only in the mid-1970s, when I began to work with Les Steffe on children's conception of number, was I drawn into a domain where my kind of conceptual analysis found some resonance.

This conference, therefore, is a most welcome occasion for me to acknowledge my debt to Les Steffe, John Richards, Paul Cobb and Pat Thompson. None of us will forget the intensity of our discussions and the pleasure of forging the agreements that provided the launching pad for the constructivist model in the field of mathematics education. Today, it is immensely gratifying to see that the model has been taken up by so many vigorous, independent thinkers who seem to have found it useful.

The papers collected in this volume show a remarkable consensus on some very basic ideas. Even more interesting, however, they also show a variety of individual perspectives. This is exactly how it should be. Radical constructivism is not a dogma, but a tool that anyone can use as he or she chooses. Above all, it is by no means a finished product. Much remains to be done to enhance its usefulness and to enlarge the range of its applications.

Ernst von Glasersfeld

To my mind, there are at present two aspects that need to be developed further. One of them is to find new ways of expressing the fundamental instrumentalist idea in order to make it less prone to metaphysical misinterpretation. The other is to achieve a far more detailed analysis of the complex area covered by the generic term 'social interaction'.

Forestalling Misinterpretation

Given the vast literature in which Piaget's *genetic epistemology* has been trivialized in order to fit it into the framework of traditional theories of knowledge, it is difficult to convey the fact that I have not called the constructivist position *radical* for political reasons, but because it requires a drastic modification of the concepts of cognition and its products. Although Piaget said dozens of times that, in his theory, 'to know' does not mean to construct a picture of the real world, most of his interpreters still cling to the notion that our knowledge must correspond to a world thought to be independent of the knower. This attachment is not surprising. The quest for a 'true' representation has been an essential feature of the tradition that has dominated Western philosophy for two and a half millennia. The sceptics, of course, forever reiterated irrefutable logical arguments against this realist conviction, but they did not succeed in shaking it, because they failed to come up with a plausible substitute for the concept of knowing.

Radical constructivism does suggest such a substitute. It holds that knowledge is under all circumstances constructed by individual thinkers as an adaptation to their subjective experience. This is its working hypothesis and from it follows that for a constructivist there cannot be anything like a dogmatic body of unquestionable knowledge. The task is to show *that* and *how* what is called knowledge can be built up by individual knowers within the sensory and conceptual domain of individual experience and without reference to ontology. What matters in the end is that the constructs actually work and do not involve contradictions. Radical constructivism, therefore, cannot be a metaphysical system, nor can it claim to be 'true'. Indeed, radical constructivists never say: 'This is how it is!' They merely suggest: 'This may be how it functions.'

Alexander Bogdanov, a remarkable forerunner of both cybernetics and constructivism, provided an excellent metaphor in his dialogues on the philosophy of science:

A. *If a tool you are successfully using to work on certain materials turns out to be useless with others, would you throw it away?*
B. *No, I would not throw it away as long as I don't have a better one. (Bogdanov, 1909, p. 26)*

A crucial aspect of this metaphor is that there are two ways for one tool to be better than another. It can be more successful in its use on a given set of materials, or it may be useful with a wider range of materials. In both senses a new tool may supersede the old one, but whether it does or does not depends on a variety of practical and social circumstances.

When this instrumentalist principle is applied to cognition, realists still insist that 'better' should be interpreted as 'closer to the truth'. They refuse to concede that knowledge can be considered as a *mere* tool in the knower's struggle towards equilibration, because they are unwilling to relinquish the notion that it must somehow reflect the structure of reality. What they choose to believe is of course their affair. But trouble arises when they criticize the constructivist position and ignore the fact that 'knowledge' in this context does not have the same representational connotation which they attribute to it in their own realist epistemology.

This stubborn refusal to consider an explicitly stated constructivist definition of knowledge (because it differs from the traditional one) is often reinforced by the spurious assumption that when constructivists speak of experience they intend nothing but sensory experience (e.g. Matthews, 1992). This, too, is an odd interpretation if one considers the great weight Piaget has always given to *reflective abstraction.* It can also be illustrated by the work of Steffe's group on the concept of number. The major emphasis in these writings is on mental operations that generate conceptual structures which are thoroughly abstract in the sense that they do not contain sensory elements.

Insofar as these misunderstandings are honest, they seem to be caused by conceptual blinders the traditional epistemology has placed on the readers. As with panicky horses, the blinders shut out perturbing sights and insights. Nevertheless, I have not given up the hope that one of us will one day find a way of making the basic points of constructivism so clear that even inveterate realist critics will not be able to misconstrue them.

Phil Lewin, in his contribution to this volume, brings up a related question. Characterizing my point of view, he says that constructivism concerns nothing but *knowing* and therefore is in no position to grant what he calls a 'permission to be'. To me, this seems the proper interpretation. Lewin goes on to explain that he agrees when constructivism insists on distinguishing experiential reality from an *ontological* one, about which it can have nothing to say. But he would nevertheless like an experiential space that provides some room for *being.* 'If that being is not ontological, so be it,' he says. 'If it is only existential . . . it is still being nonetheless.'

I think I understand what he intends. It is an important suggestion. But I would want to formulate it differently – and this presents a difficulty I am not sure how to overcome. As agents (authors) of our own experiential reality we attribute continuity to ourselves as its constructors. We cannot do otherwise, because the world we come to know is based on the creation of regularities which we are able to impose on the flux of experience. Regularities require repetition. An active entity that conserves itself must segment its experience, compare chunks, and institute lasting individual identities. However, from my constructivist perspective, it is this very agent who constructs the notions of space and time, and I am therefore reluctant to refer to the agent's continuity as 'existence'. The words 'to be' and 'to exist' are far too firmly linked to the philosophers' traditional ontology in which they are intended to describe a world that *is* and *exists* in itself. The continuity I have in mind, in contrast, is a phenomenological construct of the experiencer and, as such, warrants no conclusions about an ontological reality.

In another context (Glasersfeld, 1979, 1993) I have tried to use the notion of experiential sequence as an elementary building block of the concepts of space and time.[1] In the same vein, I would now avoid 'existence' and speak of *continuity* as the factor that situates the knower in his or her experiential world. Given this change in the formulation, I fully agree that this continuity 'carries ethical commitments with it' and that I have so far failed to produce a model of how these commitments might arise. Such a model is one of the things that need to be worked out; but as far as I am concerned, its construction cannot be guided by Heidegger's metaphor of 'thrownness'. This metaphorical term inevitably suggests a pre-existing ready-made world, a given structure *into* which all knowers are thrown. From my point of view, the generation of ethics will have to be part of the model we design to grasp our interactions with the experiential constructs we call 'others'.

The Social Element

The present interest among educational researchers and philosophically inclined psychologists in social interaction and its role in the process of learning need not pit them against radical constructivism. This topic certainly requires investigation and its investigation should not be hampered by the unwarranted fabrication that there is a conceptual contradiction between the principle of subjective cognitive construction and the experiential reality of the phenomena that are called social. Constructivism, as has been amply explained, is a theory of knowing that attempts to show that knowledge can and can only be generated from experience. If social constructionists take for granted (explicitly or tacitly) that 'society', i.e. the others in our experiential world, are a ready-made ontological given, existing as such and independently of subjective experience, they are making a metaphysical assumption. Though I see no need to make such an assumption, I feel that everyone is free to invent his or her own metaphysics. However, as far as a theory of knowing is concerned, I consider metaphysical assumptions vacuous as long as they do not specify a functional model of how ontology might determine the experiences from which we generate our knowledge. To say that something exists does not explain how we come to know it.

Alfred Schütz, one of the deepest thinkers in modern sociology, was quite clear about the fact that the basic problem of how we come to *know* of others is an epistemological problem that would have to be investigated by psychologists (cf. Schütz, 1932). Unfortunately, Piaget's work in that area is all but unknown in the English-speaking world. My own access to it has been very recent, through the Italian edition which the translator sent me (Piaget, 1989). Let me translate a few passages that seem very appropriate to the question of education:

> What has not been acquired through experience and personal reflection can only be superficially assimilated and does not modify any way of thinking. The child acculturates itself in spite of adult authority and not because of such an authority. (Piaget, 1989, p. 252)

> [A]lso on the elementary school level the child assimilates only those concepts that correspond to the operatory structures of which he has already acquired mastery, while he remains indifferent to those for which he can find no connections to his 'spontaneous' structures.[2] (ibid., p. 346)

In his discussion of children's socialization, Piaget uses many examples taken from a school setting. He did this, I imagine, because it is easier there to distinguish the two mechanisms he considers primary in social adaptation. One of them he sees in the imitation of certain physical actions or behaviors (which may include speech acts) owing to *coercion*; the other, he specifies as the generation of mutually compatible actions and mental operations as a result of reflection and understanding which take place in the context of *cooperation*. The distinction is a parallel to the one I have been making in the educational context between training and teaching.[3]

Earlier in the book, Piaget applied this distinction to the process of linguistic interaction. He begins by asking how a statement uttered by one person could be agreed to by another:

> How could such a convergence be established? The two subjects necessarily have different, non-interchangeable perceptions: they exchange ideas, that is to say, judgments concerning perceptions but never the perceptions themselves! (ibid., p. 189)

He comes to the conclusion that *meanings* are a matter of 'private symbolism' and agreement cannot manifest itself except through reactions due to mutually compatible mental operations. This is obviously not the place to present Piaget's detailed model of the child's construction of linguistic meanings in the course of interaction with others. However, the passages I have quoted may suffice to show how far ahead he was in the years between 1941 and 1950, when he wrote these essays. He even dealt with the claim, revived today by certain social constructionists, that knowledge and language do not reside in individuals but are preformed in society:

> The preformation [of social characteristics] is, as in other contexts, nothing but a commonsense illusion consolidated by the Aristotelian philosophy of potentiality and action. (ibid., p. 340)

Ernst von Glasersfeld

The fact that much of the contemporary literature on social interaction targets radical constructivism as an inimical orientation, however, does raise a problem. Since its authors are neither illiterate nor foolish, there must be something lacking in the way we present our ideas. I am not sure what exactly it is, but one particular problem comes to mind. Piaget sometimes mentioned the danger of confusing an observer's view of an organism in its observed environment and observer's inferences about the view the organism generates within the domain of its own experience. In his own writings, Piaget did not always make this distinction clear, and I think that we ourselves quite often do not pay enough attention to it.

Especially in discussing education, we tend to focus on the child or the student as we see them, and we may not stress often enough that what we are talking about is but *our* construction of the child, and that this construction is made on the basis of our own experience and colored by our goals and expectations. This is compounded by the fact that we have not yet come up with a sufficiently detailed model of how children may come to *socially interact* with other autonomous entities they have constructed in their experiential world.

My two suggestions can be summed up as follows: the radical constructivist agenda should include an effort to develop viable theoretical models in the areas of ethics and social interaction; and when we describe our constructivist orientation, we should take even more care to stress and repeat that we are constructing a model that should be tested in practice, not another metaphysical system to explain what the ontological world might be like.

Notes

1 This was suggested by Berkeley in the notebook he wrote when, at the beginning of the eighteenth century, he was a student at Trinity College in Dublin.
2 As Piaget wrote these essays between 1928 and 1963, he should not be blamed for using the masculine pronoun generically. (An English translation of his sociological essays is available.)
3 The coercion, of course, may be subtle and diffuse, as for example in the case of children's acquisition of the standard number word sequence as an empty verbal routine.

References

BOGDANOV, A.A. (alias N. Verner) (1909) 'Science and philosophy', in *Abhandlungen zur Philosophie des Kollektivismus*, pp. 9–33, S. Petersburg. (German tr. I. Maschke-Luschberger, in GLASERSFELD, E. VON, *Grenzen des Begreifens*, Bern: Benteli, 1996.)
GLASERSFELD, E. VON (1979) 'Cybernetics, experience, and the concept of self', in OZER, M.N. (ed.), *A Cybernetic Approach to the Assessment of Children: Toward a More Humane Use of Human Beings*, Boulder, Col.: Westview Press, pp. 67–113.

GLASERSFELD, E. VON (1993) 'Notes on the concept of change', in MONTANGERO, J., CORNU-WELLS, A., TRYPHON, A. and VONÈCHE, J. (eds), *Conceptions of Change Over Time*, Geneva: Foundation Archives Jean Piaget, pp. 91–6.
MATTHEWS, M.R. (1992) 'Constructivism and the empiricist legacy', in PEARSALL, M.K. (ed.), *Scope, Sequence, and Coordination of Secondary School Science*, Washington, DC: The National Science Teachers Association, pp. 183–96.
PIAGET, J. (1989) *Studi Sociologici* ('Sociological studies', tr. and ed. P. Barbetta and W. Fornasa), Milan: Franco Angeli.
SCHUTZ, A. (1932) *Der Sinnhafte Aufbau der Sozialen Welt* ('The meaningful construction of the social world'), Frankfurt: Suhrkamp paperback, 1974.

2 The Topic of Entity as it Relates to Ernst von Glasersfeld's Constructivism

Edmond Wright

It is not possible within the scope of this chapter to mount a full-scale philosophical defence of radical constructivism. What is possible is an attack from the radical constructivist point of view using a weapon readily adaptable to a wide range of opponents. But these terms of defence and attack bespeak a kind of adversarial attitude to scientific discussion which is inappropriate. What we learn from Ernst von Glasersfeld is that human agents work together with viable constructs from their experience until discrepancies appear (Glasersfeld, 1982), until the external source of experience produces constraints that reveal that the motor sequences so far deemed to be advantageous suddenly prove disadvantageous. It is therefore much more a matter of discovery and inquiry that must be set in motion when there are such 'problematic happenings' as Stephen Toulmin (1971, p. 29) calls them, and the solution is more likely to take a dialectical form than that advance that is made through revealing some logical inconsistency in the opponent's case. The very construct of constructivism itself can surely be shown to be viable even though a number of opponents have come to believe that it is vitiated by a hidden idealism and, worse, a theoretically embedded relativism. This is how they read his agreement with Vico that facts are made and not given (Glasersfeld, 1984, p. 27), that between the constructs we have and the external there is no kind of correspondence (ibid., 1982, p. 615), that the regularities upon which our agreements in truth are based can only be assumed and not finally believed (ibid., 1989, p. 438), that ontological reality cannot be straightforwardly assigned to everyday objects – and, worse, in their view, to selves (ibid., 1989, p. 445). An anti-Piagetian such as D.W. Hamlyn (1971) insists that 'Experience itself always involves confrontation with particulars' (p. 21). There is something deeply disturbing to the realist mind in the contemplation of the notion that objectivity might not have the reassuring actuality that one would like it to have, and it arouses deep suspicions of an ingrained relativism, particularly among philosophers, to read someone who boldly sets out to analyse such a fundamental concept, declaring that objects had better be looked upon as 'instrumental hypotheses and tentative models' (Glasersfeld, 1989, p. 447). Furthermore, his belief that it is out of experience that the constructs are made lays his theory open, it is argued, to accusations of subjective idealism and hence of solipsism.

The Topic of Entity

Why should there be this general suspicion? After all, none of us is sure about our identifications. As we go on sorting and re-sorting our world into these *re-cognizable* entities called subjects and objects, including that entity we call the self, we naturally wish to be as secure as we can, since the set of entities we select from the field of experience represents the set of our intentions with regard to that experience – expectations, plans, courses of intended action. Glasersfeld has followed Jean Piaget in stressing the motor aspect of our concepts, for they are bound to the demands of what he calls 'attentional pulses', selections from experience that are driven by pain and pleasure, desire and fear. There is, therefore, a natural fear of the suggestion that we might not have got them right, particularly those blessed by the authority of the best habitual usage. Now the tough-minded want to hold on to two beliefs: first, the central tenet of all realisms, that there is something in virtue of which these vital selections are true; second, that the coincidence of our public meanings is reliable, not to be disturbed by relativist claims of difference between one agent and another. Both of these lead to an attitude which sets itself against scientific inquiry into the evolutionary bases of knowledge. There appears to be a stubborn prejudice against the very notion of knowledge inquiring into its own origin, as if an examination of its genesis would not only threaten established authority but would fatally undermine the very process of knowledge acquisition.

Ernst von Glasersfeld has been exposed to attacks from the tough-minded on precisely these counts. An example of the first would be that of Stephen Wilcox and Stuart Katz (1981), who, conceiving of reality in terms of given Gibsonian invariants, ready-made structures and things, accuse him of being unable to formulate his own theory because it uses as premises the very elements which the theory is supposed to deny, namely, a given world of recognizable entities. They argue that a constructed scheme could never be self-evaluated unless an array of external entities pre-existed the constructed ones. It will be readily seen that this is a version of the Solipsist Objection against the old Sense-Datum theory of perception, and indeed, Wilcox and Katz went on elsewhere to attack the notion of internal sensory fields, producing the same performative paradox as their weapon, that one cannot argue for an internal construction of entities without employing the very notion of external entity to do so. In fact, it was through my being a philosopher of perception who does believe that it is possible to argue without self-contradiction for internal sensory fields that I came to attack Wilcox and Katz (Wright, 1986), discovering thereby that I was allying myself with Ernst von Glasersfeld.

An example of the tough-minded philosopher's second attack, that of claiming that constructivism implies the unreliability of relativism, would be that of Christine Atkinson (1983). Piaget, she says – and hence, we may presume, Glasersfeld – neglects the social aspect of objective knowledge and, consequently, the human communication dependent upon it. She makes appeal, as others do, to Ludwig Wittgenstein, claiming that Wittgenstein established that the notion of a subjective rule makes no sense, that meanings are guaranteed by the 'form of life', the public meaning. To quote Wittgenstein:

> If language is to be a means of communication there must be agreement not only in definitions but also (queer as this may sound) in judgements. (*Philosophical Investigations*, Remark 242)

This is as much as to say that, once a public meaning has been established by normal teaching processes, any subjective aspects drop out of consideration, absorbed into the public understanding of the utterance. Notice the decided assertion: that equivalence in publicly tested objective agreement is the same as equivalence in subjective private judgement once the recognized learning procedures have been observed. The guarantee of objectivity can thus not be a matter of subjective interiorized structures, merely compatible across agents. According to Atkinson, this would leave the way open for 'different realities for different subjects' (1983, p. 196), which she clearly regards as self-evidently ridiculous.

Now to the dialectical shifting of the context. This can be derived from the latest developments in the philosophy of perception (Wright, ed., 1993), refined to a position best called new critical realism, in recognition of the work of Roy Wood Sellars (1969 [1916], 1922, 1932), an American philosopher of the first half of the twentieth century, whose views on perception were remarkably prescient. It also draws on insights from the sociologist Alfred Schutz (1962), and the psycholinguist Ragnar Rommetveit (1968, 1974, 1978, 1983). But the very first move towards this entirely new approach to perception can be found in an article on representation in perception by J.B. Maund (1975). First, I shall give in outline a key distinction that he has made, using the most recent statement of his position (Maund, 1993), and then I shall endeavour to show how it can be dovetailed with radical constructivism to resituate within epistemology the whole notion of entity and its intersubjective nature. I shall begin with Maund's own analogy for a sensory field, that of a Movitype screen. The analogy will be applied to the visual field as illustrative, but the same can be said *mutatis mutandis* for all the sensory fields without exception.

A Movitype screen consists of a matrix – or 'raster', as the neuroscientists prefer to call it – that is made up of an array of tiny light sources. A computer-led input can excite these lights so as to give the impression of letters passing from right to left, or even, on the more advanced forms now commonly used in advertisements, to show moving pictures. Let us suppose that you are watching an advertisement such as the one I saw recently at the railway station at Munich, which showed a sequence of statements in German that ended up with the slow appearance out of random sparkles of a picture of a Seven-Up can.

Now it is obvious, says Maund, that there are two ways of describing what you are seeing. We could adopt the everyday public language and say, 'I saw some German sentences, followed by a picture of a Seven-Up can'. Although that is the perfectly adequate way of describing the sight, nevertheless there is a scientific way of describing it which bears no relation whatsoever to this *common-sense* description. One could ask the electronics engineer to

The Topic of Entity

provide us with a computer print-out staged across the seconds that you were watching it of the point-states of the raster of lights. This would no doubt be a long and complex document, with the state of each tiny light source given its place in the sequence. The interesting aspect of this list is that, although it would give a comprehensive description of the state of the screen, nowhere in that list would be a mention of German words or a Seven-Up can. What this makes clear is that there are two ways to describe such a screen, an '*object*-determinate' description, the 'common-sense' one, in which publicly recognizable objects are mentioned, and a '*field*-determinate' description, which gives an accurate account of the actual state of the field, but makes no mention of what any passer-by would make of it. For example, because my German is limited, I was unable to translate much of what appeared. As regards the picture, though, I might have an advantage over a German-speaker who had just arrived on the platform – because the advertisement endlessly repeated itself, it became possible for me to recognize 'the' Seven-Up can as it formed out of the random sparkles *before* someone who was seeing the sequence for the first time. To put it in a simple form, I might, as we say, 'see the can' before there was for the new arrival on the platform any 'can' to see. Nevertheless, in spite of these epistemic variations from person to person, the state of the raster was the same for both, and could be given the same field-determinate description.

So what are the empirical consequences of such a distinction? – for the analogy is taken to apply to human sensory fields in the cortex, which is where many modern neuroscientists now place them. What is it then that the field-determinate description describes? Notice that it certainly does not describe the world in terms of things, objects, persons, selves. It is no more than a record of a distribution of intensities. There is no facsimile of any kind: there is only the structural/formal isomorphism of an intermediary. This matches Glasersfeld's insistence that the internal fields are not replicas of any kind. Maund uses the analogy of a contour map: there is some principled causal connection between the input and the state of the field, but *there is no information about entities anywhere upon it nor any copying of properties.* What exists outside us are isomorphic fields of energy and mass distributions that do not possess those sensory properties at all. Robert Boyle, three hundred years ago, was thus correct: we sense indirect cortical results of what has no colour or tone or smell or taste or feel. There is therefore no pictorial resemblance. The isomorphism is of that structural kind that one finds, say, between the grooves on an old gramophone record of Schubert's Ninth Symphony and the laser pulses going on inside a CD player playing the same music. Glasersfeld (1986, p. 111) is concerned with a similar point when he examines the isomorphisms that exist between one sensory modality and another.

Consider the following various states of excitation of a TV screen: (1) no more than interference snow on what we call a 'blank' screen; (2) input from a randomizing computer program that shows a surreal succession of patterns; (3) input from a computer program that projects apparent landscapes or dinosaurs

13

or whatever; (4) input from a broadcast cartoon film; (5) input from a personal camcorder of actual scenes; (6) input from a video fiction film; (7) input from a so-called live TV broadcast. In every case a real description of the state of the raster can be given which bears no logical relation at all to what is, as we say, perceived to be on the screen. Even the question of whether what is on the screen is objective or illusory or fictional is beside the point when one is giving the state of the raster pixel by pixel. The field is real whatever one does or does not pick out from it. After all, I might have walked on to that Munich platform and the alterations on the Movitype screen might have gone on within my field of vision but outside the scope of my attention. Take it that I was searching the people getting off a train for a friend that I was expecting. All its variations, then, might have gone on entirely uninterpreted. For that part of my vision I was seeing all right, but not looking. I was in the state of the autistic child whose condition has been described by an expert as being able to 'see and hear' but not 'listen and look' (Hermelin, 1976, p. 137). The epistemic judgements 'objective' and 'illusory', bound to the adjustments of the common-sense language, have no bearing upon the field-determinateness of the screen.

For all organisms with a sensory field there is such a raster describable, one presumes by its point-states, without reference to what the organism may or may not be perceiving in it. At the level of the agnosic, the brain-damaged person who sees but cannot label any entity within her field of vision, sensing exists in a pure non-epistemic state – the whole field uninterpreted, not merely some part to which she does not happen to be attending. It is obviously possible for an organism to be born which completely lacks the ability to select perceptual units from the field, even to arrive at a concept of itself. Notice that this empirical possibility is of a sensing internal to the cortex without a self of any kind. Thus one cannot mount the old solipsist objection against it, for there is no '*solus-ipse*' there to wonder whether it alone exists. Indeed, it is a Cartesian illusion to think that sensing must be attended by a conscious self. It makes the mistake of bringing in an epistemic feature upon what is wholly non-intentional, the most sensitive epistemic feature of all, the concept of a self. It needs stressing that there is no information of any kind upon the raster; it can only be regarded as a natural sign in the uncontroversial sense given to the term by H.P. Grice (1957): just as a distant cloud can be taken by someone in the know as a sign of rain, so too distributions over the field can be taken as a sign that certain motor performances are likely to be adaptive, that is, only if the organism possesses the pain-pleasure/desire-fear module that enables it to embed significant distributions in memory.[1] To bring out the radical nature of this claim one can say that all visual sensing – and that includes the 3-D stereoscopic field as well as the colour experiences you are having now – is a part of the non-intentional material real, not in itself *mental* at all. Furthermore, it is therefore not even 'given' to anyone, since the concept of a self is subsequent to it. Such fields occur in organisms, but there is no guarantee that they are even confined to single organisms – could not Siamese twins be born sharing a visual cortex? Thoughts of this kind are strange to the Cartesian mind for it has not imagined that sensing can go on without a self there to select percepts from it. Descartes himself, though, having wondered whether all was a dream, did on the very next page of Section I of his *Meditations* confusedly toy with the notion that we might have to 'admit the reality . . . of certain real colours'. Had he pursued that thought, he would have seen that there was something that resisted the notion that all internal presentations could be dismissed as a dream. Because a cartoon appears on the TV screen we are not thereby led to think that the phosphor glowings behind the glass have suddenly become illusory. There is a systematic ambiguity here that has been overlooked by the too-logically minded (J.L. Austin is an example here; Austin, 1976), and there is a special reason for their ignorance, which we shall come to later.

That experience in itself is not something known is precisely Glasersfeld's (1986, p. 115) claim when he comes to consider the accusation that constructivism is idealist, laying itself open to the solipsist objection. That there is an ontological reality is proved by the fact that percepts are only viable: they are constrained by the external, which is not to be regarded as something known. Perceptual knowledge is an operation upon the non-epistemic sensory fields, and they are sensed, not perceived; perceiving is what goes on within them at the instigation of the 'attentional pulses'. As Roy Wood Sellars repeatedly said, 'Being is one thing and knowledge is quite another sort of thing' (1919, p. 407). It will be clear why Glasersfeld naturally rejects James J. Gibson's view that the ontological reality is already discrete, divided into given objectified invariants. The non-epistemic field is just that: it has no information on it, and to use the word 'information', as Gibson does, for the input, is to slide on a metaphor. Gibson was misled by his own success in identifying automatic visual processes such as edge-enhancers, but none of them can bestow knowledge, however much they may facilitate it in some circumstances, for in others they can prove maladaptive.[2]

The seven epistemic states of a TV screen I mentioned before can be matched by the visual field, for it can be read as showing: (1) interference – an example would be the fortification patterns that migraine sufferers see; (2) the random computer program is matched by hypnagogic imagery, which develops in some people before the onset of sleep without regard to interpretation, and is often completely non-objectified; (3) the pictorial computer program is matched by mental imagery of a purely imaginary kind, as when one sees fantasy landscapes, cities, animals, plants; (4) dreams parallel the cartoons, experiences, which, *pace* the philosopher Norman Malcolm (1959), can be made out of material, not only provided *internally* from the brain, but sometimes by extraordinary interpretation of *external* input, for it is not an uncommon experience for someone to fall asleep with their eyes open and to dream with the input from the retinas; (5) one can re-run, as from a camcorder, memory sequences, sometimes with remarkable accuracy, sometimes discovering in the sensed field what had not been noticed before; (6) one can daydream, producing episodes as fictional as any video; and (7), finally, one can open one's eyes to the outside world and see live, so to speak. Nevertheless, whatever the state of the raster, it remained perfectly real no matter what it was caused by, just as the Movitype lights and the TV screen's phosphor matrix remain real whatever is perceived or not perceived to be upon them. This is the level of non-epistemic sensing, and it exists for all of us all the time, hidden of course under the current interpretations we happen to be making, but ready to startle us when we discover that the criteria that we have been operating with prove a disappointment in new circumstances. These are the moments of discrepancy and perturbation that Glasersfeld speaks of (Glasersfeld, 1982, p. 618); the same point was made by John Dewey (1896) and George Herbert Mead (1910), who pointed out that it is discrepancies between action and result that lead to adjustments of selection in perception, an adaptive feedback. For perceiving is the region of Ernst von Glasersfeld's viabilities, those selections from the field that initially pain and pleasure, and subsequently desire and fear, maintain according to what one might call a practical hypothesis in the hope that they will not prove unreliable. We have of course to learn to distinguish those occasions when the input is not live, but that does not mean that the other conditions, from after-images to dream, do not have adaptive advantages to offer. The mirage that J.L. Austin dismissed as an illusion could be taken as a rough-and-ready guide to air temperature; the famous Bent Stick Illusion could reveal to a practised eye whether the liquid it was submerged in were water or petrol; the appearance of fortification patterns interfering with normal vision are nevertheless reliable causal indicators of the near onset of a migraine headache. Illusion and truth at the epistemic level have no purchase at the level of the non-epistemic field, which presents its variations as blankly as waves on a pool. Richard Kitchener's claim against Glasersfeldian constructivism that there is 'nothing upon which the transformations could be performed' (1986, p. 114) forgets just this, the non-epistemic sensory base. Gibson actually said that visual sensations were a mere 'luxury' (1971, p. 31), ignoring Ludwig Feuerbach's warning long ago that sensation is no 'mere luxury or trifle' (1966 [orig. 1843], p. 50). Feuerbach's target was Hegel, but there are many philosophers today who seem not to appreciate that the world is first of all sensed and not known.

Now why is it that if one accepts this new proposal from neuroscience (Edelman, 1992; Smythies, 1993) and from the philosophy of perception that at a meta-level it can be seen that there really are no such things as entities except as useful tools of the mind and particularly of minds working in common? Consider the full structure of the intersubjective situation. Of two persons, each has an empirically private registration at the sensory level that differs from the other's in registration features, sensitivity, degree of acuity, range, and so on. There is already a systematic ambiguity at this level, which might prove significant for mutual action. If my son and I are listening out for a high-pitched whistle, I shall certainly trust him if he says he hears it, though I do not, since I am well aware that my hearing range cuts off at about 15 kilohertz whereas his goes on up to 20 kilohertz. Notice against Wittgenstein, that I am conceding an agreement although I have positive evidence that my subjective judgement is not the same as his. So it is actually impossible to align two persons' sensory experiences so that they perfectly match. At the registration level there are differing perspectives. Then there will be differences in actual percept from person to person, even though they may be assuring each other that there is no difference in their criteria. To put it in Glasersfeldian terms, we all have a different fit to the same rough region of the flux, though we assure each other that we have achieved a match. Glasersfeld quotes Ludwig Fleck as saying that the creation of knowledge 'resembles a traditional myth' and points out that this arises from our 'imputing our schemes to others' (1989, p. 130).

Wittgenstein's underestimation of the sensory prevented him seeing that agreements in definitions can never produce agreement in judgements. Discrepancies in action may exist that neither party has as yet noticed because the circumstances have not made them salient. The irony of this situation can produce odd adaptive advances, for it may be person A who has selected a more adaptive percept, but it may be person B who comes to notice that person A has that very advantage. As I have pointed out many times, the structure of the intersubjective relationship is that of all jokes, all stories, for without exception they all hinge on a reinterpretation of a portion of the always uninterpreted fields. Georg Simmel (1968, p. 31) spoke of feedback effects producing 'uncanny' results, where the homely and familiar turn shockingly into the unhomely.

I mentioned earlier that I would point out the reason for the insidiousness of the Wittgensteinian mistake. As Schutz and Rommetveit have perspicuously argued, in order to make our differing percepts coincide upon those rough portions of the flux in which we are interested, we have to take for granted, that is, hypothesize, pretend for the time being that we have already achieved the perfect coincidence of focus we should like to have achieved. Although there are no referents, we have to go on the assumption that there are in order to effect the corrections that feedback has brought into prominence. We have to assure each other that we have selected the same referent although we are perfectly aware that there are no such things, only viscosities in the flux of varying rates of transitoriness. To use Glasersfeld's phrase, we have to impute our schemes to others in order to get a coinciding of our differing perspectives. *The danger lies in believing our useful hypothesis.* So Glasersfeld is right to insist that there are no ready-made structures, no Gibsonian invariants, no *Dinge an Sich*, but is equally right in claiming that there is an existent ground from which we are all selecting our own versions of what we call objects and persons.

To trope a Kantian term: we sense the Noumenon through the Phenomenon. So this is a version of realism, for there is certainly something in virtue of which our assertions can be tested for their viability. And this is why we are talking, *in order to adjust those percepts hopefully to a more adaptive stance.* The relativity of perceptions from one person to another is in fact the foundation of our continuing evolution in speech itself. The danger arises in philosophy when a philosopher takes this wise methodological counsel, that we must assume that there are objects while never believing in them, but removes the concessive phrase 'while never believing in them'. When Atkinson says that we must learn from Wittgenstein that there is no sense in talking of a subjective rule, she is only exhorting us into the needful *play* of reference. One way of putting it is to say that a needful faith is being mistaken for certainty, and, if that has a theological ring about it, perhaps this is no accident. Neither she nor Wittgenstein is able to detach existence from objectivity. We can even be sure that our personal selection exists, but to what degree it corresponds with someone else's as regards adaptive value we can never wholly know.

It is precisely the Glasersfeldian constraints that become obvious when the viability breaks down that reveal the underlying non-epistemic real to us, particularly when another can change our perspective upon significances in the context. To trope the Kantian terms again, there is the Noumenon *in* the Phenomenon: in plainer terms, not only do we have causal links to the external continuum through the non-epistemic fields, but the fields themselves are part of that same real continuum, a non-mental existence within our own brains. This is the answer to Kitchener's objection that Glasersfeld is committed to idealism by his constructivism. To say, as Glasersfeld does, that 'we function without referring to "objective" entities' (1986, p. 112) is perfectly correct; all we can achieve are fuzzy coincidings on the real, but these are adaptively valuable since we can endlessly correct each other through language about that real continuum, and as we do so, we not only become apprised of *the independent existence of what is causing the distributions of the whole sensory field* regardless of any currently viable objectification we may be making, but we have thence every right to be convinced of *the independent existence of the non-mental field itself* from which we made the new and surprising categorical adjustment at the behest of a mind outside our own. This is as far from subjective idealism as can be for it proves the sensory fields to have an existence independent of the self that is made from them. Furthermore, the experience of mutual correction, if accepted (interestingly whether it proves successfully viable or not), in which another agent proves him or herself capable of virtually stepping into our sensory field and showing us how a sensed but so far unperceived portion of it is to be safely viewed, also proves: (1) that others have sensory fields for they have demonstrated that they have access to what causes ours; (2) that other agents like ourselves must therefore exist; (3) that the external flux exists, whatever the success or otherwise of our mutually maintained coincidence of perspectives may be, that is, even if a presumed 'objectifying' proves 'illusory'. So this is a realism of the flux, not of what can now be seen to be merely viable entities. When Dr Johnson kicked a stone to disprove Berkeley, he only demonstrated the viability of the mutual selection of 'the stone'; at the next moment someone standing by might have been able to show him that it was not a stone, but a brick, that person having noticed what Dr Johnson had not, say, its texture, or that it was not even one stone,

The Topic of Entity

but two. Kitchener's fear and Dr Johnson's are the same: both can now be seen to be an illicit extension of the Schutz–Rommetveitian requirement that we hypothesize together that we have identified the same entities just in order that we may adjust our categorizations. It is not surprising that in the past the commonly accepted objectifications came to be hallowed beyond their inescapably hypothetical character: how easy to slide from the need to pretend a coincidence to a belief, after repeated mutual practical successes, that a logically perfect coincidence had been achieved. After all, the selection *we have personally made* exists, but it can never perfectly coincide with that of another, whose *different* selection also exists; and, therefore, nor can we ever be sure that we are apprised of all that is or may be relevant within it, which is precisely Glasersfeld's point about viability. It is so easy to forget the purpose of the original hypothesis, to permit the endless recategorizations to proceed. It is precisely this continual disambiguation effected by the mutual corrections of language that make us human. It is the essential feature of every informative statement that is ever spoken.

A Mathematical Addendum

One cannot in this volume leave this topic of entity without a reference across to mathematics, to the concept of number. If, strictly speaking, there are no entities, if 'they' are a product of our need to home in on portions of the real continuum by means of a mutual imagining of separate and fixed re-cognizable units, then units are no more than *a feature of that method.* They are aspects of the language game, and derive from it; they do not correspond to sets of discrete units in the real continuum but are elements of the human process of knowledge adjustment. To speak of the unit as such in Glasersfeldian terms, it represents our open agreement to imagine together that what is in fact only viable represents a permanent fixity in the real. Units are thus created in a needful imaginative game: their reality lies only in the actual sequences of that game, in which we might observe how a group of agents behave *as if* there were such units – at least, that is, until evolution provides its moments of correction, at which point, with the adjustments performed (which can involve radical re-counting), the game of mutually identified units can carry on as before, this time with new versions of these apparently rigid referents. In pure mathematics, however, the procedures of the game are lifted away from their practical application and played within their own right, a doubly imaginative shift. They are operated with as a ghost of mutual agreement, and the rule of this meta-game is that we shall proceed *as if* no mutual corrections were ever necessary, that is, although we talk as if the units had real reference, we shall withhold ourselves from ever making a real reference to a portion of the continuum. *Pro tempore*, viability is artificially turned into eternal fixity. This is why Gödel's Proof works: if the proof is examined, it will be discovered that mathematics is in fact used to refer to something, namely, elements

19

within *itself*; for the proof depends upon making numbers refer to numbers, which inevitably results in a paradox, for the very initial assumption within pure mathematics was that *there should be no such reference*, and, in addition, in referring to numbers we are referring to something that does not exist, except as a feature of the hypothetical method we employ in knowledge adjustment.

When we use the unit game in the real world, there is something that exists, the fuzzy region of the continuum upon which our differing projections are falling in hopeful coincidence. But there we are always ready to adjust our Glasersfeldian constructions when the new challenge from the real presents itself. In pure mathematics all we can adjust are the ghosts of agreement from which we begin the game, the axioms that we promise each other that we shall never query; what we cannot do in this meta-game is alter a reference in the middle. We cannot say, for example, that the variable x in the previous line has a different value from its appearance in the next line – say, because the printer has used a sans serif version of 'x' in one line and not in the other – for mathematics takes a view from nowhere, a pure anonymity representing an unchanging Cartesian subject that will see any mathematical object as timelessly unique, even an 'irrational' number.

Notes

1 See Gerald Edelman here on the need for a value system in the brain that enables it to store and modify gestalts selected from the fields (Edelman, 1992, pp. 102ff).
2 For more on this error of Gibson's, see Wright (1983).

References

ATKINSON, CHRISTINE (1983) *Making Sense of Piaget: The Philosophical Roots*, London: Routledge & Kegan Paul.
AUSTIN, J.L. (1976; orig. 1962) *Sense and Sensibilia*, ed. WARNOCK, G.J., Oxford: Oxford University Press.
DEWEY, JOHN (1896) 'The reflex arc concept in psychology', *Psychological Review*, 3, pp. 357–70.
EDELMAN, GERALD M. (1992) *Bright Air, Brilliant Fire*, London: Allen Lane/Penguin Press.
FEUERBACH, LUDWIG (1966; orig. 1843) *Principles of the Philosophy of the Future*, tr. VOGEL, M.H., Indianapolis: Bobbs-Merrill.
GIBSON, JAMES J. (1971) 'The information available in pictures', *Leonardo*, 4, 2, pp. 27–35.
GLASERSFELD, E. VON (1982) 'An interpretation of Piaget's constructivism', *Revue Internationale de Philosophie*, 142–3, pp. 612–35.
GLASERSFELD, E. VON (1984) 'An introduction to radical constructivism', in WATZLAWICK, P. (ed.), *The Invented Reality: How Do We Know What We Believe We Know? Contributions to Constructivism*, New York and London: W.W. Norton, pp. 17–40.

GLASERSFELD, E. VON (1986) 'Preliminaries to any theory of representation', in JANVIER, C. (ed.), *Problems of Representation in the Teaching of Mathematics*, Hillsdale: Lawrence Erlbaum, pp. 215-25.
GLASERSFELD, E. VON (1989) 'Facts and the self from a constructivist point of view', *Poetics*, 18, pp. 435-48.
GRICE, H.P. (1957) 'Meaning', *Philosophical Review*, 66, pp. 377-88.
HAMLYN, D.W. (1971) 'Epistemology and conceptual development', in MISCHEL, T. (ed.), *Cognitive Development and Epistemology*, New York: Academic Press, pp. 3-24.
HERMELIN, B. (1976) 'Coding and the sense modalities', in WING, L. (ed.), *Early Childhood Autism: Clinical, Educational and Social Aspects*, Oxford: Pergamon Press, pp. 135-68.
KITCHENER, RICHARD F. (1986) *Piaget's Theory of Knowledge: Genetic Epistemology and Scientific Reason*, New Haven and London: Yale University Press.
MALCOLM, N. (1959) *Dreaming*, London: Routledge & Kegan Paul.
MAUND, J.B. (1975) 'The representative theory of perception', *Canadian Journal of Philosophy*, 5, pp. 41-55.
MAUND, J.B. (1993) 'Representation, pictures and resemblance', in WRIGHT, E. (ed.), *New Representationalisms: Essays in the Philosophy of Perception*, Aldershot: Avebury Press, pp. 45-69.
MEAD, G.H. (1910) 'Social consciousness and the consciousness of meaning', *Psychological Bulletin*, 7, pp. 397-405.
ROMMETVEIT, R. (1968) *Words, Meanings and Messages*, New York: Academic Press.
ROMMETVEIT, R. (1974) *On Message Structure: A Framework for the Study of Language and Communication*, London: John Wiley.
ROMMETVEIT, R. (1978) 'On negative rationalism in scholarly studies of verbal communication and dynamic residuals in the construction of human intersubjectivity', in BRENNER, M., MARSH, P. and BRENNER, M. (eds), *The Social Contexts of Method*, London: Croom Helm, pp. 16-32.
ROMMETVEIT, R. (1983) 'On the dawning of different aspects of life in a pluralistic social world', *Poetics Today*, 4, 3 (in WRIGHT, E. (ed.), *The Ironic Discourse*), pp. 595-609.
SCHUTZ, A. (1962) *Collected Papers*, Vol. I: *The Problem of Social Reality*, The Hague: Martinus Nijhoff.
SELLARS, R.W. (1969; orig. 1916) *Critical Realism: A Study of the Nature and Conditions of Knowledge*, New York: Russell & Russell.
SELLARS, R.W. (1919) 'The epistemology of evolutionary naturalism', *Mind*, 27, 112, pp. 407-26.
SELLARS, R.W. (1922) *Evolutionary Naturalism*, Chicago and London: Open Court Publishing.
SELLARS, R.W. (1932) *The Philosophy of Physical Realism*, New York: Macmillan.
SIMMEL, G. (1968) *The Conflict in Modern Culture and Other Essays*, ed. Etzkorn, K.P., New York: Teachers' College Press, Columbia University.
SMYTHIES, JOHN R. (1993) 'The impact of contemporary neuroscience and introspection psychology on the philosophy of perception', in WRIGHT, E. (ed.), *New Representationalisms: Essays in the Philosophy of Perception*, Aldershot: Avebury Press, pp. 205-31.
TOULMIN, STEPHEN (1971) 'The concept of "stages" in psychological development', in MISCHEL, T. (ed.), *Cognitive Development and Epistemology*, New York and London: Academic Press, pp. 25-60.

WILCOX, S. and KATZ, S.T. (1981) 'The ecological approach to development: An alternative to cognitivism', *Journal of Experimental Child Psychology*, 32, pp. 247–63.
WITTGENSTEIN, L. (1967) *Philosophical Investigations*, Anscombe, G.E.M. (trans.), Oxford: Basil Blackwell.
WRIGHT, E. (1983) 'Pre-phenomenal adjustments and Sanford's Illusion Objection against sense-data', *Pacific Philosophical Quarterly*, 64, pp. 266–72.
WRIGHT, E. (1986) 'Wilcox and Katz on indirect realism', *Philosophy and the Social Sciences*, **6**, 1, pp. 107–13.
WRIGHT, E. (ed.) (1993) *New Representationalisms: Essays in the Philosophy of Perception*, Aldershot: Avebury Press.

3 Ernst von Glasersfeld's Philosophy of Language: Roots, Concepts, Perspectives

S.J. Schmidt

The development of linguistics and of the philosophy of language since the late 1950s can roughly be characterized by an increasing understanding of the cognitive as well as the social aspects of language and communication. This cognitivist and sociological turn took place in strict opposition to the two paradigms which had dominated the intellectual life in the United States until then, viz. behaviorism and first order cybernetics. And one of the most consistent protagonists in this consequential turn has undoubtedly been Ernst Glasersfeld. Glasersfeld describes the situation at the end of the 1930s as follows:

> The bulk of linguistic research, having chosen to follow Bloomfield – rather than Sapir, his teacher – developed a militant disregard for the *function* of the phenomenon it was studying. Interest was focused on those manifestations that could be called directly observable or physical. Phonology thrived and semantics, the study of meaning, which is at the core of the communicatory function of language, was thwarted. (1975, p. 2)

From its very beginning, Glasersfeld's interest in language and communication has been motivated by an epistemological position which he himself named radical constructivism, which he saw embedded in the skeptical and instrumentalist traditions of European philosophy (since Democritus and Sextus Empiricus), in the psychology of Jean Piaget or George Kelly, and in Silvio Ceccato's and Heinz von Foerster's second order cybernetics. Radical constructivism,[1] in Glasersfeld's view, is essentially a theory of knowing which has helped to draw up a coherent and homogeneous approach to language, communication, and epistemology.[2] In what follows I shall concentrate on the essentials of this approach.

Basic Concepts

The basic concepts and arguments of Glasersfeld's theory of language and communication can be found in an article published in 1974, 'Signs, communication, and language'. As the starting points of his argumentation, Glasersfeld provides a thorough and, above all, a very fair reading of S. Langer's,

N. Wiener's, C. Shannon's, and C. Cherry's ideas about language and communication, in which he concentrated on the following issues:

> N. Wiener made the point that '... it is completely impossible to understand social communities ... without a thorough investigation of their means of communication....' (Glasersfeld, 1974a, p. 466)

> C. Cherry emphasized that communication is '... the establishment of a social unit from individuals by the use of language or signs', where communication is characterized by 'the sharing of common sets of rules, for various goal-seeking activities. (There are many *shades of opinions*).' (Cherry's italics) (ibid.)

> Langer stressed the difference between the use of a significatory item as an instrument of action and its use as an instrument of reflection and contrasted 'signs' with 'symbols': 'To conceive a thing or a situation is not the same as to "react toward it" overtly or to be aware of its presence. In talking *about* things we have conceptions of them, not the things themselves; *and it is the conceptions, not the things, that symbols directly "mean."*' (Langer's italics) (ibid., p. 472)

By reformulating A. Hofstadter's assumption that a teleological actor is characterized by the inseparable combination of ends, sensitivity, and technique, in cybernetic terms (with end = reference value, sensitivity = sensory function, and technique = effector function), Glasersfeld prepares the ground for defining communication as an instrumental, goal-directed, and therefore purposive process.[3] He thus overcomes the behaviorist banning of goals and purposes without simply returning to outdated teleological positions (Glasersfeld, 1975, p. 3).

Through an analysis of C. Hockett's once well-known thirteen descriptive criteria of language as well as of S. Langer's concept of symbol, Glasersfeld reaches his own definition, which reads as follows:

> To sum up this discussion of linguistic communication, I would suggest three criteria to distinguish 'language', all of which are necessary but individually insufficient:
> (1) There must be a set (lexicon) of communicatory signs, i.e. perceptual items whose meaningfulness 'semanticity' is constituted by a conventional tie 'semantic nexus' and not by an inferential one.
> (2) These signs must be symbols, i.e. linked to representations, 'symbolicity;' therefore they *can* be sent without reference to perceptual instances of the items they designate, and received without 'triggering' a behavioral response in the receiver. As symbols they merely activate the connected representation.
> (3) There must be a set of rules 'grammar' governing the combination of signs into strings, such that certain combinations produce a new semantic content in addition to the individual content of the component signs. (1975, pp. 20ff.)

Reference and Representation

Glasersfeld's cognitive approach to language and communication concentrates on a new theoretical modeling of basic semantic problems, above all of the problems of reference and representation. Of the problem of reference, Glasersfeld states that 'The theory of reference, according to which questions about the meaning of words can be answered only by answering questions concerning things in the "real world", still casts a potent spell over semantic analysis' (1972a, p. 90). Contrary to this seemingly plausible assumption, Glasersfeld holds the view 'that the analysis of meaning must, under all circumstances, be closely linked to an analysis of concepts or mental constructs' (ibid., p. 91). He agrees with the assumption shared by researchers like Piaget, Ceccato, Kelly or Bridgman 'that the objects and events we "perceive" or "know", and that is the objects and events we refer to when we communicate linguistically, are *constructs* or, in other words, are the result of mental operations' (ibid.).[4] Objects, for example, are regarded as constructs (at least for an organism) because they have to be actively abstracted from a sequence of experiences in such a way as to keep stable a finite/definite but flexible constellation of characteristic features (which in themselves admit some variation). According to Glasersfeld (1979), most psycholinguists believe that a child must first produce/build a concept before it can associate a name with it. Accordingly, in all kinds of translations 'there is no way of passing from the surface structure of one language to the surface structure of another without delving into the substrate of conceptual understanding' (Glasersfeld, 1972a, p. 92). It follows from these assumptions that semantic analyses should be performed in terms of cognitive analyses, looking for 'the *conceptual* items the linguistic statements invoke and the relations that are posited between them' (ibid.), instead of looking for objects or truth values as the only proper aims of semantic analyses.

As Glasersfeld demonstrates in his own analyses, the specification of a verb's meaning or translation has to dig out the specific characteristics of all the situations to which the verb is applicable. By 'situation', Glasersfeld means 'conceptual situation':

> i.e. a structure made up of certain items and certain relations, whose locus is the language user's mind regardless of whether the structure could be said to have originated in perception, in imagination, or even as an illusion. (Glasersfeld, 1972a, p. 93)

In a more detailed analysis of the relation between reading, understanding, and conceptual situation, he comes to the conclusion that

> in order to understand even relatively simple sentences we must integrate such information as the sentences yield, with information that we have to provide ourselves. This additional information need not be linguistic information. . . . It frequently is, and sometimes can only be, experiential information. (1972b, p. 122)

And he sums up his analyses by saying:

> For the crucial step in the interpretation of ... language is not the step from one linguistic structure to another, but the step from a linguistic expression to a non-linguistic conceptual representation. (ibid., p. 126)

In other words, 'To understand a text means to be able to map information gathered from single words or phrases onto larger pre-existing conceptual structures' (ibid., p. 127).

In a seminal paper on problems of representation, Glasersfeld specifies concepts as those conceptions that

> have been honed by repetition, standardized by interaction, and associated with a specific word. (1987b, p. 219)

And he underscores the fact that concepts or mental representations must be thought of as dynamic in terms of

> relatively self-contained programs or production routines that can be called up and run. (ibid.)

This outline of a cognitivist semantics has also served as a basis for computational analyses of linguistic structures, called 'the correlational approach to language'.[5] Whereas in traditional grammars the lexical items of a natural language are classified and described according to their morphological features and generic syntactic functions, in correlational grammar they are classified

> exclusively according to the actual roles they can play in phrase or sentence structures – and these roles are differentiated and described by reference to the items (concepts) the words designate and to the relations into which they are put. (Glasersfeld, 1970, p. 393)

Such a grammar is not designed for the generation of sentences, but for their interpretation. I cannot go into the technical details of this kind of grammar.[6] Its design, however, makes quite clear that the epistemological focus on cognitive construction in and by the individual redirects research from the allegedly objective structures or entities of behaviorism to their active construction by individuals in experiential situations they share with others.

Evolutionary Aspects of Language

Since Glasersfeld explicitly relates linguistic elements and their 'meanings' to mental constructs or cognitive representations,[7] the question poses itself how these constructs arise in the course of human evolution. With regard to evolutionary aspects, Glasersfeld offers the following argument: Although we do not yet have any real evidence for the origin of language, we can look for basic preconditions of its emergence. Among these preconditions, Glasersfeld counts (a) the embedding of one feedback loop[8] in another (which, for instance, allows tool-making), and (b) the creation of a reference item that is a representation. A representation is defined as

> a cluster of recorded signals which, though originally composed of perceptual material, need no longer be identical with the signals that are at present available in the channels of sensory perception. (Glasersfeld, 1975, pp. 10f.)

Once this level of evolution has been reached, communicative signs can emerge as tools for coordinating the activities of two or more agents, and for organizing the division of tasks, thus providing the basic precondition of larger social communities. This hypothesis rests on comparable views formulated by B. Malinowski as well as by C. Cherry.[9]

> According to this view, communicatory behavior is a *mode of action*, its function is to link concerted activity, and it is indispensable because without these links there could be no *unified social action*. Thus it is an *instrument*, which is to say, a *tool*. (ibid., p. 12)

In other words, what led to the evolution of language was its instrumental function, not its function as an instrument of reflection which it acquired later. For Glasersfeld, the most important feature of language is its symbolic capacity to evoke ideas of things, actions, and situations in the speaker apart from actually experiencing them. The elements of language are symbolic, i.e. they are arbitrarily chosen to stand for something else. According to Glasersfeld, a 'something else' is not an object in the real world, but a segment of experience. In other words: signs or symbols are regarded as unitary experiential items intended to refer to a 'segment of experience that, also, has been isolated from the rest of experience as a discrete and distinguishable piece' (Glasersfeld, 1987b). Without this mechanism no semiotic relation could ever have been established.

Based on these hypotheses, Glasersfeld rejects N. Chomsky's belief that the acquisition of language is genetically caused by an innate capacity of *homo sapiens*. He holds, furthermore, that language did not in any way *significantly* contribute to the survival of primitive man (Glasersfeld, 1992, p. 7). On the other hand, there is no doubt that the human species has demonstrated the power of language as a tool. But, as Glasersfeld skeptically remarks, '[I]f, today, we look at what we have done with the help of that splendid tool, one may begin to wonder whether, at some future time, it will still seem so obvious that language has enhanced the survival of life on this planet' (Glasersfeld, 1975, p. 23).

Indeterminacy in Linguistic Communication

As I have tried to demonstrate, Glasersfeld relates semantics to representations in the sense of cognitive constructs in the individual. This basic constructivist hypothesis, however, immediately raises the question of how communication and understanding can be explained (or at least theoretically modeled) in such a subject-oriented conceptual framework. Glasersfeld is, naturally, aware of this problem when he writes: 'There seems to be a blatant contradiction between the claim of "communication" and the apparently irrefutable subjectivity of meaning' (Glasersfeld, 1983a, p. 211). Before we look at Glasersfeld's attempt at resolving this contradiction, let us first examine his claim that meaning is irrefutably subjective. According to Glasersfeld, the proof is provided by the process of language development in children, that is, by the fact that children gradually acquire the meaning of a word by abstracting elements from their variable experiences (activities, interactions, communications) (Glasersfeld, 1990a, p. 35). The child must accommodate his or her concepts to the use of related words in diverse contexts. 'In fact,' Glasersfeld concludes, 'the process of accommodation and refinement of the meaning of words and linguistic expressions continues for each of us throughout our lives and no matter how long we have spoken the language, there will be occasions when we realize that we have been using a word in a way that turns out to be idiosyncratic in some particular respect' (ibid., p. 36).

Once we realize the inescapable subjectivity of linguistic meaning, we have to abandon the notion that words convey ideas or knowledge – an insight which C. Shannon had already reached – and that understanding means forming similar conceptual structures.

> Instead, we come to realize that understanding is always a matter of fit rather than match. Put in the simplest way, to understand what someone has said or written means to have built up a conceptual structure that, in the given context, appears to be compatible with the structure the speaker had in mind. This compatibility, as a rule, manifests itself in no other way than that the receiver says and does nothing that contravenes the speaker's expectations. From this perspective, there is an inherent and inescapable indeterminacy in linguistic communication. (Glasersfeld, 1990a, p. 36)

Whereas in technical signaling systems the identity of code and meaning can be assured by means that lie outside the communication system, this is not the case in non-technical systems. Here the receiver of a piece of language has to build up its meaning out of conceptual elements which he or she already possesses. This meaning can fit into the meaning the speaker or writer had in mind only insofar as both have built up a consensual domain (in H.R. Maturana's sense), i.e. a domain in which both (together with other native speakers) have adapted their conceptualizations to those of others by a succession of interactive experiences. The appropriate category for comparing these conceptualizations can never be sameness, but at best compatibility or viability. Glasersfeld concludes:

> We believe to have 'understood' a piece of language whenever our understanding of it remains viable in the face of further linguistic or interactional experience. Only a subsequent statement or a speaker's reaction to our response can

indicate to us that an interpretation we have made is not compatible with the speaker's intended meaning. (1983a, p. 213)

But however often we encounter situations where the meaning we have attributed to a word or a linguistic expression seems to fit a speaker's intention, this is neither a proof of *the* conventional meaning nor does it demonstrate that our understanding actually *matches* a speaker's intended meaning. This is to say that 'a linguistic message, under any circumstances, can be interpreted only in terms of the receiver's experience' (ibid., p. 212). Consequently, successful communication presupposes comparable experiences of the communicators within a consensual domain. Conventional rules of language use resulting from social interaction are produced in a consensual domain, rules which orient communicators in their uses of language. In the context of this argument, Glasersfeld (ibid.) introduces the important distinction between what a text says and what a text means. He argues that knowing the conventional linguistic meaning of a sequence of words does not imply that we are also able to *interpret* them. For that purpose we need further information regarding the kind or type of text we encounter, the communicative context,[10] or the experiential world the communicators share. Accordingly, there is no true meaning in/of a text, and the reference to an author's intended meaning remains spurious.

Due to the essential and inescapable subjectivity of meaning, and, consequently, to the inherent indeterminacy in linguistic communication, conceptual discrepancies generate perturbations in the interaction, particularly, of course, when a conversation turns to abstract matters. These discrepancies remain insurmountable unless the participants take something like a constructivist view, only if they begin by assuming that 'a speaker's meaning cannot be anything but subjective constructs', and that 'a productive accommodation and adaptation can mostly be reached' (Glasersfeld, 1990a, p. 36). Thus, a constructivist theory of meaning can provide a theoretical explanation for the many communication difficulties we experience daily, and it can at the same time change education in order to help students build their own viable cognitive constructs.

Linguistic Competence

A good deal of Glasersfeld's scholarly work has been devoted to the analysis of primates' communicative abilities in the Lana Project (Glasersfeld, 1973, 1992). In his reports on this project, Glasersfeld underscores that any answer to the question whether or not primates or other animals, e.g. bees, have developed a language, essentially depends upon a sufficiently clear definition of 'language', so that one could induce their linguistic competence from the observation of their behavior. Neither the learning of conventional reactions to specific triggers nor the learning of conventional behavior in search of specific environmental conditions proves linguistic competence, since either may result from mere association. According to Glasersfeld, linguistic competence can be attributed to animals only in cases where the organism is able to apply a learned sign under *new* conditions and with respect to new, i.e. non-conventional, reactions of others or of the environment. Only then does a sign become a symbol (in the sense specified above). This is the reason why bees, for instance, have developed an elaborate system of communication but no language.

> [T]he messages are always produced with reference to a specific target location from which the sender has just returned and to which the recruits are to go. . . . To qualify as language, the bees' dance would have to be used also *without* this one-to-one-relation to a behavioral response. . . . In short, a communicative system that allows for *imperatives* only . . . should not be called a language. (Glasersfeld, 1977, p. 65)

With regard to chimpanzees, the Lana Project has indicated that chimpanzees indeed possess the neurophysiological prerequisites for linguistic competence. Nevertheless, they have obviously not developed a language although they are able to learn and use a communicative system which they *find* in their environment. Quite obviously language is neither a necessary precondition for surviving nor for living together in relatively stable communities (Glasersfeld, 1992).

Summary

Although Glasersfeld has never presented a fully elaborated theory or philosophy of language, his ideas on this topic, scattered throughout a large number of articles and conference papers, have deeply influenced recent constructivist efforts in this field. The brief review of his pertinent ideas which I have tried to give in this chapter shows that he has been among the first scholars to have realized that language and communication have to be described in terms of the purposive behavior of communicators in their praxis of living who, as H.R. Maturana has formulated, are always immersed in language (or languaging).[11]

According to Glasersfeld, meaning is not contained in texts or utterances and simply transported by communication from speakers to listeners or from writers to readers. Instead, it has to be attributed to linguistic items through interpretation, i.e. through relating linguistic items to cognitive constructs (concepts), and this can only be performed by active cognitive systems. Thus, on the one hand, Glasersfeld emphasizes the subject-dependency of all meaning without falling prey to blatant subjective idealism; on the other hand, however, he makes it perfectly clear that concept formation in autonomous cognitive systems can only happen in social interaction and must rely on viable experiences within consensual experiential domains.

Recent efforts to elaborate a more detailed constructivist theory of language and communication[12] follow this path of argumentation linking both evolutionary and structural perspectives. In light of this argumentative strategy it turns out that the seeming contradiction between cognitive autonomy and social control, between the subjectivity of cognition and the intersubjectivity (or sociality) of communication, can be resolved by showing how, in the phylogenesis of mankind as well as in the individual's ontogenesis, the construction of personal as well as of social experiential worlds is interwoven. Linguistic items turn out to be semiotic materializations of social experiences resulting from interactions, and they in turn 'impregnate' the individuals' linguistic and non-linguistic experiences throughout their lives. Consequently, the cognitive construction of meaning strictly relies on personal experiences and takes place in autonomous cognitive domains. But the rules and constraints of this fabric follow social rules, expectations, and legitimations which are part of the overall system of symbolic orders we may call the culture of a society (Schmidt, 1992). Thus language – as an important mechanism of culture and society – is imperative with regard to the set of possible selections (in terms of meaning-production), but at the same time leaves space for subjective creativity in selections and combinations in the ever varying contexts of living.

As far as I can see, a comprehensive philosophy of language and communication would be well advised to observe and to analyze its subjects under a fourfold perspective, viz. a biological, a psychological, a sociological, and a culture-theoretical one, integrating genetic and structural points of view, respectively. The man who has paved the way to this important insight is Ernst Glasersfeld. He has been the trailblazer out of the behaviorist desert into cognitive constructivist pastures with inspiring new perspectives, and an abundance of new interesting problems. I think Ernst Glasersfeld has proved that radical constructivism is much more than one approach among others: it is a philosophy which opens up the way to a better, more human way of living – a truth that Ernst Glasersfeld himself has impressively verified.

Notes

1 For a detailed presentation of his radical constructivism, see Glasersfeld (1987a).
2 See Glasersfeld's preface to the German collection of his articles (ibid.).
3 'For a long time, any mention of "purpose" was considered taboo by many scientists. ... The concept of "purpose" is essential for the definition of communication, and the purpose has to be on the side of the source or sender' (Glasersfeld, 1977, p. 61).
4 '[W]hat the observer calls an "object", is for the organism an inseparable component of an activity cluster' (Glasersfeld, 1975, p. 8).
5 For a description of the progression of this approach, derived from the pioneering work of Silvio Ceccato, see Glasersfeld (1970a).
6 See e.g. Glasersfeld (1970a, 1970b, 1972a).

7 'I want to emphasise that 'representation' in the constructivist view *never* refers to a picture of an experience-independent 'outside' world; instead it is intended literally

to indicate a *re*-construction of something that has been constructed at some prior experiential situation. Although the word 'concept' must not be understood in the way which it has frequently been used by learning psychologists, i.e., as referring simply to a perceptual dimension such as colour, shape, size, etc.; instead, 'concept' refers to any structure that has been abstracted from the process of experiential construction as recurrently usable, for instance, for the purpose of relating or classifying experiential situations. To be called 'concept' these constructs must be stable enough to be represented in the absence of perceptual 'input'. (Glasersfeld, 1982, p. 194, fn 6)

8. Note that Glasersfeld – in accordance with e.g. McKay or Powers – views organisms as 'hierarchical systems of control loops, in which the reference value of one unit is itself controlled by another' (1977, p. 63).
9. 'B. Malinowski said: "Speech is a necessary means of communion; it is the one indispensable instrument for creating the ties of the moment without which unified social action is impossible." And Cherry defined the term "communication" as "The establishment of a social unit from individuals, by the use of language or signs. The sharing of common set of rules, for various goal-seeking activities."' (Glasersfeld, 1975, p. 11)
10. 'Context' is defined by Glasersfeld as 'aspects of his [the receiver's] own present state, aspects of the sender's state, and above all an implicit or explicit hypothesis as to *why* the message was sent' (Glasersfeld, 1977, p. 60). Normally the communicative context reduces potential meanings to one – cases of unresolvable ambiguity are very rare.
11. See Glasersfeld (1990b).
12. See e.g. S.J. Schmidt (1994).

References

GLASERSFELD, E. VON (1970a) 'The correlational approach to language', *Thought and Language in Operation*, **I**, 4, pp. 391–8.

GLASERSFELD, E. VON (1970b) 'The problem of syntactic complexity in reading and readability', *Journal of Reading Behavior*, **3**, 2, pp. 1–14.

GLASERSFELD, E. VON (1972a) 'Semantic analysis of verbs in terms of conceptual situations', *Linguistics*, **94**, pp. 90–107.

GLASERSFELD, E. VON (1972b) 'Reading, understanding, and conceptual situations', in GREEN, F.P. (ed.), *21st Yearbook of the N.R.C.*, Milwaukee, pp. 119–27.

GLASERSFELD, E. VON, RUMBOUGH, D.M. and GILL, T.V. (1973) 'Reading and sentence completion by a chimpanzee (Pan)', *Science*, **16.11**, 182, pp. 731–3.

GLASERSFELD, E. VON (1974a) 'Signs, communication, and language', *Journal of Human Evolution*, 3, pp. 465–74.

GLASERSFELD, E. VON (1974b) '*Because* and the concepts of causation', *Semiotica*, **12**, 2, pp. 129–44.

GLASERSFELD, E. VON (1975) 'The development of language as purposive behavior', paper presented at the Conference on Origins and Evolution of Speech and Language, New York Academy of Sciences.

GLASERSFELD, E. VON (1977) 'Linguistic communication: Theory and definition', in *Language Learning by a Chimpanzee. The Lana Project*, New York/San Francisco/London: Academic Press, pp. 55–71.

GLASERSFELD, E. VON (1979) 'Cybernetics, experience, and the concept of self', in OZER, M.N. (ed.), *A Cybernetic Approach to the Assessment of Children: Toward a more Human Use of Human Beings*, Boulder, Col.: Westview Press, pp. 67–113.

GLASERSFELD, E. VON (1981) 'Feedback, induction, and epistemology', in LASKER, G.E. (ed.), *Applied Systems and Cybernetics*, New York: Pergamon Press, pp. 712–19.

GLASERSFELD, E. VON (1982) 'Subitizing: The role of figural patterns in the development of numerical concepts', *Archives de Psychologie*, **50**, pp. 191–218.

GLASERSFELD, E. VON (1983a) 'On the concept of interpretation', *Poetics*, **12**, pp. 207–18.

GLASERSFELD, E. VON (1983b) 'Learning as constructive activity', in BERGERON, J. and HERSCOVICS, N. (eds), *Proceedings of the 5th Annual Meeting of the International Group for Psychology in Mathematics Education*, Montreal 1983.

GLASERSFELD, E. VON (1987a) *Wissen, Sprache und Wirklichkeit: Arbeiten zum Radikalen Konstruktivismus*, Braunschweig-Wiesbaden: Vieweg.

GLASERSFELD, E. VON (1987b) 'Preliminaries to any theory of representation', in JANVIER, C. (ed.), *Problems of Representation in the Teaching and Learning of Mathematics*, Hillsdale, NJ: Lawrence Erlbaum, pp. 215–25.

GLASERSFELD, E. VON (1990a) 'Environment and Communication', in STEFFE, L.P. and WOOD, T. (eds), *Transforming Children's Mathematical Education*, Hillsdale, NJ: Lawrence Erlbaum, pp. 30–8.

GLASERSFELD, E. VON (1990b) 'Die Unterscheidung des Beobachters: Versuch einer Auslegung', in RIEGAS, V. and VETTER, C. (eds), *Zur Biologie der Kognition*, Frankfurt: Suhrkamp, pp. 281–95.

GLASERSFELD, E. VON (1992) 'Warum sprechen wir, und die Schimpansen nicht'? Paper presented at the Bozen conference, Sprachen des Menschen – Sprachen der Dinge.

SCHMIDT, S.J. (1992) 'Media, culture, media culture: A constructivist offer of conversation', *Poetics*, **21**, pp. 191–210.

SCHMIDT, S.J. (1994) *Kognitive Autonomie und Soziale Orientierung*, Frankfurt: Suhrkamp.

Section Two

Construction of the Self, Ethics, and Paideia

In his opening chapter Lewin raises several issues which he claims Glasersfeld's constructivism fails to address. Specifically, he urges Glasersfeld to consider that constructivism should entail an explicit ethics. He argues that ethical considerations are already tacit in many of Glasersfeld's positions, but they remain to be extricated. Lewin also wants constructivism to address more than the fact that people 'know' their world. He wants constructivism to address the question of what it means to exist in the world one knows – and this issue points directly to two additional questions. They are: (1) what can we mean by 'personal existence in a social world,' and (2) what is the 'self' and how can we describe its total formation (*paideia*). Lewin also argues that the construct of viability – in a hard sense of meeting with dire personal consequences of one's actions – is insufficient to account for why people develop feelings of what is and is not appropriate behavior relative to various contexts. Lewin claims that this, too, points to constructivism's need to address explicitly the nature and effects of social interaction. In his expansion of viability, Lewin suggests that the social context of mathematics and science is different from that prevailing in the humanities and social science. In mathematics and science, constraints on how the community operates are well understood and hence are made an explicit part of inquiry, whereas in the humanities and social sciences the community's constraints on individual interpretation are less well understood and hence discussions of them must occupy a greater part of critical inquiry. All this is aimed at sensitizing us to the need to consider the total education of our children, their *paideia*.

Larochelle (Ch. 5) wonders whether Lewin's position on ethics might not push constructivism toward becoming an ideology. Kieren (Ch. 6) suggests that Lewin's distinction between hard constraints (in the sciences) and soft constraints (in the humanities and social sciences) is less clear than one might imagine, and grounds his observations in discussions of instruction aimed at fostering young children's construction of fractional relationships. Gash (Ch. 7) augments Lewin's discussion by noting that constructivism can also be thought of as an ethical system consisting of consciously adopted first-person constraints.

> This collection is important for mathematics and science education because of the humanistic perspective Lewin brings to the discussion. His concern is that we not shut ourselves away from students' total education, focusing only on their scientific intellectual development.

4 Constructivism and *Paideia*

Philip Lewin

As I write, I am thinking back some twenty years to a time when I was a graduate student at Emory University in what I called 'epistemology' (and which Emory, not knowing what to make of it, covered its bets by calling 'general studies'). My thoughts stray to the implications for my own education which arose as I encountered Ernst's work. At the time, I knew I was interested in Piaget and in Kant, in Gregory Bateson and in cybernetics, in Heidegger and phenomenology; for me they were parts of the same puzzle. But, alas, apart from my intuitions and the hopeful support offered by a cohort of similarly confused peers, this was a puzzle which lacked academic legitimation – lacked legitimation, that is, until I met Ernst von Glasersfeld.

I want to discuss the implications of Glasersfeld's epistemology as it applies to education. One might say, without stretching the truth, that I – the kind of person I am, the kind of thinking I do – am at least in part one of those implications. I will be critical in some of my comments, but please understand that mine is criticism made from within a frame of respect and gratitude and continuing affection. The power of constructivism lies in how it underwrites viability, in how it extends permission for being. Ernst granted me that permission at a key moment in my education and for that I will always be grateful.

But Glasersfeld might quarrel with my rhetoric. He might want to say, as he does in the essay 'Knowing without Metaphysics', that 'constructivism deals with *knowing* not with *being*' (Glasersfeld, 1991, p. 17), that if anything, he granted only 'permission to know' but not any such metaphysical condition as 'permission to be'. Such ontological permission, he might say, flies in the face of the concept of viability and of a useful understanding of the nature of constraints. At best, he might want to maintain that he allowed an epistemic permission, a space within which I was free cognitively to operate.

Glasersfeld and I agree that there is no pure cognitive space, that all knowing is situated. He has spoken passionately and often of the distinction between an experiential reality and an ontological reality, and of how constructivism addresses the former but has nothing to say, because it can have nothing to say, of the latter. To this extent we have no quarrel. But I want more from an experiential space. For me, such a space is not solely epistemic. It too is implicated with being. If that being is not ontological, so be it; if it is only existential, only ontic, it is still being nonetheless. It is the space, as Heidegger (1962) noted, of my being-in-the-world, of my already finding myself situated. Traditional academic philosophy distinguishes epistemology from ethics and ontology. But because the being of concern to constructivism is the space of lived existence, such separation is not possible.

The epistemology of knowers who are existentially situated carries ethical commitments with it (whether they are explicitly acknowledged or not). This is so because 'to be situated' is to be situated with respect to a culture, a gender, a language, a bloodline – to the whole complex of conditions which constitute our 'thrownness' (Heidegger, 1962). Indeed, we already find ourselves enacting our thrownness – encultured and engendered, speaking a language, continuing a bloodline – long before we engage in any conscious reflection about these distinctions. It is in how we live within our thrownness, in the choices we have already made and the actions already undertaken, that our ethics become manifest.

Glasersfeld might also find my ready invocation of the first-person to be somewhat problematic. What is the referent of this 'I' in the phrase 'the kind of person I am'? Glasersfeld, it would seem, wants no part of such locutions. He has maintained that,

> As to the concept of self, constructivism – as an empirical epistemology – can provide a more or less viable model *for the construction of the experiential self*; but the self as the operative agent of construction, *the self as the center of subjective awareness, seems to me to be a metaphysical assumption and lies, at least for this constructivist, outside the domain of empirical construction.*
> (Glasersfeld, 1989, p. 447; his italics)

These remarks raise two symmetrical disagreements I have with Glasersfeld. They concern how constructivism is entailed with being (and not just knowing), and how it is implicated in questions of the self. These questions entail each other experientially (even if they do not do so syllogistically). How one thinks about one's situatedness with respect to the world and how one thinks about who one is are two sides of the same thinking, mutually co-arising. That is, 'the construction of the experiential self' is not separable from the 'operative agent of construction, the self as the center of subjective awareness'. While the 'experiencer' and 'the self as the center of subjective awareness' are separable in that lived experience is not always accompanied by reflective self-awareness, I maintain that they are jointly implicated in the act of construction. My disagreements with Glasersfeld in both cases are minor, matters of emphasis and clarification more than anything else. After all, perhaps Glasersfeld's favorite insight of Piaget's is the latter's claim that 'Intelligence . . . organizes the world by organizing itself' (Glasersfeld, 1982, p. 613). But to me these disagreements are worth addressing because they mark regions within which a philosophical position of constructivism overlaps with our existential situatedness in time. Constructivism, it seems to me, is the epistemology which is necessary (not just desirable) for knowers who are temporally embedded. It is what such knowers do epistemically, whether or not such doing reaches conscious awareness. Without some understanding of how our being arises from our situatedness in time, we are cut off from understanding our conditions as biological organisms and historical persons.

It is in this larger sense that I want to raise the question of education, not so much education as it takes place through formal schooling but education as what the Greeks called *paideia*, the complete process of education through which one became a competent participant within culture. For the Greeks, such *paideia* eventuated in a life of full involvement as a citizen in the *polis*. I wish to slightly expand *paideia*'s meaning to include education for life as a whole, as that education through which one's character is formed. It is the education that guides our ethics, our actual behavior (whether or not that ethics is compatible with its articulation, indeed whether or not that ethics ever reaches articulation). And because such a process of character-formation, of complete education, takes place whether we are aware of it or not, whether its outcome for ourselves or for others is what we consciously intend or not, I find it necessary to speak of a self, not as a metaphysical assumption or a marker of subjectivity, but as that region of *psyche* which undergoes *paideia*. While I will not articulate a concept of soul or deep self here, I will suggest as a horizon for my remarks that what we call character might be understood as the fluid composite of structures and habits of being which have arisen as *psyche* has undergone, and derived meaning from, its experience of living.

Viability and Hard Constraints

In one of Glasersfeld's essays, 'Learning as Constructive Activity,' he writes,

> Interpretation implies awareness of more than one possibility, deliberation, and rationally controlled choice.... To do the right thing is not enough; to be competent one must also know what one is doing and why it is right. (Glasersfeld, 1988, p. 328)

While the context for this remark is a discussion of learning in mathematics, the principle being set forth applies more generally and more deeply. What can it mean to 'know what one is doing and why it is right'?

Glasersfeld frequently cites organic thinkers such as Vico and Piaget, but here his remarks call to mind that other organic theorist, Aristotle. In the *Nicomachean Ethics*, Aristotle (1962) argues that practical intelligence, *phronesis*, consists in knowing how to apply the right rules at the right time in the right way. Acquiring such intelligence is not easy. To do so entails knowing that our choices must be sensitive to context and nuance, to degree and circumstance. And to do so is also a question of how we come to make the kinds of choices we do, of how we learn to recognize context and circumstance in the first place. This is a question of character, where I use 'character' in its literal meaning of 'how a thing is etched or marked'. I ask us to consider the question of character as a question of how we have been marked by our living, by our experience. To put it another way, I want to raise the question of how constraints function in those acts of constitution through which we become who we find ourselves to be.

My focus on the role of constraints is intentional. Glasersfeld, beautifully and appropriately, has used the notions of viability and constraints to deconstruct the notion of adaptation in the three Piagetian (1971, 1985) contexts of epistemology, cognition, and biology; that is, in contexts where the focus of attention is, respectively, the relation of truth to how it is formulated, the relation of knowers to that which they would know, and the relation of organisms to their environment. Let me review some of Glasersfeld's insights about these domains. (For ease of expression, I will use a biological vocabulary of 'organism' and 'environment' to stand for all three domains.)

Adaptation carries with it implications of perfect adjustment and of functional completeness: perfect adjustment in the sense that an adaptation is seen as the univocal solution to a problem in an organism's environment, where that problem can be identified as such by an external observer prior to the intervention of the organism; and functional completeness in the sense that an adaptation is taken always to serve a purpose, namely, to solve the pre-existing problem. The value and power of adaptationist discourse should be clear; it allows external observers to become experts, to understand the experience of organisms prior to and better than those organisms can understand it themselves. Speaking in terms of adaptation is the triumph of observation over participation. It gives us a Panglossian world (Gould and Lewontin, 1979) in which everything is just as it is because it could not possibly be any other way; if it could be, it would be. Indeed, the only shortcoming of adaptationist discourse is that it is wrong.

First, it is wrong epistemologically because it ignores the experience of the organism, who does not encounter 'problems' in its environment but rather experiences resistances, irritations, felt senses of incongruity or inappropriateness or unfitness. It is through these lived interactions that problems as such come to be conceptualized; the problems do not precede the interactions.

Second, adaptationist discourse is wrong empirically since it ignores how already existing structures of the organism – biochemical, skeletal, physiological, neurological, cognitive, affective, behavioral – negotiate what is experienced as resistance and so come to 'solve' what an external observer has called a 'pro-blem'. Constraints are internal as well as external, and organismic responsivity mediates both. But responsivity need not be, and ordinarily is not, either univocal or entirely functional. A variety of responses will ordinarily ameliorate a given disturbance. Because pre-existing structure must be taken into account, the response chosen may well optimize, addressing a number of factors, rather than maximize, satisfying only that factor which has become differentiated as the problem.

Glasersfeld has argued that the criterion of biological 'success' is any response which sustains organismic or cognitive integrity. The criterion of concern cannot be 'adaptation' in the sense of a univocal best response to a static environment; it can only be viability, any one of the many possible responses that are compatible with the ongoing organization of the biological or cognitive entity over time, with what Maturana and Varela (1980) call the continuing autopoiesis of the system. To use Lévi-Strauss's (1966) distinction, organisms and knowers are not engineers who predesign perfect solutions and then import the appropriate materials to the worksite; they are *bricoleurs* who fabricate acceptable responses out of the materials at hand, the resources available to them in their living. Constraints in epistemic or cognitive or biological contexts are not objectively existing conditions that can be defined as such, prior to and independent of activity on the part of the knower or organism. Instead, a constructivist perspective suggests that constraints emerge as a consequence of how a knower constructs invariances in its living. That is, constraints become apparent as resistances and disequilibria in particular domains of inquiry and interaction are experienced, and accommodations to them – biochemical, cognitive, behavioral – are undertaken. What we think of as learning is the process through which accommodations to perturbations are progressively assimilated and, at times, internalized at deeper and deeper levels of *psyche*, eventually becoming manifest as structure; that is, as habits of construal and behavior, as preferred ways of giving meaning to experience, as predispositions and aversions and anticipations, as character.

A rhetoric of viability (rather than one of adaptation) helps clarify the nature of constraints. But at the same time it makes clear the necessity for a further consideration which I believe Glasersfeld has underplayed, namely, the necessary inclusion of the sociocultural within the epistemology of radical constructivism. Just as radical constructivism has incorporated a theory of biology, so it also requires the supplement of an explicit social theory. The viability of constructions that are specifically cultural entails this. Indeed, as we move from biological to cognitive to cultural domains of epistemic construction, epistemic strategizing that seeks even an optimal response (let alone a univocally adaptive one) becomes less and less tenable as specific historical factors increase the range of possible construals within which viable epistemic construction can take place. Let me try to show why this is the case.

Adaptation, as I have said, implies an already existing environment to which an organism or knower must accommodate. The model of adaptation is ahistorical; it presupposes a situation into which an organism is born, a condition within which a knower already finds itself. Speaking biologically, the rhetoric of adaptation implies constraints that are already taken to exist as such, as so-called 'objective' features in an environment. For instance, a moist and oxygenated atmosphere is taken by this measure to pre-exist the seedling that will grow in it.

As I have already tried to indicate, we know that this perspective is incorrect; we know that biology is historical, that the moist bioclime of a seedling is in part a consequence of generations of forest that have held moisture rather than allowing it to erode the soil, and that the oxygenated atmosphere is the result of millions of years of photosynthesis. Earlier flora, that is, have helped create and continue to sustain the conditions necessary for seedlings to flourish. We know, in other words, that the ahistorical perspective of adaptation is incorrect, and that constraints become manifest in conjunction with the activity of the organism. The behavioral and structural features of the organism develop in congruence with the affordances (Gibson, 1966) of an environment through which the viability of the organism may be sustained. What we call 'constraints' and what we call 'the means through which an organism negotiates its continuing existence' co-arise; one does not precede the other. We also know that from the perspective of an observer, constraints are both external to the organism (as resistances and resources) and internal to it (as structures resulting from accommodations internalized over both ontogenetic and phylogenetic time). Yet given the enormously long extensions of phylogenetic and evolutionary time in comparison with the lifetime of any given organism, it is understandable why some would make the mistake of thinking of constraints as pre-existing features to which an organism must adapt.

It is easier to see that an ahistorical perspective is incorrect in cognitive settings, that the model of pre-existing constraints which permit viability is dangerously incomplete, when we shift our attention from the biological to the human. Human knowers, like all organisms, want to get by, but the variety of responses that will allow them simultaneously to satisfy external pressures and internal affects are legion. Such will surely be the case as well in formal school settings. We know, for instance, that the particular responses which evoke a teacher's approbation are historically contingent, that, to give one example, the 'right' answer to the question of 'Why do things fall'? will be 'desire for natural place' in one historical regime, 'gravitational attraction' in a second, 'gravity waves' in a third. Yet within each historical locus, the 'right' answer appears to be timeless and univocal.

Moreover, in the cognitive domain social factors come into play that enormously complicate what may seem the most straightforward of situations. I may choose to give one of a whole range of responses to the question of why things fall, from the currently accepted version of the scientific to the mockingly insolent, depending on my purposes in answering the question. If part of my concern is to impress my adolescent peers with my wit, or not to embarrass them if I know the answer and they don't, or to avoid singling myself out as 'a brain,' or to express my contempt for the teacher's expectations or for the entire school setting of examinations, I may choose a response that may appear to be non-optimal and even self-destructive. But such responses may carry with them a variety of associated features which contribute to their being viable in the long run.

In the epistemic domain as well a similar complication concerning historically situated conditions of inquiry may exist. This is particularly likely in those domains within which knowledge is explicitly presumed to be ahistorical such as mathematics and the natural sciences. While knowledge within these domains does change over time, among the presuppositions of those practices which we call scientific are that such changes within these domains of inquiry increasingly approximate toward a truth that is timeless and universal, that is not historically contingent. Let me emphasize that this is not an empirical claim about scientific knowledge; it is, rather, a transcendental claim, a claim about one of the conditions under which it is possible to do science. So long as we accept the premises of atomic theory, for instance, an atom of carbon has six protons in its nucleus whether we live in Topeka or Hiroshima, whether we practice organic chemistry in 1899 or 1999. The corpus of knowledge within science and mathematics is taken as ahistorical, pre-existing and independent of any particular inquiry, surviving any particular inquirer. And this is as true in instances of paradigm change as it is in those of normal science. While a change of paradigms may alter every single one of the fundamental assumptions governing the former disciplinary matrix, the new paradigm will be understood, in its turn, to provide its own ahistorical and universally adequate context for inquiry.

Scientific knowledge is taken as ahistorical, that is, not because of the time scales involved (as in the cases of cosmological or geological or biological time) but because of its epistemology. To practice science successfully, one simply must assume that basic facts about the world remain constant over time. It therefore follows that to do science, one ought to define, operationalize, and control variables in a way that elicits unambiguous data. This is the point of Popper's (1934) criterion of falsifiability. However idealized the criterion is as a description of actual scientific practice, it still serves as a regulative ideal. It suggests how useful it can be to operate with constraints that are both defined exactly and assumed to be timeless and unchanging. The most productive science will be that in which critical experiments can be performed; the condition for these is precisely that the conditions of inquiry are so rigorously specified as to permit only univocal responses (i.e., where all variables are isolated and controlled and none conflated). Indeed, it has been argued by scientists as well as philosophers that true scientific talent consists less in the ability to theorize or even to execute experiments and accumulate data than it does in the ability to set up conditions of inquiry in such a way that experimental outcomes are unambiguous.

As a result of this presupposition of ahistoricity in logico-mathematical and scientific inquiries, something very curious happens to epistemology, especially when it is brought into an educational setting: one may be radically constructivist in intent and still hold forth for a correctness of response that is essentially univocal. One may invoke a rhetoric of viability and still allow in practice for only one possible solution. All the work of specification will have been done by the teacher drawing upon the reigning tradition in establishing the conditions of inquiry while the student/knower is conceptualized as creative and inventive. In some ways, this 'paradox of happy agreement' may seem the best of all possible epistemic worlds. Given specified boundary conditions, each student independently pursuing his or her own best intuitions comes up with a solution identical to all the others. Each concludes that (given a Euclidean framework) alternate interior angles are congruent; that (given the imaginary numbers) the square root of -1 exists; that (ignoring evaporation and the limits of eyeball measurements) the tall, thin beaker contains the same amount of water as the short, broad one; that (having internalized stoichiometry and abandoned eyeball measurements completely) a mole of carbon and a mole of magnesium contain the same number of atoms.

In other words, if the boundary conditions specifying a domain of inquiry are so well demarcated as effectively to preclude all but one solution, the claim that knowledge is constructed by a student/knower who has not participated in specifying these boundary conditions but who simply has been taught to accept them as given must be understood in two distinct senses, an epistemic sense and a sociocultural sense. Epistemologically, each knower constructs his or her own knowledge; socioculturally, each knower accepts authoritatively endorsed knowledge as timelessly true. The danger is that these two senses may become conflated. Should that occur, the specification of boundary conditions that made univocity inevitable will be forgotten or become invisible to itself, and the contingency of knowledge that is historically variable will be taken as universally and ahistorically true. We know that domains and their boundary conditions are themselves historically constituted; in some cases (most notably, the domains of scientific and mathematical inquiry), they are specifically constituted as ahistorical. But those acts of constitution must not be forgotten or ignored in the educational setting.

I note in passing that this apparent paradox between the epistemic and the socio-cultural permeates Piaget's work: given a presupposed and historically constituted set of initial conditions which define a domain of inquiry, each of us as independent knowers is taken to construct what we agree is the same reality. It is because of this paradox that there has been so much discussion over whether or not Piaget's genetic epistemology is a realist epistemology (e.g. Richards and Glasersfeld, 1980; Lewin, 1988). Piaget left the question *aporetic*. Resolving it would have required him to undertake an investigation into the nature of those epistemic acts through which the boundary conditions that specify domains of inquiry were themselves constructed.

If the conditions of inquiry are taken to be rigorous and unchanging – that is, if they specify a domain of inquiry as universal and timeless – then the student/knower can be permitted an apparently untrammeled freedom that is actually quite limited since only a few or even one 'solution' or 'adaptation' will suffice. In these instances, viability approaches adaptation as a limit; the only solutions will be optimal. Even Glasersfeld permits this ambiguity to appear. In one of his discussions of the implications of constructivism for education, for instance, he argues that 'the constructivist teacher will not be primarily interested in observable results, but rather in what students *think* they are doing and *why* they believe that their way of operating will lead to the solution of the problem at hand' (Glasersfeld, 1991, p. 24). But this may be tantamount to affirming that insofar as the boundary conditions of inquiry are well defined, the unconstrained freedom of the knower can be endorsed not because of any authentic interest in students' constructions but despite them. Because the chreodes of these particular selection landscapes are so deeply grooved, the happy conclusion of equifinality, of many paths to the same end, will prevail. In these cases, we have the *aporetic* luxury of speaking both of the importance of students' constructions and of there being 'the solution of the problem at hand'. It thereby becomes a simple matter to trivialize the power of

Constructivism and Paideia

construction in comparison with the criterion of getting the right answer. However unwittingly, constructivism can encourage a pedagogy that undermines its best insights. It should be clear that this is the direct opposite of Glasersfeld's intent, and the passage I quote goes on to emphasize that

> if one wants to generate understanding, the reasons why a student operates in a certain way are far more indicative of the student's stage of conceptual development than whether or not these operations lead to a result that the teacher finds acceptable. (Glasersfeld, 1991, p. 24)

My point, though, is that if even Glasersfeld can be mis-read due to the paradox of happy agreement, far less circumspect writers and readers may actively if unwittingly contribute to the mis-understanding of radical constructivism. It is due to the conflation of epistemic and sociocultural factors that subtle inquiries into how sociomathematical norms are negotiated in the classroom (like those reported in this volume) become germane, and that the focus of concern turns, as Glasersfeld notes, from 'observable results' to 'what students think they are doing and why'.

Viability and Soft Constraints

The epistemic situation becomes even more elusive if the constraints in a selection landscape are primarily cultural. What if, that is, our concern is education in more amorphous domains of inquiry such as philosophy or sociology, or even with the education known as *paideia* with respect to one's participation within culture? Here viability will have a much different meaning than it does in mathematics and the physical sciences, not because there will be no solutions to support authentic construction, but because there may be both too many that are viable and none that is optimal to the problem at hand. Within mathematics and the physical sciences, conditions of inquiry are ordinarily well defined; scientists delight in confounding each other's pet theories (as Popper implied), and even the most Rogerian of teachers sometimes will think, even if they dare not say, 'wrong'. Within the living experience of biology, constraints may be almost as clearly demarcated; for all their genomic variability and organismic resourcefulness, species are far more likely to become extinct than to survive over geological time. But within culture, conditions of survival are often too weak or too slowly acting for their effects to guide behavior in the present. I must eat, but what shall it be? I must work, but at what? And when I eat, how long can I indulge my gluttony or my anorexia before I sicken from either? And when I work, shall it be at law or medicine, or at embezzlement or drug dealing? When will the consequences of my choices become apparent?

Further, living in time alters the situatedness of the knower as the grounds of viability are redefined as a result of earlier operations. An ethics will accompany our living not in the sense of an explicit moral code (that, even when it is articulated, may be irrelevant to our actual behavior) but in the sense of an implicit set of guiding orientations for how particular behaviors and actions that we undertake have been chosen. At the same time, the consequences of poor choices may be postponed indefinitely in a way that is not likely in either scientific contexts (where poor choice results in swift refutation experimentally or from one's peers, or both) or biological ones (where poor choice results in injury, sickness, or death).

Epistemically, the culinary choices of an anorectic and a triathlete are equal; epistemically, the behavioral choices of a John Gotti and of a Morris Dees are equal; epistemically, the corporate choices of an Exxon Corporation and of a Ben & Jerry's are equal. In these cases and any number of others we might consider, viability has been maintained as a result of the particular choices each has made. But does it seem likely that the constraints enacted by how each has lived in the past would be experientially neutral in terms of epistemic construals for the future? Is it not instead more likely that how an anorectic has behaved epistemically in the past will partially constitute the constraints through which future construals will be made, that part of how food is perceived results from a history of how food has been perceived? Do we really believe that each time John Gotti faced a certain resistance in the conduct of his affairs that his prior behaviors had not sedimented in a way that marked how he anticipated his options for the future? Is it not possible that the manner in which the Exxon Corporation has sought to present a benign face to the general public did not lead it to underestimate the initial severity and continuing environmental impact of the Exxon Valdez oil spill in Prince William Sound? It is not only 'intelligence [that] organizes the world by organizing itself', but the self in the sense of character also does so; it too organizes the world by organizing itself.

Culturally, many solutions permit viability. John Gotti is still alive, and Exxon is still posting profits. An analysis in the cultural domain that limits itself to a criterion of viability is not so much incorrect as incomplete, if for no other reason than that viability *per se* lacks the rigor that obtains for it in biological and epistemic contexts. Do we make choices only with consideration of immediate needs and desires, or should we also consider family or community or country? Should the highest value be to gratify temptation, or should we instead honor 'higher' values of restraint and sacrifice? From the perspective of viability, many answers are equal. Indeed, a rhetoric of (mere) viability arguably is compatible with a life and ethics of nihilism. This is not an intended consequence of constructivism but it is correlative to the ambiguity that characterizes cultural life, especially if we limit our epistemology to a consideration of the experiential reality of the cognizer and thereby minimize or ignore coordinate ontic commitments that involve how a knower manages to survive, day by day, from within his or her thrownness. As Glasersfeld has noted,

> ethics itself cannot actually be based on the viability of schemes of action or thought, because this viability is always gauged in the context of specific goals – and it is in the choice of goals that ethics must manifest itself. (1995, p. 127)

Constructivism and Paideia

It is ironic that the possibility of nihilism increases as the degree of cultural complexity advances. In contemporary Western culture, we are buffered to an extraordinary degree from those immediate constraints to which non-human organisms are subject. Those of you reading this chapter, I would guess, are not immediately subject to starvation or death by exposure; with our sophisticated medical technology, we survive many of the most severe injuries and illnesses; in the avenues of the city which we as members of a particular socio-economic class travel, death by predation remains rare. Yet ethically any of us may stumble from one love affair to the next, from one belief system to another, from one career to the next, acting alternatively as maximizers of what we construe to be our self-interest or as selfless sacrificers for the public good, or simply as passive players in the larger cultural drift, all the while remaining at best half-aware of the implications of our actions upon other people, upon the world, upon our deeper selves – and all while maintaining our viability. The moral blindness compatible with cultural life is one of the latter's most curious features.

Where does this leave constructivism? That the constructions of the knower will generate their own constraints is a central cybernetic tenet. This process has been acknowledged as well in a number of other contexts. Freud invoked it to account for the ontogenesis of the superego out of the vicissitudes of the instincts; Winnicott speaks of it in the formation of the compliant or 'false self'; it is at the heart of Kelly's (1955) psychology of personal constructs. We see it as well in attachment behaviors, or, for that matter, in the whole range of phenomena that fall under the rubric of cultural learning – gender-specific or class-specific behaviors, social distance, courtesy, facial expression, and so on. All these behaviors illustrate what Bateson (1972) referred to as 'learning to learn' or 'deutero-learning'; all draw upon that dynamic described by Castoriadis (1987) through which *psyche* is enveloped within the 'social imaginary', and whose result establishes what Bourdieu (1985) has called the 'habitus'. Similarly, poststructuralists and feminists have begun to explicate how the person is constituted through its situatedness within cultural practices. But if the variety of processes through which internal constraints are generated has begun to be widely acknowledged, there is little in this variety that precludes the compatibility of such constraints with nihilism.

There is a necessarily ethical dimension to epistemic construction which we fail to acknowledge at our peril, yet constructivists have sometimes sought to do just that. There is an *aporia* here. On the one hand, constructivists have reproduced the value-free rhetoric of positivist science and have maintained that constructivism is an epistemic position, not an ethical one. On the other hand, constructivism has had an implicit ethics all along. That is, the behaviors valued quite explicitly by constructivism are of active knowers practicing freedom of inquiry, demonstrating spontaneous creativity and resourcefulness. These behaviors, not by chance, are in dynamic resonance with some of the most cherished illusions of contemporary culture. Who, in this clime, would advocate passive knowing or rote memorization? Who would not champion creativity?

Philip Lewin

Just as today everyone claims to be an environmentalist (for no one boasts of harming the natural world), so we find that pedagogically and perhaps even epistemologically everyone has become a constructivist. As in 'the paradox of happy agreement', constructivists seem to have the best of both worlds: they operate by an ethics that is so thoroughly endorsed by society at large that they can claim to be beyond ethics altogether. The implicit ethics of constructivism coincides so completely with the hegemonic values of our time that constructivist ethics may have become invisible to itself, while simultaneously, some who call themselves constructivists argue that the task of ethical legitimation is epistemologically untenable.

Glasersfeld is aware of this overall problematic: witness his frequent references to the tradition of skepticism and of the historical situatedness of knowledge described by Vico. It is reflected, as well, in his interest in second-order cybernetics, the cybernetics of an observer who recognizes his or her own involvement in the process of knowing. But a cybernetics of the knower's involvement in knowing is actually a cybernetics of complicity, a cybernetics that would take as its focus the responsibility of the knower for creating and sustaining the conditions under which epistemic inquiry proceeds. It is a cybernetics of those boundary conditions which so often become invisible, mere background, to inquiry. Glasersfeld has resisted pursuing the implications of complicity for radical constructivism. Yet to the extent constructivism fails to reflect upon the ethics which will arise through complicity as a necessary (and not merely adventitious) consequence of epistemic construction, others will be free to find whatever ethics they please within it, or no ethics at all.

Indeed, it seems to me that the rush to fill such a vacuum lies behind the excursions into ethics that Maturana has undertaken in the last decade. Maturana has maintained, for instance,

> that love is the emotion that constitutes social phenomena; that when love ends, social phenomena end; and that interactions and relations that take place between living systems under other emotions different from love, are not social interactions or social relations. Therefore, when I speak of love I do not speak of a sentiment, nor do I speak of goodness, nor recommend kindness. When I speak of love I speak of a biological phenomenon; I speak of the emotion that specifies the domain of actions in which living systems co-ordinate their actions in a manner that entails mutual acceptance, and I claim that such operation constitutes social phenomena. (1988, pp. 64–5)

The performative ambiguity surrounding this notion of love arises, it seems to me, from failing ontologically to reckon with the different conditions of viability within biology and culture. Emphasizing that they are different is one of the chief concerns of this chapter. To specify 'love' as a biological category is to smooth over the complex and agonizing forms it takes culturally, and to ignore the diversity of constraints within which it appears. Moreover, stipulating a definition of love only exacerbates the difficulty of thinking clearly about this

Constructivism and Paideia

most profound of affects since the everyday meanings of the word, with all their semantic complexity, continue to linger. Thus, to argue as Maturana does that

> Slavery does not constitute an ethical problem in a society in which master and slave sincerely accept slavery as a manner of living in mutual acceptance, or as a legitimate manner of entering in a work agreement. (1988, p. 73)

is simply to have forgotten or ignored deutero-learning. It is to have covered over and rendered invisible how it is that all of us, including slaves, are marked by our living, and how the sedimentations of past construals and behaviors become the internal constraints anticipatory and defining of our present realities. Ironically given the sophistication of Maturana's epistemology, there is no memory of a history of interactions in his claim. The master and slave, despite utterly opposed formative experiences, are presented as though they have freely entered into their social arrangement. Indeed, by these terms, a wife who remained with an abusive husband, a shopkeeper who paid protection money to the local thugs, a Holocaust survivor who acted as a kapo, all existed in relations of love with their oppressors for all entered into relations of 'mutual acceptance' with them.

Constructivism and Ethics

But if Maturana can be faulted for overstating the domain of ethics, Glasersfeld is guilty of understating it. In *Radical Constructivism*, he introduces the topic of ethics as a secondary concern in a discussion of the role other people play in the construction of social and self-knowledge. He states,

> If it is others from whose reactions I derive some indication as to the properties I can ascribe to myself, and if my knowledge of these others is the result of my own construction, there is an inherent circularity in that procedure. In my view, this is not a vicious circle, because we are not free to construct others in any way we like. As with all other constructs, the 'models' we build up of others either turn out to be viable in our experience, or they do not and have to be discarded.
>
> This dependence on viability in our construction of other individuals has a consequence that leads into the direction of ethics, a realm that is no less opaque for constructivism than for other rational theories of knowledge. Nevertheless, the fact that the individual needs the corroboration of others to establish the intersubjective viability of ways of thinking and acting, entails a concern for others as autonomous constructors. If we force them in any way to conform to our ideas, we *ipso facto* invalidate them as corroborators. (Glasersfeld, 1995, p. 127)

Philip Lewin

Glasersfeld explicitly links his position to the Kantian imperative always to treat others as ends rather than as means. He observes that

> Strictly speaking, [the Kantian imperative] is not an 'ethical' precept but a prerequisite for ethics. It simply asserts that we have to consider other people's humanity and that we ought not to treat them as objects. All philosophy of ethics is implicitly based on this assumption. Yet it does not say why it should be so. (ibid.)

Seeking to provide an epistemic basis for what he sees as a meta-ethical principle, Glasersfeld continues (concluding with the observation I have already quoted concerning the limitation of viability for ethics):

> Constructivism provides at least one basic reason. From its perspective, the concern for others can be grounded in the individual subject's *need* for other people in order to establish an intersubjective viability of ways of thinking and acting. Others have to be considered because they are irreplaceable in the construction of a more solid experiential reality. This in itself does not constitute an ethical precept either, but it does supply a rational basis for the development of ethics. Let me emphasize that ethics itself cannot actually be based on the viability of schemes of action or thought, because this viability is always gauged in the context of specific goals – and it is in the choice of goals that ethics must manifest itself. (ibid.)

Glasersfeld's discussion raises several points. First, it should be noted that his analyses of both knowledge and of ethics are remarkably Kantian in character. As in Kant, the domain of knowledge is constrained by the limitations and capacities of the knower, and the domain of morality is understood to be separate from knowledge. The Kantian dualism between a phenomenal realm subject to empirical law and therefore to epistemic investigation, and a noumenal realm of freedom within which moral judgment resides but about which we can know nothing, is implicitly reaffirmed. Yet stepping beyond Kant, Glasersfeld takes reason to ground ethical practice. How this grounding rests within a Kantian framework is unclear.

Second, I believe Glasersfeld's effort to preserve a sharp separation between ethics and epistemology fails (though I believe this to be a happy failure). It fails in part precisely as reason is taken to provide a ground for ethics; the boundary between them is already blurred. But we can see its failure more clearly if we examine Glasersfeld's injunction that we view others 'as autonomous constructors'. This claim is certainly consistent with a Kantian ethic but it does not follow from constructivism. All a constructivist can know is that others produce ways of knowing and being. He or she can have no idea how these came about; there is certainly no basis for thinking of these ways as having arisen autonomously, especially if one simultaneously maintains that a process of social interaction is partially responsible for them. As I have noted above, a major theme of contemporary thought has been to render suspect

Constructivism and Paideia

the so-called autonomy of a knower with respect to their social and cultural inscription, and Glasersfeld himself acknowledges that 'it is others from whose reactions I derive some indication as to the properties I can ascribe to myself'.

Similarly, with respect to the claim that others help one construct a 'more solid experiential reality', the question arises from a constructivist perspective of what it would mean to say that one's experience of reality had become 'more solid'. How would one know? Presumably, a 'more solid experiential reality' is one that has become less subject to perturbation. But since this is a reality that has been intersubjectively negotiated, it cannot be 'more solid' in an ontological or epistemic sense, but only in the social sense that one successfully exists in a consensual domain with others. Such a way of existing may or may not be a desirable one as a basis for ethics. It may underwrite a concern for social justice but it may also warrant adhering to unexamined common sense or even to extreme prejudice and discrimination. Indeed, it is not merely compatible with the status quo, but insofar as it values consensus, it may place a higher value on avoiding social embarrassment than it does on social advocacy. In this reading, a social reality that receives the most intersubjective affirmation, that is the least contentious or controversial, would be the most solid. Or, to put it another way, there is nothing in an ethical posture that entails it will encounter less perturbation. Indeed, the opposite is far more likely to be the case, as one's ethically based actions encounter the disequilibrations of those who resist. Social consensus, in other words, cannot of itself secure a 'rational basis for the development of ethics'.

Glasersfeld concludes this discussion by saying that 'the individual has a need to construct others and to keep these models of others as viable as possible because only viable others can lend the highest level of support to the subject's experiential reality' (ibid., p. 128). But this seems to be a misstatement. Viability (for a constructivist) is not a matter of degree; one is not more or less viable, one is either viable or one is not. Moreover, even taken at face value, why should it be true that one's models of others should be kept as viable as possible? There are any number of examples one could cite – from climbing a corporate hierarchy to succeeding in politics, from getting out of an uncomfortable marriage to getting out from under unwanted possessions, from holding on to one's racism and prejudice to holding on to one's affirmation of multicultural identity – in which it is in the subject's interest to construct others in stereotypical ways, to see them as less worthy of respect than oneself, to deny them the same viability one grants oneself, and thereby to make one's current experiential reality more impervious to perturbation. In other words, Glasersfeld's claims, insofar as they are epistemic, seem to me to be untenable. They seem to conflate two meanings of viability: (1) viability as taking sufficient account of others to 'get by' in one's dealings with them; and (2) viability as respecting others as autonomous constructors.

But though Glasersfeld's conflation may be untenable epistemically, it would certainly be appealing as a foundation for ethics if it could be defended. That is, I see Glasersfeld's argument as covertly inserting ethical premises that,

Philip Lewin

in accord with Kant's moral imperative, would treat others with respect, as ends and not means. In this way, Glasersfeld can both maintain a Kantian framework and ground a desirable ethics within constructivist epistemology. But, again from a Kantian perspective, this is precisely what he cannot do: the phenomenal domain of epistemology has no warrant to lay ground for the noumenal domain of ethics. Indeed, Kant expressly forbids epistemology from doing so due to reason's tendency to overreach itself.

I see a problem, then, in how Glasersfeld formulates the relation between constructivism and ethics. I see him as wanting both to be faithful to Kant and to go farther than Kant, both to sanction ethically neutral epistemic claims about viability and to support a Kantian ethic that treats persons a priori as morally autonomous. On the one hand, Glasersfeld acknowledges that even if constructivism is primarily an epistemological position, it must, at the very least, lay a foundation for the further development of an ethics. It requires this as a consequence of its concern with the formation of an experiential self (not to mention its interest in mounting a pre-emptive defense against those who charge radical constructivism with relativism and nihilism). But on the other hand, Glasersfeld's reluctance to specify an ethics leaves his position vulnerable, both affirming and denying an ethics, both asserting the epistemic limits of constructivism for ethics while simultaneously transgressing these limits. This is a pity, for the epistemological value of radical constructivism is far too great to allow it to founder over its incomplete conceptualization of ethics. Instead, I would argue that constructivism already harbors a covert ethics, and while the fact that it is already ethical is a good thing, the fact that its ethics is covert is not.

Constructivism requires an explicit ethical posture. The normative ethics of Kant, however, cannot provide it. Insofar as Glasersfeld seeks to appropriate Kant for his own project, he too becomes subject to the Kantian separation between ethics and epistemology which, I have tried to show, the development of his ideas does not sanction. But perhaps the virtue ethics of Aristotle can help radical constructivism avoid the pitfalls into which a too-strong allegiance to the normative ethics of Kant has led it. Earlier I pointed out that in the *Nicomachean Ethics*, Aristotle argues that practical intelligence, *phronesis*, consists in knowing how to apply the right rules at the right time in the right way, and that such sensitivity was already part of Glasersfeld's sensibility. Let me follow Aristotle's suggestion a bit further.

Phronesis can only be achieved insofar as it has been lived, insofar as one's own experience, rightly understood, has come to function as the tacit guide to one's ethos, one's behavior. It emerges out of our immersion in time, out of a personal history that defines for each of us the particular nuances of our experiential realities. Aristotle's answer to the question of rightly understanding one's experience was that to do so meant understanding how one's choices contributed to the formation and maintenance of the kind of human community of which one would want to be a part. For us, of course, this perspective is of uncertain value. Knowing that the kind of community which Aristotle idealized was one in which women and slaves and foreigners and even manual laborers could never achieve full citizenship might well lead us to feel that these are not the kinds of social orders with which we wish to be associated. We have no guiding vision of a perfect society to which we piously adhere. We may have no guiding vision at all except the one that we imperfectly and teleonomically develop through our practices in our daily creation of ourselves.

If we take radical constructivism seriously, if we understand that constraints are internally generated through our living in time, then it seems to me we must equally take seriously how the sedimentation of those constraints anticipates our behaviors in the future. It seems to me that the relative coherence of those constraints constitutes 'character', an internal region of epistemic and ethical inertia. It does not merely lay the ground for ethics; it already is an ethics.

Heinz von Foerster has also suggested the desirability of an implicit ethics, an ethics that does not parade itself in moral codes and commandments, but that resides instead within language and action, within sensitivity to the other, within structures of trust. He has formulated as a kind of ethical imperative the maxim to 'act so as to *increase* the number of choices' (1992, p. 16). I would alter his maxim by construing it psychologically. The ethical task that I would recommend then becomes one in which increasing the number of choices serves as a means of richly recovering one's own past, with all its choices and choice points, all its decisions and indecisions, all its failures and mistakes. It serves as a way to rediscover, in its fullness, all of who we have been so that we might know who we are. As a psychological guide, I would rephrase von Foerster's maxim to read 'act so as to be fully conscious of all the choices one has already made and already lived'.

Glasersfeld's radical constructivism has focused on the spontaneity of knowers as they meet their future. I would invite us to consider how our epistemic spontaneity is situated with respect to how we have been already marked in our living. It is there that the implications of constructivism for education will be found.

References

ARISTOTLE (1962) *Nicomachean Ethics*, tr. M. Ostwald, Indianapolis: Bobbs-Merrill.
BATESON, G. (1972) 'Social planning and the concept of deutero-learning', in *Steps to an Ecology of Mind*, New York: Ballantine Books, pp. 159–76.
BOURDIEU, P. (1985) *Outline of a Theory of Practice*, tr. R. Nice, Cambridge: Cambridge University Press.
CASTORIADIS, C. (1987) *The Imaginary Institution of Society*, tr. K. Blamey, Cambridge, Mass.: MIT Press.
FOERSTER, H. VON (1992) 'Ethics and second-order cybernetics', *Cybernetics and Human Knowing* 1, 1, pp. 9–19.
FOUCAULT, M. (1977) *Discipline and Punish. The Birth of the Prison*, tr. A. Sheridan, New York: Random House.

GIBSON, J.J. (1966) *The Senses Considered as Perceptual Systems*, Boston: Houghton Mifflin.
GLASERSFELD, E. VON (1982) 'An interpretation of Piaget's constructivism', *Revue Internationale de Philosophie*, 142-3, pp. 612-35.
GLASERSFELD, E. VON (1988) 'Learning as constructive activity', in *The Construction of Knowledge*, Salinas: Intersystems Publications, pp. 310-38.
GLASERSFELD, ERNST VON (1989) 'Facts and self from a constructivist point of view', *Poetics* 18, pp. 435-48.
GLASERSFELD, ERNST VON (1991) 'Knowing without metaphysics: aspects of the radical constructivist position', in STEIER, FREDERICK (ed.), *Research and Reflexivity*, Newbury Park, California: Sage Publications, pp. 12-29.
GLASERSFELD, E. VON (1995) *Radical Constructivism: A Way of Knowing and Learning*. London: Falmer Press.
GOULD, S.J. and LEWONTIN, R. (1979) 'The Spandrels of San Marco and the Panglossian Paradigm', *Proceedings of the Royal Society of London*, 205, pp. 581-98.
HEIDEGGER, M. (1962) *Being and Time*, tr. J. Macquarrie and E. Robinson, New York: Harper & Row.
KELLY, G. (1955) *The Psychology of Personal Constructs*, New York: W.W. Norton.
LEVI-STRAUSS, C. (1966) *The Savage Mind*, Chicago: University of Chicago Press.
LEWIN, P. (1988) 'Richard Kitchener's, *Piaget's Theory of Knowledge. Genetic Epistemology and Scientific Reason*', *Journal of Mind and Behavior*, 9, pp. 89-96.
MATURANA, H. (1988) 'Reality: The search for objectivity or the quest for a compelling argument', *Irish Journal of Psychology*, **9**, 1, pp. 25-82.
MATURANA, H. and VARELA, F. (l980) *Autopoeisis and Cognition*, Dordrecht: Reidel.
PIAGET, J. (1971) *Biology and Knowledge*, tr. B. Walsh, Chicago: University of Chicago Press.
PIAGET, J. (1985) *The Equilibration of Cognitive Structures*, tr. T. Brown and K. Thampy, Chicago: University of Chicago Press.
POPPER, K. (1934) *The Logic of Scientific Discovery*, New York: Harper & Row.
RICHARDS, J. and GLASERSFELD, E. VON (1980) 'Jean Piaget, psychologist of epistemology: A discussion of Rotman's *Jean Piaget: Psychologist of the Real*', *Journal for Research in Mathematics Education*, **11**, 1, pp. 29-36.

5 Radical Constructivism: Notes on Viability, Ethics and Other Educational Issues

Marie Larochelle

Constructivism could come in for severe questioning if, as with certain other schools of thought, it did not show its epistemological colors, which is to say, the limitations, both constraining and empowering, within which it operates. On that point, it seems to me that radical constructivism, as conceived by Glasersfeld, is relatively clear: it is not a theory of the world, but rather of the organism which constructs for himself or herself a theory of the world (Glasersfeld, 1987a, 1995). Furthermore, this organism is not seen as an agent or an actor in his or her psycho-sociological totality, but rather as an observer or an 'ordinary'[1] subject of which the historicity and sociality are also of 'ordinary' variety (wherein historicity refers to a sort of operative genesis whereas sociality refers to the constitution of the 'I and you' via the reciprocity of routine experiences shared by subjects).[2]

From this perspective, constructivism might appear to some as a theory which contains an 'impoverished conception' of the actor. At least such an impression is conveyed by Lewin's repeated criticisms (Ch. 4) concerning the 'cold' rationalization of 'self' as shown, for example, in the way constructivism purportedly deals with the 'self' only in experiential terms. It is true that constructivism does not aim to elaborate a 'unified theory' of the actor; moreover, were it to do so, it would, to put it mildly, be placing itself in an uncomfortable position in terms not only of its epistemological premises but also of its deliberate option in favor of action, that is to say, in favor of processes rather than the 'states of the subject' or the 'states of the world'. Just as constructivism has rejected the illusion of the object, it must not allow itself to lapse into accepting the illusion of the 'knowable subject', as Morf (1998) defines it, for fear of simply making a metaphorical shift along the same ontological continuum. However, this does not signify that the question of the self, to continue with this example, is devoid of interest for constructivism. Nevertheless, its stance on reflexivity obliges it to approach the question of the self *other-wise*, most probably by adopting an approach which diverges from that favored by Lewin and which also appears to me to derive from what certain sociologists call the concern for ontological security.

Accordingly, a radical constructivist does not attempt to know what the self *is*, nor to locate it relative to a supreme faculty or a center of subjective consciousness (Glasersfeld, 1987b), let alone to a somewhat supernatural psychic force which could be thought of as exercising unilateral control over all the subject's actions. In this respect, the process of sedimentation that Lewin mentions seems to me to be of critical importance. It goes without saying that this metaphor points to the fact that how a subject acts or figures things out is not independent from his or her own history and experiences, as radical constructivism has also maintained. However, Lewin's imagery is tinged with a certain fatalism which causes these experiences to be viewed statically, as if the subject were no longer functioning in the present and had not been transformed by his or her experience. Moreover, by way of analogy, the concepts of 'self' and 'sedimentation' appear to me, accordingly, as a psychological version of the determinist sociological theories, with the 'hidden forces' of social structures and institutions being transferred to the 'self'. Constructivism of the kind I am referring to questions the origin of the self, the conditions of its coming-to-be, as well as of its actual invention, and, finally, how the concept, *via* language and transactions between subjects becomes a way of interpreting experiences and identifying similarities and invariants within these experiences. To be sure, constructivism questions the effects of the recurrence of these invariants on the experience of a stable world which these invariants make possible, a stable world which gives the impression of an identity, of 'Eigen values'. In short, to my way of thinking, constructivism views the issue of self as a reflexive and recursive construction, 'a reflexive ordering of narratives of the self or of self identity', in Giddens' expression (1993, p. 460).

In addition, this type of constructivism keeps its distances with regard to the issues involving self and identity, for a number of reasons. For one, the whole question has been weighted down with particularly heavy meanings throughout history (fixedness, causality). As well, the actions of the subject have been ascribed the curious status of 'outer shell' to some inner latent core, as if the subject's meanings and ways of making sense of action escape his or her control and understanding. Certainly, I am not saying that the subject masters all the conditions and consequences of his or her undertakings, nor that actions are only realized piecemeal; I want to emphasize, rather, the dangers of theorizations which in a way are based on a conspiracy, be it couched in psychoanalytical or social terms, and which at the same time obscures not only the active, reflexive and oriented character of action but also its potential for renewal and innovation. Furthermore, there is also the risk of petrification which threatens all discursive production, as has been brought out by Foerster (in Segal, 1986). In education circles, the interpretation of the works of Piaget serves to demonstrate the continued need for vigilance within constructivism. For example, the concept of operating stage or structure, which was an analytic tool in the original work, has, through the multiple usages to which it has been subjected, acquired *'une épaisseur de réalité'* (the characteristics of a substance) according to the expression of Moscovici and Hewstone (1984),[3] thus causing this concept to be transformed into a sort of logico-mathematical homunculus, to paraphrase Foerster (in Segal, 1986).

Even within such constraints, however, constructivism seems to me to provide fertile ground for the renewal of educational practices. Having noted the promise of constructivism, we obviously continue to be faced with the task of translating its notions, articulating their interconnections and placing them within contexts. It cannot be otherwise, for epistemological constructivism is not a teaching model. In light of the preceding considerations, it is my goal in the remainder of this chapter to pursue a number of tangents already alluded to. In particular, I will address certain questions raised by Lewin, notably the 'educational handling' of the concept of viability and the *siren song* of ethics.

About Viability

To begin with, it should be pointed out that I subscribe to Lewin's point of view when he raises the question of how constructivism in education is on its way to being identified with 'epistemological correctness' in the absence of a serious and thorough examination of the ins and outs of this theory and of our interpretative habits as well. Indeed, as Bednarz and I have elaborated elsewhere (1998), constructivism anticipates thoroughgoing questioning of basic principles and epistemological 'breaks' (*ruptures*) of a kind that are much more disquieting than complacent affirmations of the sort, 'If there is more than one way to get to Rome, all roads do eventually lead to Rome!' Nevertheless, generally speaking, it is this 'weak' version of constructivism which seems to have won the favor of actors in education, thanks to such earthshaking principles concerning the active participation by students in the construction and learning of knowledge.

Generally speaking, it can be said that renewed interest in the knowledge of students seems to have barely changed the usual conventions of teaching activity, whatever the level of instruction. It is certainly true that the student's point of view is more often sought than was previously the case (that is, in fact, *the* major effect of so-called constructivism on educational practices; see Morf, 1998). However, more often than not, the concern for what the student has to say is limited to a normative perspective rather than to one which aims to clarify the conditions in which the student's point of view first arises and then takes root. In this context, listening is engaged in only so as to spot 'what's gone wrong' in the student's point of view – *vis-à-vis* official knowledge, of course – without regard for the fact that the nature and scope of this knowledge are potentially quite distinct from the view developed by the student. All in all, it is as if the legitimacy and relevance of knowledge were not dependent upon a context. The important thing, then, is not the 'complexification' of the student's knowledge nor his or her openness to other realms of possibility, using the terms of Piaget (in Inhelder et al., 1977), but, rather, the narrowing of the gap between what the student knows and what he or she ought to know, as is shown by analyses of teaching episodes carried out by, among others,

Marie Larochelle

Geddis (1988), Gutierrez et al. (1995), Voigt (1985), and Larochelle (1998). Thus, it is still the same *schema of docility* (Foucault's expression, 1975) to established knowledge which commands respect, and the same tendency to bracket off student knowledge which continues to be favored, although all this is done more subtly than was the case with the traditional perspective of 'transmission of knowledge'; as before, re-institutionalization of the social hierarchy of knowledge and the preservation of orthodoxy in this area emerge victorious.

In other words, even if the realist rhetoric concerning 'knowledge as the reflection of reality', or 'knowledge *of*', which underlies traditional educational practices has given way to the constructivist rhetoric of 'knowledge *that*' (Rorty's distinction, quoted in Boudon, 1990, p. 57), which implies that knowledge is always knowledge *that* a person constructs, the principle of symmetry which caused this split is nevertheless 'forgotten'. To a certain degree, we are dealing here with the methodological expression of the concept of viability, which presupposes that the various forms of knowledge under discussion should be explained using the same criteria or the same concepts. Now, it is on just this point that discourses of an avowedly constructivist cast are ambiguous. In fact, it seems as though the knowledge of students does not enjoy the same epistemological immunity or the same 'adaptive function' as do scholarly types of knowledge. It seems as if the coherency and overall organization of the models proposed by scholarly knowledge (one model for a group of problems) carries greater weight than models developed by students, and, moreover, that students would be better off trading in their eclectic knowledge for a more high-powered variety or at least a variety considered as such within a particular milieu. But is this plausible? How can modes of knowledge which are based on different postulates and which pursue different ends be interchangeable? In addition, how is this ideal of substitution to be articulated in connection with one of the key concepts of constructivism, i.e. the concept of viability?

Indeed, when the viability of a schema or a structure is established by a subject, this entails that the subject perform an operation of *reflexive monitoring* of his or her experiences and cognitive paths. By the same token, the action which results from reflexive monitoring is, at least in principle, consistent not only with this operation of coordination but also with the understanding that the subject has of the conditions of his or her action. In other words, it is plausible to think that the subject *has indeed good reasons* to do what he or she does or to believe what he or she believes, even if from the point of view of a particular community this belief is not valid. However, what happens to the student's competency at differentiating and rationalizing (within Giddens' meaning of the word) in the above-mentioned practices? Is such competency not confined merely to displaying, as best as he or she can, a gamut of intellectual operations which allow him or her to reenact a scenario, replete with a prearranged script and stage?

In the same vein, one might also wonder what importance is to be accorded to competencies in rationalization underlying the scholarly types of knowledge upon which teaching is based. Indeed, if during the practices of substitution mentioned earlier, the student can eventually realize that he or she is the creator of his or her knowledge, it is not at all clear that the student would be also able to realize that the knowledge which is being presented to him or her is also the 'knowledge *that*' another person (or a 'community of persons') has constructed, in light of the habitual tendency toward reification which occurs whenever scholarly modes of knowledge undergo transposition and become knowledge-to-be-taught (Hodson, 1988; Lemke, 1993).

As we have written elsewhere (Larochelle and Désautels, 1991), one might wonder whether it is still scholarly knowledge that is being referred to in the practices concerned. To begin with, this type of knowledge cannot be reduced to empirical and methodological certitudes. Furthermore, epistemological reflection is an integral part of scholarly activity, contributing to the precision and the cognitive range of this knowledge (Piaget, 1967). Finally, this activity is not conducted in a social void and, for that reason, does not exist isolated from the projects and tensions that mark the social field in which it is, as a particular activity, included. It is common knowledge, as sociology and the history of the sciences have taught us, that two competing theories can very well originate from a work which conforms to the rule book but that, nevertheless, one theory will compel recognition and the other will not! What role is to be played by the conditions which make the production of scholarly knowledge possible within the above-mentioned practices? Are these conditions not linked instead to an idea of knowledge-in-final-form that has been 'purified' of the contingencies, alliances and interdependencies which nevertheless provide it with depth and meaning, and which have cleared its path toward social recognition? And how is the student going to be able to understand this knowledge-in-final-form if he or she does not know which question it is an answer to, what its epistemological connections are, and, more generally what worldview it is based on? Is there not a risk that the student will ritualize the meaning precisely because he or she is not able to problematize it, to call it into question?

In other words, even if more and more educational practices are called constructivist, their engagement *vis-à-vis* constructivism seems to me to be lukewarm and takes a form which appears to be more psychological than socio-epistemological. The position of the constructivist teacher is certainly not a simple one: he or she must take an interest in the 'epistemological innovations' of students (Confrey's expression, 1998) in a way that extends beyond a desire for new intellectual scenery, while at the same time being sure to familiarize students with 'scholarly epistemological innovations', within a perspective of 'epistemological democracy'. Indeed, if it is true that teaching practices cannot simply make do with nodding approvingly at students' knowledge, it is every bit as true that these practices can no longer be envisaged as 'the colonization of student's knowledge by that of scholars' (Terhart's expression, 1988), notably by masking the fact that scholarly knowledge is constructed and negotiated, too. Let us not forget that throughout their education, students learn *what kind of knowledge counts*, indeed, this is the way that intellectual *habitus* are instilled, as Lewin and many authors, following Bourdieu, have suggested (Muller and Taylor, 1995). This is also how, depending on the case, the student will either be prone to accept the social hierarchy of knowledge uncritically, indeed to think that the production of this symbolic capital is reserved for a minority of 'gifted' persons, or how, on the contrary, he or she will tend to gain consciousness of his or her ability 'to create a difference', to 'act otherwise', that is to say, 'to be able to intervene in the world or to refrain from such intervention, with the effect of influencing a specific process or state of affairs' (Giddens, 1984, p. 14). In the first case, as Bourdieu has explained (1980), we are dealing with an obvious power nexus of symbolic domination, to the extent that, over the course of their education, students are gradually led to fabricate a depreciative image of themselves as knowing subjects, and to apply the dominant criteria of evaluation (scientific or pseudo-scientific) to their practices of knowledge (Roth and McGinn, 1998). The following comments by an adolescent are an eloquent illustration of the stakes of this situation, both socially and cognitively, namely the possibility of establishing an inhibiting relationship to scholars, and the problem of understanding with which students are confronted whenever other fundamental characteristics of scientific knowledge are ignored, i.e. its relational qualities, how it proceeds by producing models (thus, how it is a product of the imagination as well as of negotiation with peers and of alliances of all kinds, thereby ensuring a viable future for the models in question).

> I have a lot of difficulty seeing how scientists can deal [with things we cannot see]. They [the teachers] explain it to us and we understand how [the scientists] could see that. They say: 'the distance from the moon to the earth is such and such ...'. I don't know it by heart. But how did they measure that? They don't have a measuring tape that long! I have a lot of difficulty with that. . . . And the guy who discovered it: how did he do it? It happened just like that one morning? I don't get it. I understand when it has been explained, but this guy nobody ever gave an explanation to, how did he do it? He must have been really gifted. One must necessarily be gifted, interested, intelligent. Some are more intelligent than others. It is like the law of nature we were talking about: Some trees grow while others will always stay small. (Désautels and Larochelle, 1989, p. 155)

In the second case, it is a matter of a completely different relationship to knowledge which is at work. What counts here is not the restatement of knowledge by students but rather an epistemological process for delving deeper into knowledge games and for enabling students to move from the exploration of one game to another in an informed but liberated manner. Furthermore as we remarked in an earlier research paper,[4] the re-presentation of knowledge games in symmetrical fashion (*re-symétrie*) seems to facilitate among students the establishment of a relationship between the process of official knowledge production and that of their own. This 're-symmetrization' encourages the development of better informed and much less fatalistic representations of both types of knowledge, as the following point of view expressed by one student leads one to believe:

> I admit I had never thought of the process of production. At first, I thought it was something like an inspiration from heaven. I rapidly changed this simplistic view of the process of production. My ideas about science have really changed since the beginning of the course. To me, scientists were geniuses, two to three times more intelligent than the rest of us. My idea was that they woke up one morning and said to themselves, 'Today, I have this problem to solve'. They would then sit in front of a piece of paper and their intelligence would function by itself. They then produced scientific knowledge. But, from my own experiences, I realized that it was not that way at all. You have to work at it, go by trial and error; it is by working really hard that you can arrive at something. . . . I have learned that knowledge is much more a type of questioning than cramming the brain with facts and figures. (Larochelle and Désautels, 1992, pp. 235, 230)

This type of relationship to knowledge is also different because learning transactions no longer focus on setting in motion cognitive activities alone which are then strengthened through repetition and application. The aim of education consists, then, as Morf has emphasized (1998), in encouraging knowledge development which shows a potential for spin-off, that is, which leads toward invention and research, or which according to Foerster (1992) allows for the 'multiplication of potentialities'.

These comments only go to show that I have made a decision concerning not only the meaning and orientation of educational practices but also the 'multiplication of potentialities' which radical constructivism has made it possible to entertain. It is quite possible that what I advance here will not win over the partisans of constructivism. In any event my choice presents a certain family likeness to those undecidable questions which Foerster (1992) has dealt with – those undecidable questions that are indeed decidable. Radical constructivism itself approaches an essentially undecidable question as though it were decidable, namely, whether we are 'discoverers' (in which case, according to Foerster, we are looking as through a peephole upon an unfolding universe) or whether we are the 'inventors' (in which case we see ourselves as the participants in a conspiracy for which we are continually inventing the customs, rules and regulations). Radical constructivism does indeed take a position and opts for the latter view.

It is in light of such decisions that the tangents mentioned at the beginning of this text must be understood, because, in order to reflect on educational practices, it is not enough to draw inspiration from the 'cold' version of epistemological constructivism. It is necessary 'to put constructivism in the educational context' from a perspective which of course emphasizes a process of dialecticizing rather than one of subordination. Obviously, we are not working with 'ordinary' subjects but rather with social actors; nor is it the case that we are working with 'ordinary' educational tools, since these tools, whether they be programs or textbooks, also belong to a category of actors inasmuch as they are the expression of those who invented them, and, as a result, are able to impose a certain type of interaction on other actors (Latour, 1989; Callon, 1989). At that point, what is now at stake is one's ability to make viable choices (theoretically and empirically speaking) for which one is ready to assume, simultaneously, epistemological, ethical and social responsibility.

In this light, we must thoroughly examine the logical underpinnings of the particular communicative and educational contract we favor (Brousseau, 1986; Schubauer-Léoni, 1986). This is so because, as the above-mentioned studies of Geddis, Gutierrez et al., and Voigt, and the preceding comments of the students all show, it is plausible to think that the representations that a person constructs concerning taught knowledge might also be dependent not only on the position which is assigned to him or her over the course of his or her education, but also on the epistemological status which is accorded to his or her own knowledge. But that is not all. As I have already mentioned, we must also examine the contents of teaching activities as well as the conventions of language used to give this content form; it goes without saying that such habits are inescapably affected by an epistemological, social and ethical representation of the forms of knowledge concerned. Otherwise, confronting students with 'knowledge coming from nowhere' not only mystifies the human endeavors from which it has derived, it also obscures the fact that the transformation of this knowledge into established forms of knowledge, that is to say, into a norm, implies a decision: in order for knowledge to become a norm, someone must see to this (Fourez, 1992)!

It is in connection with this last point that I will conclude my remarks, and indicate how, in my view, radical constructivism does not shy away from ethics.

The Siren Song of Ethics

If constructivism is indeed a reflexive theory (i.e. one that practices what it preaches), it cannot then present itself as a meta-perspective dictating what ethics should be without simultaneously running the risk of lapsing into the very thing it denounces. Again, constructivism maintains that it is impossible to have an all-encompassing view; this precept applies to all discourses, including one of a constructivist type. This does not mean, however, that constructivism teaches us little more than the relativization of points of view; it also teaches that holding a point of view is a matter of choice, which amounts in a way to adopting a back-handed approach to ethics – that is to say, constructivism does not propose a moral code, but instead strives to make evident the fact that ethical issues are indeed at stake. Granted, as long as we believe that we encode reality in terms of substances and phenomena which are independent of our actions; as long as facts are believed to speak for themselves; as long as knowledge is considered a mere reflection of ontological reality and language simply a tool for denoting it; in short, as long as we conceive of ourselves as the mouthpieces of reality rather than the artisans creating it, then the effects of our discourse and practices will give us no pause for reflection (Larochelle and Bednarz, 1994), and the chances that these practices will be problematized in epistemological terms will remain slight. However, if, as constructivism has indicated, we act according to our understanding, we will have an entirely different situation on our hands. By reintroducing 'the properties of the observer into the description of his or her observations', we recognize at the same stroke that these observations are consequent upon the choices and distinctions that the observer makes; that is, they are consequent upon his or her way of reflecting on and working out the reasons, values, ideologies and representations that he or she agrees to promote.

Just as with the issues surrounding the self, constructivism can constitute a powerful tool for deciphering the epistemological and ethical premises and effects not only of those kinds of discourse which present themselves officially as having some bearing on these questions, but also of those discourses in which epistemology and ethics act like stowaways. Now it seems to me that unavowed claims and programs are smuggled into the practices of teaching scholarly knowledge on a regular basis. Most of the time, this knowledge, notably in the scientific and the mathematical areas, is presented as if it were untouched by such 'impurities', as if it were a type of knowledge which does not pose any problems – in other words, as if it constitutes a 'knowledge of'. It follows from this that it is of epistemological and ethical interest to examine our linguistic habits and practices in this area, as Mathy (1997) and Sutton (1996) have also emphasized. Who knows, perhaps in the process of examination we will be able to determine how, regardless of our option in favor of constructivism, such linguistic practices and habits conflict with constructivism in the form of continuing *to separate what is connected* (I am paraphrasing Bateson here), and by also asserting that by means of 'the syntax of subject and predicate, "things" have qualities and attributes' instead of saying that they are 'produced' (Bateson, 1980, p. 67), and that these things actually represent, as Foerster says, 'keys which are useful to unlocking problems' (in Segal, 1986, p. 33).

The epistemological work done by Fourez (1985, 1988) on a text on ecology for students is instructive in this connection. As the following excerpts illustrate, his research not only clearly demonstrates that 'school language' constantly eliminates the observer from its descriptions, but, also, that 'some very different visions of the world [and of the sciences] can be transmitted when teaching the same material' (ibid., p. 39).

For example,[5] the following statement presents the goal of the exercise to students,

> '*Learn to observe nature scientifically.* . . . *The scientist carries out numerous measurements, notes and samplings; he [or she] attempts to understand the functioning of his [or her] natural environment.*'

Marie Larochelle

This statement conveys a representation of science and its practices which is very different from the one that underlies the following 'modified' version:

> '*Learn to utilize observation techniques that biologists use in the field . . . The scientist carries out numerous measurements, notes and samplings, he [or she] tries to understand the response of this environment toward specific experiments or projects.*'

Now, the first statement, besides perpetuating an idyllic image of scientific practices, can also be a source of considerable confusion for students with its appeal to an idea of nature. As Stengers (1992) states, there is an essential difference between exercises in the critical observation of 'natural' beings and the type of observation conducted in accordance with the programs and apparatus of experimentation. In the first type of exercise, ants, spiders, etc., are not theoretical objects of science, but sources of questions and curiosity, whereas in the second, scientists attempt to present phenomena for which, by definition, the right way to observe and to reach conclusions has been devised, that is, according to Stengers, the way 'which was devised to take precedence over all others' (ibid., p. 8). The modified version of the above statement avoids the naturalistic trap and also widens the range of possible approaches to the subject by incorporating into its own approach the potential effect of the scientists' interests and projects, which can occur in connection with widely differing preoccupations (emotional, economic, etc.). By proceeding thus, the statement conveys a different idea of scientists' procedures by showing how their approach is particular and 'infused' with a project: knowledge is always *someone's* knowledge and never simply, to borrow a metaphor, *anonymous* knowledge. Continuing along the same lines, this statement also conveys the idea that observation is an active process rather than a contemplative one: there are techniques involved (hence, there are conditions under which observation is rendered operative). Furthermore, these conditions are convention-bound in that they refer to criteria and distinctions which are recognized by the group of practitioners involved.

The modification of statements which follow are equally interesting in terms of the possibility of reintroducing the observer into the description of his or her observations. For example, substitute the following statement '*You must be able to distinguish the characteristics of the biotope from the biocoenosis*' for '*You must distinguish the characteristics of a natural milieu the way scientists do*'. The second statement would have us believe that all observation refers to certain criteria determined by the various scientific communities, thus conveying an idea of objectivity quite different from that which characterizes conventional educational discourses on the sciences. Likewise, the following statement '*We will specify what an ecosystem is*' presents an ecosystem as something which could exist 'independently'. By slightly modifying this statement '*We will specify what it is we call an "ecosystem"*', it is the analytical activity underlying the formulation of a concept which is emphasized. In its new form, the statement

Radical Constructivism

indicates that to speak of an ecosystem is to perform a certain interpretation of it, in connection with the convention-bound language that has been devised by scientists and placed in relation to their particular projects.

In conclusion, if I return to the implications of radical constructivism for education, I can only stress that they necessitate problematization of a much deeper kind than that which confines 'students' knowledge' and the appropriation of scholarly knowledge within a purely psychological framework. Our educational practices, our own relationship to knowledge, in short, our *reflexive monitoring* is also concerned. On that score, I believe constructivism holds out the promise of a powerful ethical project since – and this is not, as Audet (1993) has warned against, to fall prey to the naive belief that we can exercise mastery over everything, including ourselves – constructivism reminds us that it is *we who constitute our world* (to borrow an expression from Giddens, 1993). We *do* have the capacity to decide, which is what we do in teaching on a daily basis *anyway*, consciously or not.

Notes

I would like to thank Paul Cairns and Donald Kellough for translating my text from French into English.

1 This qualification, borrowed from Morf (1998), signifies that the characteristics of the subject – notably the categories inherited from psychology – do not enter into the description of knowledge.
2 It should be noted that, in accordance with its premises and its project of elaborating a *rational* model of cognition, constructivism envisages this 'identity' of subjects from an epistemological perspective rather than a social one, in the sense that if the social realm is referred to (Glasersfeld, 1991), it does not however undergo theorization. Constructivism does not, at any rate, claim to constitute a social theory. However, this absence of a fully developed theory occasionally gives rise to some curious interpretations and, indeed, shortcuts, in which whatever qualifies as social is referred to as a factor (for example, Lewin (Ch. 4), speaks of 'social factors'), and not as something as inescapably constitutive of the identity in question. It is possible that through the use of this expression, an attempt is being made to avoid the 'thingified subject' or the 'cognitive puppet', terms that are otherwise current among certain deterministic social theories. However interesting this avoidance might be, it does not solve all problems and actually helps perpetuate the belief, particularly widespread in psychology, that 'whatever is social is exterior', as Van Haecht puts it (1990, p. 112), hence, that the individual is not social.
3 The tendency to transpose the 'ideas, words and relationships' of scholarly knowledge into the everyday material world of 'things, qualities and forces', as Moscovici and Hewstone have emphasized, can certainly be seen as a manifestation of an empirico-realist epistemology. However, this tendency might also be interpreted as a way of making particularly counter-intuitive knowledge easier to digest, somewhat in the manner of the amateur scholars so acutely portrayed by Flaubert in his unfinished novel, *Bouvard et Pécuchet* (c. 1880). The same tendency has been abundantly

demonstrated in the vast research project that has been conducted since the 1970s about the 'spontaneous conceptions' made by students of all ages who have taken science courses (for a listing of studies on the subject, see Pfundt and Duit 1994). Furthermore, it has also been documented in the studies of students' representations of science and scientists. See, among others, Désautels and Larochelle (1998); Driver et al. (1996); Ryan and Aikenhead (1992); Roth, McRobbie and Lucas (1998).

4 This research project aimed at familiarizing young adults with the scientific endeavor, particularly by means of an in-class simulation of a scientific community and through the re-creation by peers of a number of issues and interrogations which accompany the production of scholarly knowledge and its recognition (Larochelle and Désautels, 1991b, 1992; Désautels, 1998).

5 The very first example has already been presented in Larochelle and Bednarz (1994).

References

AUDET, M. (1993) 'Introduction', in AUDET, M. and BOUCHIKHI, H. (eds), *Structuration du Social et Modernité Avancée. Autour des Travaux d'Anthony Giddens*, Québec: Presses de l'Université Laval, pp. 1–25.

BATESON, G. (1980) *Mind and Nature*, New York: Bantam.

BOUDON, R. (1990) *L'Art de se Persuader des Idées Douteuses, Fragiles ou Fausses*, Paris: Seuil.

BOURDIEU, P. (1980) *Le Sens Pratique*, Paris: Éditions de Minuit.

BROUSSEAU, G. (1986) *Théorisation des Phénomènes d'Enseignement des Mathématiques*, Ph.D. thesis, Université de Bordeaux I, Bordeaux, France.

CALLON, M. (ed.) (1989) *La Science et ses Réseaux*, Paris: La Découverte/Conseil de l'Europe/Unesco.

CONFREY, J. (1998) '"Voice and perspective": Hearing epistemological innovation in students' words', in LAROCHELLE, M., BEDNARZ, N. and GARRISON, J. (eds), *Constructivism and Education*, New York: Cambridge University Press, pp. 104–20.

DÉSAUTELS, J. (1998) 'Constructivism-in-action: Students examine their idea of science', in LAROCHELLE, M., BEDNARZ, N. and GARRISON, J. (eds), *Constructivism and Education*, New York: Cambridge University Press, pp. 121–38.

DÉSAUTELS, J. and LAROCHELLE, M. (1989) *Qu'est-ce que le Savoir Scientifique? Points de Vue d'Adolescents et d'Adolescentes*. Québec: Presses de l'Université Laval.

DÉSAUTELS, J. and LAROCHELLE, M. (1998) 'The epistemology of students: The "thingified" nature of scientific knowledge', in FRASER, B.J. and TOBIN, K. (eds), *International Handbook of Science Education*, Dordrecht: Kluwer, pp. 115–26.

DRIVER, R., LEACH, J., MILLAR, R. and SCOTT, P. (1996) *Young People's Images Of Science*, Buckingham: Open University Press.

FLAUBERT, G. (1979) *Bouvard et Pécuchet*, Paris: Gallimard.

FOERSTER, H. VON (1992) 'Ethics and second-order cybernetics', *Cybernetics & Human Knowing*, 1, 1, pp. 9–19.

FOUCAULT, M. (1975) *Surveiller et Punir. Naissance de la Prison*, Paris: Gallimard.

FOUREZ, G. (1985) *Pour une Éthique de l'Enseignement des Sciences*, Lyon/Brussels: Chronique Sociale and Vie Ouvrière.

FOUREZ, G. (1988) 'Ideologies and science teaching', *Bulletin of Science, Technology and Society*, 8, pp. 269–77.

FOUREZ, G. (1992) *Éduquer. Écoles, Éthiques, Sociétés*, Brussels: De Boeck-Wesmaël.
GEDDIS, A.N. (1988) 'Using concepts from epistemology and sociology in teacher supervision', *Science Education*, 72, 1, pp. 1–18.
GIDDENS, A. (1984) *The Constitution of Society*, Cambridge: Polity Press.
GIDDENS, A. (1993) 'Identité de soi, transformation de l'intimité et démocratisation de la vie', in AUDET, M. and BOUCHIKHI, H. (eds), *Structuration du Social et Modernité Avancée. Autour des Travaux d'Anthony Giddens*, Québec: Presses de l'Université Laval, pp. 455–76.
GLASERSFELD, E. VON (1987a) 'An interpretation of Piaget's constructivism', in *The Construction of Knowledge. Contributions to Conceptual Semantics*, Seaside, Calif.: Intersystems Publications, pp. 231–58.
GLASERSFELD, E. VON (1987b) 'Cybernetics, experience, and the concept of self', in *The Construction of Knowledge. Contributions to Conceptual Semantics*, Seaside, Calif.: Intersystems Publications, pp. 145–87.
GLASERSFELD, E. VON (1991) 'Introduction', in VON GLASERSFELD, E. (ed.), *Radical Constructivism in Mathematics Education*, Dordrecht: Kluwer, pp. xiii–xx.
GLASERSFELD, E. VON (1995) *Radical Constructivism: A Way of Knowing and Learning*, London: Falmer Press.
GUTIERREZ, K., RYMES, B. and LARSON, J. (1995) 'Script, counterscript, and underlife in the classroom: James Brown *versus* Brown v. board of education', *Harvard Educational Review*, 65, 3, pp. 445–71.
HODSON, D. (1988) 'Toward a philosophically more valid science curriculum', *Science Education*, 72, 1, pp. 19–40.
INHELDER, B., GARCIA, R. and VONÈCHE, J. (eds) (1977) *Hommage à Jean Piaget. Épistémologie Génétique et Équilibration*, Neuchâtel/Paris: Delachaux & Niestlé.
LAROCHELLE, M. (1998) 'La tentation de la classification. Ou comment un apprentissage non réflexif des savoirs scientifiques peut donner lieu à un problème épistémologique', *Recherches en Soins Infirmiers*, 52, pp. 72–80.
LAROCHELLE, M. and BEDNARZ, N. (eds) (1994) 'À propos du constructivisme et de l'éducation', *Revue des Sciences de l'Éducation*, 20, 1, pp. 5–19.
LAROCHELLE, M. and BEDNARZ, N. (1998) 'Constructivism and education: Beyond epistemological correctness', in LAROCHELLE, M., BEDNARZ, N. and GARRISON, J. (eds), *Constructivism and Education*, New York: Cambridge University Press, pp. 3–20.
LAROCHELLE, M. and DÉSAUTELS, J. (1991a) '"Of course, it's just obvious!" Adolescents' ideas of scientific knowledge', *International Journal of Science Education*, 13, 4, pp. 373–89.
LAROCHELLE, M. and DÉSAUTELS, J. (1991b) 'The epistemological turn in science education: The return of the actor', in DUIT, R., GOLDBERG, F. and NIEDDERER, H. (eds), *Research in Physics Learning: Theoretical Issues and Empirical Studies*, Bremen: University of Bremen and Institute for Science Education at the University of Kiel, pp. 155–75.
LAROCHELLE, M. and DÉSAUTELS, J. (1992) *Autour de l'Idée de Science. Itinéraires Cognitifs d'Étudiants et d'Étudiantes*, Québec/Brussels: Presses de l'Université Laval and De Boeck-Wesmaël.
LATOUR, B. (1989) *La Science en Action*, Paris: La Découverte.
LEMKE, J.L. (1993) *Talking Science, Language, Learning and Values*, Norwood: Ablex.
MATHY, P. (1997) *Donner du Sens aux Cours de Sciences. Des Outils pour la Formation Éthique et Épistémologique des Enseignants*, Brussels: De Boeck.

MORF, A. (1998) 'An epistemology for didactics: Speculations on situating a concept', in LAROCHELLE, M., BEDNARZ, N. and GARRISON, J. (eds), *Constructivism and Education*, New York: Cambridge University Press, pp. 29–42.

MOSCOVICI, S. and HEWSTONE, M. (1984) 'De la science au sens commun', in MOSCOVICI, S. (ed.), *Psychologie Sociale*, Paris: Presses Universitaires de France, pp. 539–66.

MULLER, J. and TAYLOR, N. (1995) 'Schooling and everyday life: Knowledges sacred and profane', *Social Epistemology*, **9**, 3, pp. 257–75.

PFUNDT, J. and DUIT, R. (1994) *Bibliography: Students' Alternative Frameworks and Science Education* (4th edn), Kiel: Institute for Science Education.

PIAGET, J. (1967) 'Les courants de l'épistémologie scientifique contemporaine', in PIAGET, J. (ed.), *Logique et Connaissance Scientifique*, Paris: Gallimard, pp. 1222–71.

ROTH, W.-M. and MCGINN, M.K. (1998) '>unDelete Science education: /lives/work/ voices', *Journal of Research in Science Teaching*, **35**, 4, pp. 399–421.

ROTH, W.-M., MCROBBIE, C. and LUCAS, K.B. (1998) 'Four dialogues and metalogues about the nature of science', *Research in Science Education*, **28**, 1, pp. 107–18.

RYAN, A.G. and AIKENHEAD, G.S. (1992) 'Students' preconceptions about the epistemology of science', *Science Education*, **76**, 6, pp. 559–80.

SCHUBAUER-LEONI, M.L. (1986) *Maître – Élève – Savoir: Analyse Psychosociale du Jeu et des Enjeux de la Relation Didactique*, unpublished Ph.D. thesis, Université de Genève, Geneva.

SEGAL, L. (1986) *The Dream of Reality. Heinz von Foerster's Constructivism*, New York: W.W. Norton.

STENGERS, I. (1992) *Le Rôle Possible de l'Histoire des Sciences dans l'Enseignement*, Montréal: Université du Québec à Montréal, Cahier du CIRADE no. 65.

SUTTON, C. (1996) 'Beliefs about science and beliefs about language', *International Journal of Science Education*, **18**, 1, pp. 1–18.

TERHART, E. (1988) 'Philosophy of science and school science teaching', *International Journal of Science Education*, **10**, 1, pp. 11–16.

VAN HAECHT, A. (1990) *L'École à l'Épreuve de la Sociologie. Questions à la Sociologie de l'Éducation*, Brussels: De Boeck-Wesmaël.

VOIGT, J. (1985) 'Patterns and routines in classroom interaction', *Recherches en Didactique des Mathématiques*, **6**, 1, pp. 69–118.

6 Constraints, *Paideia* and Occasioning[1]: Can Mathematics Teaching be Part of *Paideia*?

Thomas E. Kieren

This chapter could well have been entitled 'Dancing the Structural Dance'. Such a name would at once acknowledge that this contribution and the work of Glasersfeld point to individuals using their own structures in shaping their experience and using that experience reflectively to change or shape their structures. It would also point to the continuing interplay between the personal actions of the individual and the variety of occasions, and constraints from those occasions, in the environment of experience. In this chapter this structural dance will involve individuals, their teacher, their peers and all the elements of a community as each member of the community brings forth a piece of a mathematical world with others.

Lewin defines *paideia* as 'the complete process of education through which one became a competent participant within culture'. In what sense can the activity in a mathematics classroom be part of *paideia*? From Lewin's chapter I use questions of knowing what one has done and why such doing is right; and of the nature and functioning of constraints in Glasersfeld's constructivism to explore constructive activity in a mathematics classroom. Lewin suggests that working with mathematical ideas provides an experience of strong constraint for mathematics learners. A consideration of activities of students working in a space for learning fractions is interpreted as showing that students experience various levels and kinds of mathematical constraints related to the nature of their changing mathematical understandings. Within a classroom setting such constructing is done while experiencing a variety of other constraints as well. I suggest that it is this complex of experienced constraints, both mathematical and non-mathematical, that allows us to observe the on-going mathematical activity as part of *paideia*. Looking at the issue of constraints from the point of view of the classroom and the teacher, while the student is constructing or bringing forth a mathematical world determined by their own structures and viable in terms of the student's own experienced constraints, one can observe some of the teacher's constructions as providing the occasion for the students constructions as well as the student's constraints. Such a view of teacher activity suggests that while part of what a teacher is doing is constructing models of student mathematics, she or he is also constructing a mathematical setting to occasion student mathematics. In addition the teacher is constructing a

Thomas E. Kieren

community and a culture with the students. Hence decisions underlying such occasioning and culture making, being part of *paideia*, are essentially ethical ones.

Constraints in Action

A class of middle school students has been exploring fractional numbers with aid of a 'fraction kit' which consists of two unit pieces and two units worth of halves, thirds, fourths, sixths, eighths, twelfths and twenty-fourths as shown below. They have engaged in such activities as covering one piece with, say,

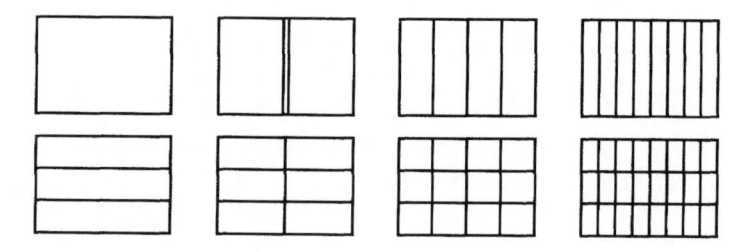

one third or with other pieces, and making up appropriate equations showing additive or equivalence relations. Now the teacher asks the children:

'*Try to find out how much was shown by these expressions*:
$$\frac{1}{3} + \frac{1}{16} \text{ and } \frac{2}{24} + \frac{3}{12} + \frac{1}{6}.$$'

Nearly all the children immediately engage in what could be observed as appropriate activity. A few of the children know how to 'add fractions' from previous experiences and do so; but for most this is new and interesting. The teacher circulates among the students responding to their queries. Occasionally she sends a student to the chalk board and asks, 'Why don't you show your working to the rest of us?' Soon there are a large number of 'works' on the board. These vignettes are cases of middle school students constructing or bringing forth their mathematical worlds based on their own histories and structures. That is, the actions of the students are evidence of their own constructive

VAN: $\frac{1}{3} + \frac{1}{6} = \frac{2}{4}$
TEACHER: *Why do you think that?*

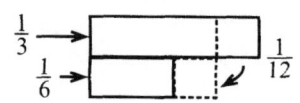

VAN: *Take $\frac{1}{12}$ off from $\frac{1}{3}$; and add $\frac{1}{12}$ to $\frac{1}{6}$. Then you have two fourth-pieces.*

Constraints, Paideia *and Occasioning*

PETER: $\frac{1}{3} + \frac{1}{6} = \frac{3}{6}$

TEACHER: *Can you explain that?*

PETER: *Just cut the* $\frac{1}{3}$ *into* $\frac{2}{6}$ *and you get it.*

ANDREA: $\frac{1}{3} + \frac{1}{6} = \frac{6}{12}$

TEACHER: *Why does that work?*

ANDREA: *You can cut* $\frac{1}{3}$ *into* $\frac{4}{12}$ *and cut* $\frac{1}{6}$ *into* $\frac{2}{12}$. *So* $\frac{6}{12}$.

JANE: $\frac{1}{3} + \frac{1}{6} = \frac{2 \times 1}{2 \times 3} + \frac{1}{6} = \frac{3 \div 3}{6 \div 3} = \frac{1}{2}$

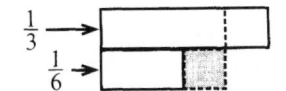

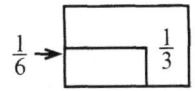

TEACHER: *Can you explain that to the rest of us?*

JANE: *It's simple. You find the least common denominator; that's sixths. So two sixths plus one sixth make three sixths and that reduces to one half.*

STEVE: *You can use a half piece.*

TEACHER *(sounding puzzled):* *What are you trying to do?*

STEVE: *There... That's it.*

activity based on their own histories of experience and not attempts to mirror some pre-given outside world. To do such constructive cognizing or bringing forth, an organism and these students in particular would, of necessity, have the capabilities outlined by Glasersfeld:

- The ability and, beyond it, the tendency to establish recurrences in the flow of experience [which for him entails]
- remembering and retrieving (re-presenting) experience, and the ability to make comparisons and judgments of similarity and difference;
- apart from these . . . the organism likes certain things better than others, which is to say that it must have some elementary values. (1993, p. 17)

The variety of the student responses shows these features at work and indicates that what might appear to an observer to be a 'closed' mathematical task – adding two fractions – can and does allow for a variety of constructive activity by students.

But what, one might ask, is the role of the environment – the materials, the queries, the teacher, the fellow students – in such constructive activity? Lewin

Thomas E. Kieren

(Ch. 4) in his contribution raises several questions which elaborate this matter. He does so in the context of the notion of *paideia*: 'the complete process of education through which one became a competent participant within culture' (p. 39). The almost direct tie between *paideia* and cognition can be seen in the enactivist definition of cognition from Varela, Thompson and Rosch posed through two questions:

> What is cognition? Enacting: A history of structural coupling [through which an individual with others] brings forth a world. How do I know when a cognitive system is functioning adequately? When it becomes part of an ongoing existing world (as the young of every species do) or shapes a new one (1991, pp. 206–7)

This definition of cognition, together with Lewin's definition of *paideia*, leads one to note that participation in *paideia* is a test for the viability of persons' (and particularly children's or young peoples') cognitive activity. Before turning to Lewin's questions specifically directed at constructive cognition, the idea of *paideia* raises other questions for mathematics education:

> Is mathematics education part of *paideia per se*? Is this so for all students or just for some or perhaps a select few? Or does one simply turn to mathematics to acquire some disembodied skills which might be useful tools for engaging in *paideia*?

One answer to these questions will be provided by interrogating on-going classroom activity through the eyes of Lewin's more specific questions relating *paideia* to constructivism. Lewin's first question arises from his attention to the elements of cognitive activity as expressed by Glasersfeld above. In particular, Lewin focuses on the fact that such activity appears to involve rational choice making. In fact, Glasersfeld (1993) suggests that successful cognition does not simply involve doing the right thing; the student needs to know what they are doing and why such doing is right. These criteria lead to Lewin's first question:

> What can it mean to know what one is doing and why it is right? (Ch. 4, p. 39)

Glasersfeld (1993), using ideas drawn from Piaget, has underwritten the concept of viability as a means of a person (and an observer of that person) 'knowing what is right' in action. But Glasersfeld's idea of viability raises for him the questions of constraints. The person tests the viability of her or his actions against their perceived and felt constraints. Lewin (Ch. 4) raises the following question, which forms the second question about constructive cognition and brings us directly to the function of the environment in constructive cognition:

Constraints, Paideia *and Occasioning*

I want to raise the question of how constraints function in those acts of constitution through which we become who we find ourselves to be (p. 39)

Viability and Constraints

To investigate further the ideas of viability and constraints we return our attention to the classroom discourse which started this chapter. These brief dialogues are drawn from the field records of a teaching experiment/teacher development project in an urban middle school. The class members have a variety of ethnic backgrounds and have been characterized by the school as having a wide variety of past mathematical performance. The teacher has an undergraduate degree in mathematics education and has taught for five years. The children are studying fractional numbers; here most of the students are just starting to look at them as elements in an additive structure, although a few, including Jane, come to this experience with more formal algorithmic knowledge of addition of fractions. As suggested above, the teacher and the students are going over items from an assigned homework activity which they were free to approach as they saw fit. Although from casual inspection the task itself looks to be a closed one, both the students and the teacher took these to be open questions. Now as (Ch. 4) has observed, mathematical questions, perhaps especially these, come with strong constraints. But by considering a number of the children's responses as well as their reasoning (verbal and diagrammatic) with respect to their actions, I wish to have us move beyond these strong historical mathematical constraints and explore what we might observe these students to take as constraints. Using the language of Lewin, I want to explore how the children's mathematical knowing in action and the possible underlying conceptions co-arise with the constraints and indeed elements or aspects of the environment of action. Finally as a consequence of this, I wish to explore the role which the teacher played in these activities.

Let me point to just a few features of these actions and interactions as they pertain to viability and constraints. But let me remind you that these interactions were not events isolated from one another. All but two of the twenty-eight students involved had produced a response to the teacher's intervention and those shown above were by no means unusual. Further, picture that these responses were drawn out and visible to all, and the interchanges between the teacher and individual students were done publicly. In fact, many of the interchanges above prompted other questions from other students.

Of course it is easy to see the strong mathematical constraints at work here. While it seems evident to me that each student is using her or his own schemes to perceive and then take structure-determined constructive action in this situation, one could also say that these constructions are all leading to the 'same answer'. Indeed, it was on the teacher's agenda that the students would not only compare their work with that of others but see the products of their work as equivalent in some way. This is the strong mathematical constraint against which all of the students' action/results might be compared. Thus at that level Jane and Steve and Van's sums, for example, prove to be the same – they are all equal or equivalent to one half.

But is that the whole story? It appears to me that this strong mathematical constraint is a type of second order constraint or formal constraint. There are less formal constraints which are clearly in operation here. This was seen in the frequent questions between students or from students as to whether their action/results were actually the same or about in just what ways they were the same as some of the other students' responses. This occurred not because most students were not aware of what they had done or how they had done it – most were – nor because they could not explain why their action/result was viable – many students could do this. This questioning occurred because something other than strong mathematical constraint was also observable here.

Even within these less formal mathematical actions one can distinguish different kinds or qualities of action/results and possible evidence for differing constraints at work. For example, one might interpret Van as acting and thinking with the fraction pieces in finding his solution of two fourths. But his response to the teacher can be interpreted as showing an 'equivalence in action' reasoning underlying his confidence in his response; and as an ability to 'prove' informally that two fourths could be deduced from his actions. So while his first response may have been physically determined, the teacher's question signaled for Van another kind of constraint. In this setting Van felt a responsibility to defend his actions – to know why they worked. But it appears that the teacher's question also provoked Van to think, or at least talk, about his response in a way which involves an abstraction from his previous action. In contrast, consider Steve's response and solution. In Steve's case, fractional amounts were very closely tied to actions on pieces. He actually found a piece, one half, and showed how one sixth and one third as pieces (with some transformation) could be fitted to it. His 'same amount' image seemed much more tied to actual regions than to the fractional amounts as numbers. Viability for him was literally a matter of physical fitting. In later discussion it is not surprising that Van could comprehend Jane's formal solution while Steve was limited to the world of his actions. Put differently, while Van's reasoning – that which appeared to be elicited by the teacher's question – referenced actions in the physical world, Steve's reasoning directly included physical actions. In terms of constraints, one might observe Steve as feeling only the necessity of the physical constraints of the kit (which to an observer have the strong mathematical constraints built in). On the other hand, Van appeared to feel the constraint actually to 'prove' that two fourths could be developed from one sixth and one third. While such a proof might be thought of as part of the constraint of mathematics itself, it is more explicative to see it as a felt constraint inherent in belonging to this particular mathematical community.

To conclude this part of the discussion, the point of the interpretations above is to demonstrate that while knowledge of mathematics could be experienced as a strong constraint in this environment, it was operating only in an indirect way for most of these students. In fact, at this point in the instruction, probably only a small number of students, such as Jane, acted directly with the mathematics itself as a constraint. Even for her, because her response to the teacher's query had a mechanical quality, the mathematical constraint had a rather narrow procedural meaning. Perhaps the sedimentation of experienced constraints from her life in 'school mathematics' cultures, which were narrower than the one she was experiencing here, is observable in what Jane took to be viable in her reasoning actions in this setting as well. But what of the constraints which were operational in the more informal mathematical constructive activity of the other students in the dialogues above? Looking at the materials themselves one might say that the strong mathematical constraints were built directly into them by the teacher and hence the students would be almost obliged to experience them. I would argue that from the diverse complexity of the responses, the students' perceptions of these features were likely different from the mathematics 'put into the pieces' by their creator.

Occasioning and Constraints

In the discussions above the role of the teacher in this mathematical action has been left at an implicit level. Interpretation of the dialogue below, as well as reinforcing and extending the discussion above, will consider the interactive dynamics between the student and the environment, especially the teacher. To do this I will use the term 'occasion' as a verb to describe her actions, and indeed the function of all the elements of the environment with respect to the constructive mathematical actions of the individual students. Kieren, Davis and Sumara (1994) would say that while each student acted constructively based on her or his structure (which reflects her or his history of interactions and thus includes sedimented constraints (Lewin, Ch. 4)), the environment – the kit, the questions themselves, but especially the way in which the teacher listened and acted in the classroom – *occasioned* that constructive action. Bickhard (1989) uses the term 'selection pressure' to describe such environmental impacts. The word 'occasions' is an attempt to highlight the students' knowledge in action, their bringing forth of a mathematical world with others, as co-arising with the environment. Such constructed knowledge in action is seen as a co-emergent phenomenon. The dialogue below allows us to observe the complex of constraints experienced by Peter in his constructive actions as well as to observe the 'structural dance' (Maturana and Varela, 1987) in which the teacher's activity provides the occasions for Peter's actions and in turn his constructive activity provides occasions for the teacher's and his fellow classmates knowing in action.

Thomas E. Kieren

Protocol: Peter's Solution of $\frac{3}{12} + \frac{2}{24} + \frac{1}{6}$

PETER: *Use eights[sic]. Four eights[sic]. (Making this drawing)*

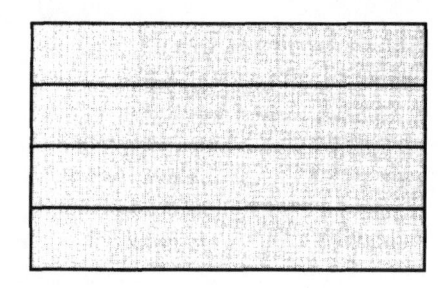

TEACHER: *Wow! How did you ever think of that?*
[brief pause]
PETER: *Half of a twelfth plus one twenty-fourth plus one fourth of a sixth is an eighth – and that happens twice.*
Half of a twelfth plus half of a twelfth plus a fourth of a sixth is an eighth – and that happens twice.
Altogether there are four eighths.
TEACHER: *(Like nearly all of the class and the observer): What?*
PETER: *See; I'll show you. (Makes this drawing)*

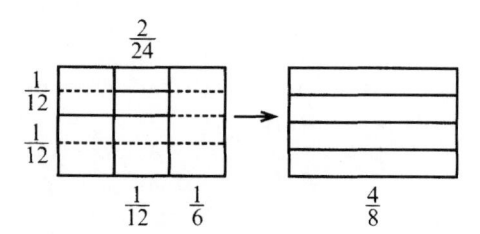

The Questions of Constraints in Action

Peter's many constructive actions in this dialogue can be interpreted in light of Lewin's questions with which this chapter was started. Clearly, Peter acted in a manner which was appropriate to the situation; he knew what he had done and why what he had done was right. He could draw his ideas (re-present them) and explain them in terms which referenced the pieces or his image of them; but, in fact, his explanation was independent of his actions on the pieces. It appears from the drawing under Peter's last comment that Peter's later reasoning was constrained differently from his initial actions. Initially, he acted to have pieces (eighths) fit on his physical pattern of other pieces. But his response to the first question of the teacher justified that action/result on other grounds. It could be argued that Peter, in his second answer, is engaged in formulating a sort of proof that a state of four eighths can be rearranged to be the same as that of three twelfths plus two twenty-fourths and one sixth. One might go even further and say that Peter's first two responses were anticipated by him to be viable in this classroom space. They fitted with his perception of activity which would be acceptable and with his expectation that sense-making activity was valued in this classroom. They also fitted with his wish to be seen as doing 'something different' (as four eighths had yet to be offered as a response in the class). In other words, his actions fitted with the constraints of his construction of social contracts with the teacher and his peers.

What can we 'conclude' about constraints in action from this episode and those like it shown in less detail in the student responses which opened this chapter? First, that although constraints induced by the mathematical nature of the episodes can be considered 'strong' either in terms of some perceived nature of mathematical truth or because some elements of the situation were designed on a mathematical basis, such experienced mathematical constraints are by no means monolithic. They are moderated by the natures, models and levels of students' mathematical cognitive structures (Glasersfeld, 1987; Pirie and Kieren, 1992). But that does not diminish the impact of such experienced constraints on the constructive activity. It appears in the work of many students, but particularly so in Peter's work above, that the teacher's question prompted him to accommodate his mathematical construction of fractions to what he appeared to see as new constraints. He simply could have observed, like Steve in the first set of responses, that four eighths fit on his arrangement of fractional pieces. But he chose to alter his actions and his reflections on his actions to make his actions viable in a new way. Put another way, the teacher's query appeared to prompt Peter to review his previous scheme of equivalence – fractions are equivalent if their amounts match physically, and begin to alter it in some way – fractional amounts can be reasoned to be equivalent. Notice, however, that in neither case did he use the 'standard' notion of fractional equivalence.

A second conclusion is that mathematical constructive activity, at least in a classroom such as this, is itself not a monolithic or singular phenomenon. It is clear that Peter was engaged in many constructions at once. In a sense such a view muddies the constructivist waters when we wish to apply its concepts and tenets to practical educational settings rather than using them as tools in the study of mathematics learning by individuals. In the 'controlled' environment of a teaching experiment, the researcher can try to 'isolate' observations of these felt constraints by manipulating the situation, changing the questions asked of the student, or simply by interviewing the student on the spot about some possible constraint. But the teacher or a researcher in a regular classroom situation observes that such constraints could be acting all at once to influence the actual actions of the student. The 'effects' or impacts of such constraints cannot be observed as independent by the observer nor are they likely to be felt in that manner by the student.

But I, with Lewin, take an optimistic view of this complexity of constraints. If mathematically related constraints can be seen to come in many levels of strength and if mathematical construction by persons in classrooms is seen as this many-sided, all-at-once phenomenon, then it is also easier to see mathematics education as part of *paideia* rather than simply as an arena, rather divorced from *paideia*, where one picks up a 'tool kit', albeit an important one, for *paideia*. In a representationist view of mathematics learning the student is simply trying to mirror or match a pre-given idea or procedure. Such a view seems congruent with the 'math as tool kit' position. But constructing a mathematical world or a mathematical reflective abstraction appears to involve one not only with the strong constraints of mathematics as a body of knowledge (Davis, 1994), but also involves realizing in ones actions the felt constraints of logical language and validation, and of the quest for membership in a community. Acting under such felt constraints in an 'all-at-once' way does appear to be part of *paideia*.

The Structural Dance of Occasioning

The dialogue above shows a continuing interplay between Peter's personally constructed actions (some of which are obviously mental in nature) and a variety of occasionings offered by the world around him. Peter had experienced in this setting doing other exercises with the kit and had taken part in and observed previous interactions related to such work between the teacher and fellow students. Constraints sedimented from such experience; the kit and the particular exercise all occasioned his first response. Peter's action surprised the teacher but also provided the occasion for her own action which was determined by her sense of the situation; an observer might interpret what she did as showing that she was not looking for pre-given 'answers', but rather for personal solutions which 'fit'. Hence, she asked a proscriptive or 'fitting' question: 'How did you ever think of that?' This question appears to have elicited a more sophisticated kind of understanding on Peter's part. The teacher's genuine puzzlement in understanding Peter's reasoning shows that Peter's 'proof' was not simply a match for some pre-given mathematics. But this puzzlement experienced by his teacher and peers provided an occasion for Peter to feel the constraints of membership in this 'mathematical community' and take yet another alternative action in order that his 'proof' might be seen as 'fitting' in this community. Both Peter and the teacher acted and appeared conscious of their actions (i.e. knew what they were doing and why they were doing it); both showed their thinking and knowing in action. Their co-arising action may well be an example of what Maturana and Varela mean when they say:

> Everything we do is a structural dance in the choreography of coexistence. (1992, p. 248)

Concluding Remarks

It has been my purpose in this chapter to interpret several vignettes of classroom mathematical activity first to show the viability of a constructivist view of such on-going activity. But beyond that, these interpretations were intended to show also how constraints worked in such activity. In this regard I have attempted to make two points. First, although one could observe strong mathematical constraints at work in these situations, these manifested themselves in a wide and personally determined way in the actions of students. Further, it appeared that these students experienced and acted on many other kinds of constraints as well. Second, it was observed that these constraints were not experienced independently of one another but in an all-at-once fashion. Finally, through these interpretations, I have attempted to show how the teacher acted to provide the occasions for student construction and that these teacher activities were also the result of constructions occasioned by her perception of student activities. Thus the mathematical cognition could be observed to co-arise in a complex fashion within the environment and community around it.

This complex, co-arising view of constructive mathematical cognition suggests to me that mathematics education is indeed part of *paideia*. I think Lewin would argue that the teacher's purposes in the actions described above were ethical ones and that constructivism *à la* Glasersfeld can be a basis not only for a teacher or researcher's better understanding and modeling of students' mathematical constructions, but also provides a sound basis for the mathematics teacher's participation in the *paideia* of her students.

Note

1 Research behind this chapter is sponsored in part by Grant 410 93-0239 of the Social Sciences and Humanities Research Council of Canada.

References

BICKHARD, M. (1989) 'How does the environment affect the person'? in WINEGAR, L.T. (ed.), *Children's Development within Social Contexts: Metatheoretical, Theoretical and Methodological Issues*, Hillsdale, NJ: Lawrence Erlbaum.

DAVIS, B. (1994) *Listening to Reason*, unpublished Ph.D. thesis, University of Alberta, Edmonton.

GLASERSFELD, E. VON (1987) 'Learning as a constructive activity', in JANVIER, C. (ed.), *Problems of Representation in the Learning and Teaching of Mathematics*, Hillsdale, NJ: Lawrence Erlbaum, pp. 3–18.

GLASERSFELD, E. VON (1993) 'Piaget's constructivist model of knowing and learning', Amherst, Scientific Reasoning Research Institute, University of Massachusetts.

KIEREN, T., DAVIS, B. and SUMARA, D. (1994) 'Catch my evolutionary drift: Four essays on enactivism and curriculum', paper set presented at the Annual Meeting of the American Educational Research Association, New Orleans, April.

MATURANA, H. and VARELA, F. (1987/1992) *The Tree of Knowledge*, Boston: New Science Library/Shambhala.

PIRIE, S. and KIEREN, T. (1992) 'Creating constructivist environments – constructing creative mathematics', *Educational Studies in Mathematics*, 23, 5, pp. 505–28.

VARELA, F., THOMPSON, E. and ROSCH, E. (1991) *The Embodied Mind*, Cambridge, Mass.: MIT Press.

7 Epistemological Origins of Ethics

Hugh Gash

Lewin's chapter focuses on the need for a constructivist ethics. His position calls for an analysis of ways in which knowledge and relationships are associated. This response is concerned with the following themes: first, connections between ways of knowing and ways of relating in constructivist writings; second, some constructivist issues in Lewin's chapter; and third, I describe a series of constructivist intervention studies designed to apply constructivist educational strategies for ethical reasons.

Ways of Knowing and Ways of Relating

A number of constructivist theorists have drawn attention to the ethical and social implications of their epistemology. For Kelly (1955) ways of knowing were ultimately ways of relating. This follows from the anticipatory and dynamic nature of knowing. Kelly saw behaviour as governed, not simply from what people anticipate in the short term – but by where the choices will lead in the longer term. What we know about people bears on the ways in which we relate to them. The constructions that we make determine the nature of our interdependencies. Maturana (1988, 1991) has been clear about the ethical implications of two types of explaining and Foerster (1991) has shown how thoughts about one's relationship to experience have ethical implications. Which is the primary cause, the world or my experience of it? Foerster adopted the position that his experience is the primary cause and the world the consequence. This ties him inseparably and inevitably to his responsibility. Finally, Glasersfeld has noted that constructivism leads to greater tolerance in social interactions. This tolerance arises when one realizes that neither problems nor solutions are ontological entities but arise out of ways of constructing. A world arises out of a way of seeing, a way of experiencing. That is not to say that we find all ways or all worlds equally likable (e.g. Glasersfeld, 1991, 1995).

I would like to draw attention to three features of constructivism before turning to some specifics of Philip Lewin's contribution. First, constructivism emphasizes the role we have in organizing our experience, the way in which we make our understandings. Glasersfeld (1995), by his use of the word 'radical' in the phrase 'radical constructivism', signalled a break with a tradition that has been dominant for about two thousand years. Further, by showing the connections that the constructivist epistemological position has with cybernetics, he displayed both it's plausibility and power. To those whose implicit epistemology reflects the traditional view, one of the most unsettling of the implications is that different ways of understanding, different answers, may not be wrong. Instead, they may reflect an alternative way of looking at experience. Second, constructivism invites an openness to consider the ideas of other people and an openness to reconsider one's own ideas. Such openness requires both tolerance for uncertainty, and respect for others. Third, in coming to understand something new, there is a fragility in the learner stemming from the need to let go of previous knowledge. As adults we know how hard it is to change. So constructivist teaching requires respect for this fragility in the learner. Respecting learners in this way has two desirable consequences. First, it will allow students to grow to trust their own processes. Second, this trust in turn will allow them to develop confidence to examine their worlds responsibly.

Constructivist Issues

The Problem with Viability

As Lewin pointed out in the first part of his chapter, the constructions of the learner generate their own constraints. This is an essential part of an individual's development. The choices people make in life leave their marks on them. These choices depend on the reflexive interaction between a person's prior organization of past experience and the perceived opportunities in ongoing experience. Once one moves from considering an individual's constructions to considering how these are perceived by another, one can enter the ethical domain. From an ethical point of view, it is not enough to say that viability will be the criterion of choice. There can be an unsettling moral blindness compatible with cultural life and indeed with viability.

I agree that there is a need to attend to the ethical domain. It is certainly possible to avoid it, but as Glasersfeld has remarked, when one understands constructivism it touches everything. There is a dilemma in that ethical issues, being about right and wrong, provide a challenge to the respect that constructivism gives to different ways of understanding. There are a number of reasons why this dilemma has not been resolved. First, as Lewin has pointed out, there is a coincidence between the values of constructivism and of contemporary culture. Another reason is that many people understand constructivism to imply a profound relativism.

Towards a Constructivist Ethics of Mutual Respect

In the two years I spent at Georgia (1973–5) there was a series of informal interdisciplinary seminars we called 'constructivist evenings', which were organized by Ernst von Glasersfeld. The metaphorical nature of the word 'reality' was a

Hugh Gash

recurring theme. Reality, to use Robert Pirsig's (1973) word, was a 'cleavage' term: one's attitudes to constructivism and its implications seem predictable from one's attitude to the word 'reality'. Indeed, the interpretation of 'reality' is central to the distinction between adaptation and viability (e.g. Glasersfeld [1980]1987, p. 67). So while I agree wholly with Lewin that to forget the historical nature of constructions entails a loss of coherence, the distinction between hard and soft constraints perturbs me. I wonder if there is a way to express Lewin's intention that does not seem to allow reality to reappear in the guise of hard constraints.

'Reality without Parenthesis'

If I were not being constructivist, I could put this in another way. My first and unguarded reaction is to attack the possibility of distinguishing between hard constraints and soft constraints! That distinction seems to me either (1) to be the result of a realist epistemology, or (2) to invite or make legitimate such an interpretation. Sensing the emotions associated with threat, my discourse switches to 'reality without parenthesis'. This is a moment to notice that there were many 'war arenas' in our world in the 1990s. The relation between threat and rigidity seems to be a general phenomenon. I want to draw attention to the way that the emotion I experience on interpreting the text is an important determinant of my response.

I pause and decentre

I remember the value of mutual respect, and I rephrase my response: my concern is that the introduction of hard and soft constraints invites precisely that trivialization of constructivist insights that Lewin (Ch. 4) decries (pp. 44–5 above). The problem is that the terms 'right', 'wrong', and 'error' carry heavy non-constructivist connotations. Hard/soft constraints (and right/wrong) require an observer; and can only be observed after an individual has done something. There is a difficulty in specifying the meaning of 'correctness' within constructivist theory. In this paragraph, my emotion is respect, and a desire to discuss the distinctions hard/weak, and correct/incorrect. As a result, my response is not dismissive. The emotion or construct under which I operate plays a powerful role in determining my response.

Notice, however, that I have introduced in the preceding paragraphs what I find to be an important ethical corollary of the constructivist position. Namely, the grounds or implicit epistemological assumptions in an argument are braided-interwoven with the form of one's social relations and with the emotions at play in social interaction. I will return to this later. At present I am proposing decidability/undecidability as an alternative to hard and soft constraints.

Lewin wrote about hard and soft constraints in ways that acknowledge ideas of scientific orthodoxy (hard) and the right of individuals to differ on

Epistemological Origins of Ethics

cultural matters (soft). I think there are problems with this view. First, scientific orthodoxy is no remedy for the durability of misconceptions of scientific concepts in nonspecialists. So the existence of so called 'hard constraints' is no guarantee that these constraints will actually constrain. There are similar problems with soft constraints. Cultural rules may be variable and so qualify for the appellation 'soft constraint'. However, there are severe consequences to ignoring cultural rules in cultures with clear social rules (e.g. business or religious cultures). Compare 'liaisons' of President Clinton and President Mitterrand, and public reaction in each case. Clearly there are differences in the cultural construction of boundaries between individual and social domains. For me, the distinction hard/soft distracts from constructivist insights into the role of the individual's activity in knowing and invites 'creeping realism'. However, I do acknowledge the important role of social support for ideas an individual constructs and expresses.

Consider from a constructivist stance some uses of the term 'correct' as a prelude to introducing (un)decidability as an alternative to soft and hard constraints. People construct their descriptions of wine from a particular bottle, their gender stereotypes, and their responses to '$9 \times 7 =?$'. What can be said about correctness in each case? It is often difficult, and I include myself, to remember consistently to eschew rightness/wrongness, correctness/incorrectness, and espouse viability. There is much cultural support for the idea that *one* way is best.

I act regularly as a judge in wine competitions. In this capacity I have noticed that people's judgments may differ radically (but legitimately) from their peers'. Tasters may, for example, simply apply different categories (with different meanings and associated criteria of validation) to the experience. Application of different categories to their experiences of a wine by two individuals would not be wrong. I have also observed a social consensus emerging in groups of wine tasters who meet regularly. In the case of gender stereotypes, constructs (e.g. emotional, dependent, and strong) differ developmentally and culturally. I have samples of data from 8- and 11-year-old children in different countries illustrating such differences in perceptions of personal–social gender stereotypes. Again, difference does not imply incorrectness, and again social support for an individual's stereotyped views plays an important role (see Gash, 1993).

It is clearer that a person can be *wrong* about their numbers. However, an answer to a mathematics problem may be wrong either because of processing errors, or because the wrong 'items' were manipulated. Again, however, as in the other two examples, while it is the constructed entities and the actions of an individual on them which create the error, ultimately the error is social. Following Maturana (1988), the error is only recognized after the event when the mathematical expression has moved from the level of experience to the level of explanation. So agreement about correctness in mathematics stems from agreement about items and which operations on them are permissible.

An alternative way in which we can look at constraints is to use 'decidability/undecidability', just as Heinz Foerster did in defining metaphysics: 'We turn

83

into metaphysicians . . . whenever we decide on questions that are in principle undecidable' (1991, p. 63). The advantage of this is to provide a way to expose the items and operations in any position. There are various ways to proceed in solving a problem, negotiating a perturbation, or generally adopting a position. In addition, the results may not be viable. However, there are ways of *deciding* whether the procedures used are viable. We can decide whether a number is divisible by seven, no matter what its size. It took centuries to provide the procedure to decide that $x^n + y^n = z^n$ has no solutions in positive integers for n greater than two (Fermat's theorem). Now, thanks to Andrew Wiles, this is decidable. More generally, if we examine disagreements in terms of process, then we look at the ways in which the positions have been constructed. Positions taken will have been constructed from individual viewpoints. These positions may contain undecidables. But by searching the process and examining both the items and the operations one can hope to see where the difference lies, and on what it is based. For all these reasons I prefer and advocate decidability/undecidability as an alternative to the distinction between hard and soft constraints.

While Lewin has made his distaste for some of Maturana's views explicit, I suspect Lewin's criticism stems in part from his view of Maturana's reconstrual of terms such as 'love'. I would like to offer a positive perspective on a way Maturana (1988) described the intersection of epistemology and ethics. He distinguished two types of explanation. I identify one of these 'explanatory paths' with a constructivist orientation, the path of reality in parenthesis. In the other 'explanatory path' reality is without parenthesis. What Maturana says about these types of explanations offers a basis for a constructivist ethics.

'Reality in and without Parenthesis'

When we operate in an explanatory path of 'reality in parenthesis' we accept responsibility for the making of our statements and their limitations. In addition we offer explanations based on the procedures needed to arrive at them. In disagreements there is a recognition that the other may have been applying different criteria of acceptability in their explaining. Further, in conversation we may cease to differ by recognizing the different domains in which we have been operating.

On the other hand, when we operate in an explanatory path of 'reality without parenthesis' we do not accept responsibility for our statements. Tolerance is jettisoned. Our cognitive processes are hidden. We do not have to base statements on their constitutive operations. The truth of statements is not in question. In disagreements the other is wrong, and power is exerted to demand compliance with what is self-evidently true. I think the use of decidability/undecidability avoids invoking the 'reality without parenthesis' which seems to be implied by hard constraints.

Would it be possible to promote the important ethical consequences achieved by adopting the explanatory path of 'reality in parenthesis'? Could parents learn, for example, to interact in this way with their children? It is my suspicion that learning to be tolerant of others may be learned most easily in infancy in transactions with parents and others. At some stage in development I believe it becomes more difficult to be tolerant. If we can judge by the global political situation, it seems very difficult for many adults to learn.

Deuterolearning: Learning to Learn

Lewin identified early learning experiences as critical for the future education of young people. It is by means of education that we hope to pass on what we have found valuable in our experience. Bateson (1972) described how a process of *multilevelled* recursive learnings provided a framework to explain how personality is formed. I used Bateson's formulation in thinking about children's learning of gender stereotypes (Gash, 1993), and, with my colleague Vincent Kenny, I have tried to develop general ways of reducing prejudice (Gash and Kenny, 1997).

Is it the case that the powerlessness to which Philip Lewin has referred arises because of the implications of the radical constructivist model? Is it that the varieties of ways to explain experience, which are all legitimized by constructivism, have paralysed our sense of evaluation? Have we become afraid to adopt positions ourselves? If this is so for some, let us accept the challenge to differ, and offer encouragement to all to make explicit what they feel is valuable. It is a truism that each generation in any culture must pass on its insights to the next generation. If we believe in the theories we work with, we will work to pass on what is valuable. I believe that the increase in awareness of the validity of different viewpoints is reflected in a variety of contemporary cultural phenomena. These include constructivist writings, and the collapse of dominant totalitarian systems (e.g. Communism, the USSR, and many families). At present in Ireland there are tensions between (a) old authoritarian forms of control such as the Church, and (b) the democratic desire for a pluralist society. The international community will be aware that these tensions are explosive in the North of Ireland. Yet constructivist insights offer a way out, if people can see how to put these insights into practice. At this time our hopes for peace are high in the Republic of Ireland.

The constructivist model of learning and development provides an account of the conditions needed for change. It is in a system's interest to change if it will become more viable after the change. This could be explained in many ways. In what follows I delve into one example introduced above – parenthesizing reality.

If we adopt the explanatory path of 'reality in parenthesis', the limits of statements are transparent. We can allow others the space to hold different viewpoints within this explanatory path. Different viewpoints imply different domains of reality. If we allow others with different viewpoints to go unchallenged, we concede power and choose not to represent our own viewpoint. In my experience, there are ideas central to constructivism that are difficult to communicate. In my courses I try to make these ideas interesting, even intriguing, but the cultural support for modernist ways of thinking is deeply ingrained in my students. I suspect this is as true of American students as it is of Irish ones (e.g. Schommer, 1990). In spite of these difficulties, one way that teachers are ready to accept that there are different realities is with examples of developmental differences. Children's worlds and understandings are different from those of teachers' in easily identifiable ways. The developmental metaphor is a useful one in introducing constructivist insights. Elementary teachers, in particular, recognize the need to 'teach' gently and with mutual respect. I have found this a good example to use to communicate the fragility of the child when she or he is coming to understand something new.

During the past few years, I have been engaged in a series of constructivist projects designed to promote attitude change in different domains. The fundamental idea has been to stimulate intra-individual conflict by means of questioning and counter-examples. This is to strive to promote different realities in the classroom. The initial project was to investigate the feasibility of promoting more flexible approaches towards gender stereotyping in elementary school children. Teachers used tactics such as questioning and providing counter-examples to create conflict between the children's ideas and their experience. If, for example, a child has a fixed idea about a gender stereotype the teacher invited or provided a counter-example. This provided evidence to the contrary; it gave an example of a different reality. We encouraged the teachers to try to find children who could provide counter-examples. If this failed, teachers could provide counter-examples themselves.

The initial project on gender demonstrated the effects of the constructivist teaching programmes that provided opportunities for the children involved in the experiment to reconsider their views on gender stereotyping. The control children had their regular classes. The programme was evaluated by comparing the children in the experiment group and the control children on a standard measure of personal–social gender stereotypes. The children in the experiment had lower scores than the control children. In other words, the children in the former group were less rigid, and more flexible, about assigning stereotypes exclusively to males or females. Further, there was evidence that the lower scores of that group were durable. For example, a sample group of children who had participated in the study was retested one year later and the difference between the experimental and control groups remained significant. (An account of this project can be found in Gash and Morgan, 1993 and Gash et al., 1993.)

More recently I have been involved in extending these approaches to other cognitive domains: these have included attitudes towards mental disability (Gash, 1993), attitudes towards special needs (Gash, 1996), attitudes towards children from the Third World (Gash, 1995), conceptions of the heroic (Gash and Conway, 1997), and the child's self concept. Initially these classroom intervention projects were undertaken to promote positive attitudes towards a particular target group. There have been explicit prosocial aims in each project. These aims have been to invite children to reconsider the ways in which they have come to think about a particular issue by providing them with alternatives, and considering the implications of each view.

The aim of two of the projects, on the child's self concept and on the concept of the hero and heroine, was rather different. In the first of these we were concerned to provide opportunities for developing the self concept. The hypothesis was that children with secure self concepts will not have a need to feel good by putting down others. We all need to feel important some of the time. If people feel good about themselves and what they do, I believe they will not learn to feel good by humiliating others.

The final domain I mentioned was the heroic. We hoped that it would be possible to refocus the concepts of heroes and heroines held by the children who were 9 and 10 years old. The initial context for this study is that in our culture certain aspects of the heroic are promoted to the neglect of other more prosocial dimensions. A casual examination of the offerings in some of my local video stores illustrates the prioritizing of violence in that domain in my local Irish culture. The heroic has both connections with the self and with culture, and comparisons of boys and girls in the US and Ireland have provided additional examples of differing cultural constructions (Gash and Conway, 1997).

The self is a construct to which, as Glasersfeld has said, we do not have direct access. Glasersfeld wrote about the self in this way: 'the self is a relational entity ... which manifests itself in the continuity of our acts of differentiating and relating and in the intuitive certainty we have that our experience is truly ours' (1987[1970], p. 187). Bateson (1972) has provided an analysis of the way in which continuity in the patterning of experience is acquired. He explained it as second-level learning, or the learning of the contexts of viable first-level learnings. Contextual specification is, as I understand it, very largely a way of organizing social experience. It is at the boundary between intra-personal experience and inter-personal experience.

The historical learnings that constitute the self are notoriously difficult to change. This is partly the result of social support for individual identity. Friends will notice if you change. We are mirrored in the expectations of our friends, and that mirroring constitutes a powerful part of our identity. So choice is constrained by group identity. Heinz Foerster, for example, provided the story of the man who had seen himself through the eyes of his wife. He was seeking help, very depressed because of his wife's death. 'All his life, in the union of these two humans, the man had seen himself through the eyes of his wife. When she died, he was blind. But when he saw he was blind, he could see! So it is with us: we see through the eyes of the other' (Foerster, 1991). In this example one can see how an individual's identity can be contextualized and change. Such change is possible but seems difficult in ordinary circumstances. It seems to involve changing levels, if we understand levels as Bateson explained them. Such changing of levels or, in another metaphor, altering of boundaries, is often accompanied by a great release of energy in an individual. Consider the examples of falling in love, and of religious conversion. If this is so, let us hope for new defining of boundaries and changes of level through reading the proceedings of this conference. Then we can resume our lives with more energy!

Conclusion

So to complete the circle I return to Lewin's contribution. I agree with him and support his drawing attention to a number of issues: that there is a need to use constructivist approaches to consider ethical ideas; and that historical personal constraints have inevitable ethical implications. I have referred to arguments that constructivist processes involved in knowing are simultaneously social ways of relating to others and entail an ethics of mutual respect. I would like to finish by suggesting that there may be stage-like sequences in coming to understand and apply constructivist insights in our practice and living. In my own development as a constructivist, I believe there have been shifts in levels of awareness, shifts which resemble stages.

The first stage involves coming to recognize the validity and authority of the different realities of cultures, age groups, and individuals. Radical constructivism has played an important role in highlighting this and the consequent importance of intra-personal interpretations. A shift occurs in understanding the importance of the inter-personal social support for the ideas and beliefs an individual holds. However, to be fully open to our possibilities may imply a third stage that entails responsibly considering and working out the social consequences of our decisions. In the initial section of his chapter Lewin raised the following issue: How have we been marked by our experience in that region of the psyche which undergoes *paideia*? An answer may be offered along lines implicit in the stages that have just been outlined. As an example at the first level or stage, I suggest that the nihilism Lewin feared in contemporary culture may be avoidable if people can be challenged to examine the bases of their actions and to understand their role in understanding the world. Such nihilism stems from the failure to consider the circumstances, constructs or framework within which decisions are made (cf. Maturana, 1991, p. 51).

It seems a short step from recognizing the role of individuals in constructing their worlds (stage one) to beginning to examine the role of social support for constructs (stage two). The self is a construct that has difficulty existing in isolation from its social network – so it is relevant to ask how viable are the relations with this network? Under what emotions and constructs is this balance conserved? Questions of this type are likely to provide opportunities for allowing different realities to coexist responsibly. I hope that individuals who have been marked by constructivism will exhibit ways of retaining spontaneity and finding viable alternatives in difficult circumstances. A guide to providing such alternatives has been provided by Boxer and Kenny (1990) in a detailed account of ways in which different limited perspectives interact socially in systemic ways. This leads to the third level in which the social embeddedness of constructs invites consideration of the ethical dimension. One suggestion is that we could teach people to follow the rule proposed by Heinz Foerster (1992): 'For any discourse I have, say, in science, philosophy, epistemology, therapy, et cetera, to master the use of my language so that ethics is implicit.' However, the danger of talking about ethics on its own, is that one will unavoidably become prescriptive of a reality without parenthesis. Heinz Foerster (1992) avoided this in his reading of Wittgenstein; I paraphrase: 'the reward of good action is in the action itself.' And I conclude with a quotation from Glasersfeld:

> From the constructivist point of view, it makes no sense to assume that any powerful cognitive satisfaction springs from simply being told that one has done something right, as long as 'rightness' is assessed by someone else. To become a source of real satisfaction, 'rightness' must be seen as the fit with an order one has established oneself. (1987[1983], p. 329)

References

BATESON, G. (1972) *Steps to an Ecology of Mind*, New York: Ballantine.
BOXER, P. and KENNY, V. (1990) 'The economy of discourses: A third order cybernetics?' *Human Systems Management*, 9, pp. 205–24.
FOESTER, H. VON (1991) 'Through the eyes of the other', in STEIER, F. (ed.), *Research and Reflexivity*, London: Sage.
FOESTER, H. VON (1992) 'Ethics and second-order cybernetics', *Cybernetics and Human Knowing*, 1, 1, pp. 9–20.
GASH, H. (1993) 'Stereotyping and constructivism: Learning to be men and women', *Cybernetics and Human Knowing*, 1, 4, pp. 43–50.
GASH, H. (1995) 'Attitudes of Irish primary school children to European and Third World children', in HACKETT, M. (ed.), *Intercultural Education – Celebrating Diversity*, Drumcondra Education Centre: Dublin, pp. 44–65.
GASH, H. (1996) 'Changing attitudes towards children with special needs', *European Journal of Special Needs Education*, 11, pp. 286–97.
GASH, H. and CONWAY, P. (1997) 'Images of heroes and heroines: How stable'? *Journal of Applied Developmental Psychology*, 18, pp. 349–72.
GASH, H. and KENNY, V. (1997) 'The implementation of a constructivist approach to the resolution of prejudice', http://www.oikos.org/kenpred.htm
GASH, H. and MORGAN, M. (1993) 'School-based modifications of children's gender-related beliefs', *Journal of Applied Developmental Psychology*, 14, pp. 277–87.
GASH, H., MORGAN, M. and SUGRUE, C. (1993) 'Effects of an intervention and school type on gender stereotypes', *Irish Journal of Education*, 27, pp. 60–70.
GLASERSFELD, E. VON (1987) *The Construction of Knowledge*, Seaside, Calif.: Intersystems Publications.
GLASERSFELD, E. VON (1991) 'Knowing without metaphysics: Aspects of the radical constructivist position', in STEIER, F. (ed.), *Research and Reflexivity*, London: Sage.
GLASERSFELD, E. VON (1995) *Radical Constructivism*, London: Falmer Press.
KELLY, G. (1955) *The Psychology of Personal Constructs*, New York: W.W. Norton.

MATURANA, H. (1988) 'The search for objectivity, or the quest for a compelling argument', in KENNY, V. (ed.), 'Radical constructivism, autopoiesis and psychotherapy', *Irish Journal of Psychology*, 9, pp. 25–82.

MATURANA, H. (1991) 'Science and daily life: the ontology of scientific explanations', in STEIER, F. (ed.), *Research and Reflexivity*, London: Sage.

PIRSIG, M.R. (1973) *Zen and the Art of Motorcycle Maintenance*, London: Bantam.

SCHOMMER, M. (1990) 'Effects of beliefs about the nature of knowledge on comprehension', *Journal of Educational Psychology*, 82, pp. 498–504.

SPENCER-BROWN, G. (1972) *Laws of Form*, New York: Dutton.

8 Perspectives on Issues Concerning the Self, *Paideia*, Constraints and Viability, and Ethics

Leslie P. Steffe

Lewin raises four major issues for constructivism in the opening chapter of this section: how we think of 'self' within a constructivist framework; how constructivism addresses the notion of *paideia* – 'the complete process of education through which one becomes a competent participant within a culture'; how science and mathematics differ from the humanities because of different constraints and forms of viability in them; and whether constructivism should produce an ethics of the field. Lewin's concern with 'self' is that without some understanding of how our being arises from our situatedness in time, we are cut off from understanding our conditions as biological organisms and historical persons. Although asking questions about what constitutes self may seem unrelated to mathematics and science education, the way in which students construct their relationship to knowledge (mathematical or scientific) and to their learning and doing of the knowledge in question is one of the major problems confronting constructivist educators in these fields.

Issues Concerning the Self

There are two basic issues surrounding the way in which Lewin framed the question of the self and the distinction that Glasersfeld (1995) makes between the experiential self and the self as center of subjective awareness. The first concerns Lewin's introduction of being into the concept of the self, and the second concerns Glasersfeld's notion of the experiential self. Glasersfeld restricts the experiential self to that part of the 'self' which is experienced on the sensory-motor level, e.g. the kitten biting its own tail, or a human seeing his or her hand (the human is the only one getting tactual signals from it). Of the self as center of subjective awareness, Glasersfeld explained that 'it is precisely this awareness of what one is doing or experiencing that is the foundation of what we ordinarily call our *self*. It does not have to be thinking in any elevated sense. If you are becoming aware of tying your shoe laces, you also become aware of the fact that there is a you who is doing it' (1995, p. 122).[1] In contrast to the experiential self,

Leslie P. Steffe

> The other and more important 'self'[2] is the one that has my memories, the one that thinks and reasons whenever I do these (remembered) things, and the one that just now has pains in its shoulders because it struggled to mend a garage door yesterday. It's a wholly mysterious entity – mysterious in a sense different from the garage door, which certainly had its own mysteries for me! This self is capable of remembering, reflecting, feeling, liking, and disliking – all things that are mysterious, but about which one knows certain effects. In this regard, I am an unrepenting dualist and until someone offers me a plausible model of 'consciousness', I see no reason to change my view. (Glasersfeld; personal communication, 22 October 1998)

A Sense of Continuity

By introducing the notion of 'being' into this mysterious self, Lewin suggests that it is not solely epistemic, but that it is also entailed with being or existence. Glasersfeld (Ch. 1) interpreted Lewin's suggestion by noting that as authors of our own experiential realities, we attribute continuity to ourselves as its constructors. In amplification of why he is reluctant to refer to the agent's continuity as 'existence', he notes that it is this very agent who constructs their 'notions' of space and of time (Piaget, 1964). So, for Glasersfeld, 'existence' is an epistemic affair. Larochelle (Ch. 5) apparently agrees that the experiential self is a construction of an acting agent: '[A] radical constructivist does not attempt to know what the self *is*, nor to locate it relative to a supreme faculty or a center of subjective consciousness' (p. 55). Interpreted further, Larochelle's comment implies that the experiential self is not a static affair of existence or being. Rather, it is a complex of dynamic, changing and multifarious selves dependent on the acting agent's own history and experiences as well as on the narrative scripts provided by the community at large. Lewin commented that 'this is my view too; this is what living in time means' (Lewin; personal communication, 21 October 1998). So, starting with the dawning awareness of space and time in the individual, there would seem to be agreement among Larochelle, Lewin and Glasersfeld concerning the epistemic nature of the experiential self, an agreement that turns on Glasersfeld's interpretation of 'existence' as a sense of continuity of the self in the construction of experiential reality.

Levels of Experience

There is still an issue, however, concerning the experiential self as a complex of dynamic, changing and multifarious selves because Glasersfeld restricted the experiential self to that part of the 'self' which is experienced on the sensory-motor level. However, re-presentation, which is the regeneration of sensory material in its immediate absence, opens the possibility of levels of experiencing, of which Glasersfeld (personal communication, 23 October 1998) said, 'I certainly agree that you can introduce various "levels of experiencing" – and I am looking forward to seeing your classification'. This opens up a fundamental research problem in mathematics and science education, because mathematics and science are extraordinarily experiential and, unfortunately, it is the kind of experience that all too many people have learned to avoid.

Larochelle (Ch. 5) believes that connecting the experiential self to the 'conditions of its coming-to-be, as well as of its actual invention, and, finally, how the concept, *via* language and transactions between subjects becomes a way for interpreting experiences and for identifying similarities and invariants within these experiences' (p. 56), helps us to place the question of the experiential self into the realm of human construction and investigation. Larochelle's idea of the experiential self becoming a way for interpreting experiences of others extends the core experiential self of which Glasersfeld speaks to the social self (Glasersfeld, 1995, p. 126). Likewise, the core experiential self needs to be considered in relation to the child's construction of mathematical and scientific experiences. One way to establish such a relation is to maintain the spontaneity of spontaneous development in mathematics and science learning in the schools. Not only do children construct space and time, they also construct a multitude of other mathematical concepts and operations before they are seven or eight years of age. This spontaneous construction, when coupled with a spontaneously constructed 'system of physics peculiar to the child'[3] (Piaget, 1964, p. 1), indicates that mathematical or scientific experiences are already implicated in children's spontaneous development and hence are constitutive aspects of children's construction of a stable reality that includes mathematical or scientific aspects. To the extent that a child is aware of its actions or interactions that an observer would call 'mathematical' or 'scientific', the observer can legitimately speak of the child's awareness of itself as an agent of mathematical or scientific action or interaction, which does extend the child's basic concept of self.

When the spontaneity of spontaneous development is maintained within children's mathematics learning, Kieren (Ch. 6) speaks of students 'constructing or bringing forth their mathematical worlds based on their own histories and structures' rather than 'attempts to mirror some pre-given outside world' (pp. 70–1 above). As spontaneous development occurs in part as a result of autoregulation of children's interactions in their socio-cultural as well as their physical milieu (Piaget, 1964), it is in principle possible to connect school learning in mathematics and science with the products of spontaneous development by bringing those products forth in the educational setting. Although the systems that spontaneous development produces are distinguishable from those of mathematicians or scientists, this does not disqualify these systems as serving in the mathematics and science education of children.

The problem of how to maintain the spontaneity characteristic of spontaneous development in school learning is a critical one because the way in which children regard their mathematical or scientific experiences is largely a matter of school learning. Children do eventually become aware of their mathematical or scientific experiences[4] and establish a relationship between their selves as

Leslie P. Steffe

centers of subjective awareness and these experiences. In the usual conventions that constitute mathematics and science teaching, these subjects are regarded as 'hard constraints' in the sense which Lewin explains. In this view, mathematics and science teaching is not based on the products of children's spontaneous development outside of school, and thus it does not contribute to the continuation of this spontaneous constructive activity. This raises major issues for the continued evolution of the relationship of the self to mathematical and scientific knowledge throughout childhood and beyond into young adulthood, because the rejection of one's sense of oneself as an agent of mathematical or scientific action or interaction may create a disturbance in the self as a center of subjective awareness that can handicap further learning in mathematics or science. In fact, it can lead easily to a rejection of those parts of one's experience.

Issues Concerning Constraints and *Paideia*

Separating the experiential self and the self as center of subjective awareness is crucial because it allows us to account for how an individual, for example, might maintain a sense of tolerance or viability of the self given what might be considered as hard constraints. According to Lewin (personal communication, 21 October 1998), what makes a constraint hard is the degree to which the boundary conditions establishing the constraint are assumed as given. Moreover, in the sciences and mathematics Lewin claims that inquiry takes place under conditions of well-defined constraints. In the same communication, Lewin further elaborated:

> Scientists and mathematicians agree ahead of time on the nature of the conditions under which their inquiry will be regarded as valid. In the case of science, this question is the question of method and experimental design ... In the case of mathematics, the presuppositions of the field of inquiry are simply accepted.

Hard Constraints in Mathematics and Science Teaching

Kieren (Ch. 6) not only addresses the issues concerning the self, but also the issue of how constructivism addresses *paideia*, and in doing so, addresses issues concerning hard constraints. Kieren's primary concern is whether mathematics education can be seen as 'part of *paideia* rather than simply as an arena, rather divorced from *paideia*, where one picks up a "tool kit", albeit an important one, for *paideia*' (p. 78 above). In this, he explicitly questions the separation of mathematics and *paideia*, and implicitly questions the necessity of strong constraints as emerging from accepting certain presuppositions of mathematics as given.

Kieren is quite successful in painting an image of a practice of mathematics education that *occasions* constructive action on the part of students, which,

Perspectives on Issues

in turn, provides occasions for the teacher's and other students' knowing in action. Rather than speak in terms of hard or soft constraints, Kieren chooses to emphasize a complexity of socio-mathematical constraints which are of the nature that children experience in their spontaneous mathematical and scientific development. He accomplishes what he sets out to do because he works in a framework (enactivism) compatible with a radical constructivism rather than with what Larochelle refers to as the 'weak' version of constructivism – a constructivism in which mathematics and science are regarded as givens. In the weak version of constructivism, Larochelle (Ch. 5) appropriately comments that 'renewed interest in the knowledge of students seems to have barely changed the usual conventions of teaching activity, whatever the level of instruction' (p. 57 above). This is in contrast to the recursive image of mathematics teaching that Kieren develops – the teacher acts to provide occasions for student construction, and these teaching acts are the result of constructions occasioned by perceptions of student activities.

Lewin believes that 'Science and math are frequently taught as though the constraints were hard, when they are only presupposed. But the sociocultrual conditions under which education takes place are always operative, and to that extent, teachers in mathematics and science must be attuned to how the boundary conditions of instruction affect the content of instruction even (and especially) when the content of instruction seems straightforward to them' (Lewin; personal communication, 21 October 1998). In Kieren's work (Ch. 6), these boundary conditions are decidably different from what would be the case if he regarded the presuppositions of mathematics as being simply accepted and therefore as constituting hard constraints. He explicitly questions the necessity of teachers regarding inquiry in mathematics as taking place under conditions of well-defined constraints. When discussing the 'hard constraints' he as a teacher could see in fractional tasks, Kieren (Ch. 6) commented that 'Although constraints induced by the mathematical nature of the episodes can be considered "strong" either in terms of some perceived nature of mathematical truth or because some elements of the situation were designed on a mathematical basis, such experienced constraints are by no means monolithic. They are moderated by the nature, modes, and levels of students mathematical understandings' (p. 77 above).

Further, Kieren (Ch. 6) sees no reason why a teacher must, a priori, establish the nature of the conditions under which inquiry in his or her classroom will be regarded as valid.

> A consideration of activities of students working in a space for learning fractions is interpreted as showing that students experience various levels and kinds of mathematical constraints related to the nature of their changing mathematical understandings. Within a classroom setting such constructing is done under the experience of a variety of other constraints as well. It is suggested that it is this complex of experienced constraints, both mathematical and non-mathematical, that allows us to observe the on-going mathematical activity as part of *paideia*. (p. 69 above)

Leslie P. Steffe

Kieren's comment opens the issue concerning how (not whether) a teacher might use his or her knowledge of mathematics in mathematics teaching. That this is a major problem in mathematics education is made clear by Lewin (Ch. 4).

> One may invoke a rhetoric of viability and still allow in practice for only one possible solution. All the work of specification will have been done by the teacher drawing upon the reigning tradition in establishing the conditions of inquiry while the student/knower is conceptualized as creative and inventive. In some ways, this 'paradox of happy agreement' may seem the best of all possible epistemic worlds. (p. 43)

Such a practice is consequent upon the choices and distinctions that the teacher makes; that is, they are consequent upon his or her way of reflecting on and working out the reasons, values, ideologies and representations that he or she chooses to promote (Larochelle, Ch. 5). In making these choices, Larochelle (Ch. 5) commented that, 'it seems to me that unavowed claims and programs are smuggled into the practices of teaching scholarly knowledge on a regular basis. Most of the time, this knowledge, notably in the scientific and mathematical areas, is presented as if it were untouched by such "impurities", as if it were a type of knowledge which does not pose any problems – in other words, constitutes a "knowledge of"' (p. 63).

Decidability-Undecidability

Concerning 'soft constraints', Lewin commented that: 'I explicitly do not ground the idea of soft constraints in the frame of reference of a single actor. It is precisely the negotiation of constraints with other knowers that makes constraints in the sociocultural domain soft' (personal communication; 21 October 1998). Larochelle and Kieren opened the question whether the hard constraints of mathematics and science aren't also negotiable. Gash (Ch. 7) explicitly stated his position concerning this question in the following passage.

> While I agree wholly with Lewin that to forget the historical nature of constructions entails a loss of coherence, the distinction between hard and soft constraints perturbs me. I wonder if there is a way to express Lewin's intention that does not seem to allow reality to reappear in the guise of hard constraints. (Ch. 7, p. 82)

Gash's (Ch. 7) advocacy of decidability-undecidability as replacing hard and soft constraints finds some justification in the thinking of Max Born. After rejecting the thesis that the sense perceptions of different individuals are identical in his famous comment,

> Thus it dawned upon me that fundamentally everything is subjective, everything without exception. That was a shock (Born, 1968, p. 162),

he went on to say, 'The problem was not to distinguish the subjective from the objective, but to understand how to free oneself from the subjective and to arrive at objective statements' (ibid., p. 162). Using methods of thinking of the physicist rather than the philosopher, Born said of his approach to the problem, 'I suggest the expression "decidability" for a fundamental rule of scientific thinking (although I did not find the word in the dictionary): use a concept only if it is decidable, whether it can be applied in a special case or not' (ibid., p. 170), and used what he regarded as the kernel of Einstein's theory of general relativity as illustrative.

> An observer in a closed box can therefore not decide whether the acceleration of a body relative to the box is due to a gravitational field or to an acceleration of the box in the opposite direction. (ibid., p. 171)

In this case, to decide involves a second observer, as pointed out by Foerster in his statement of the principle of relativity, which

> rejects a hypothesis when it does not hold for two instances together, although it holds for each instance separately. (Foerster, 1984, p. 59)

Von Foerster (1984) goes on to remind us that the principle of relativity is not a logical necessity nor can it be proven to be either true or false.

> [T]he crucial point to be recognized here is that I am free to choose either to adopt this principle or to reject it. If I reject it, I am the center of the universe, my reality is my dreams and my nightmares, my language is monologue, and my logic monologic. If I adopt it, neither I nor the other can be the center of the universe. (ibid., pp. 59–60)

Given the acceptance of the principle of relativity, the practice of science and mathematics, as well as the practice of teaching science and mathematics, certainly relies on negotiation in making decisions concerning establishing objective statements. In this context, the idea that constraints are internally generated through our living in time (Lewin, Ch. 4, p. 53), or its equivalent – the constructions of the learner generate their own constraints (Gash, Ch. 7, p. 81) – takes into consideration the frame of reference of the actor. In this frame of reference, the attitude that constructions of the learner generate their own constraints is not simply an appropriate attitude. Rather, it is necessary because constraints emerge only as *experienced* constraints. However, in the observer's frame of reference, the observed constraints of the actor are in the experiential field of the observer.[5] Including the observer as well as the actor clarifies the relative nature of constraints in radical constructivism, because to arrive at an 'objective statement', the principals involved must perform tests on which to base their decisions (Born, 1968, p. 173). In radical constructivism, then, although the subjectivity of experienced constraints is irrefutable, it is possible in principle to make tests which lead to decisions of compatibility or incompatibility.

Leslie P. Steffe

Constraints and Decidability

If decidability is regarded as the means to understand how to free oneself from the subjective and to arrive at objective statements, constraints and this idea of decidability are distinguishable and cannot be reduced to one another. It helps to understand the relationship between them if the idea of constraint is placed in the context of adaptation. Like Glasersfeld, Lewin (Ch. 4) rejects adaptation as adaptation to a pre-existing and mind-independent world. However, Glasersfeld (1995) reformulates adaptation in the context of experiential reality, and this contributes to what I regard as the negative and the positive role of constraints.

Knowledge, rather than being regarded as true only if it reflects a real world, is regarded as viable only if it has not clashed with obstacles or constraints. 'This knowledge of clashes or constraints and failures describes reality in "negative terms"' (Glasersfeld, 1995, pp. 72-3). Often overlooked in this negative description of reality is the additional condition that knowledge remains viable only if it finds some confirmation in experience. I regard these confirmed conceptual structures as the positive aspect of Glasersfeld's model of knowing and they complement the negative aspect. Glasersfeld articulates the positive aspect of his model in terms of schemes, and specifies accommodations of those schemes as being induced by whatever constraints the knower may encounter in their use.

The concept of accommodation is a part of the notion of adaptation, and hence, of learning. Learning in the context of adaptation is regarded as those more or less permanent modifications of the involved schemes that eliminate perturbation induced by experienced constraints.[6] In this idea of learning, the term 'constraint' has two meanings – 'constrained by' and 'constrained to'. The former meaning pertains to the negative aspect of constructivism and the latter to the positive aspect. A scheme is constrained by clashes with reality, and constrained to those experiential situations in which it is used (or confirmed). In this context, 'decidability' refers to whether a certain scheme either fits or does not fit within an experiential situation – to whether it can be used or not by making tests. On the other hand, 'undecidability' refers to whether no decision of fit can be made – to those cases where the test fails to provide a basis for decision.

Although 'constrained by' and 'constrained to' may seem dichotomous, they can function together.[7] For example, even when the listening agent seemingly understands the utterances of another, this may involve coordinations of previously unrelated concepts or operations, coordinations which may remain outside of the awareness of the listener. In this case, the listener may be constrained to his or her perceptions of the utterances of the other and believe he or she understands,[8] but from the observer's perspective, would not have understood without making the coordination or modification. So, accommodation can and does occur in the context of social interaction. Moreover, what seems to be a constraint in the 'constrained by' meaning can be in retrospect a confirmation of a superseding scheme.

It seems essential to retain the above distinctions between 'decidability' and 'constraints'. There is a further distinction between 'decidability' and 'viability' which also seems essential. For example, in a famous metaphor concerning reality in radical constructivism, Watzlawick (1984, pp. 14–15) recounted a story of a captain sailing his ship through an uncharted channel devoid of beacons and other navigational aids. The course of the ship chosen by the captain would remain viable while sailing only so long as the ship did not run into obstacles hidden beneath the water. Without the proper navigational aids, the captain could not make tests to find the hidden obstacles and use the results of the tests in making decisions concerning the course of the ship so it would not meet these obstacles. Sailing without navigational aids eliminated the possibility of deciding on a viable course.

Foerster has spoken repeatedly in terms of the distinction between problems that are in principle decidable and those that are in principle undecidable (Foerster, 1991). He grounds ethics in the consideration of those problems which are left to us to decide without navigational aids or for which tests are inconclusive. This is compatible with Glasersfeld's (1995, p. 127) assertion that ethics must be manifest in the choice of goals, and viability of schemes of action or thought in the context of specific goals.

On an Ethics of the Field

In the frame of reference of the actor, ethics lies outside of the domain of viability. In the observer's frame of reference,[9] the choice of goals does not seem to be any more or less rational than Born's principle of decidability. So, an ethics of teaching mathematics or science can in part be based on rational choice of the teacher, if the teacher is considered as Maturana's (1978) second-order observer, or an observer of the circumstances of observation. That is, the teacher must make decisions or tests prior to teaching concerning the choice of goals he or she might subsequently test for appropriateness in the teaching context. Such decisions should be regarded as involving schemes of action or thought which the teacher uses in making tests prior to teaching. In this case, decidability pertains to more than decidability at the experiential level. It involves a second level of decidability that follows on from the second level of viability explained by Glasersfeld (1995). A conceptual item is viable on the second level if it fits within a coherent conceptual network of structures which, at their point of experience, have turned out to be viable in the experiential sense. This second level of viability depends on doing thought experiments or tests to decide if a conceptual item fits within a goal structure. These decisions serve as a basis for establishing viability at the second level.

Establishing viability of a chosen goal structure in interactive communication with students involves a second-order (not level) of viability (Glasersfeld, 1995). When a conceptual item is found viable not only in our own sphere of actions, but also in that of another, this establishes a second-order of viability

Leslie P. Steffe

to the conceptual item. A second-order of decidability, then, involves von Foerster's statement of the principle of relativity in making tests on which decisions concerning the compatibility of our conceptual constructs with those of the other are based.

Clarification of the first and second *levels* of viability, and of the first and second *order* of viability, serves as a basis for a first and second level of decidability and a first and second order of decidability. These are important distinctions to make in establishing goal structures pertaining to mathematics and science teaching. They are also important distinctions to make in a consideration of ethics because ethics is usually thought to begin with consideration of the other. For example, Gash (Ch. 7) commented that 'Once one moves from considering an individual's constructions to considering how these are perceived by another, one can enter the ethical domain' (p. 81). Moreover, Glasersfeld (Ch. 1) commented that 'From my point of view, the generation of ethics will have to be part of the model we design to grasp our interactions with the experiential constructs we call "others"'. In contrast, a second-order of decidability at the second (conceptual) level of decidability is necessary to establish a goal structure because the teacher needs to contemplate a particular goal in the context of its appropriateness for students. Of course, this still involves a consideration of the other, but it is a conceptual consideration that does not involve an experiential other. There are also ethical considerations in building a goal structure through decisions that are not referenced to another. These decisions involve considerations of internal consistency in those cases that cannot be decided on the basis of logical necessity.

In his critique of the lack of an 'explicit ethical posture' in radical constructivism, Lewin (Ch. 4) capitalizes on the possibility of the development of an implicit ethics within the individual in the following comment,

> If we take radical constructivism seriously, if we understand that constraints are internally generated through our living in time, then it seems to me we must equally take seriously how the sedimentation of those constraints anticipates our behaviors in the future. It seems to me that the relative coherence of those constraints constitutes 'character', an internal region of epistemic and ethical inertia. It does not merely lay the ground for ethics; it already is an ethics. (p. 53)

Lewin argues that

> [t]he behavior we call ethical arises as a consequence of how a person has made sense of their experience. As a result of our experience, certain preferred ways of acting and thinking come to be developed [second level of decidability but within subject]. We can refer to these preferred modes of construal as habit or sedimentation or tacit knowledge or deutero-learning or any of a number of other terms. This is the constructivist part; we make sense of our experience on the basis of how we have constructed ways of making sense of experience in the past. Some of this constructive process depends on a kind of

100

individual creativity and personal preference [first- and second-levels of viability]; some of it depends on social and physical constraints, on the demands others make of us or the limitations of the physical world [second- and first-order decidability, respectively]. Note that much if not most of this process takes place without conscious awareness or intention, especially since virtually all of it takes place by about age five, and that it is usually extremely difficult to alter or modify this early learning – this *paideia* – in any fundamental way later on in life. (personal communication, 31 October 1998; parenthetical comments added)

According to Lewin, then, ethics does not simply begin with considering how an individual's constructions are perceived by another. Rather, an ethics is implicit in the constructions of the individual. As such, they seem to arise from the same presuppositions that Glasersfeld (1995, p. 68) made concerning the construction of schemes which served as a core consideration of Kieren (Ch. 6) in his argument that mathematics education be considered as a part of *paideia*:

- the ability and, beyond it, the *tendency* to establish recurrences in the flow of experience;
- this, in turn, entails at least two further capabilities: remembering and retrieving (re-presenting) experiences, and the ability to make comparisons and judgments of similarities and differences; and
- the presupposition that the organism 'likes' certain experiences better than others; which is to say, it must have some elementary values.

Lewin (Ch. 4) has argued that a starting point for an ethics in radical constructivism that begins with notions such as respect for the other and openness, or tolerance and mutual respect (Gash, Ch. 7, p. 81) is based on the normative ethics of Kant, which, he asserts, Glasersfeld's ideas do not sanction. In making his argument, Lewin (Ch. 4) deconstructs the Kantian imperative that one should always treat others as ends rather than as means. We can see that Glasersfeld's three postulates would not lead necessarily to that imperative. Although it is an appealing imperative for any number of reasons, it can easily be subordinated to, for example, a goal of climbing a corporate hierarchy, where people are often treated as means rather than ends. There may have been an ethical reason for the choice of this goal rather than some other goal which honored the Kantian imperative, depending on one's values. Although Lewin chooses to cast his argument in terms of viability without a consideration of goals, his example carries the force of his argument that there is not a sharp separation between ethics and epistemology, and that an ethics emerging from constructivism would be a model of ethics consistent with constructivism rather than a constructivist ethics that begins with ethical precepts.

Larochelle (Ch. 5) apparently agrees with Lewin on this point. '[I]t [constructivism] teaches that holding a point of view is a matter of choice, which amounts in a way to adopting a back-handed approach to ethics – that is to say, constructivism does not propose a moral code, but instead strives to make evident the fact that ethical issues are indeed at stake' (p. 62). Constructivism does not dictate that everyone will adopt a particular ethics. Rather, it predicts that ethical considerations will emerge naturally as humans interact and form communities. Gash (Ch. 7) expresses this idea as an important ethical corollary of the constructivist position: 'Namely, the grounds or implicit epistemological assumptions in an argument are braided-interwoven with the form of one's social relations and with the emotions at play in social interaction' (p. 82). Constructivism does impose constraints on those people who chose consciously to adopt constructivism as a stance.

Notes

1. Glasersfeld reinterpreted Descartes' pronouncement 'I think, therefore I am' as 'I am *aware* of thinking, therefore I am'.
2. The self as center of subjective awareness.
3. See Larochelle (Ch. 5) and Glynn and Duit (1995) for references concerning children's scientific conceptions.
4. The spontaneous development of the systems of mental operations 'peculiar to the child' in the mathematical or scientific realm occurs in the main outside of the awareness of the child.
5. In the observer's frame, the environment of the actor is everything in the experience of the observer that is not the actor.
6. Glasersfeld (Ch. 1) points out that experience is more than sensory experience.
7. Clashes with reality are experienced most often in the context of a scheme being used.
8. Such a belief may not have involved a conscious decision. In that case, it would not be an interpretation. Not until the subject becomes aware of possible interpretations can we say that decidability operates.
9. The observer may be the actor observing his or her own actions.

References

BORN, M. (1968) *My Life and My Views*, New York: Charles Scribner's.
FOERSTER, H. VON (1984) 'On constructing a reality', in P. WATZLAWICK (ed.), *The Invented reality*, New York: W. W. Norton, pp. 41–62.
FOERSTER, H. VON (1991) 'Through the eyes of the other', in STEIER, F. (ed.), *Research and Reflexivity*, Newberry Park, Calif.: Sage, pp. 63–75.
GLASERSFELD, E. VON (1995) *Radical Constructivism: A Way of Knowing and Learning*, London: Falmer Press.
GLYNN, S.M. and DUIT, R. (eds) (1995) *Learning Science in the Schools*, Mahwah, NJ: Lawrence Erlbaum.
PIAGET, J. (1964) 'Development and learning', in RIPPLE, R.E. and ROCKCASTLE, V. N. (eds), *Piaget Rediscovered: A Report of a Conference on Cognitive Studies and Curriculum Development*, Ithaca, NY: Cornell University Press, pp. 7–19.
WATZLAWICK, P. (1984) 'Introduction', in WATZLAWICK, P. (ed.), *The Invented Reality*, New York: W.W. Norton, pp. 13–15.

Section Three

Practice of Mathematics Education

Mathematics teaching, taken at its extremes, can have two fundamentally different goals. One is that students *become facile* with prescribed rituals, some of which involve writing marks in various configurations, in response to commands to perform them. The other is that students *develop insight* into their natural world, their interactions with it, and their reasoning about it. The first goal typifies what we imagine as 'traditional' mathematics. The second goal is less common, and requires social systems that typically do not exist. The chapters in this section definitely exemplify issues surrounding the latter goal – that of transforming the mathematics education of school practice to one that fosters insight into significant mathematical ideas, coherence in students' understandings of various topics, and dispositions that are propaedeutic for greater mathematical and scientific literacy.

J. van den Brink (Ch. 9) shares with us an approach to teaching geometry that grows out of Freudenthal's didactic realism. He illustrates an approach to mathematics education, shared in large extent by the other chapter authors in this section, that places mathematizing at the center of students' and teachers' activities. It is distinct among the three, however, in that Brink draws strongly from issues in mathematics to structure his thinking about interactions with students. Wright (Ch. 10) also emphasizes issues of mathematical understanding, but in a very different setting than the others. His chapter is about a recovery program for students who had been unsuccessful in other settings, and draws on the constructivist-based research of the Interdisciplinary Research on Number project. Cobb (Ch. 11) situates many of the issues addressed by Brink and Wright within a perspective that attempts to account for the social context of students' emerging sophistication and how addressing it might bring it into service of mathematics education goals.

9 Students' Constructions: A Necessity for Formalizations in Geometry

Jan van den Brink

What contributions can Ernst von Glasersfeld's epistemology make to the teaching of geometry and, in particular, to formalization in geometry? I have found a number of striking ideas described by Glasersfeld and, among them, a basic idea that is shared by radical constructivism and didactic realism, which was developed in The Netherlands. Both of these frameworks stress the *'students' constructions'*. This chapter is a report of a didactic phenomenological investigation into spherical geometry in mathematics education for 16 year olds. The research demonstrates that the students' intuitive constructions and viewpoints, which were inspired by various types of geometry (spherical geometry, plane geometry, solid geometry) contributed to the process of formalization. Without the students' intuitive ideas no genuine formalization in geometry is possible.

Geometry for Clarification in an Unfathomable 'Reality'

Spherical geometry is the geometry of the surface of a sphere. This probably brings to mind the *analytical* measurement of spherical triangles and all sorts of theorems in goniometric[1] terms regarding such triangles. But that's not the only thing that is involved in the study of spherical geometry. Quite the contrary. We can also study it in a non-analytical way, and there are a number of convincing arguments for a study of this type, which is a study of *synthetic* spherical geometry.

In 'daily life', for instance, phenomena can be found which remain unclear and mysterious without interpreting them in terms of spherical geometry in general and great circles in particular. Take the fact that an airplane bound for Atlanta from Amsterdam does not depart in a southwesterly direction (which, given a world map, would seem logical), but, rather, in a northwesterly direction – as if taking a detour alongside the North Pole. 'Strange,' one might say. Why should this be? Another phenomenon which can be explained on an elementary geometrical level is the fact that the great circle indicates both the shortest distance between two points on earth and their initial direction. 'The shortest distance?' one might ask. But how can the fact be explained that one must constantly readjust one's compass course while moving towards the destination in the shortest possible distance? How can one explain that the shortest distance

Jan van den Brink

is on a great circle? Another question is, 'Are there straight lines on the earth?' What may they be on the curved surface of the earth? And, finally, consider parallel lines straight ahead around the earth. Do they exist?

The answers to these questions depend on how one regards the world, because one's knowledge about the world depends also on how one regards it. Geometrical knowledge can provide clarification of such phenomena and – as was the case in Antiquity – can include discussions about 'the construction of paths of action and thinking that an unfathomable "reality" leaves open for us to tread' (Glasersfeld, 1983, p. 2).

Different Types of Geometry, Great Circles, Poles and Antipoles, and Map Projections

A number of topics within spherical geometry are suitable for classroom use. For example: great circles, poles and antipoles, map projections, and different types of geometry.

Great Circle

The *great circle* is an important topic. In analogy, a great circle is to a two-dimensional spherical surface what a straight line is to a flat surface; it is the determinant of both the shortest distance and the shortest direction between two points. But it is also the greatest cross-section of a sphere in the three-dimensional space. So, the great circle can be defined in different ways depending upon the space (two-dimensional or three-dimensional) one has in mind.[2]

In the new mathematics curriculum for school children in The Netherlands,[3] great circles are found exclusively in the unit entitled 'Mecca' (Brink and Meeder, 1991; Brink, 1993a and 1993b). The unit is well suited to the curriculum, and forms a special topic in continuation of 'solid geometry' (cross-sections), 'geometry of vision lines', 'orientation and location' and 'calculating in geometry', which are the four main chapters in the geometry curriculum (Team W12–16, 1992, p. 14).

Pole and Antipole

Pole and antipole is another topic specific to spherical geometry. The North and South Poles serve as models. A geometric link can be made between poles, antipoles, the centre of the earth, and great circles. In addition to poles and antipoles, a sphere also contains 'planes' and 'opposing planes' (the hemispheres, for instance, or the time zones), and lines and 'opposing lines' (the prime meridian and the date line, for example). These 'opposing' concepts are characteristics of spherical geometry.

Map Projections

The 'representation' of the spherical surface on a flat surface is the third of the topics which can make spherical geometry a fascinating subject for all students. Two map projections catch the eye – the Mercator projection[4] (a world map) and the central projection[5] (gnomic map, e.g. a polar map) are particularly appropriate for further investigation. What does a straight line drawn on a world map mean on the globe (a rhumb-line[6] with fixed compass direction, a loxodromic line)? And drawn on a polar map (a great circle: the shortest direction)? There are two different directions on the globe, according to the two map projections.

Different Types of Geometry

Spherical geometry, plane geometry and solid geometry are formalized backgrounds that can be used to appreciate the differences between students' ideas (e.g. about what a great circle might be). To understand the meaning of a student's remarks, one has to know differences among various types of geometry. These differences are not only differences in formal systems of axioms. Rather, they are also different ways of regarding the world and, accordingly, of constructing knowledge about it. We can see the world as a flat, two-dimensional surface close around us or as a spherical two-dimensional surface from the viewpoint of a satellite (a great circle is seen as a straight line). We can also see the world as a filled three-dimensional globe (a great circle may be a greatest secant circle cutting through the globe).

The knowledge constructed from these different worldviews produces different geometrical laws. For example, in plane geometry for every two different points there is one and only one straight line that joins them. But in spherical geometry, a pole and its antipole are incident to an infinite number of straight lines (great circles). Glasersfeld points to the disturbance that can be generated by such seemingly *contradictory* experiences (Glasersfeld and Cobb, 1983). The disturbance not only engenders discussions, it engenders different formalizations in the classroom as well. These formalized systems produced by the students are related to Glasersfeld's idea of *'subjective environment'* (Glasersfeld, 1983): not only is the knowledge of a phenomenon constructed in an individual way, but so is the whole environment in which the phenomenon fits.

Lessons in Spherical Geometry

The topics of great circle, pole and antipole, map projection, and different types of geometry occupied six lessons in the school year. The sixth lesson was an exam. The lessons were given by one teacher, Wim Schaafsma, in three 10th grade MAVO[7] classes at the Greydanus school in Zwolle, The Netherlands. A

Jan van den Brink

total of seventy-five 16-year old students participated in these lessons. They made use of globes, Styrofoam balls, a half-sphere of transparent plastic (Lénárt, 1993), an Islamic prayer rug, and a student's textbook, entitled *Mecca*.

Where is Mecca?

I developed this textbook as an example of how mathematics can be enriched for all children by choosing topics from different cultures; for instance, from the Islamic culture. The book deals mainly with spherical geometry on the globe.

> *There he was: the Imam,* [so begins the textbook.]
> *I asked him my question right away:*
> *'When you pray, you pray towards the East, don't you?'*
> *'No, towards Mecca,' he answered.*
> *'But how do you know where Mecca is? I can find the East, but Mecca. . . .'*

Figure 9.1 Mecca-meter at 250

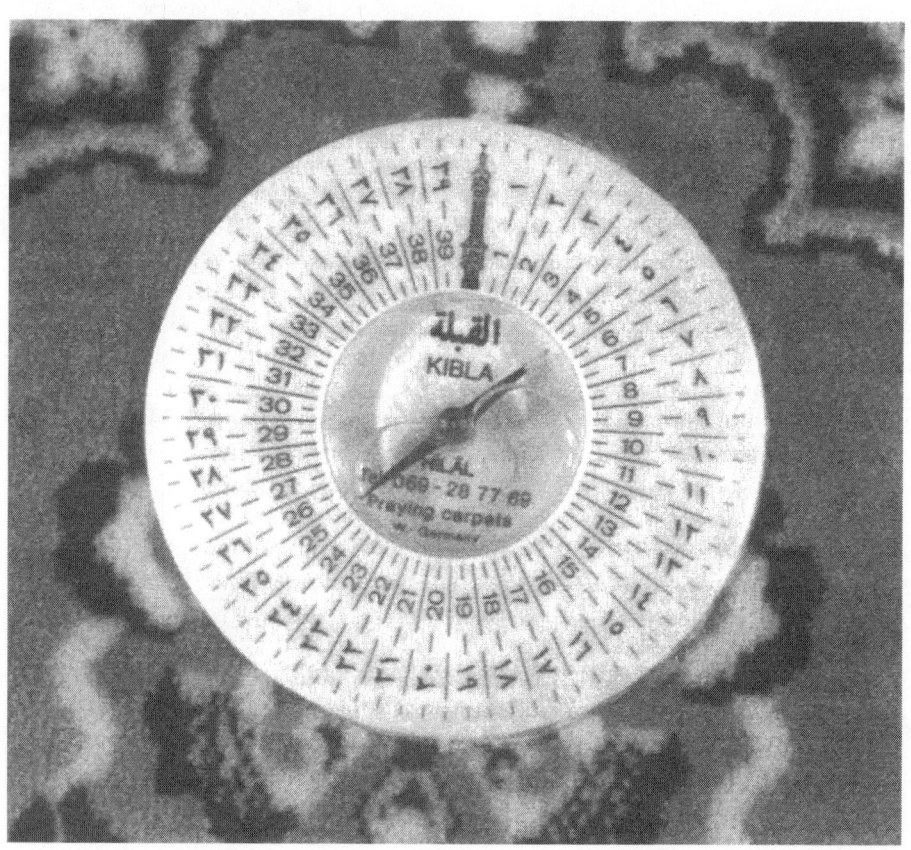

'You can find Mecca in three ways,' the Imam explained to me. 'First of all, you can tell by the sun. But you don't see the sun so often here in Holland. So there's a second way.' I was amazed when he told me that he could find the direction of Mecca with a sort of compass.
'But when you can't see the sun and you don't have that compass,' the Imam continued, 'there's also a third way: your feeling of solidarity with Mecca.'
'But then a Muslim in Amsterdam prays in a different direction from a Muslim in, for instance, Turkey, Morocco or Indonesia,' I interrupted him. The Imam nodded; 'Yes.' And as though he'd suddenly thought of something, he asked me to wait a moment, left the room, and returned carrying a beautiful rug. In the middle of this rug was indeed a compass, which we later called the 'Mecca-meter'.
'Kibla' was written on the Mecca-meter. 'The direction of Mecca,' explained the Imam. But however the rug was turned, the needle of the compass naturally kept pointing to the North. What was to be done? From a pocket on the underside of the rug the Imam pulled out a little book full of cities and numbers. He leafed through it until he found: '250 Amsterdam'.
He then turned the rug so that the needle of the Mecca-meter pointed to 250 (see Figure 9.1).
'Kibla,' he said, and laughed as he drew our attention to the minaret of the Mecca-meter that was now pointing towards Mecca.

Was the Kibla Correct? The Perils of a Designer

While designing the workbook, an emotional moment occurred when I realized that the Kibla, as shown in the Imam's little book, was not correct. What should I do? My purpose was not to criticize the Kibla or Kibla constructions, but I couldn't simply ignore it. According to the Imam's book, from Havana you should pray compass direction due east; but the great circle, on the other hand, indicated the shortest direction northeast (Figure 9.2).

Studying the history of Islam produced results. In the Islamic faith, the Kibla is a basic concept that indicates more than just geographical direction: 'Kibla' means in the first place solidarity with Mecca. Another reassuring fact was that determining the Kibla has been a major issue for Islamic scholars since the beginning of Islam. Most of the 200 Islamic manuals for astronomy that appear between AD 750 and AD 1750 devote at least one chapter to this subject. But – and this is the crux of the matter – a number of different constructions were available for determining the Kibla. In some of these constructions the earth was regarded as a flat surface in a small area surrounding Mecca. For certain locations, these 'flat constructions' provided a good approximation of the direction. Arab astronomers – none of whom ever assumed the earth to be flat – were also familiar at that time with great circles for indicating distance and direction according to the shortest route. In other words, exact constructions of the Kibla which were based on great circles generally indicated a different direction from the abovementioned flat constructions, which were indeed viewed by Arab scholars as mere approximations.

Jan van den Brink

Figure 9.2 Havana–Mecca bow

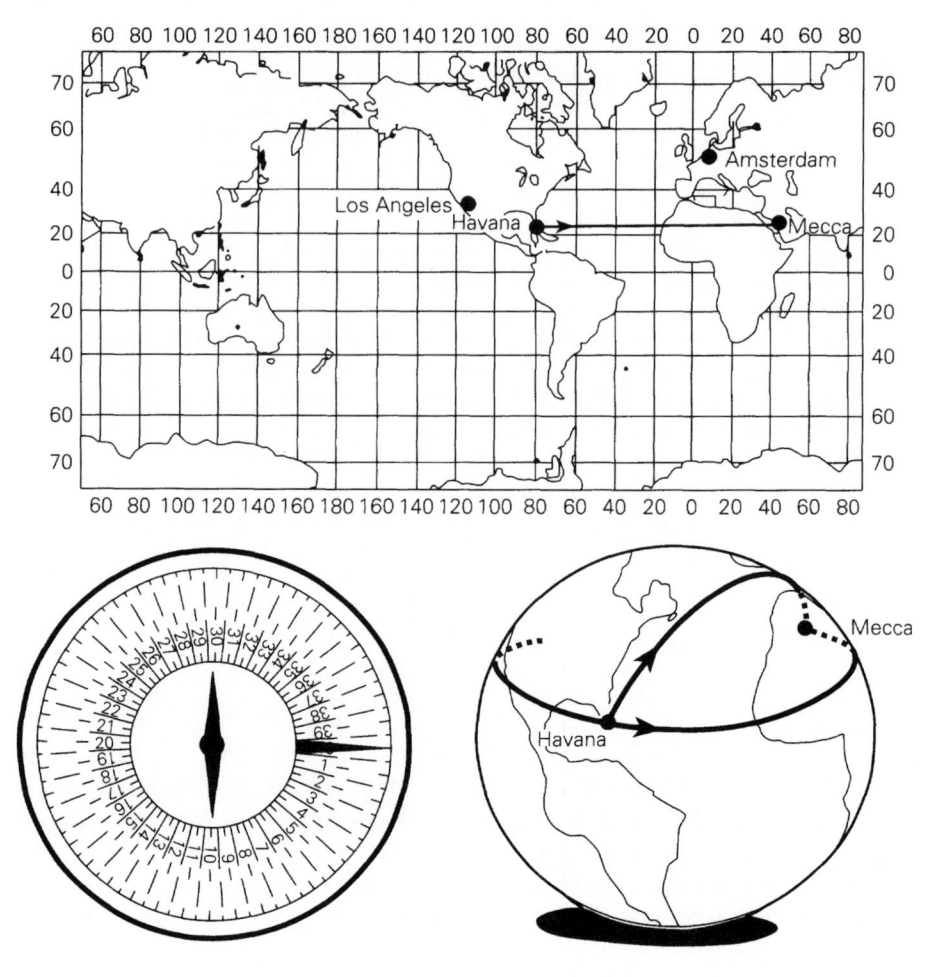

To my astonishment, this historical issue for the Kibla of 'flat constructions' and 'great circle constructions' fitted precisely into what we had in mind for the workbook *Mecca*: comparing the flat map of the world with the globe as different models for the earth.

In the Classroom

I observed the given lessons and took detailed notes in order to improve the workbook. Teacher Wim and his students made striking comments that often shed new light on geometrical concepts.

Students' Constructions in Geometry

Figure 9.3 A world map

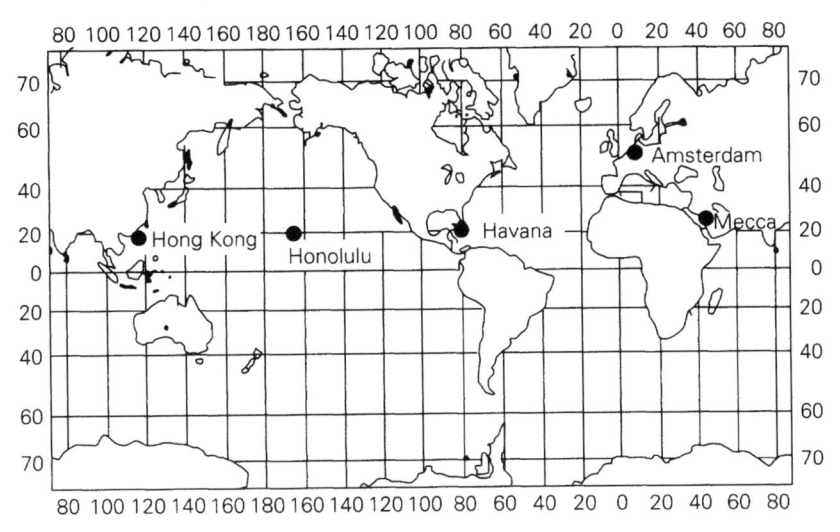

'Direction and Direction is Two'

During the third lesson, three students, Peter, Betrick and Bart are looking over each other's work. Bart had missed the first two lessons due to illness and the other two are now explaining everything to him. Betrick is telling Bart about the prayer rug; about how the Mecca-meter (the compass on the rug) is used together with the Imam's booklet. Then they turn to worksheet 1 (Figure 9.3).

Bart draws straight arrows on this world map from various places (Amsterdam, Havana, Honolulu, Hong Kong) to Mecca.[8]

- *Peter explains to him: 'They're looking from those places in different directions'.*
- *Bart looks at him in amazement. 'No, all in the same direction,' he says, 'all towards Mecca.'*
- *'No, that's not the same direction,' snaps Betrick.*
- *'No, that's obvious,' replies Bart, irritated. 'They're looking at the same place but not in the same direction.'*

Evidently, the students are already implicitly aware that 'direction' has various meanings: the direction straight to the city of Mecca (the shortest direction), but also the direction to Mecca in relation to another point – the North Pole, for instance (the compass direction). In the second case, the direction varies for different places, unless we (theoretically speaking) take Mecca itself as the North Pole, then continual course adjustment along a great circle to Mecca is not necessary. Obviously one of the 'mysteries' mentioned in the first section of the chapter (constantly readjusting the course) has been solved.

111

Jan van den Brink

Great Circles on the Two-Dimensional Earth Surface

A bunch of circles is presented in the workbook (Figure 9.4).
Students are asked:

- *Draw new circles through points A and B*
- *What is the smallest circle?*
- *What is the greatest circle?*

Teacher Wim told me that a student (I shall call him Theo) said that if you started here on your paper, at this point **B**, and you moved to the right all the time, off the paper, underneath the earth, and then again coming up on the left side, to **A**; that would be the greatest circle you could think of on earth, going through the two points **A** and **B** on your paper.

Theo's comments directly clarify that the 'straight' line **AB** on the paper is part of a great circle and that the great circle carries the shortest distance from

Figure 9.4 A bunch of circles

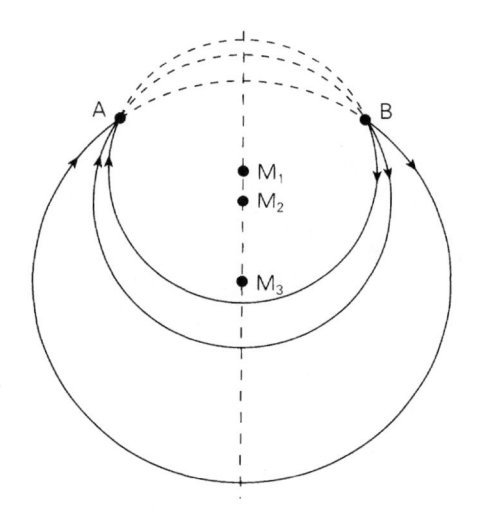

Figure 9.5 A bunch of circles and a straight line

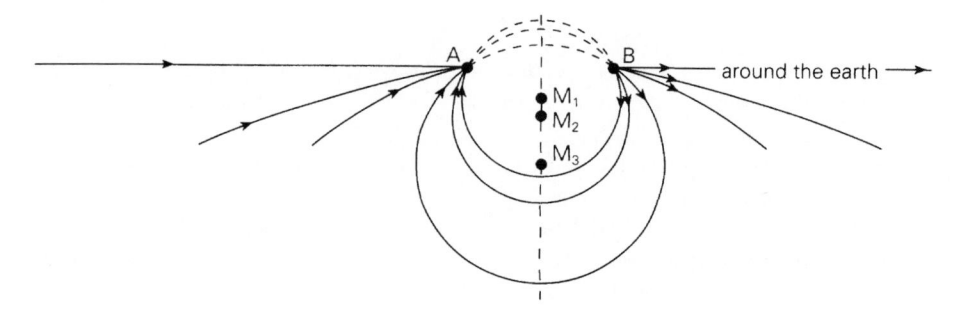

Students' Constructions in Geometry

Figure 9.6 Two cross-sections of the earth

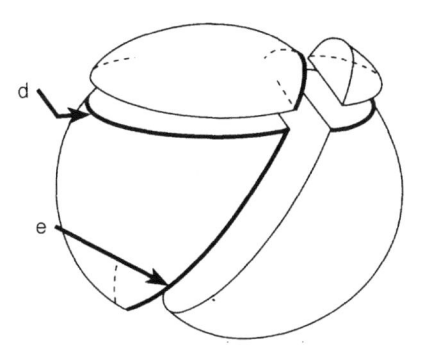

A to **B** on the spherical surface. I published Theo's story in the textbook (Figure 9.5) and students are asked what they think about his idea.

Great Circles through a Three-Dimensional Sphere

A chapter in the textbook deals with cross-sections of the sphere. In it, students are asked:

Which circle is the largest cross-section? d or e? Why? (Figure 9.6)

'Circle e,' a student says, 'because it's closer to the middle.' And another student: 'It's the middle cross-section.' This is an earliest definition of a 'great circle', and it differs from Theo's. Instead of a cross-section of the three-dimensional earth, the great circle was seen by Theo as a line straight ahead around the earth on the earth's two-dimensional *surface*. I collected a lot of such different 'definitions' of great circles, formulated by students and based on a variety of geometrical standpoints. 'Teaching becomes an adventure,' says teacher Wim, without doubt.

In the Staff Room

I meet Wim regularly in the staff room to discuss his progress and which topics are left. Wim said that he had discussed time zones in the classroom. Although this may seem to be a strange choice of topic, it fits well in spherical geometry. A sphere is an appropriate object for the discussion of poles and antipoles, lines and 'opposing lines' (the prime meridian and the date line), hemispheres and 'opposing hemispheres'. I stress to Wim, however, the great circle and its different definitions, as well as the great circle as determinant of the shortest direction, adjusting the compass course along a great circle, and flying North of the parallel circle. In addition, I show Wim a didactic idea: the 'revolving door'.

Jan van den Brink

Figure 9.7   Revolving door with axis AB

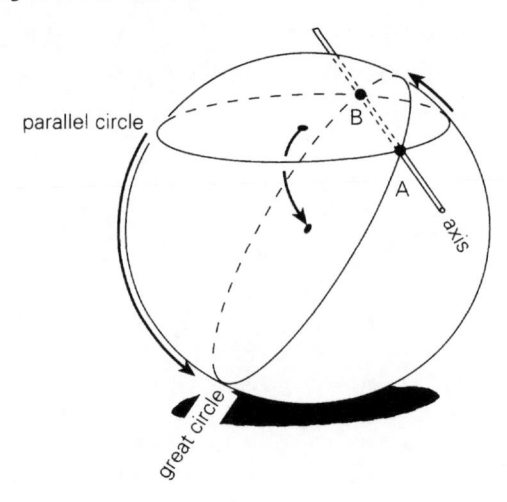

Figure 9.8   Amsterdam–Atlanta problem

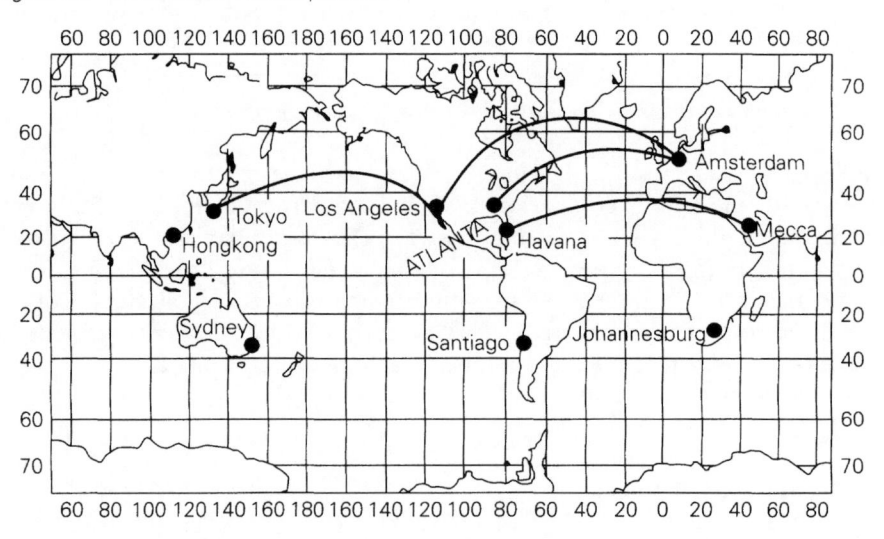

A fan of cross-sections slices the earth in circles. By this one can demonstrate that the shortest distance between two points is indicated by the great circle, and also that the great circle will move North of the parallel circle by revolving the door on its axis. The idea of the revolving door gives a solution of the Havana–Mecca problem (see Fig. 9.2) in the first section of this chapter.

At home, on a transparent plastic sphere, I drew three circles that crossed each other in two places: a parallel circle, a small circle, and a great circle.

Students' Constructions in Geometry

Figure 9.9   Three circles on a plastic sphere

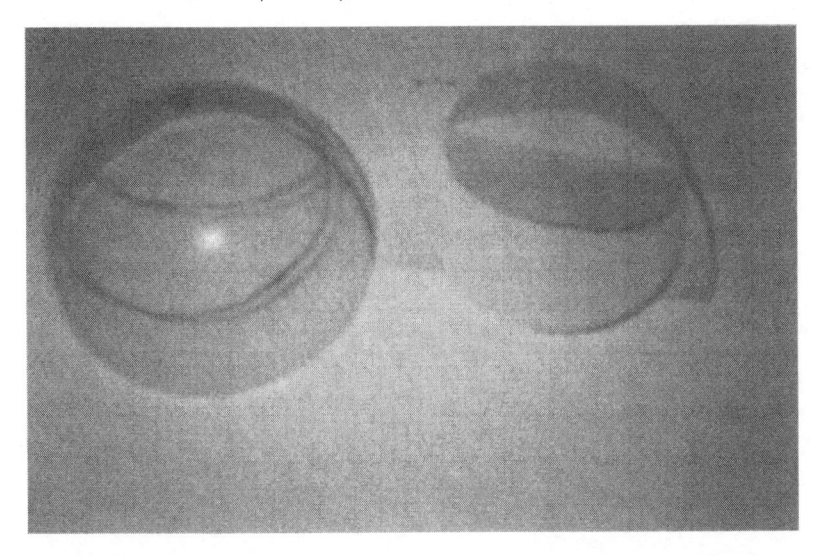

A paper revolving door of these three circles fits inside the sphere. 'Educational designing is a bit of home industry', Wim calls it. He has another suggestion: use two thumb tacks (drawing pins) to pin a piece of bicycle brake cable to a Styrofoam ball along the parallel circle. The cable is stiff enough to remain in a circle and, by sliding it, one can demonstrate that it is larger than the great circle. Whatever the solution of this didactic problem we might find, in the end, we leave it to the students to resolve our problem by making a good construction.

Students' Constructions

Map and Sphere

The students look over each other's homework in groups of four.[9]

Is the direction to Mecca from Havana to the East or Northeast?

'On the map it's to the East,' says Peter. Everyone in the group agrees. To my amazement Peter then continues: 'But it's to the Northeast on the earth because the earth is spherical'. Again there is agreement among the students. Maarten explains by saying: 'The shortest distance between two points is more towards the North, because that's always where the narrowest point of the earth is'.

It seems that the students are first visualizing a map which, in their eyes, is of more value than the globe. The fact that the spherical globe is a more 'authentic' model for our earth is not yet apparent to them. They construct a sphere out of the map by rolling it into a cylinder and then pulling it together at each pole. The distance between the points at a given latitude becomes shorter as one progresses Northwards. Therefore, in their minds, the direction

Jan van den Brink

Figure 9.10 The curve from Havana to Mecca

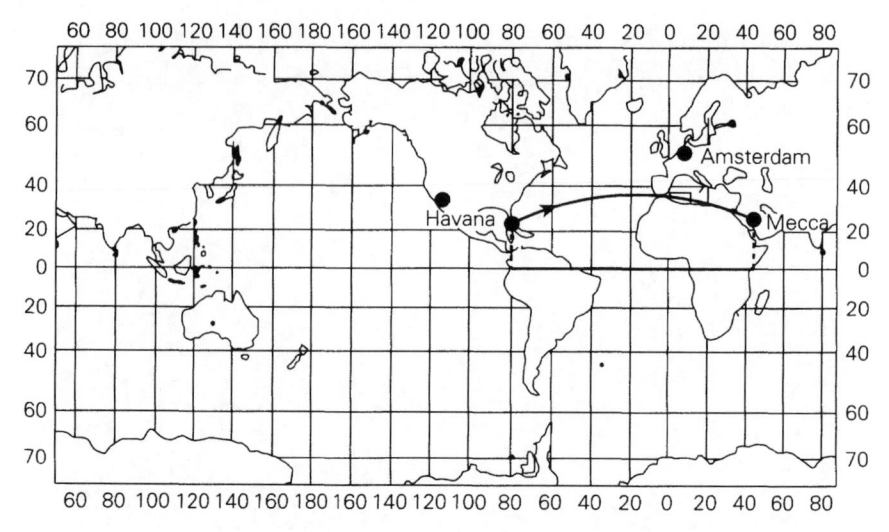

determining the shortest distance must be more Northerly. This idea, thought up by the students, is a terrific alternative for my revolving door, for which I had such difficulty finding a demonstration model.

One of the Two: 'Either on the Map, or on the Globe'

A bit later I realize that something surprising is happening here again. The students are now considering the present question:

An airplane flying from Havana to Mecca takes off to the Northeast and not to the East. Why is this?

Peter, Bart and Betrick look at the map and see the curve from Havana to Mecca (Figure 9.10).

They think up all sorts of reasons: in order to refuel in Spain, to catch a tail wind, to avoid the desert. Then Betrick discovers: 'Oh, they've done it with the globe – it's the globe direction, not the map direction. They've drawn the globe direction on the map'.

Initially, the students distinguished two different shortest directions, one on the map and one on the globe, and kept them strictly separated. The idea that globe direction can also be depicted on a map is new for them. The fact that a line on the globe can become a curved line via Spain on the map is a new idea as well. On the basis of these results, I made some improvements in the unit (indicate direction on the map, see the direction on the globe, draw the globe direction on the map) so that the students might see the difference between globe direction and map direction.

116

Intuitive Geometry for the Sake of Formalization

One Definition of Great Circle or Many Definitions?

When developing the textbook, my goal was to ask students to investigate all aspects of a mathematical object that should be taught. Therefore, I was interested mainly in different 'definitions' of great circles that the students could imagine. But there were also other reasons.

In a mathematical theory, one usually begins with one definition for an object. How the author arrived at this definition, why it was preferred over other definitions, and how to state it in precise form – in other words, the problem of formalization – remains hidden from the student. Freudenthal (1971) wrote that definitions 'are not preconceived to derive something from them, but more often they are just the last element of analysis, the finishing touch of organizing a subject. Children should be granted the same opportunities as the grown-up mathematician claims for himself' (1971, p. 424). And, he warned, 'Geometrical axiomatics cannot be meaningful as a teaching subject unless the student is allowed to perform these activities himself' (ibid., p. 426).

Experiences in primary education (Brink, 1987, 1991a and 1991b) have led me to believe that, in mathematics education, it is better not to begin with one sole definition but, rather, to ask the students to produce all sorts of different 'definitions' with all kinds of characteristics.[10] This gives the students an idea of what it means to be the author of a theory, of an arithmetic book, of a manual for a calculator, etc. They must consider the various 'definitions' and investigate which properties are essential for a definition, which are not, and which are incorrect. In Hiele's opinion (1957), by investigating geometrical properties of quadrangles and finding relationships among such objects, a student achieves a higher level if an internal network of geometrical relations is attained. In my research, from initially thinking up 'definitions' and properties of great circles, a network of relations was achieved in the sense of Hiele.

Students' Own Productions in Spherical Geometry: Definitions of the Great Circle

The students are discussing an assignment in the textbook in groups. The question is:

How would you describe what a great circle on the earth is?

Some of the answers the students gave are:

- A circle like the equator (Betrick).
- A straight line around the earth (Bart).
- A circle that goes straight around the earth (Johan's first definition).

Jan van den Brink

- Where the earth is the thickest (Johan's second definition).
- The greatest circumference of the earth (Wouter).
- 'A great circle is a circle straight through the middle of the earth that arrives at the same point' (Peter).

I could detect some weighing of the definitions by the students (Which is the 'best'? Which is the most inclusive?), as occurs in the formalization of a mathematical system. Johan formulated two different definitions, though he did not choose 'the best one'. Peter combined a cross-section through the 'spatial' globe with the lines straight across the 'surface of the globe'. That brought me to a new assignment.

Assessing Students' Own Productions

I wrote students' definitions in the textbook. The worksheet consists of eight 'definitions' of great circle which I had collected. I streamlined them somewhat and asked the students to assess them.

- *A great circle is a circle that divides the globe in two halves.* Right or wrong?
- *A great circle is the greatest possible circle on the globe.* Right or wrong?
- *A great circle is a circle that divides the globe in two pieces.* Right or wrong?
- *A great circle is a circle that goes through the North and South Poles.* Right or wrong?
- *A great circle is a circle whose centre is the earth's centre.* Right or wrong?
- *If you keep going straight while going around the earth, you'll make a great circle.* Right or wrong?
- *A great circle is a circle around the earth that is 40,000 km long.* Right or wrong?
- *A great circle is a circle on the earth that is not parallel to the equator.* Right or wrong?

I have several reasons for publishing the students' definitions in the textbook:

- The first aim of the assignment was that students search all aspects of the great circle *at their level*. So, using students' definitions provides a genuine opportunity to make such a search.
- Assessing the definitions of fellow students is not only motivating for a student, but it also provides an opportunity for him or her to explore possible misconceptions. It's a form of interaction between students (silent interaction).
- By assessing definitions and standpoints of fellow students, the authority of the teacher's geometrical viewpoint is avoided.

- It provides the students with the opportunity of weighing and revising their 'definitions' and to find a network of geometrical relations for this field. In this manner, the intuitive ideas of students play an essential role in the process of geometrical formalization. Without intuitive ideas, no genuine formalization is possible, I believe.
- Radical constructivists believe that construction of knowledge about the world is necessarily an individual affair,[11] and therefore may differ. Publishing students' different productions in a textbook is an acknowledgment of this belief.

Different Types of Geometry

Some children became particularly disturbed upon the perusal of the various definitions and vehement geometrical discussions and striking arguments arose in the classroom.

Intolerance for Different Viewpoints

Heidy, Anette, Maarten and Jan are considering the next definition:

A great circle is a circle whose centre is the earth's centre. Right or wrong?

'False!' says Heidy. I can't believe my ears. This is the very definition of great circle. False?! 'A great circle goes across the earth and not through the earth,' she says. Anette thinks differently and tries to explain it. 'If you take this ball,' she says, holding a Styrofoam ball with a seam at the equator and pretending to break it in two at the seam, 'you get two halves. So that gives you two great circles whose centre is at the centre of the earth.'

'Where you draw the line, you break through here, that's what you mean,' says Heidy in her own words. 'That's how you get the centre of the earth, yeah, I get it. But a great circle is still a straight line across the earth and not a cross-section through the earth like you mean. And a straight line doesn't have a centre. Only a circle has that.' She turns to me, asking, 'Teacher, who's right here?'

The great circle as a straight line across the earth's *surface* does not have a centre on the earth's surface, nor is it a circle on that surface. The great circle as the greatest cross-section through the earth's *sphere* has a centre, indeed. These are two ways of looking at it, each of which is correct in itself.

Something that is typically 'radical' is the constructivist criticism levelled at persons taking part in a discussion in which 'the participants believe that *their* meaning of the words they have used are *fixed entities* in an objective world outside the speakers' (Glasersfeld and Cobb, 1983, p. 10). Such discussions are common in classrooms and one such was an element in the discussion of

Jan van den Brink

Heidy and Anette. So, I told them, 'You're both right,' explaining once again both viewpoints. But this bothers them; they feel only one of them should be 'objectively' correct. But they like their own ideas as the most objective!

The Paradox of the Happy Agreement

In their negotiations, students are inclined to revise their opinions. As a result, students in the classroom construct a kind of consensus about how they as classmates will think about the objective outside world. Mental objects are of intersubjective origin, and are taken as 'shared meanings' (Bauersfeld, 1983; Cobb, 1987; Brink, 1991b). This seems to fit with what Lewin (Ch. 4, p. 43 above) calls 'the paradox of happy agreement': 'Each student, independently pursuing his or her own best intuitions comes up with the identical solution as all others.' For instance, they all conclude that 'alternate interior angles are congruent'.

Negotiations: Maintaining One's Idea or Taking a Shared Meaning?

I am not sure whether the paradox of happy agreement is inherent in radical constructivism, or whether it is forthcoming from traditional education. Tendencies for sharing meanings are characteristic of traditional mathematics education. Also, in new realistic education, whole structures may be developed by children. Individual points of view cause conflicts, which is more in the sense of radical constructivism than is the paradox of happy agreement. The example mentioned by Lewin is illustrative: alternate interior angles are congruent. Indeed, but only if parallel straight lines do exist. That is the case in plane geometry, but may differ in other geometries. For example in spherical geometry they do not exist.

There is also a difference in the reactions of young children and of more grown-up students. Grown-up students tend to maintain their different meanings even when they are in conflict with others. How? By fitting the idea in a self-made formalized framework compatible with plane geometry, spherical geometry, or solid geometry. And that is important because it benefits geometry education. In convincing fellow students, one needs to search one's own underlying system; it's consequences, its consistency, its rules and operations, and its constraints.

Formalizing: A Network of Properties

Searching Exhaustively for a Network of Properties

The fourth lesson of Mecca started with the teacher's request to 'name as many properties of great circles as you can'. Great circles, again? But the request is

Students' Constructions in Geometry

not redundant because in addition to the familiar properties, the students name a number of new ones. Moreover, they find more and more relationships among the different properties and between various concepts. In fact, they find a brand new geometry in which, for instance, parallel straight lines don't exist.

Parallelism?

- 'The great circles are all the same length,' a student says in response to the teacher's request, 'because they're all just as big as the equator.'
- 'Each great circle passes through the centre of the earth,' a girl reasons, 'because it divides the earth into equal halves. But parallel circles are different,' she continues. 'They don't divide the earth into two equal pieces, so their centres will never lie at the centre of the earth.'
- 'Every great circle is situated both in the Northern Hemisphere and in the Southern Hemisphere', a student comments.
- 'Every great circle crosses the equator,' another student concludes. 'Any two great circles will always cross each other.' (The equator is used by the students as a model for great circles.) And teacher Wim asks, 'Are there parallel great circles on earth?'

The students concluded that lines straight ahead around the earth (great circles) cannot be parallel. The parallelism depends on how one regards the world, whether a flat or a global one.[12]

Paideia *and* Paidia

The 'paradox of the happy agreement' only applies within one system if it applies at all. In plane geometry, everyone will conclude that alternate interior angles are congruent, based on visual perception. But geometry education reaches further than plane geometry. There are different geometries and different conceptual structures to modify the knowledge about the world. On that very basis no 'happy agreement' can be attained. Only 'tolerance'. Or 'democracy' (Lenart, 1993).

Looking back on the conversation between Heidy and Anette, I realize that the differences between geometries call for tolerance of the students for each other's viewpoints. Might mathematics have a pedagogical value on the level where structuring and formalizing are at issue? In a Greek dictionary I found various meanings of '*paideia*': 'upbringing', 'youth', but also 'punishment' according to certain rules. I also found the closely related '*paidia*', which means: 'playing', 'game for children', 'infantile game' and even 'joking'. *Paidia* and *paideia* have to do with all sorts of rules of play. Regarded in this way – as games – the different geometries fit wonderfully well.

It is remarkable that in discussions based on different geometrical viewpoints (spherical geometry, plane geometry, and solid geometry) about a mental

Jan van den Brink

object like a great circle, the students must be asked for tolerance and to pay attention to the constructions and viewpoints of their neighbours, for the other rules they follow, and for the other games they play. That's a pedagogical value of geometry education from a fundamental *geometrical point of view*: namely the different types of geometries.

Viability and Constraints

Piaget's adaptation implies an experiential environment in which an organism (or knower) makes accommodations (Glasersfeld, 1982; Lewin, Ch. 4). The constraints of the environment become manifest only in conjunction with the activity of the organism. Glasersfeld uses the idea of 'viability' – the continuing organization of the biological (or cognitive) system over time – as fundamental in adaptation. Applied in the cognitive field Glasersfeld's notion of the 'experiential environment' stresses the interdependence of the subject and the environment. Neither is less subjective than the other (Glasersfeld and Cobb, 1983, p. 5; Glasersfeld, 1988). 'Intelligence . . . organizes the world by organizing itself' (Glasersfeld, 1982, p. 613). The 'constraints' of the environment and 'the means through which an organism (or knower) negotiates its continuing existence' co-arise. Stressing 'further existence' in the context of viability, Glasersfeld wrote: 'We believe to have "understood" a piece of language whenever our understanding of it remains viable in the face of further linguistic or interactional experiences' (1983, p. 213).

In my geometry education, each student made his or her own subjective logical system; a network of relations, a geometry, as part of the 'subjective environments' in which a phenomenon (of a great circle, for instance) fitted. From my point of view, the constraints of different geometries became manifest in the discussions in the classroom as consequences of different ways of regarding the world. And again, *paideia* and *paidia* as 'playing' comes to the fore: which rules do my fellow students follow?

Didactic Constructivism

Conditions and Instructional Means in Geometry Education

Didactic constructivism tries to find conditions and means by which education develops in the sense of radical constructivism (Glasersfeld, 1991a, 1991b; Brink, 1991a). During the geometry lessons, students were encouraged to modify their notions, and their ideas remained viable in the exhaustive search for properties and relations. An internal structure and a higher Hiele level was achieved. But in the role of their teacher, how does one promote and stimulate these results? What were the conditions in education for this activity? In which perspective can we place these activities?

Students' Constructions in Geometry

In my view the key element was that not only one type of geometry was taken as the holy truth. This opens up possibilities for multiple conceptions and it helps keep the students' ideas viable. Six other aspects of the geometry instruction may also be mentioned:

- the '*own productions*' of the students and the use of the productions in the textbook;
- students' *assessment* of the productions of other students facilitated their subjective network of relations;
- searching exhaustively for *new properties* and relations in order to extend the subjective network;
- convincing by *opposing examples* in order to clear up misconceptions in the network;
- encouraging students to go in *search of adventures*; and
- formalizations by *comparing* different types of geometry.

Convincing by Opposing Examples

In the assignment of assessing students' own productions, problems provided an opportunity to explore convincing by opposing examples.

A great circle is a circle that passes through the North Pole and the South Pole. Right or wrong?

'It is a circle, so that's possible,' says Betrick. He gets stuck on this one particular characteristic: it is a circle. Bart supplies an opposing example to unerringly refute Betrick's answer: 'It's false,' says Bart, 'because the equator is also a great circle and it doesn't pass through the North Pole and the South Pole.'

A great circle is a circle around the earth that does not run parallel to the equator. Right or wrong?

False, according to Peter. But Betrick says, 'That's true, because if it's parallel then you get an parallel circle.' This counter example convinces Peter. The statement makes good sense if the universe is only great circles. But it is not correct if it refers to all circles on the earth, for there are circles smaller than a great circle and not parallel to the equator.

Encouraging Students to Go in Search of New Adventures for a New Perspective

In a discussion with teacher Wim, he made the following comment: 'I feel kind of insecure. I don't know where we are going. The topic isn't clear, or not yet,

Jan van den Brink

anyway. The problems are also questions for me.' I agreed with him. What is the perspective? But it amazes me that he did continue enthusiastically to go on new adventures with the class. He even thinks up some new problems and discovers aims to go to.

'Straight lines on the earth?'

For instance, he is fascinated by his discovery that straight lines across the earth's surface are not genuinely straight (sight) lines. 'Are there actually any straight lines on the earth? It would be great if they discover those differences between plane and spherical geometry,' he says. 'Are there actually any straight lines on the earth?' he asks the class casually, hoping they will reply in the negative. But they mention a number of examples, such as the sun's rays and the doorposts, in confirmation of their affirmative answer. It is true that vertical lines – such as doorposts – do not follow the earth's curvature. The question is whether two vertical doorposts are in fact parallel, for, viewed spatially, they both point to the centre of the earth. In the ensuing discussions, student Henk resolves the issue: 'If you make the line on the floor go straight ahead, then it will leave the earth.' He considers a tangent to the earth. 'And if it doesn't leave the earth, then it's not a straight line,' he continues.

The balloon above Mecca – the great circle as determinant of direction

According to the vertical straight lines Wim says: *'Imagine that a huge helium balloon on a string rises above Mecca. Will it rise up like this?'* He draws Figure 9.11 on the board.

> *'No, in that way it's going towards the North,'* says a student. *'The balloon has to go to the right'.*
> *'To the right?'* asks Wim and waits. The children search for a better formulation for what we know as *'upwards'* or *'vertical'*.
> *'Straight away from the earth,'* says another.

Figure 9.11 Balloon northwards and Amsterdam

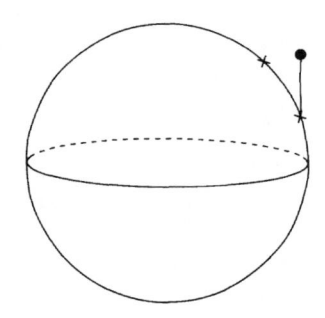

Students' Constructions in Geometry

Figure 9.12   Four drawings

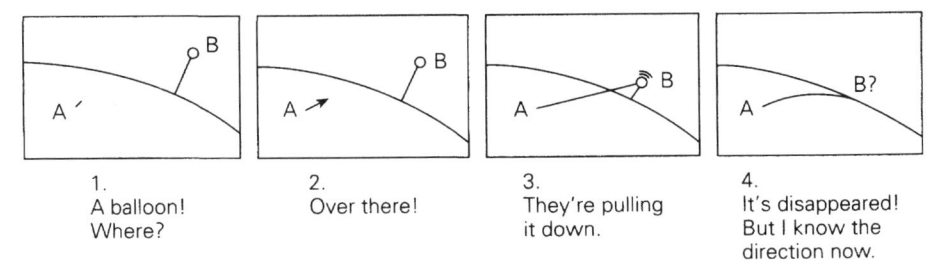

1.	2.	3.	4.
A balloon! Where?	Over there!	They're pulling it down.	It's disappeared! But I know the direction now.

Figure 9.13   Central projection

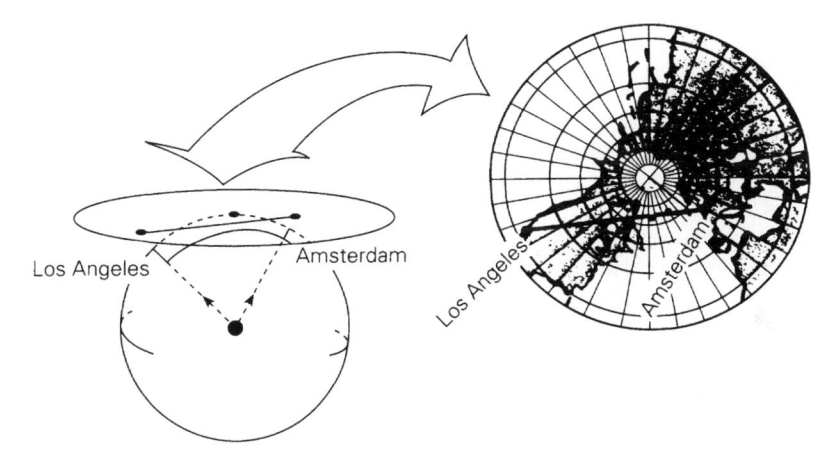

> '*Actually we are all little balloons*', says Wim, '*all stuck to the earth with our feet towards the centre.*'
> '*Then the balloon descends,*' he continues, '*and the sight line from Amsterdam follows a sight plane that cuts through the earth as a . . . ?*'
> '*Great circle,*' guesses a student. For it will cut the earth in its centre.
> '*So the great circle is not only the shortest distance, but it also indicates the shortest direction from, for instance, Amsterdam to Mecca,*' Wim states succinctly. I have my doubts whether everyone has understood his explanation.

In the textbook four drawings present this story on the balloon above Mecca in order to demonstrate (as the Star above Bethlehem) that the great circle is the determinant of the shortest direction between two places on earth.

'*Changing course along a straight line?*'

In the textbook a polar map[13] introduces another remarkable phenomenon of the great circle: going straight ahead along a great circle you have to adjust the compass course continuously (Figure 9.13).

125

Jan van den Brink

Figure 9.14 Line of course and arrow

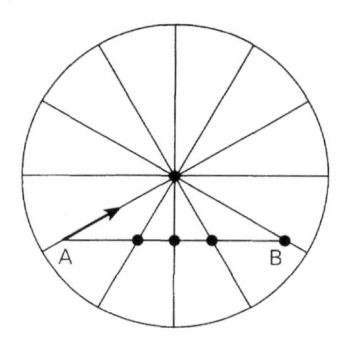

The arc of the great circle passing through Los Angeles and Amsterdam changes into a segment which intersects the map in a straight line.

> 'You're looking down over the North Pole', says Wim, 'and then you see this'.

He draws the 'star' of Figure 9.14 on the blackboard. Wim suggests that the students imagine themselves standing above the North Pole and looking down over the globe so that they see a disc which is not quite the same as the polar map. But for the benefit of the considered phenomenon it does not matter.

> 'An airplane flies from point A to point B', says Wim. 'Along this line AB straight ahead. Which direction is it heading at takeoff, which directions during the flight, and which direction as it nears point B?'
> 'It starts flying Northeast,' suggests one student.
> 'OK,' says Wim. 'Pay attention, 'cause you won't believe your eyes. Farther on, the compass is pointing in another direction.'

He draws a new compass needle pointing again towards the North Pole. But the flying direction is rather East!

> 'In which direction is it flying?' he asks at each new compass needle he draws along the whole route. 'The same direction?' Silence. You can hear a pin drop. Then: 'How's that possible? I don't get it.'

It's true, they can't believe their eyes. You fly in a line straight ahead, along a great circle, but in an ever changing direction of the compass needle. This phenomenon could be easily explained by walking past a street lamp, which is viewed from an ever changing angle. It is, in fact, the very same problem as posed by Bart: Going towards Mecca in relation to the North Pole.

> 'The shortest distance without changing course'

At the end of the lesson, Wim takes the students on another adventure.

Students' Constructions in Geometry

'Are there two places on earth between which you can travel without having to change course?' he asks.
'Along a meridian,' answers a girl.
'Along the equator,' says another.
Wim discusses the answers: *'Yes, because then you either keep going northwards (along the meridian) or eastwards (along the equator)'.*
'Or if you follow a parallel circle,' says a third student, *'that also goes eastwards.'*
'No,' says Wim, *'because that's not the shortest distance between two points.'*

So the answer is not simply a line upon which the course has been fixed (a 'loxodrome'), but a line which is both a loxodrome and a great circle (shortest distance). A parallel circle is indeed a loxodrome, but not a great circle. The students can find no more examples of this type of lines.

After this I improved the textbook by the meaningful use of two map projections: the mercator projection (on which a straight line is a rhumb-line or loxodromic line) and the central projection (a straight line is a great circle).[14]

Comparing Plane Geometry and Spherical Geometry (a Perspective)

After the lessons the students like to have an overview of the different types of geometry. So, I added a worksheet in the textbook in which both types are compared.

	Complete the Second Column	
Geometry in the Plane		**Geometry on the Sphere**
Point in the plane		Point on the sphere
Straight line		Great circle
1. Infinite number of straight lines through a point		1. ....
2. Only one straight line through two points		2. ....
3. Two straight lines have one point in common or are parallel		3. ....
6. Two points divide a straight line into three parts		6. ....
7. Only one of these three parts can be used for defining distance of two points		7. ....
8. There is no greatest distance between two points		8. ....

Jan van den Brink

Examination

Preparation for the Examination

An examination was given in the sixth lesson. We – Wim and I – liked to know which of the geometrical properties had become the students' own. I wrote the examination covering the following topics:

- great circles, antipoles and opposing planes;
- map projections;
- discussions of plane geometry, spherical geometry and solid geometry.

Some Exam Problems and their Results

We examined familiar as well as brand new properties of the great circle. The familiar ones were, indeed, familiar, for 93 per cent of the students answered these questions correctly. The children scored low in areas that were strictly technical and algorithmic, such as working with coordinate systems. This was true also for topics based on the revolving door (which had not been dealt with), such as the shortest distance and a flight path's northerly course.

On the other hand, the students were easily able to work with great circles, and poles and antipoles, in all sorts of *new* situations. They quickly formed links between these concepts and thought up relationships that had not been explicitly discussed in class. One property, not covered in the lessons, was tested in the following question:

> *For every point on a great circle its antipole also is on the same great circle.*
> True or false?

Of the students, 97 per cent answered this problem correctly. Although Wim had occasionally made use of great circles when drawing on the board, he had never explicitly established the link between poles, antipoles and great circles.

We included the two problems presented in Figures 9.15 and 9.16.

Figure 9.15 Draw the antipoles of points A, B and C

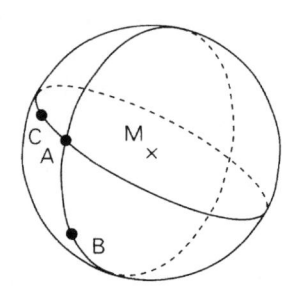

Students' Constructions in Geometry

Figure 9.16 Construct the centre of the sphere using the antipoles pictured

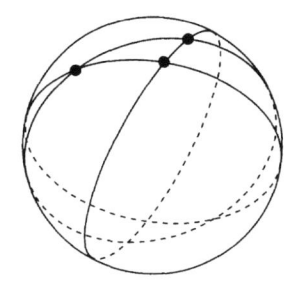

Figure 9.17 Erik's method: M = middle point

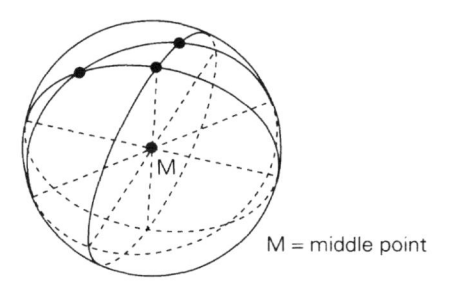

M = middle point

Of the students, 76 per cent answered the first problem correctly. In solving the second problem, 61 per cent of the students constructed the centre in the correct fashion, while 23 per cent first drew only one line from a pole to its antipole and then found the middle of this line as the centre of the sphere (a less satisfactory solution). One student, Erik, used imaginary intersections of the great circles and their antipoles in order to find the centre – an original method (Figure 9.17).

General Conclusions

Some main points in the mathematics curriculum for students from 12 to 16 years of age were demonstrated in these investigation lessons.

a. Focusing on mathematics in contextual frameworks, familiar to students

Not only as applied mathematics, but also for conceptualization and insight. For example, the question 'Where is Mecca?' is familiar to many of the Islamic students at school. It was used as a motivating introduction.

b. Encouraging the constructions and productions of students

Not only in 'doing exercises' in a certain geometrical structure (e.g. plane geometry), but also in developing the structures themselves (e.g. the structure

Jan van den Brink

of the spherical geometry) based on the students' experiences. The students did obtain insight into spherical geometry concepts such as great circles, poles and antipoles, and map projections.

c. *Stressing interaction and conflict situations*

When constructing a geometrical structure, the student has to argue against geometrical experiences of a deviating type. For example, spherical geometrical experiences often conflict with planar geometrical experiences. Encouraging conflictive experiences in mathematics education within a radical constructivist epistemology is done so the students understand that knowledge is constructed via one's own experience and one's own way of regarding the world as well as to confront them with counter examples of taken-as-given geometrical laws when appropriate. The various types of geometry that emerged in the unit stimulated powers of reasoning.

d. *Encouraging formalization*

In discussions on topics based on the various types of geometry that emerged, the students took a number of different geometrical standpoints and were able to defend and modify these standpoints using a variety of geometrical representations and formulations. The process whereby the students' designed and assessed their 'own productions' and chose from a number of these turned out to be an excellent method of furthering abstraction and formalization abilities in geometry education.

- In the struggle to convince fellow students of a point of view or way of seeing a geometrical phenomenon, students often formalize their ideas by constructing relations between geometrical concepts.
- The students' constructions were starting points for further formalizations.

'Intuitive' geometry played an essential role pointing the way towards more formal geometry. Without the intuitive geometrical ideas of students no genuine formalization is possible.

Notes

1. For instance the spherical theorem of Pythagoras: $\cos a \cdot \cos b = \cos c$ with a, b and c sides of a triangle of which the angle opposite to c is 90 degrees.
2. The common definition of a great circle on a sphere is the circle's center is the center of the sphere.
3. Some main points in the new mathematics curriculum for students from 12 to 16 years of age are: (a) focusing on mathematics in contextual frameworks familiar to students; (b) encouraging the constructions and productions of students; (c) stressing interaction and conflict situations; (d) encouraging formalization.

4 A Mercator projection is often used in making world maps.
5 In a central projection (gnomic projection), the center of projection is the center of the sphere and the sphere is projected onto a flat plane positioned tangentially to the sphere. A great circle of the sphere is projected onto a straight line in the plane.
6 A loxodrome or rhumb-line is the path of a ship which cuts the meridians at a constant angle, e.g. 90 degrees due East, sailing alongside a parallel circle.
7 Junior general secondary education.
8 In lesson 5, they will think that the straight arrows must be replaced by curved ones ('greatcircle' arrows) and they improve their previous work. Improving on their ideas after-the-fact makes them feel that they have really learned something.
9 Working in groups is a good way of working. By looking over each other's work, the students must justify their own answers. For the designer/researcher it provides an ideal situation for collecting unexpected ideas, which can be used to improve the material. But one has to avoid the temptation of wandering around the classroom like a teacher, because the information collected then tends to be rather fragmented. One can better listen and think with one group.
10 'Abstraction' means 'relinquishing specifics' (Parreren, 1978). In my opinion, this puts the teacher on the wrong track if it is the teacher who relinquishes specifics. My experience in primary school teaching was quite the opposite. In order to help children abstract the 'bus arrow-language' into bare 'arrow language', it was necessary *not* to relinquish specifics (like 'wheels' and other drawings) but to include them. Abstraction of the arrow-language was obtained by allowing the children themselves (as 'arithmetic book authors') to think up an expansion of specific situations and contexts where arrow-language functioned, and to embellish the arrows. The students' own productions supplied the bare arrows with a variety of contexts and also enabled them to see the similarities.
11 The reader might interpret this statement as leaving out social interaction. This is not what is intended. Rather, the statement should be interpreted with reference to individuals in interaction of some kind, including social interaction. Even a 'co-construction' is a construction by someone, perhaps one or more of the participants in the interaction which lead to the co-construction.
12 Euclid began his work with definitions and axioms. He had five axioms, e.g. 'an interval can be prolonged indefinitely' and the famous 'parallel axiom', interpreted in Figure 9.18.

    If angles a and b together are less than two right angles, the lines l_1 and l_2 will meet each other. In spherical geometry both axioms are denied: every interval is of finite length and angles a and b may be two right angles and yet l_1 and l_2 (e.g. meridians) will meet each other (at a pole). They will never be parallel.

    Two non-Euclidean geometries (the hyperbolic and the elliptic ones) satisfy all of Euclid axioms except those two mentioned above. The mathematician F. Klein modified spherical geometry into a model for elliptic geometry, by taking each pair of antipodal points on a sphere surface as one 'elliptic' point (Struik, 1980).
13 A polar map is a central projection (gnomic projection), where the center of projection is the center of the globe. The Northern Hemisphere is projected on to a plane. The textbook contains a description of how the great circle on the globe is mapped into a straight line on the map.
14 In navigation a loxodrome (e.g. a parallel circle) is preferred above a great circle. Alongside a loxodrome changes in compass direction are not necessary. However, a loxodrome generally is not a great circle and therefore not the shortest distance.

Jan van den Brink

Figure 9.18   Three lines and two angles

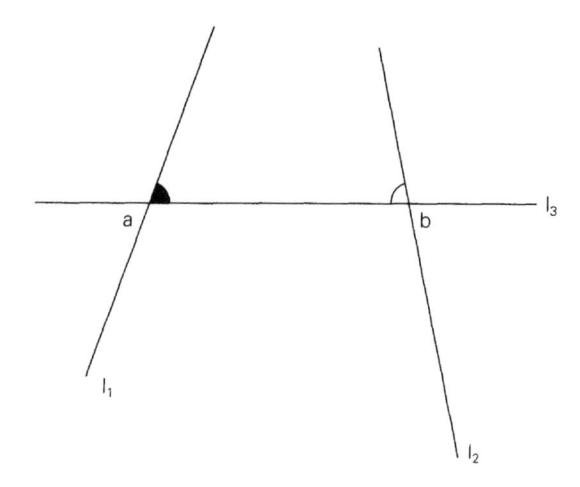

To meet both requirements (a fixed course and the shortest distance), a 'composed track' is mapped out. Ikos, who is a navigating officer, explains:

> First I map out a straight line on the central projection map. That straight line is a great circle. I then copy the points of intersection with the meridians on a Mercator projection and connect these points with straight lines that are loxodromic on the Mercator projection. Thus, I navigate on a loxodromic line to the points of a great circle. We call this a 'composed track'.

Then he gives an assignment to prove that the projections of the parallel circles at a central projection are different kinds of conic sections.

References

BAUERSFELD, H. (1983) 'Subjektive Erfahrungsbereiche als Grundlage einer Interaktionstheorie des Mathematiklernens und -Lehrens', in *Lernen und Lehren von Mathematik*, Cologne: Aulis, pp. 1–57.

BRINK, J. VAN DEN (1987) 'Children as arithmetic book authors', *For the Learning of Mathematics*, 7, 2, pp. 44–7.

BRINK, J. VAN DEN (1991a) 'Didactic constructivism', in GLASERSFELD, E. VON (ed.), *Radical Constructivism in Mathematics Education*, Dordrecht: Kluwer, pp. 195–227.

BRINK, J. VAN DEN (1991b) 'Realistic arithmetic education for young children', in STREEFLAND, L. (ed.), *Realistic Mathematics Education in Primary School*, Utrecht: Freudenthal Institute, pp. 77–92.

BRINK, J. VAN DEN (1993a) 'Different aspects in designing mathematics: Three examples from the Freudenthal Institute', *Educational Studies in Mathematics*, 24, pp. 35–64.

BRINK, J. VAN DEN (1993b) *Mecca* (student text and teacher's guide; English version), Utrecht: Freudenthal Institute.

BRINK, J. VAN DEN and MEEDER, M. (1991) 'Mecca', *Mathematics Teaching*, 137, pp. 20–3.

COBB, P. (1987) 'Information-processing psychology and mathematics education – A constructivist perspective', *Journal of Mathematical Behavior*, 6, pp. 3–40.

FREUDENTHAL, H. (1971) 'Geometry between the devil and the deep sea', *Educational Studies in Mathematics*, 3, pp. 413–35.

GLASERSFELD, E. VON (1982) 'An interpretation of Piaget's constructivism', *Revue Internationale de Philosophie*, 142–3, pp. 612–35.

GLASERSFELD, E. VON (1983) 'On the concept of interpretation', *Poetics*, 12, pp. 207–18.

GLASERSFELD, E. VON (1988) 'Environment and communication', in STEFFE, L.P. and WOOD, T. (eds), *Transforming Children's Mathematics Education: International Perspectives*, Hillsdale, NJ: Lawrence Erlbaum, pp. 30–8.

GLASERSFELD, E. VON (1991a) 'A constructivist's view of learning and teaching', in *Research in Physics Learning – Theoretical Issues and Empirical Studies*, International Workshop, Bremen, March 1991.

GLASERSFELD, E. VON (ed.) (1991b) *Radical Constructivism in Mathematics Education*, Dordrecht: Kluwer.

GLASERSFELD, E. VON and COBB, P. (1983) 'Knowledge as environmental fit', *Man-Environment*, 13, pp. 4–15.

HIELE, P.M. VAN (1957) *De Problematiek van het Inzicht, Gedemonstreerd aan het Inzicht van Schoolkinderen in Meetkunde-Leerstof* (Problems of insight, demonstrated on the insight of school children in geometry subject matter), Amsterdam: Meulenhoff.

LENART, I. (1993) 'Alternative models on the drawing ball', *Educational Studies in Mathematics*, 24, pp. 277–312.

PARREREN, C.F. VAN (1978) *Niveaus in de Ontwikkeling van het Abstraheren* (Levels in the development of abstraction), Groningen: Wolters-Noordhoff.

STRUIK, D.J. (1980) *Geschiedenis van de Wiskunde* (History of mathematics), Utrecht: Spectrum.

TEAM W12-16 (1992) *Achtergronden van het Nieuwe Leerplan Wishunde 12–16, Deel 2*, (Backgrounds of the new curriculum in mathematics for 12–16 year olds, Part 2), Utrecht: Freudenthal Institute/SLO, Enschede.

10 Professional Development in Recovery Education[1]

Robert J. Wright

The focus of this chapter is an applied research and development project in children's early arithmetical learning. This project, known as Mathematics Recovery, draws in a very significant way on the early number research program undertaken in the 1980s at the University of Georgia (e.g. Steffe et al., 1983; Steffe and Cobb, 1988). In Mathematics Recovery, theory and methods which resulted from the research program in early number are applied by teachers at the lower elementary level. These teachers have undertaken or are undertaking a professional development program focusing on specialist teaching to advance the arithmetical knowledge of low-attaining first graders. Mathematics Recovery was developed during the period 1992 to 1995, and involved twenty teachers in eighteen schools in the north coast region of New South Wales, Australia. Since January 1995, Mathematics Recovery has been implemented on a significant scale in school districts in the southeast of the United States (Wright et al., 1998) where approximately eighty teachers have undertaken the Mathematics Recovery professional development program. Since 1996, teachers in two local education authorities in the United Kingdom have also undertaken this program. In New South Wales, since 1996 Mathematics Recovery theory and techniques have been adapted as the basis of a systemic, large-scale, classroom-based project which has involved several hundred schools and thousands of students across all forty educational districts in the state (Bobis and Gould, 1998; Stewart et al., 1998). Finally, in New Zealand in 1998, Mathematics Recovery theory and techniques have been adapted as part of a major nationally funded project, the first phase of which involves seventy-two teachers.

Background to the Mathematics Recovery Project

At-risk Students

Levin (1989) highlighted the urgent need to address the problem of too many children experiencing chronic failure at school. Levin calls for additional funding for programs 'to bring at-risk students into the educational mainstream by improving their school success to the level of other students' (ibid., p. 48). At-risk students are 'those who lack the home and community resources to benefit

Development in Recovery Education

from conventional schooling practices' (ibid., p. 47). The problem is urgent because poverty is a major indicator of at-risk populations, the proportion of at-risk students is high and increasing rapidly, and the degree of their disadvantage is increasing.

Recovery Education

Recovery education can be regarded as one important response to the need to provide better education for at-risk students. The term 'recovery education' is closely aligned to but can be distinguished from 'early intervention' because the latter is applied to programs in the preschool years and to children for whom identification of potential learning problems has occurred in the first three years of life (Meisels and Shonkoff, 1990, p. xvi). Recovery education is distinguished from remedial education because the former involves: (a) identification after one year of school (i.e. 6-year-olds) of children who are apparently unable to benefit from classroom teaching; and (b) intensive individualized teaching to advance the learner to an average level for their class. By way of contrast, remedial education typically applies to older children and often involves group teaching. As is typical in remedial education, recovery education is undertaken by teachers who have undertaken a specialized, post-initial training program. Recovery education is best known in the area of children's learning to read. The Reading Recovery Program which originated in New Zealand almost twenty years ago (e.g. Clay, 1979; 1987; 1990; 1992; 1993) and is now well established in the United States (e.g. DeFord et al., 1991; Lyons, Pinnell and DeFord, 1993; Pinnell et al., 1990) and elsewhere (Dombey, 1992; Smith, 1986) can be regarded as a beacon in recovery education. Reading Recovery continues to attract widespread support that extends well beyond those directly involved with it (e.g. Wasik and Slavin, 1993; *The Literacy Challenge*, 1993). The Mathematics Recovery Program is organizationally similar to Reading Recovery, and aims to advance the mathematics learning of least advanced first-grade children.

Differences in Levels of Mathematical Knowledge of Young Children

That there are profound differences in the levels of children's mathematical knowledge when they begin school has been established by research in Australia (Wright, 1991c; 1994a), New Zealand (Young-Loveridge, 1989) and the United Kingdom (Aubrey, 1993). Also supported by research (Wright, 1994a; Young-Loveridge, 1991) is the fact that, by and large, children maintain their relative levels of achievement as they progress through the lower, middle and upper elementary years. Thus low achievers remain as the low achievers, average achievers continue to achieve at an average level, and so on. Additionally, in a given class or school, the difference in ability levels of the lowest and highest achievers is much greater at the end of the elementary years than at the beginning. Thus a three-year difference (Wright, 1991c) at the beginning of schooling is transformed into a seven year difference (Cockcroft, 1982) at the end of the elementary years. The term 'three-year difference' at the beginning of schooling refers to the fact that, in a given class or school, some children learn mathematics by the age of four that others do not learn until they are seven.

Coping with Children's Ability Range

Coping with a relatively wide range of ability levels is one of the most difficult challenges for classroom teachers. This is particularly so in classes of twenty-five to thirty or more students that are common in Australian schools and elsewhere. What is frequently claimed in curricula, professional development courses and books about mathematics teaching is that teaching approaches can be developed which successfully take account of a range of ability levels. These approaches typically involve collaborative, problem-based and activity-based learning. These sources argue that, because of the open-ended nature of learning activities, students are able to solve problems and complete activities using strategies commensurate with their level. Further, it is also claimed that instructional methods can be adopted which allow children at different levels to learn successfully together, and that this results in students learning significantly from more or less able peers; for example, learning other students' methods of solving problems from their explanations and discussions. This author would certainly agree that collaborative learning among students of mixed abilities can be quite successful, but what also seems reasonable is that it tends to be less successful as the range of ability widens.

Basic Skills Testing and Remediation

In Australia's largest state, New South Wales, mandatory basic skills testing in literacy and numeracy at third- and sixth-grade levels was introduced in government schools in 1989 (Doig and Masters, 1992; Masters et al., 1990) and this program of annual testing has continued at third-grade level and at fifth- rather than sixth-grade level. One purpose of the basic skills testing program is to monitor progress in learning at school, class and individual levels. Additionally, the instigators of the program in part justify it in terms of the information it provides to schools to enable them to address areas of class or individual weakness in students' learning. One question that arises about the basic skills testing program and its significance in addressing the problem of chronic school failure in mathematics is the following: to what extent do third-graders identified in the basic skills test as requiring remediation score significantly better on the fifth grade test? That is, what success are schools having in the middle and upper elementary years in addressing the problem of chronic school failure in mathematics?

Development in Recovery Education

Remediation in Mathematics at the Elementary Level

In many elementary schools in New South Wales there are established programs of remediation undertaken by teachers working in a specialist position classified as Support Teacher Learning Difficulties (STLD). These programs usually involve children in the third to sixth grade range, and involve small group teaching rather than individualized instruction. What also seems typical of these programs is that language and literacy remediation are accorded a higher priority than mathematics remediation. The mathematics instruction that occurs in these programs typically involves memorizing basic facts of arithmetic and practicing methods of computation – methods that have long been characteristic of remedial programs in mathematics. Clearly, the task that these teachers have in trying to bring about significant accelerated learning of least advanced students in the third to sixth grade range is an almost impossible one. While many of these teachers are sympathetic to newer approaches to mathematics instruction that take account of children's current meanings and strategies, these teachers simply do not have opportunities to learn theory or practice associated with implementing these new approaches. Indeed, the necessary application by researchers of current theories of learning and teaching of mathematics to specialist remedial settings has not been undertaken. In these circumstances there is little wonder that STLD teachers may seem somewhat overwhelmed by the problems of failure in school mathematics that they are endeavoring to address.

Basic Skills Testing in a Political Context

That basic skills testing was introduced in New South Wales elementary schools with: (a) virtually no support from classroom teachers, academics or teachers' professional associations; (b) little enthusiasm from school and system administrators; (c) some opposition from parent groups; and (d) strong opposition from teachers' unions, can be understood in politico-educational terms. During the campaign prior to a New South Wales state election held a year or two after the introduction of basic skills testing in 1989, both the governing party and the opposition promised to maintain the testing program. One can conclude from this that politicians and their advisers have determined by the usual means that there is significant electoral support for basic skills testing. Perhaps much of this support comes from parents' disillusionment with an education system which they believe has failed their child and failed to inform them of their child's lack of progress early enough to take adequate steps to redress it.

Legitimizing the Inevitability of Failure

The question of whether differences in school achievement are attributable to congenital or life experience factors has long been pondered. The nature versus nurture debate has a long and respectable history (e.g. Plomin et al., 1988). In New South Wales government schools third-graders undertake a mandatory basic skills test in mathematics the results of which are reported to parents as a quartile rank. One can take the view that children whose score falls in the lowest quartile do not have an innate ability to learn mathematics very well because they have not been able to take advantage of classroom instruction in the first four years of school. This view accords with the long history of widespread failure in school mathematics and more broadly with our society's ready tendency to celebrate innumeracy – for example, to take pride in the fact that one has had difficulty with and lack of success in learning mathematics. An alternative view might hold that: (a) the particular nature of children's cognitive experiences in the years before school has a profound effect on the level and nature of their knowledge when they start school and this is largely what determines their progress in the first years of school; and (b) children who in the first three years of school find that they are unable to succeed in school mathematics may develop, and have reinforced, strategies that are counterproductive to successful mathematics learning (cf. Pinnell, 1989, p. 182). Educational administrators implement basic skills testing because they believe it will make schools and teachers more accountable and provide valuable information to parents, teachers and school systems. Unfortunately, formally assessing children's mathematics knowledge at third- and fifth-grade levels may well be equivalent to 'shutting the gate after the horse has bolted' and, worse, may serve mainly to confirm perceptions of parents and teachers that some children are unable to learn mathematics very well and are unlikely to learn it successfully in the future. Thus basic skills testing serves to legitimize the view that there is an inevitability about widespread failure in school mathematics. In other words, the adult generation of innumerates imposes or supports basic skills testing and unknowingly creates the next generation in its own image.

Theoretical Bases of Mathematics Recovery

Children's early arithmetical learning has been an area of intense research activity over the past twenty years (e.g. Carpenter et al., 1982; Fuson, 1988; Steffe et al., 1983; Steffe and Cobb, 1988). Since the mid-1980s researchers' efforts in early childhood mathematics have been directed at the need to integrate research on learning with research on teaching (e.g. Carpenter and Fennema, 1992; Cobb et al., 1991; Cobb et al., 1992; Yackel et al., 1991; Fuson, 1992a; Fuson et al., 1992; Resnick, 1992). This has resulted in classroom-based research projects which take account of the results of the earlier research into children's learning. The research by Steffe and colleagues in early arithmetical learning is distinctive because it was primarily about conceptual change (Glasersfeld and Steffe, 1991, p. 99). Of interest in this research were children's advances in learning as observed during interactive and individualized teaching sessions. Children participating in these teaching sessions were taught

Development in Recovery Education

several times per week in teaching cycles of duration of 18 to 20 weeks, during their first and second years of school. This research had the purpose of documenting children's conceptual progress over time by describing children's current arithmetical strategies and ways in which these strategies were reorganized in the course of solving arithmetical problems. The participants in these research projects were beginning first-graders and, by and large, were assessed as lower attaining. These children are of similar age and achievement levels to participants in the Mathematics Recovery Program and this is one reason why the methods and results of this constructivist research program are particularly suited for application to a recovery program in mathematics. Additionally, the earlier research program included individualized teaching, that is, the instructional approach used in Mathematics Recovery (and of course, in Reading Recovery as well).

Teaching and assessment in Mathematics Recovery focus on several aspects of young children's arithmetical knowledge, aspects which have been described in detail elsewhere (Wright, 1994a; 1998a). A brief summary is presented here. The first and primary aspect is labeled 'the Stage of Early Arithmetical Learning'. Assessing this stage involves eliciting the most sophisticated strategies used by the child to solve what, from an adult's perspective, are simple addition or subtraction problems. For example, a child might be limited to counting visible objects (Stage 1), might count-on without requiring visible objects to solve an additive task (Stage 3), or when working out 8+9, might use 8+8 and not use counting by ones (Stage 5). This five-stage model is adapted from the earlier constructivist research program (e.g. Steffe et al., 1983; Steffe and Cobb, 1988). Other aspects of children's arithmetical knowledge which are the focus of assessment and teaching in Mathematics Recovery are facility with number word sequences both forward and backward, and ability to identify numerals (Wright, 1998b). Children's understanding of tens and ones (Steffe and Cobb, 1988; Cobb and Wheatley, 1988), ability to sequence consecutive numerals, and subitise (e.g. Glasersfeld, 1982) are also of significance.

Underlying the work of Steffe and colleagues is Glasersfeld's (1984, 1991) radical constructivist epistemology, which has its roots in the work of Piaget. According to Glasersfeld (1991), a tenet of all constructivist epistemologies is the notion that originated with Socrates, viz that 'knowledge is the result of a learner's activity rather than of the passive reception of information or instruction' (ibid., p. xiv). Distinctive in the constructivist epistemology espoused by Glasersfeld is

> the revolutionary attitude pioneered in the 1930s by Jean Piaget. . . . This attitude is characterised by the deliberate redefinition of the concept of knowing as *an adaptive function* [emphasis in original]. . . . This means that the results of our cognitive efforts have the purpose of helping us to cope in the world of our experience, rather than the traditional goal of furnishing an 'objective' representation of a world as it might 'exist' apart from us and our experience. (Glasersfeld, 1991, p. xiv)

Robert J. Wright

An Overview of the Development and Procedures of Mathematics Recovery

Why Have Recovery Education at the First Grade Level?

In planning Mathematics Recovery the following question was considered: At what age or grade are children at risk of chronic failure in mathematics best suited to undertake a recovery program? Given that there is a relatively wide range of abilities when children begin school and that this range increases as children progress through elementary school it seems reasonable to argue that intervention should occur as soon as possible after the child starts school. On the other hand there are reasons why a Mathematics Recovery program should not occur in the first year: (a) at this time children are coping with the transition to schooling and for this reason may not benefit from or cope well with a program of intensive, individualized teaching; (b) some children judged to be among the least advanced at the beginning of schooling may make relatively large gains as a result of classroom teaching and thus may not require a recovery program. Thus the second year of school (i.e. first grade) was considered to be the most appropriate for Mathematics Recovery.

School-Based Phases of the Project – 1992, 1993 and 1994

As stated earlier, Mathematics Recovery was developed during the period 1992 to 1995, and involved twenty teachers in eighteen schools in the north coast region of New South Wales, Australia. This development involved separate school-based phases in each of the three school years of 1992, 1993 and 1994. In the 1992 school-based phase, a teacher in each of six schools worked half-time on the Mathematics Recovery Project for the period from mid-August until mid-December – sixteen weeks of the school year. In 1993, the school-based phase of the project also ran from mid-August until mid-December and involved ten schools. In 1992, the sixteen-week phase consisted of an initial six-week, half-daily professional development program; an eight-week teaching cycle during which four children were taught in individualized sessions four mornings per week; and a final two-week period during which participants and comparison children were reassessed and concluding professional development meetings were held. In 1993, the sixteen-week phase was structured as it had been in 1992. In 1994, the project involved a teacher in each of eleven schools and ran for most of the school year rather than for a sixteen-week phase as it had done in 1992 and 1993.

The Initial Phase of the Professional Development Course

Since 1995, there have been several implementations of Mathematics Recovery as a professional development course. This course typically involves an initial phase of teacher learning, prior to commencing teaching cycles with first-graders. The initial phase is structured as follows. First, teachers learn a method of assessing young children's arithmetical knowledge which was developed and used extensively by the author in recent years (Wright, 1991c; 1994a; 1994b; 1998a; Wright et al., 1996; 1998), and which draws on the earlier research program (e.g. Cobb and Steffe, 1983; Steffe et al., 1983; Steffe and Cobb, 1988). Learning the assessment method involves assimilating detailed explanations of principles underlying the interview method and purposes of interview tasks, discussing videotaped excerpts of assessment interviews, and conducting trial assessments. Second, teachers learn a range of instructional activities that have been developed in Mathematics Recovery. As in the case of learning the assessment method, videotaped excerpts of teaching sessions are discussed so that teachers may understand better the teaching methods and specific instructional activities used in the project. The third and final part involves: (a) assessment of a cohort of first-graders which includes likely candidates for Mathematics Recovery as nominated by class teachers; (b) selection of up to four participants on the basis of the assessment; and (c) using the results of assessment to plan individualized teaching programs for each participant. These teaching programs are provisional only and are revised on a daily and weekly basis as a result of the child's progress in the teaching cycle.

Teaching Cycles and Teaching Sessions

After completing the initial phase of the professional development course, teachers administer individualized teaching programs to participating students. In these programs, students are withdrawn from class and taught in an individualized program involving teaching sessions of 25–30 minutes duration, daily, for teaching cycles of 12–15 weeks. Typically, the daily starting time for each child's session is varied in order to minimize the likelihood that the child is absent from classroom work of a very similar nature over many days. For several important reasons, all teaching and assessment sessions are routinely videotaped. Teachers use videotapes of teaching sessions to review their teaching and also to monitor children's progress. In the first week of the teaching cycle, a version of 'roaming the known' is used. This allows the teacher to take a reasonably flexible approach to choosing particular instructional activities, to present activities similar to those presented during the assessment interview, and to know better the kinds of activities that are routine for the child, those that are problematic but perhaps within a zone of proximal development (Vygotsky, 1978, p. 86), and those that seem to be well beyond this. Teachers write daily plans for their teaching sessions which list instructional activities selected from a bank of activities studied in the initial professional development course. A typical daily plan includes four to six instructional activities.

Robert J. Wright

The Instructional Activities

A detailed description of the instructional activities that have been developed during the course of the project is presented in Wright (1998a). Some examples of these activities are: (a) additive and subtractive tasks involving collections or rows of counters some or all of which are hidden; (b) activities involving copying or counting sequences of sounds or movements; (c) activities using numeral cards arranged either singly or in numeral tracks or grids; (d) ascribing number to spatial patterns which are briefly displayed; (e) activities using collections of tens and ones; (f) activities that promote more sophisticated use of finger patterns in adding and subtracting; (g) number word sequence activities such as reciting sequences forward and backward, and stating number words before or after a given number word; (h) activities involving combining and partitioning small numbers without counting (Cobb et al., 1995); (i) activities that invoke quinary-based strategies (Gravemeijer, 1994); and (j) notating and symbolizing in ways that accord with students' strategies (Gravemeijer et al., in press). Many of these were used in constructivist teaching experiments undertaken with 5- to 8-year-olds in earlier research projects (Steffe et al., 1983; Steffe and Cobb, 1988; Wright, 1989; 1991a; 1991c; 1994a).

Modus Operandi *and Guiding Principles for Mathematics Recovery Teaching Sessions*

In working with Mathematics Recovery teachers the following is emphasized as a *modus operandi* for the teaching sessions. First, the teacher must hypothesize about the child's current ways of thinking. This is informed by prior observations in a current or earlier teaching session or in an earlier assessment session, and may concern, for example, the child's current arithmetical strategies, facility with number words or numeral identification. Second, the teacher tests their current hypotheses by posing a task or asking a question and closely observing the child's response. Third, the teacher modifies his or her hypothesis on the basis of the child's response, and so the cycle continues. Additionally, the teacher must continually monitor the child's willingness to tackle problems and how comfortable or at ease the child seems to be. Through practice and reflection teachers can learn to adjust, in subtle but important ways, the pace, difficulty and degree of variation and challenge when interacting with the child according to perceptions of the child's ease and satisfaction when responding to the instructional activities. Teaching should be tailored as closely as possible to the initial and on-going assessment, and should be at the 'cutting edge' of the child's knowledge. Activities should be genuine problems for the child and teachers must routinely make micro-adjustments to planned activities on the basis of the child's responses. The child should be continually challenged, with the teacher aiming to bring about reorganizations in the child's thinking. These reorganizations are manifest in new and more sophisticated strategies. The teaching sessions are intended to be intensive. However, our observation is that for the vast majority of children the teaching and interview sessions are usually a very positive experience. Children seem to experience intrinsic satisfaction from thinking hard and solving problems and their enthusiasm for the sessions increases as the weeks progress. Additionally we believe that individualized teaching is necessary to achieve the intensity that is required in the teaching sessions.

Children's Learning

We have observed that, as a result of participating in teaching sessions, important and positive changes in attitude to mathematics can occur as children develop a new sense of their ability to do mathematics and a greater reliance on their own resources. Children reflecting on their mathematical activity is an important aspect of the teaching sessions and it can play a crucial role in bringing about reorganizations of current strategies. Closely related to reflecting is the importance of giving children extensive thinking time and avoiding the temptation to speak when they are solving problems. Providing ample opportunities for extensive periods of thinking hard about arithmetical problems is a key aspect of the teaching approach. Underlying the program is a belief that children in need of a recovery program in mathematics are likely to have had too few opportunities to think hard about arithmetical problems and to reflect on their thinking.

Professional Development Meetings

Implementation of Mathematics Recovery involves an initial phase of teacher learning (described above), and a series of professional development meetings once the teaching cycles have commenced. These meetings are typically scheduled weekly or every other week. Following is a description of a typical half-day professional development meeting involving up to twelve teachers and a teacher leader. There is an initial period of 30 to 40 minutes during which each teacher overviews their teaching sessions; a period of 60 to 75 minutes during which each of three or four teachers gives a 15 to 20 minute presentation focusing on children's progress, usefulness of instructional activities, and their challenges and achievements to date; and a final 20 to 30 minute discussion period focusing on issues which arose during the meeting. As in the initial phase of the professional development course, analysis and discussion of videotaped excerpts are key features of these on-going professional development meetings. For example, teachers routinely show and discuss such excerpts during their presentations at these meetings.

Robert J. Wright

Significance of Videotaping

Videotaping is a crucial tool in Mathematics Recovery and has its origins in the earlier research programs (e.g. Steffe et al., 1983; Steffe and Cobb, 1988; Wright, 1991a; 1991c; 1994a). In these research programs, the videotapes were used in micro-analyses of children's advancements in their arithmetical knowledge as it occurs in interactive teaching situations (see Cobb and Steffe, 1983; Glasersfeld and Steffe, 1991; Steffe, 1991). In Mathematics Recovery, the videotapes form the basis of research into children's learning, research into teaching, assessment of children's arithmetical knowledge, and documentation of children's progress over time. Further, videotaped records are used extensively in evaluation of instructional activities and in the professional development course for teachers. Mathematics Recovery does not incorporate use of a one-way mirror to enable an instructor and colleagues to observe each trainee's teaching sessions. Rather, in Mathematics Recovery, observation and analysis of assessment and teaching sessions are undertaken via review of videotaped records of the sessions.

Mathematics Recovery – On-going Developments and Outcomes

When Mathematics Recovery commenced in 1992, the initial plan was to work with six schools and to develop instructional activities as time progressed. Several years earlier, the researcher (Wright, 1989; 1991a; 1991b) had conducted a ten-month teaching experiment involving individualized teaching sessions conducted weekly with four children in their kindergarten year who were among the least advanced in their class (5- to 6-year-olds). The approaches and the instructional activities initially used in the Mathematics Recovery teaching sessions were drawn from the earlier research programs. The assessment method developed for Mathematics Recovery also drew on this work and was used by the researcher in an earlier study focusing on arithmetical development in the first two years of school (Wright, 1991b; 1994).

Children's Progress in 1992

A detailed analysis of the progress of the 24 participants and its comparison with the progress of 66 counterparts has been completed and a report based on this analysis is available (Wright, Stanger, Cowper and Dyson, 1996). Nineteen of the 24 participants made major advancements and four of the remaining five made significant advancements during teaching cycles of eight-weeks' duration. In each of the six schools the advancements of the participants were notably greater than those of their counterparts who were initially at levels similar to those of the participants (i.e. prenumerical).

Participating Teachers' Reactions To The Project In 1992

As is to be expected there was strong enthusiasm amongst the six project teachers at the beginning of the program. For all of the teachers this enthusiasm was maintained and strengthened during the project. All of the teachers expressed the belief that they had learned significantly as a result of their participation and that this learning would be of benefit, either as a specialist recovery teacher or in classroom teaching. This is documented in professional journals maintained by the teachers during their time on the project.

Learning From the First Years of the Project

Given the experimental nature of the project, the achievements of the first year (1992) were regarded as very promising. In the first year significant insight was gained into: (a) the amount of progress that is achievable, (b) the usefulness of instructional activities, (c) an appropriate *modus operandi* for teaching sessions, and (d) the ways in which teachers interpreted theory and related this to their practice. All of these were used to revise the Mathematics Recovery professional development program for 1993, and this kind of revision has occurred in subsequent years as well. In Mathematics Recovery it is increasingly apparent that, as appears in reports of children's progress in Reading Recovery, children's progress is typically accompanied by major changes in their general learning strategies and their perceptions of themselves as successful learners who develop ways of learning mathematics which are significantly less teacher dependent.

Mathematics Recovery Outcomes

Detailed reports of children's progress in the major implementations of Mathematics Recovery are available elsewhere (Wright, 1994b; Wright et al., 1994; 1996; 1998). Typically, virtually all participating students make significant progress, around 75 per cent of participating students make major progress and advance to at least average attainment levels for their class, and about one-third of that 75 per cent (25 per cent of participating students) advance to significantly above average levels.

The Potential of a Recovery Program

In the course of working in schools on implementations of Mathematics Recovery in Australia, the United States and the United Kingdom, the author has come to understand better the potential of the program directly to benefit all students in a school rather than merely the least advanced first-graders who participate. In some implementations of Reading Recovery the proportion of a year cohort selected to participate in the program is as high as 30 per cent (Clay, 1990, p. 64). Given wide ranges of mathematical achievement in even the earliest years of schooling, it seems reasonable to claim that in a good number of schools, a similar percentage of children require a program of intensive individualized learning in early mathematics. Consider a school with ninety first-graders which implements Mathematics Recovery in which a specialist teacher teaches four of the least advanced first-graders individually each day, in 30 minute sessions. On the basis of several implementations of Mathematics Recovery, the most effective implementation would involve two specialist teachers each working five half-days per week on the program. Experience indicates that: (a) the lowest achieving students, i.e. the two or three least advanced among ninety, may require more than two terms (20 weeks) in a recovery program to reach a level at which they can learn successfully in class; (b) students more advanced than these but still candidates for Mathematics Recovery are likely to reach an appropriate level in a significantly shorter period, around 12 to 15 weeks. Thus with an implementation involving two half-time teachers, up to twenty-five students are likely to participate over the course of the school year, whereas with an implementation involving one half-time teacher, eight to ten students are likely to participate. Having two half-time specialist recovery teachers is preferable to having one full time because the teaching is very intensive and demanding on the teacher. An implementation as described allows more classroom instructional time for average and high-attaining children, and thus there is a good potential for all students to benefit significantly.

Broader Impact and Significance of Mathematics Recovery

In the initial years (1992-4) of the development of Mathematics Recovery, the focus of the project by and large was limited to instructional programs for individualized teaching of low attainers. As the years progressed, it became increasingly apparent that many Mathematics Recovery teachers were applying their new found knowledge and techniques in significant reorganizations of their classroom teaching. Many of the teachers found themselves to be regarded as key resource people in early mathematics teaching for colleagues in their own or other schools. What became very apparent after a few years of the program was that Mathematics Recovery was very successful as professional development, and was applicable to classroom teaching and to average and able learners as well as to low attainers. Accordingly, in New South Wales in 1996 Mathematics Recovery theory and techniques were adapted as the basis of a systemic, large-scale, classroom-based project in the government school system. This project, which is entitled 'Count Me In Too', has the goal of providing teachers with better understanding of young children's mathematical thinking and ways of developing more sophisticated mathematical strategies in their students. The project has involved several hundred schools and thousands of students across all forty educational districts in the state. It has been judged to be successful (Bobis and Gould, 1998; Stewart et al., 1998) and seems to be highly regarded by teachers and principals in participating schools. In a similar vein, significant positive and broader outcomes have been observed in the case of the implementation of Mathematics Recovery in the United Kingdom.

Conclusion

An important focus of the Mathematics Recovery Project in 1992–4 was to work collaboratively with teachers to find ways of providing for the least advanced young children. Individualized learning environments were developed in which the children undergo a program of intensive learning of early arithmetic. This involved taking a reflective and problem solving approach which includes identifying key questions about the children, and continually questioning one's assumptions about young children's arithmetical thinking and how best to provide opportunities for its advancement. There are several aspects of the project which have been rewarding in both personal and professional senses. These include the continuing challenge to improve methods and to understand better children's arithmetical learning and thinking, the very obvious progress of virtually all of the participants, dramatic changes in the participants' attitudes to doing mathematics, continuing enthusiasm for and commitment to the program from participating teachers, and interest and support from groups such as parents, principals, administrators and other teachers.

Note

1   The research project which is the major focus of this chapter is funded by Grant No. AM9180064 from the Australian Research Council and by contributions in kind from government and Catholic school systems of the North Coast Region of NSW. Additional support has been provided by research grants from Southern Cross University. The author expresses his gratitude to the children, teachers and schools involved.

References

AUBREY, C. (1993) 'An investigation of the mathematical knowledge and competencies which young children bring into school', *British Educational Research Journal*, 19, pp. 27–41.

BOBIS, J. and GOULD, P. (1998) 'The impact of an early number project on the professional development of teachers', in KANES, C., GOOS, M. and WARREN, E. (eds), *Proceedings of the 21st Annual Conference of the Mathematics Education Research Group of Australasia*, Brisbane: Griffith University, pp. 106–13.

CARPENTER, T.P. and FENNEMA, E. (1992) 'Cognitively guided instruction: Building on the knowledge of students and teachers', *International Journal of Educational Research*, **17**, 5, pp. 457–70.

CARPENTER, T.P., MOSER, J.M. and ROMBERG, T.A. (eds) (1982) *Addition and Subtraction: A Cognitive Perspective*, Hillsdale, NJ: Lawrence Erlbaum.

CLAY, M.M. (1979) *The Early Detection of Reading Difficulties*, Auckland: Heinemann.

CLAY, M.M. (1987) 'Implementing reading recovery: Systemic adaptations to an educational innovation', *New Zealand Journal of Educational Studies*, **22**, 1, pp. 35–58.

CLAY, M.M. (1990) 'The Reading Recovery programme, 1984–88: Coverage, outcomes and Education Board district figures', *New Zealand Journal of Educational Studies*, **25**, 1, pp. 61–70.

CLAY, M.M. (1992) 'Reading recovery: The wider implications of an educational innovation', in WATSON, A.J. and BADENHOP, A.M. (eds), *Prevention of Reading Failure*, Sydney: Ashton Scholastic, pp. 22–47.

CLAY, M.M. (1993) *Reading Recovery: A Guide Book to Teachers in Training*, Portsmouth: Heinemann.

COBB, P. and STEFFE, L.P. (1983) 'The constructivist researcher as teacher and model builder', *Journal for Research in Mathematics Education*, 14, pp. 83–94.

COBB, P. and WHEATLEY, G. (1988) 'Children's initial understandings of ten', *Focus on Learning Problems in Mathematics*, **10**, 3, pp. 1–26.

COBB, P., MCCLAIN, K., WHITENACK, J. and ESTES, B. (1995) 'Supporting young children's development of mathematical power', in RICHARDS, A. (ed.), *Proceedings of the Fifteenth Biennial Conference of the Australian Association of Mathematics Teachers*, Adelaide: Australian Association of Mathematics Teachers, pp. 1–11.

COBB, P., WOOD, T. and YACKEL, E. (1991) 'A constructivist approach to second grade mathematics', in GLASERSFELD, E. VON (ed.), *Radical Constructivism in Mathematics Education*, Dordrecht: Kluwer, pp. 157–76.

COBB, P., YACKEL, E. and WOOD, T. (1992) 'Interaction and learning in mathematics classroom situations', *Educational Studies in Mathematics*, **23**, 1, pp. 99–122.

COCKCROFT, W.H. (1982) *Mathematics Counts: Report of the Committee of Inquiry into the Teaching of Mathematics in Schools*, London: HMSO.

DEFORD, D.E., LYONS, C.A. and PINNELL, G.S. (eds) (1991) *Bridges to Literacy – Learning from Reading Recovery*, Portsmouth: Heinemann.

DOIG, B. and MASTERS, G. (1992) 'Through children's eyes: A constructivist approach to assessing mathematics learning', in LEDER, G. (ed.), *Assessment and Learning of Mathematics*, Melbourne: ACER, pp. 269–89.

DOMBEY, H. (1992) 'Reading recovery: A solution to all primary school reading problems?', *Support for Learning*, **7**, 3, pp. 111–14.

FUSON, K.C. (1988) *Children's Counting and Concepts of Number*, New York: Springer.

FUSON, K.C. (1992a) 'Research on learning and teaching addition and subtraction of whole numbers', in LEINHARDT, G., PUTNAM, R. and HATTRUP, R.A. (eds), *Analysis of Arithmetic for Mathematics Teaching*, Hillsdale, NJ: Lawrence Erlbaum, pp. 53–187.

FUSON, K.C. (1992b) 'Research on whole number addition and subtraction', in GROUWS, D.A. (ed.), *Handbook of Research on Mathematics Teaching and Learning*, New York: Macmillan, pp. 243–75.

FUSON, K.C., FRAIVILLIG, J.L. and BURGHARDT, B.H. (1992) 'Relationships children construct among English number words, multiunit base-ten blocks, and written multidigit addition', in CAMPBELL, J.I.D. (ed.), *The Nature and Origin of Mathematical Skills*, Amsterdam: North-Holland, pp. 39–112.

GLASERSFELD, E. VON (1982) 'Subitizing – The role of figural patterns in the development of numerical concepts', *Archives de Psychologie*, 50, pp. 191–218.

GLASERSFELD, E. VON (1984) 'An introduction to radical constructivism', in WATZLAWICK, P. (ed.), *The Invented Reality*, New York: W.W. Norton, pp. 17–40.

GLASERSFELD, E. VON (ed.) (1991) *Radical Constructivism in Mathematics Education*, Dordrecht: Kluwer.

GLASERSFELD, E. VON and STEFFE, L. (1991) 'Conceptual models in educational research and practice', *Journal of Educational Thought*, **25**, 2, pp. 91–103.

GRAVEMEIJER, K. (1994) *Developing Realistic Mathematics Education*, Utrecht: CD-B Press.

GRAVEMEIJER, K., COBB, P., BOWERS, J. and WHITENACK, J. (in press) 'Symbolizing, modeling, and instructional design', in COBB, P., YACKEL, E. and McCLAIN, K. (eds), *Communicating and Symbolizing in Mathematics Classrooms: Perspectives on Discourse, Tools, and Instructional Design*, Mahwah, NJ: Lawrence Erlbaum.

LEVIN, H.M. (1989) 'Financing the education of at-risk students', *Educational Evaluation and Policy Analysis*, **11**, 1, pp. 47–60.

LITERACY CHALLENGE (1993) A Report on Strategies for Early Intervention for Literacy and Learning for Australian Children – House of Representatives Standing Committee, Canberra: Australian Government Publishing Service.

LYONS, C.A., PINNELL, G.S. and DEFORD, D.E. (1993) *Partners in Learning: Teachers and Children in Reading Recovery*, New York: Teachers College Press.

MASTERS, G., LOKAN, J., DOIG, B., KHOO, S., LINDSEY, J., ROBINSON, L. and ZAMMIT, S. (1990) *Profiles of Learning: The Basic Skills Testing Program in New South Wales*, Melbourne: ACER.

MEISELS, S.J. and SHONKOFF, J.P. (eds) (1990) *Handbook of Early Childhood Intervention*, Cambridge: Cambridge University Press.

PINNELL, G.S. (1989) 'A systemic approach to reducing the risk of reading failure', in ALLEN, J.B. and MASON, J.M. (eds), *Risk Makers, Risk Takers, Risk Breakers. Reducing the Risks for Young Literacy Learners*, Portsmouth: Heineman, pp. 178–97.

PINNELL, G.S., FRIED, M.D. and ESTICE, R.E. (1990) 'Reading recovery: Learning how to make a difference', *Reading Teacher*, January, pp. 282–95.

PLOMIN, R., DEFRIES, J.C. and FULKER, D.W. (1988) *Nature and Nurture during Infancy and Early Childhood* (1st edn), Cambridge: Cambridge University Press.

RESNICK, L. (1992) 'From protoquantities to operators: Building mathematical competence on a foundation of everyday experience', in LEINHARDT, G., PUTNAM, R. and HATTRUP, R.A. (eds), *Analysis of Arithmetic for Mathematics Teaching*, Hillsdale, NJ: Lawrence Erlbaum.

SMITH, J. (1986) 'Reading Recovery in central Victoria: What we have learnt', *Australian Journal of Reading*, **9**, 4, pp. 201–8.

STEFFE, L.P. (1991) 'The constructivist teaching experiment: Illustrations and implications', in GLASERSFELD, E. VON (ed.), *Radical Constructivism in Mathematics Education*, Dordrecht: Kluwer.

STEFFE, L.P. and COBB, P. (1988) *Construction of Arithmetic Meanings and Strategies*, New York: Springer.

STEFFE, L.P., GLASERSFELD, E. VON, RICHARDS, J. and COBB, P. (1983) *Children's Counting Types: Philosophy, Theory, and Application*, New York: Praeger.

STEWART, R., WRIGHT, R.J. and GOULD, P. (1998) 'Kindergartener's progress in the Count Me In Too Project', in KANES, C., GOOS, M. and WARREN, E. (eds), *Proceedings of the 21st Annual Conference of the Mathematics Education Research Group of Australasia*, Brisbane, Australia, Griffith University, pp. 556–63.

VYGOTSKY, L. (1978) 'Educational implications: Interaction between learning and development', in COLE, M., JOHN-STEINER, V., SCRIBER, S. and SOUBERMAN, E. (eds), *Mind in Society: The Development of Higher Psychological Processes*, Cambridge, Mass.: Harvard University Press (tr. M. Lopez-Morillas; original work published 1935).

WASIK, B.A. and SLAVIN, R.E. (1993) 'Preventing early reading failure with one-to-one tutoring: A review of five programs', *Reading Research Quarterly*, **28**, 2, pp. 179–200.

WRIGHT, R.J. (1989) 'Numerical development in the kindergarten year: A teaching experiment', PhD thesis, University of Georgia. [DAI, 50A, 1588; DA8919319]

WRIGHT, R.J. (1991a) 'An application of the epistemology of radical constructivism to the study of learning', *Australian Educational Researcher*, **18**, 1, pp. 75–95.

WRIGHT, R.J. (1991b) 'The role of counting in children's numerical development', *Australian Journal of Early Childhood*, **16**, 2, pp. 43–8.

WRIGHT, R.J. (1991c) 'What number knowledge is possessed by children entering the kindergarten year of school?', *Mathematics Education Research Journal*, **3**, 1, pp. 1–16.

WRIGHT, R.J. (1994a) 'A study of the numerical development of 5-year-olds and 6-year-olds', *Educational Studies in Mathematics*, 26, pp. 25–44.

WRIGHT, R.J. (1994b) 'Working with teachers to advance the arithmetical knowledge of low-attaining 6- and 7-year-olds: First year results', in PONTE, J. and MATOS, J. (eds), *Proceedings of the 18th International Conference for the Psychology of Mathematics Education*, Lisbon, University of Lisbon, pp. 377–84.

WRIGHT, R.J. (1998a) 'An overview of a research-based framework for assessing and teaching early number', in KANES, C., GOOS, M. and WARREN, E. (eds), *Proceedings of the 21st Annual Conference of the Mathematics Education Research Group of Australasia*, Brisbane, Australia, Griffith University, pp. 701–8.

WRIGHT, R.J. (1998b) 'Children's beginning knowledge of numerals and its relationship to their knowledge of number words: An exploratory, observational study', in OLIVIER, A. and NEWSTEAD, K. (eds), *Proceedings of the 22nd Conference of the International Group for the Psychology of Mathematics Education*, Stellenbosh, South Africa: University of Stellenbosh, Vol. 4, pp. 201–8.

WRIGHT, R.J., COWPER, M., STAFFORD, A., STANGER, G. and STEWART, R. (1994) 'The Maths Recovery Project: A progress report', in BELL, G., WRIGHT, R., LEESON, N. and GEAKE, J. (eds), *Proceedings of the 17th Annual Conference of the Mathematics Education Research Group of Australasia*, Lismore, NSW, Australia: Southern Cross University, pp. 709–16.

WRIGHT, R.J., STANGER, G., COWPER, M. and DYSON, R. (1996) 'First-graders' progress in an experimental mathematics recovery program', in MULLIGAN, J. and MITCHELMORE, M., *Research in Early Number Learning: An Australian Perspective*, Adelaide: AAMT, pp. 55–72.

WRIGHT, R.J., STEWART, R., STAFFORD, A. and CAIN, R. (1998) 'Assessing and documenting students' knowledge and progress in early mathematics', in BERENSON, S.B., DAWKINS, K.R., BLANTON, M., COULOMBE, W.N., KOLB, J., NORWOOD, K. and STIFF, L. (eds), *Proceedings of the Twentieth Annual Meeting of the North*

American Chapter of the International Group for the Psychology of Mathematics Education, Vol. 1, pp. 211–16. Columbus, Ohio: ERIC Clearing-house for Science, Mathematics, and Environmental Education.

YACKEL, E., COBB, P. and WOOD, T. (1991) 'Small group interactions as a source of learning opportunities in second grade mathematics', *Journal for Research in Mathematics Education*, **22**, 5, pp. 390–408.

YOUNG-LOVERIDGE, J. (1989) 'The development of children's number concepts: The first year of school', *New Zealand Journal of Educational Studies*, **24**, 1, pp. 47–64.

YOUNG-LOVERIDGE, J. (1991) 'The development of children's number concepts from ages five to nine. Early mathematics learning project: Phase II', Vol. 1: *Report of Findings*, University of Waikato, NZ.

11   Constructivism in Social Context[1]

Paul Cobb

In this chapter, I focus on one of the aspects of constructivist theory that Glasersfeld (Ch. 1) identifies as in need of further development. This aspect of the theory involves locating students' mathematical development in social and cultural context while simultaneously treating learning as a process of adaptive reorganization. In addressing this issue, I illustrate the approach that I and my colleagues currently take when accounting for the process of students' mathematical learning as it occurs in the social context of the classroom. In the opening section of the chapter, I clarify why this is a significant issue for us as mathematics educators. I then outline my general theoretical orientation by discussing Glasersfeld's constructivism and Bauersfeld's interactionism. Against this background, I develop criteria for classroom analyses that are relevant to our interests as researchers who develop learning environments for students in collaboration with teachers. Next, I illustrate the interpretive framework that I and my colleagues currently use by presenting a sample classroom analysis. Finally, in the concluding sections of the chapter, I reflect on the sample analysis to address four more general issues. These concern the contributions of analyses of the type outlined in the illustrative example, the relationship between instructional design and classroom-based research, the role of symbols and other tools in mathematical learning, and the relation between individual students' mathematical activity and communal classroom processes.

From Individual Learners to Participants in Communities

Sfard's (1994a) analysis of the development of the concept of concept in mathematics education research provides a useful starting point from which to clarify why I believe it is important to view students' mathematical learning as occurring in social context. Sfard divides the ways in which mathematics educators have thought about students' development of mathematical understandings into four broad, overlapping and not mutually exclusive paradigms. At the risk of oversimplifying Sfard's subtle analysis, I briefly discuss each paradigm in turn.

Single-Frame Paradigm

The research characteristic of this paradigm aims to develop a comprehensive picture of individual students' mathematical conceptions at a particular point

152

in time. Often, students' mathematical activity is compared with a normative model of mature activity, and divergences are treated as students' misconceptions (cf. Confrey, 1990).

Multiple-Frame Paradigm

As Sfard (1994a) puts it, the goal of research that typifies this paradigm is to produce a model of the birth and maturation of particular mathematical concepts by identifying sequences of developmental phases, levels or stages. In this paradigm, activities that were previously taken as indicators of misconceptions are often seen as necessary steps in students' development of mature conceptions.

Motion-Picture Paradigm

Research conducted in this paradigm questions the assumption that students' development of mathematical concepts inevitably passes through a sequence of well-defined phases or stages. Rather than identifying a sequence of *fixed* points along a developmental route, the goal of this type of research is to model the *process* by which students' mathematical concepts develop. This approach allows for the possibility that the results of these constructive processes, the mathematical understandings that students develop, can differ from one situation to another. Two of the most influential models of this type are Pirie and Kieren's (1994) recursive theory of the growth of mathematical understanding and Sfard's (1994b) own theoretical framework based on an assumed process-object duality of mathematical concepts. More generally, constructivist analyses that characterize mathematical learning as a process of reorganizing activity are at the forefront of work conducted within this paradigm (e.g., Confrey and Smith, 1995; Steffe and Wiegel, 1994; Thompson, 1994).

Sfard (1994a) argues that analyses developed within this paradigm can inform pedagogical decision-making in that teachers and instructional designers seek to influence the process by which students' mathematical understandings develop. However, she also observes that both this and the preceding two paradigms are primarily individualistic – they are concerned with the mathematical understandings of individual learners. There has, however, been a further trend in mathematics education research in recent years, one that brings to the fore the socially and culturally situated nature of mathematical activity (e.g., Bishop, 1988; Cobb and Bauersfeld, 1995; Nickson, 1992; Nunes, 1992; Voigt, 1994). This trend indicates that a fourth broad paradigm is currently emerging.

Participation in Communities of Practice Paradigm

Analyses conducted within this paradigm, like those conducted in the motion-picture paradigm, are vitally concerned with the process of mathematical

Paul Cobb

development. However, in contrast to the motion-picture paradigm, individual students' mathematical interpretations, solutions, explanations and justifications are seen not only as individual acts, but simultaneously as acts of participation in collective or communal classroom processes. Viewed in this way, mathematical learning is seen to be necessarily and inexorably located in social context. It should be acknowledged that this paradigm encompasses a panoply of theoretical positions that include various versions of constructivism, sociocultural theory and sociolinguistic theory (cf. Cobb, 1994; Confrey, 1995; Lerman, 1996; Steffe, 1996). Each of these perspectives provides an orientation on mathematical learning as it occurs in social context. However, comparing and contrasting these alternatives is beyond the scope of this chapter, and I will instead focus directly on the version of social constructivism to which I and my colleagues subscribe.

Theoretical Orientation

The version of social constructivism that has emerged in the course of our work in classrooms draws heavily on psychological constructivism as developed by Glasersfeld (1978, 1987, 1991) by incorporating both the Piagetian notions of assimilation and accommodation, and the cybernetic concept of viability. Thus, the approach we take follows Glasersfeld (1992) in using the term *knowledge* in 'Piaget's adaptational sense to refer to sensory-motor and conceptual operations that have proved viable in the knower's experience' (p. 380). Traditional correspondence theories of truth are therefore dispensed with in favor of an account that relates truth to the effective or viable organization of activity: 'Truths are replaced by viable models – and viability is always relative to a chosen goal' (Glasersfeld, 1992, p. 384). As Glasersfeld observes, this instrumentalist orientation to knowledge is generally consistent with the views both of Dewey (1981) and of contemporary neo-pragmatist philosophers such as Bernstein (1983), Putnam (1987) and Rorty (1982).

Although Glasersfeld defines learning as self-organization, he is careful to clarify that this constructive activity occurs as the cognizing individual interacts with other members of a community. Thus, he stresses that 'the most frequent source of perturbations for the developing cognitive subject is interactions with others' (1989, p. 136). In addition, he elaborates that knowledge refers to 'conceptual structures that epistemic agents, given the range of present experience *within their tradition of thought and language,* consider viable' (Glasersfeld, 1992, p. 381; italics added). In making this observation, Glasersfeld indicates the socially and culturally situated nature of epistemic agents' understandings. In other words, learning is not merely social in the sense that interactions with others serve as a catalyst for otherwise autonomous conceptual development. Instead, the products of learning, increasingly sophisticated ways of knowing, are also social through and through.

In building on this insight, I and my colleagues have turned to symbolic interactionism (Blumer, 1969) and ethnomethodology (Mehan and Wood, 1975) as developed for mathematics education by Bauersfeld et al. (1988). Bauersfeld et al.'s interactionist perspective complements Glasersfeld's psychological focus in that both view communication as a process of mutual adaptation wherein individuals negotiate meanings by continually modifying their interpretations. However, whereas Glasersfeld is concerned with individuals' construction of their ways of knowing, Bauersfeld emphasizes that 'learning is characterized by the subjective reconstruction of societal means and models through negotiation of meaning in social interaction' (1988, p. 39). In accounting for this process of subjective reconstruction, he focuses on the teacher's and students' interactive constitution of the classroom microculture. Thus, he argues that

> participating in the processes of a mathematics classroom is participating in a culture of mathematizing. The many skills, which an observer can identify and will take as the main performance of culture, form the procedural surface only. These are the bricks of the building, but the design of the house of mathematizing is processed on another level. As it is with culture, the core of what is learned through participation is *when* to do what and *how* to do it.... The core part of school mathematics enculturation comes into effect on the meta-level and is 'learned' indirectly. (Bauersfeld, 1993, p. 4)

Bauersfeld's reference to indirect learning clarifies that the occurrence of perturbations is not limited to those occasions when participants in an interaction believe that communication has broken down and *explicitly negotiate* meanings. Instead, for him, communication is a process of often *implicit negotiations* in which subtle shifts and slides of meaning occur outside the participants' awareness (cf. Cobb and Yackel, 1996). In taking this approach, Bauersfeld uses an interactionist metaphor and characterizes negotiation as a process of mutual adaptation in the course of which the teacher and students mutually establish expectations for each others' activity and obligations for their own activity (cf. Cobb and Bauersfeld, 1995; Voigt, 1985). Consequently, for Bauersfeld and his colleagues, the classroom microculture is an emerging phenomenon. The teacher and students are seen jointly to constitute classroom norms and practices in the course of their interactions. Analyses compatible with Bauersfeld's interactionist perspective therefore propose that individual students' mathematical activity and the classroom microculture are reflexively related (Cobb, 1989; Voigt, 1996). In this social constructivist view, individual students are seen actively to contribute to the evolution of the classroom mathematical practices that both enable and constrain their individual mathematical activities. This assumed reflexive relation in turn implies that neither an individual student's mathematical reasoning nor the classroom microculture can be adequately accounted for without considering the other. In general, the reflexive interdependence of students' activity and the practices in which they participate serve to differentiate the social constructivist approach that I and my colleagues take from alternatives in which social phenomena are viewed as primary and psychological phenomena are treated as secondary.

Figure 11.1 Aspects of the developmental research cycle

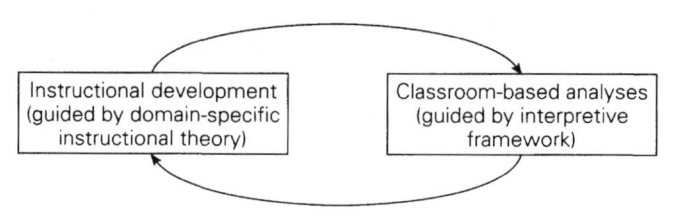

```
    ┌──────────────────────────┐      ┌──────────────────────────┐
    │ Instructional development│      │ Classroom-based analyses │
    │ (guided by domain-specific│─────▶│ (guided by interpretive  │
    │   instructional theory)  │◀─────│       framework)         │
    └──────────────────────────┘      └──────────────────────────┘
```

Criteria for Classroom Analyses

Given the basic tenets of the social constructivist approach I have outlined, the challenge of accounting for learning in social context involves analyzing both (1) the evolution of the communal practices in which students participate, and (2) the development of individual students' mathematical understandings as they participate in and contribute to the evolution of these classroom practices. Consequently, from this point of view, a first criterion when accounting for learning in social context is that such analyses should *focus on the mathematical development of both individual students and of the classroom communities in which they participate.*

Stated in this way, the rationale for this first criterion is primarily theoretical and reflects the assumed reflexive relation between individual activity and communal practices. In considering other criteria, it is important not to lose sight of the fact that we are mathematics educators. In other words, the issue of accounting for mathematical learning in social context should not be treated solely as an esoteric, purely theoretical problem. Instead, it should be grounded in our activity as mathematics educators who conduct highly interventionist research with the goal of contributing to current efforts to improve mathematics teaching and learning. In the case of myself and my colleagues, our work involves *developmental research* that combines the *development* of learning environments for students with classroom-based *research* into students' learning as they participate in classroom practices (Gravemeijer, 1994). This notion of developmental research, which was originally formulated by researchers and instructional designers at the Freudenthal Institute in The Netherlands, should be differentiated from both child development research and psychological research into the development of particular conceptions. The cyclical nature of developmental research is illustrated in Figure 11.1. Gravemeijer (1994) clarifies that this cycle occurs at a variety of different levels that range from moment-by-moment pedagogical decision-making in the classroom to the several-month time periods involved in using and revising a sequence of instructional activities. In making this observation, he differentiates developmental research from the traditional formative-evaluation approach of first implementing predetermined instructional activities and strategies and then subsequently evaluating their effectiveness.

Constructivism in Social Context

The first aspect of the developmental research cycle shown in Figure 11.1 involves the development of sequences of instructional activities for students as guided by a domain-specific instructional theory. In our case, the theory is that of Realistic Mathematics Education developed at the Freudenthal Institute (cf. Streefland, 1991; Treffers, 1987). Gravemeijer (1994) clarifies that the designer initially conducts an anticipatory thought experiment. In doing so, he or she envisions how students' mathematical learning might proceed as an instructional sequence is enacted in the classroom. The thought experiment therefore involves conjectures about both students' possible learning trajectories, and the specific means of supporting, organizing and guiding that development (cf. Simon, 1995). It is important to stress that these conjectures are tentative and provisional, and that they are continually tested and modified as the designer engages in classroom-based research. In this, the second aspect of the developmental research cycle, the designer attempts to make sense of what is actually happening as instructional activities are realized in interaction between a teacher and his or her students in the classroom.

It is within the setting of the developmental research cycle that the issue of accounting for students' mathematical learning in social context gains pragmatic force and ceases to be a matter of purely theoretical speculation. For example, in the case of myself and my colleagues, the research involves teaching experiments of up to a year in duration that are conducted in collaboration with classroom teachers who are members of the research and development team (cf. Cobb, in press; Confrey and Lachance, in press; Simon, in press; Yackel, 1995). After each classroom session, we usually hold a short debriefing meeting in which we discuss what happened and plan instructional activities for subsequent sessions. The ways in which we look at communal classroom practices and at individual students' activity and learning profoundly influence the instructional decisions we make and thus the instructional design process. As a consequence, the challenge of developing ways of analyzing students' mathematical learning as it occurs in social context is, for us, a pressing practical concern. Given our agenda as mathematics educators who conduct developmental research, a second criterion is therefore that such analyses *should provide feedback to inform the ongoing process of instructional development.*

In addition to conducting ongoing analyses of classroom events on a daily basis, we also video-record all classroom sessions so that we can conduct retrospective analyses of entire teaching experiments. The time frame of these analyses gives rise to further challenges. In particular, analyses that locate students' mathematical activity in social context often deal with only a few lessons, or perhaps focus on just a few minutes within one lesson. For example, I have contributed to entire papers about classroom episodes that are less than ten minutes long (e.g., Cobb et al., 1992). Detailed analyses of this type can make an important contribution to developmental research. However, the issue that I and my colleagues have been struggling with is that of stepping back from and coming to grips with what transpires in a classroom not during a ten-minute episode but over, say, a three-month time period. A third criterion that

157

arises when conducting developmental research is therefore that analyses should *document the mathematical learning of both the classroom community and of individual students over extended periods of time.*

Interpretive Framework

Thus far, I have attempted to demonstrate why the issue of accounting for mathematical learning in social context is pragmatically significant and have proposed three criteria that are relevant given the concerns of developmental research. Against this background, I now focus on the interpretive framework that has emerged from my own and my colleagues ongoing attempts to analyze classroom events. It is important to clarify that this framework does not reveal the structure of individual and collective classroom activity independently of situation and purpose. In line with Glasersfeld's instrumentalist view of knowing and understanding, the most we would claim is that we have found it useful as we have worked with teachers and their students in classrooms.

The framework, which was developed in collaboration with Erna Yackel, is shown in Figure 11.2 (cf. Cobb and Yackel, 1996). As the column headings indicate, it involves the coordination of social and psychological perspectives. The social perspective is the interactionist perspective on collective or communal classroom processes developed by Bauersfeld and his colleagues.

The psychological perspective reflects the basic tenets of constructivism as developed by Glasersfeld and involves analyzing individual students' and the teacher's interpretations and actions as they participate in and contribute to the development of communal practices. The entries in the column headed 'social perspective' – social norms, sociomathematical norms and classroom mathematical practices – refer to aspects of the classroom microculture that Yackel and I have found it useful to differentiate, given our research agenda. The corresponding entries in the column headed 'psychological perspective' refer to what, for want of better terminology, might be called their psychological correlates.

I will give an extended example taken from a year-long teaching experiment to illustrate how analyses can be organized in terms of the framework. This experiment was conducted in a first-grade classroom with 6- and 7-year-old students and focused on the development of core quantitative concepts. A series of three individual interviews conducted with all the students at the beginning, middle and end of the school year indicated that the experiment was reasonably successful by traditional standards. For example, at the beginning of the school year in September, all eighteen students typically attempted to count to solve several types of tasks with sums and minuends up to 20, their methods ranging from counting all to counting on and counting back. However, at least in the social context of the interviews, six of the students could not use their fingers as countable substitutes for other objects that were not directly accessible. For example, when the most elementary types of word problems were posed with numbers of five or less, the possibility of putting up

Constructivism in Social Context

Figure 11.2 An interpretive framework for analyzing the classroom microculture perspectives

Social perspective	Psychological perspective
Classroom social norms	Beliefs about own role, others' roles, and the general nature of mathematical activity in school
Sociomathematical norms	Mathematical beliefs and values
Classroom mathematical practices	Mathematical conceptions

fingers as substitutes for items mentioned in the problems statements did not arise for them.

In contrast to the September interviews, ten of the eighteen students used non-counting thinking strategy solutions to solve *all* of the tasks posed to them in interviews conducted in January. The following representative example illustrates solutions of this type.

> *Joe and Bob each take a handful of candy out of this jar [picture shown]. Joe gets 13 pieces and Bob gets 9 pieces. How many pieces should Joe put back to make it fair?*
> CHILD: *Oh – 4, 'cause take away 3 would make 10 and take away 1 would make 9.*

A further three students used thinking strategies to solve at least half the tasks presented, and the remaining five produced relatively sophisticated counting solutions.

One child's family had moved away from the school before the final interviews were conducted in May. Ten of the remaining seventeen students solved all of the tasks posed that involved sums and minuends up to 100 by producing relatively sophisticated incrementing and decrementing solutions. The following solution is representative:

> *Bob and Joe each take a handful of candy out of this jar [the child was shown a picture]. Joe gets 63 pieces and Bob gets 27 pieces. How many pieces should Joe put back to make it fair?*
> CHILD: *27 – 10 is 37, so 20 is 47, 30 is 57, three more – 33 – is 60, so it's 35.*

Three other students each developed several solutions of this type, and the remaining four students all produced thinking-strategy solutions at least for tasks with sums and minuends to 20.

The reason for outlining the interview results in terms of observed solution strategies is not to make claims about the instructional sequences developed in the course of the teaching experiment. The research team in fact had grave concerns about one of the instructional sequences and subsequently conducted a follow-up teaching experiment, in the course of which a radically modified sequence was developed (cf. Cobb et al., 1997; McClain et al., in press). My purpose is instead merely to illustrate that the students generally made significant progress. As a consequence, the data collected in the course of the experiment constitute an appropriate setting in which to explore ways of accounting for the process of mathematical development as it occurs in the social context of the classroom. In the following paragraphs, I outline the analysis of the first-grade teaching experiment by discussing first social norms, then sociomathematical norms, and finally classroom mathematical practices.

Social Norms

In line with the interpretive framework as illustrated in Figure 11.2, the first step in the analysis involved documenting the social norms to delineate the classroom participation structure (cf. Erickson, 1986; Lampert, 1990). This was accomplished by focusing on transcripts of five lessons distributed across the school year. The field notes of three observers who made daily observations indicated that these lessons were representative of the larger data corpus. The classroom participation structure in fact proved to be relatively stable by the midpoint of the school year, and can be summarized as follows:

- Students were obliged to explain and justify their reasoning.
- Students were obliged to listen to and attempt to understand others' explanations.
- Students were obliged to indicate non-understanding and, if possible, to ask the explainer clarifying questions.
- Students were obliged to indicate when they considered solutions invalid, and to explain the reasons for their judgment.
- The teacher was obliged to comment on or redescribe students' contributions, sometimes by notating their reasoning.

This participation structure is exemplified in the following brief exchange which occurred as the teacher and students were discussing solutions to a task corresponding to '14 − 6'. One child, Joseph, had explained that he had used a physical device called an Arithmetic Rack (cf. Treffers, 1990) that consists of two parallel rods on each of which are five white and five red beads. He said that he had made two collections of seven beads to show 14 (i.e. five red and two white beads on each rod), taken away six from one of these collections, and immediately recognized that eight beads were left.

T: *Raise your hand if you understand what Joseph said. Raise your hand if that makes sense to you. [Several students do not raise their hands.] OK, if that doesn't make sense to you, what could you ask Joseph to help you understand it?*
DARREN: *I don't understand how you started out with the 14....*
JOSEPH: *No, I did 7 and 7 equals 14, and I broke the 7 up into 6 and 1 and I had, I added the one to the 7 then it would be 8.*

Constructivism in Social Context

JAN: *I don't understand how you broke the six and one down.*
JOSEPH: *You know 7 plus 1 will make, I mean 6 plus 1 would make 7.*
JAN: *Yeah, but what about the 8?*
JOSEPH: *Oh, the 8, um I had, I had about 7. [T places an arithmetic rack on the overhead projector and makes two collections of seven beads.] See that 7 right there next to the other 7?*
[T separates one of the collections of seven into six and one.] I had that 1 right there and the 7 to make 8.
JAN: *Oh.*
T: *Joseph, you've done a really nice job explaining that. I think it might help some people if they could see what you're saying.*
[T moves beads on the arithmetic rack as Joseph explains his solution for a second time.]
JAN: *I get it. . . . That's a good way.*
T: *Thank you for your question, Jan. Darren, did you have a different way?*
DARREN: *Yeah.*
T: *Give your attention to Darren.*

As a point of clarification, the way in which the teacher used an arithmetic rack to enact Joseph's explanation can be viewed as an instance in which she notated a student's reasoning (Kaput, 1991). On other occasions, the teacher's notating involved both standard and non-standard written notation.

As shown in Figure 11.2, I take the psychological correlates of the social norms to be individual students' beliefs about their own roles, others' roles, and the general nature of mathematical activity in school. In line with the social constructivist approach I have outlined, these norms and beliefs are considered to be reflexively related. On the one hand, students actively contribute to the evolution of classroom norms as they reorganize their beliefs. On the other hand, students' participation in the norms both enables and constrains the ways in which they might reorganize their beliefs. This reflexive relation gives rise to the conjecture that in guiding the renegotiation of social norms, teachers are simultaneously supporting students' reorganization of their beliefs. This conjecture, it should be noted, is open to empirical investigation.

Sociomathematical Norms

It is apparent from the list of social norms given above that such norms are not specific to mathematics, but apply to any subject matter area. For example, one would hope that students might explain and justify their reasoning in science or history classes as well as in mathematics. The second aspect of the classroom microculture that we differentiate focuses on normative features of students' mathematical activity (Yackel and Cobb, 1996). With regard to the analysis of the first-grade classroom, one sociomathematical norm identified was that of what counts as an acceptable mathematical explanation. In the most general terms, acceptable explanations in this classroom had to be interpretable by other members of the classroom community as descriptions of actions on numerical entities. For example, in the sample episode, Joseph said, 'I did 7 and 7 equals 14, and I *broke* the 7 up into 6 and 1 and I had, I *added* the 1 to the 7 then it would be 8.' A second sociomathematical norm identified concerned what counted as a different mathematical explanation in this classroom. It appeared that solutions to additive tasks were judged as different if they involved either (1) a difference in quantitative interpretations (e.g. the task in the sample episode interpreted as $6 + \_\_ = 14$ rather than $14 - 6$), or (2) a difference in calculational processes such that numerical entities were decomposed and recomposed in different ways (e.g. a solution in which a student reasoned $14 - 4 = 10$, $10 - 2 = 8$ would be judged as different from Joseph's solution in this classroom).

Significantly, by the midpoint of the school year, various counting methods that would be judged as different by researchers (e.g. counting all versus counting on) were not judged as different. Instead, all such solutions were simply described as counting. This observation highlights our claim that what counts as a different explanation can vary markedly from one classroom to another, and that these variations can profoundly influence the mathematical understandings that students develop.

The third sociomathematical norm identified concerns what counted as an insightful mathematical solution. It is important to clarify that, by the midpoint of the school year, the teacher responded differentially to students' contributions, and that in doing so she indicated that she particularly valued what she and the students called grouping solutions. A detailed analysis of the teacher's proactive role in supporting the students' learning indicates that this was an important facet of her effectiveness in supporting her students' learning (McClain, 1995). In particular, it enabled the students to become aware of more sophisticated forms of mathematical reasoning, thereby making it possible for their problem solving efforts to have a sense of directionality (cf. Voigt, 1995). In accomplishing this, however, the teacher continued to accept and actively solicited counting solutions from students whom she judged were not yet able to develop grouping solutions. In doing so, she actively managed the tension between proactively supporting the evolution of classroom mathematical practices and ensuring that all students had a way to participate in those practices. Classroom observations indicate that she was generally successful in this regard (Cobb et al., 1997).

As is shown in Figure 11.2, we take students' specifically mathematical beliefs and values to be the psychological correlates of the sociomathematical norms. Elsewhere, we have argued that the process of supporting students' development of intellectual autonomy in the classroom involves guiding the renegotiation of sociomathematical norms (Yackel and Cobb, 1996). Thus, although it has not been our primary focus, we have necessarily had to address issues of ethics in the course of our work in classrooms (cf. Gash, Ch. 7; Kieren, Ch. 6; Larochelle, Ch. 5; Lewin, Ch. 4). More generally, we conjecture that in guiding the renegotiation of these norms, teachers are simultaneously supporting students' reorganization of the beliefs and values that constitute what might be called their mathematical dispositions. Once again, this conjecture is open to empirical investigation.

Classroom Mathematical Practices

The third aspect of the interpretive framework concerns the mathematical practices established by the classroom community and their psychological correlates, individual students' mathematical interpretations and actions. The objective when analyzing the evolution of classroom mathematical practices is to trace the mathematical development of the classroom community against the backdrop of the social and sociomathematical norms. We have in fact analyzed all 103 lessons that were video-recorded in the course of the teaching experiment (Cobb et al., 1997; Gravemeijer et al., in press; McClain, 1995; McClain and Cobb, in press; Whitenack, 1995). However, for illustrative purposes, I will focus on one short instructional sequence called the 'Candy Shop' that was enacted during twelve lessons midway through the school year. In traditional terms, the instructional intent of this sequence might be described as that of supporting students' development of initial understandings of place value numeration. However, given that our focus during the teaching experiment was on the quality of students' mathematical experiences (cf. Glasersfeld, Ch. 1) rather than on their acquisition of a list of topics institutionalized in textbook curricula, we found it useful to cast the instructional intent in terms of Greeno's (1991) environmental metaphor. Described in this way, the intent was that the students would eventually come to act in a mathematical environment in which numerical quantities are *invariant* under certain transformations (e.g. ten units of one taken together to make a single unit of ten). For example, in such an environment, 42 is the same quantity whether it is structured as 4 tens and 2 ones, as 3 tens and 12 ones, or as 1 ten and 32 ones. Needless to say, coming to act in such an environment is a major intellectual achievement for young children and requires proactive instructional support.

Mathematical practice I: Counting by tens and ones

At the beginning of the instructional sequence, the teacher introduced the anchoring scenario by developing a narrative with her students about a character called Mrs Wright who owned a candy shop. In the course of these initial discussions, the teacher and students established the convention of packing candies into rolls of ten. The first mathematical practice identified was that of counting by tens and ones to evaluate collections of candies. For example, in one of the first instructional activities, the teacher gave the students bags of lose unifix cubes and asked them to act as packers in the candy shop. Before

Paul Cobb

they began, however, the students were asked to estimate how many rolls of ten they thought they would make. This served to orient them to enumerate the candies/unifix cubes as they packed them. In a subsequent instructional activity, the teacher used an overhead projector to show the students a pictured collection of rolls and individual candies and asked them to figure out how many candies there were in all. In both these instructional activities and in others, solutions in which students first counted rolls by ten and then individual candies by one became routine and beyond need of justification.

The emergence of this first mathematical practice indicates that a practice does not necessarily correspond to a particular type of instructional activity but can instead cut across several activities. It is also important to clarify that the actual process of emergence typically involves a process of explicit negotiation. For example, several students participated in the first instructional activity described above in which they acted as packers in the candy shop by counting rolls by ten, 10, 20, 30, ..., 80, but then said that they had made 80 rolls. In contrast, other students counted in the same way but said that they had made eight rolls that contained 80 candies. In terms of Steffe et al.'s (1988) psychological analysis of early number development, one can speculate that the students who said they had made 80 rolls counted bars of ten unifix cubes as numerical composites of ten (i.e. each roll was a collection of ten units of one but not a single unit of ten itself composed of ones). In contrast, the bars of cubes may have been composite units of ten for the students who counted them by ten but said that they had made eight rolls that contained 80 candies. Given the intent of the instructional sequence, a mathematically significant issue therefore emerged as the teacher orchestrated discussions in the course of which students questioned each other's interpretations. An analysis of the actual process by which the practice of counting by tens and ones emerged would involve a detailed microanalysis of these discussions. It is in this regard that microanalyses of moment-by-moment interactions can play an important role in developmental research.

Mathematical practice II: Grouping ten candies mentally

A second mathematical practice emerged as the teacher and students continued to discuss solutions to tasks that involved pictured collections of rolls and candies. One task presented was:

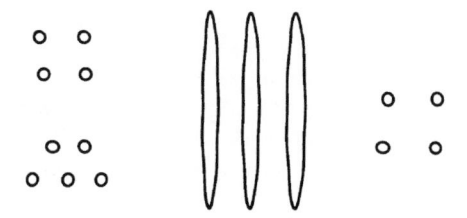

Constructivism in Social Context

The reasoning of the first student who gave an explanation, Casey, proved to be difficult for the teacher and other students to follow. However, he appeared mentally to group ten individual candies together.

T: *How did you figure it out, Casey?*
CASEY: *Well, I knew there was 13 pieces not counting the rolls, all those pieces that are loose,*
T: *OK.*
CASEY: *And then those three rolls make 30 and if you go up and I got past 10, and I got to 13, so I got past 30, and then I knew if you added 10 and 3, and I used up two of those, I mean three of those (points towards the screen from his position sitting on the floor). You have 30, and you add the 10, you used up the 10 on the 30 and then you had 3 left and that made 43.*

Casey's subsequent clarifications indicate that when he spoke of 'using up a 10 on the 30', he probably meant that if he counted ten more from 30 he would complete the 30s decade and have 40, and that three more would be 43. Thus, his reasoning seemed to be counting-based even though he did not actually count the 10 individual candies but instead anticipated the results of counting.

Not surprisingly, the teacher asked Casey to repeat his explanation.

T: *OK, come [to the overhead projector screen] and point to the 30 you're talking about. Pay close attention, I heard somebody say they didn't really understand.*
CASEY: *[Goes to the screen] Here's the 30.*
T: *OK, he pointed to these three rolls, that's 30 pieces.*
CASEY: *And then I have 5 and 5 [points to a group of 5 candies, and to groups of 4 and 1 candies], and that used up the 30 because it made 10 and I got 40, and then I have 3 left and then I have 40, and then it's 43.*

The teacher then began to redescribe his solution, possibly to verify her interpretation with him.

T: *Casey, you said this was 30 [writes 30 beneath the rolls]. Then you have 5 here [circles a group of 5 candies].*
CASEY: *Yes.*
T: *Then you had [circles a group of four candies] . . .*
CASEY: *Four, and then that 1 over there made 5. [T circles the candy he points to.] So that's 10. I used up that 30 right there, I used up that 30 with 10, you see 30 is a whole entire 10 almost, it's not really a whole entire 10 – after 39 comes 40 and that used up the 10.*
T: *So there's the 30 that he used [points]. Now does everybody see the 10 that he used? He had 5 there, and then you saw he had 4 and 1 more made another 5. So did you add the 5 and 5 to make 10?*
CASEY: *Yes.*
T: *So then you had 30 plus 10 and that got you up to 40.*
CASEY: *Yes.*

165

Paul Cobb

> T: *And then you still had these 3 more [circles the group of 3 candies] made 43.*
> CASEY: *Yes.*

In the course of this exchange, the teacher appeared to accommodate to Casey's way of speaking, saying 'there's the 30 that he used'. However, in doing so, she assumed that Casey was referring to the three pictured rolls when he in fact seemed to be referring to the 30s decade. Thus, there was a subtle difference in their individual interpretations in that Casey's reasoning seemed to be counting-based but the teacher redescribed his solution in the collection-based terms of adding first a collection of ten candies and then three more (cf. Cobb and Wheatley, 1988; Fuson, 1992). Nonetheless, Casey and the teacher communicated effectively as the exchange continued and each remained unaware of the disparities in their individual interpretations. Consequently, the initial emergence of the second mathematical practice involved a process of both explicit and implicit negotiation. I note in passing that it is in order to account for communicative interactions of this type that I and my colleagues speak of *taken-as-shared* rather than *shared* interpretations. The notion of a taken-as-shared interpretation implies that individual interpretations fit for the purposes at hand but does not imply that they necessarily match (cf. Cobb et al., 1992; Glasersfeld, 1983).

As the sample episode continued, several other students indicated that they did not understand Casey's reasoning.

> JAN: *I don't understand about the 4 and the 1.*
> T: *It's like this Jan. Pretend like this 1 is right there instead of right there [draws a candy next to the group of four and crosses out the candy she had previously circled]. Then what would you have [points to the groups of five and four]?*
> JAN: *Ten.*
> T: *Is that what you were thinking about Casey?*
> CASEY: *Yes.*
> T: *Pretending that this one ...*
> JAN: *Oh, I know what it is.*
> CASEY: *If you have 5, 5, is 10; 30, use up the 30, then you get 40, then you use this 3, 43.*

Casey's comment, '30, use up the 30, then you get 40', indicates that he had interpreted the teacher's comments in counting-based terms throughout the episode, while she had interpreted his reasoning in collection-based terms. The succinctness of Casey's final explanation when compared with his initial attempts to explain his reasoning illustrates that this exchange in which he and the teacher mutually adapted to each other's activity had been productive for him. He seemed to assume that his interpretation of the task was now self-evident and that he only needed to explain the calculational processes.

In the remainder of this lesson and in subsequent lessons, the act of mentally grouping ten pictured candies became an established classroom mathematical practice that was beyond justification. The teacher for her part indicated that such solutions were particularly valued. For example, after several students had explained their solutions to the following task, she asked, 'Is there another way that you could group to figure out 93?'

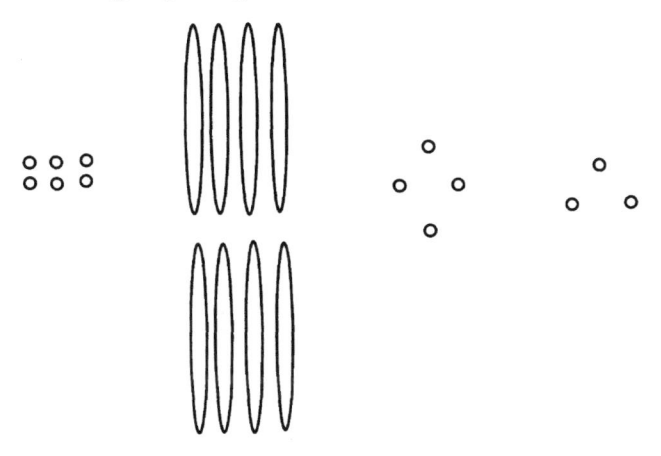

BOB: (*Walks to the screen.*) *I think it's 93 because I took this 6 [points] and I broke it up and I took 1 away and I put it with the 4 [points] to make 5 and 5, to make 10, and I knew that was 80, so it would be 90, and then 93.*

Bob's explanation indicates that, in contrast to Casey, his reasoning was collection-based. Thus, there was a significant difference in the two students' thinking even as they contributed to the development of the same mathematical practice. As Bob described his solution, the teacher indicated that she particularly valued it by writing the following arithmetical sentences to record it:

$$4 \quad 6$$
$$80 + 10 = 90$$
$$90 + 3 = 93$$

In addition, the protracted discussion of Casey's solution had also implicitly served to legitimize reasoning of this type.

It can be noted in passing that a full explanation of the emergence of this practice would have to take account of the students' participation in the practices that had been previously established by the classroom community. For example, Casey and Bob both immediately recognized a grouping of ten individual candies as five and five. This, in all probability, reflects their prior participation in practices involving the Arithmetic Rack that were established during the first part of the school year. More generally, it is essential when analyzing classroom mathematical practices to document how one practice evolves from previously established practices. Only then does the analysis describe the *process* of the classroom community's mathematical development.

Paul Cobb

Mathematical practice III: Generating alternative partitionings

The third mathematical practice identified during the 'Candy Shop' sequence emerged when the teacher introduced a new type of instructional activity in which the students generated different partitionings of a given collection of candies. The teacher explained that Mrs Wright was interrupted as she packed candies into rolls.

> T: *What if Mrs Wright had 43 pieces of candy, and she is working on packing them into rolls. What are different ways that she might have 43 pieces of candy, how many rolls and how many pieces might she have? Sarah, what's one way she might find it?*

The students, as a group, were able to generate the various possibilities with little apparent difficulty.

> SARAH: *Four rolls and three pieces.*
> ELLEN: *Forty-three pieces.*
> KENDRA: *She might have two rolls and 23 pieces.*
> DARREN: *She could have three rolls, 12 pieces, I mean 13 pieces.*
> LINDA: *One roll and 33 pieces.*

The teacher for her part recorded each of their suggestions on the whiteboard as follows:

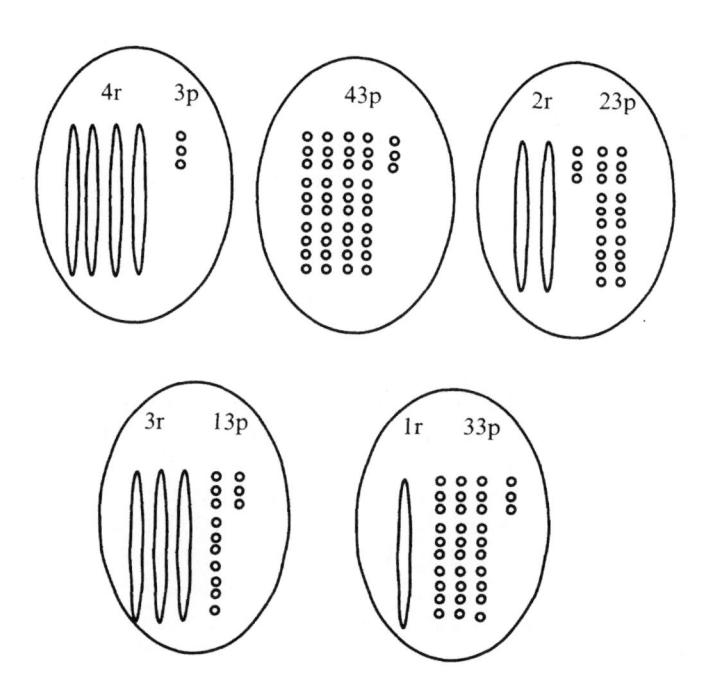

Constructivism in Social Context

Previously, the students had participated in the first and second mathematical practices by evaluating pictured collections of candies. Now, however, the teacher drew pictured collections to record the results of their reasoning as they generated alternative partitionings. It is this contrast and the fact that such reasoning was beyond justification that leads me to treat the activity of generating alternative partitionings as a distinct mathematical practice. At this point in the episode, one of the students, Karen, volunteered:

KAREN: *Well see, we've done all the ways. We had 43 pieces . . . [walks to the whiteboard].*
T: *OK.*
KAREN: *And, see, we had 43 pieces [points to 43p] and right here we have none rolls, and right here we have one roll [points to 1r 33p].*
T: *OK, I'm going to number these, there's one way . . . no rolls [writes '0' next to 43p].*
KAREN: *And there's one roll, there's two rolls, then there's three, and there's four.*
T: *(Numbers the corresponding pictures 1, 2, 3, 4.)*

Most of the students seemed to take the need to order the configurations as self-evident, and a second student proposed an alternative scheme for numbering the pictures. The discussion during the remainder of the session then focused on the merits of different ways of organizing and labeling the configurations.

Summary

This necessarily brief account of the mathematical practices that emerged during the 'Candy Shop' sequence can be summarized as follows:

- counting by tens and ones to evaluate collections of candies;
- grouping ten candies mentally when evaluating collections;
- generating alternative partitionings of a given collection of candies.

With regard to the intent of the instructional sequence, we, as observers, can see in this sequence of mathematical practices the initial emergence of the invariance of quantity under certain transformations. In particular, the students' reasoning as they participated in the third mathematical practice indicates that it was, for them, self-evident that the number of candies remained unchanged when rolls were unpacked and when individual candies were packed into rolls. It can therefore reasonably be argued that the learning of the classroom community as documented by the evolving sequence of practices was mathematically significant.

As a further point, it is again important to stress that an analysis of mathematical practices does not merely involve listing a series of activities, methods or strategies. The analysis also has to sketch the collective developmental

Paul Cobb

route of the classroom community by indicating how one practice might have emerged from others. For example, consider again Bob's reasoning when he evaluated a collection of eight rolls and 13 candies:

BOB: *I think it's 93 because I took this 6 [points] and I broke it up and I took 1 away and I put it with the 4 [points] to make 5 and 5, to make 10, and I knew that was 80, so it would be 90, and then 93.*

Here, in reasoning, '80, so it would be 90, and then 93', Bob in effect established nine units of 10 and three units of 1 as an alternative to 93 organized as 8 tens and 13 ones. This, of course, is not to say that he consciously related these alternative partitionings. Instead, the relationship was implicit in his activity as he participated in the second mathematical practice. As the third mathematical practice emerged, what was previously implicit in students' socially situated activity became an explicit topic of conversation. This example is paradigmatic in that it illustrates that an analysis of a classroom community's learning should explain how the activity of participating in a particular practice emerged as a reorganization of the activity of participating in prior practices.

Reflections

My purpose in the following paragraphs is to step back from the specific analysis of the 'Candy Shop' sequence to make three more general points. The first is to clarify the contribution of analyses that focus on the mathematical practices established by a classroom community. To this end, imagine that at the end of the school year we had interviewed not only the students in the teaching experiment classroom but also those from another first-grade classroom in the same school. I am sure that if we shuffled the video-recordings of these interviews, the reader would almost unerringly be able to identify the classroom from which each student came. It is precisely this contrast between the mathematical activity of the two *groups* of students that is accounted for in terms of participation in the differing mathematical practices established in the two classrooms.

To continue the thought experiment, suppose that we now focus on only the students in the teaching experiment classroom. The contrast set is then not one group of students as compared to another, but is instead the activity of other students in the same classroom community. This comparison brings to the fore differences in the reasoning of students who had participated in the same classroom mathematical practices. It is here that psychological analyses of the individual students' diverse ways of participating in these practices are needed in order to account for qualitative differences in mathematical reasoning within the classroom community. In a recently completed teaching experiment, we were in fact able to document several individual students' activity on an

Constructivism in Social Context

ongoing basis and are currently conducting longitudinal analyses of the process of their mathematical development as they participated in and contributed to the evolving classroom mathematical practices (Stephan, 1998).

The second more general point is to note that in documenting the evolving mathematical practices, we have in effect documented the 'Candy Shop' sequence as it was realized in interaction in the classroom. However, the students' participation in these practices also constituted the immediate social situation in which they learned by constructing increasingly sophisticated mathematical understandings. As a consequence, the analysis also documents the evolving social situation of their mathematical development. We therefore have the following situation:

Figure 11.3 Relations between mathematical practices, instructional sequences and social situation of development

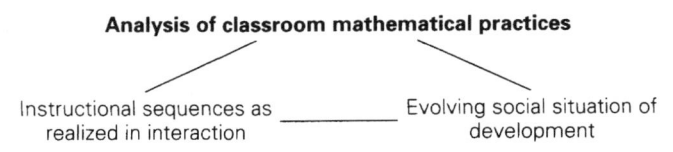

```
            Analysis of classroom mathematical practices
                    /                           \
Instructional sequences as  _____  Evolving social situation of
   realized in interaction                     development
```

These interrelations are encouraging in that they bring together the two general aspects of developmental research – instructional development and classroom-based research (see Figure 11.1). This indicates that analyses of classroom mathematical practices might make it possible to develop a common language in which to talk both about instructional design and about individual and collective mathematical development in the classroom. One of the attractive features of such an approach is that it offers an alternative to the traditional metaphor of mathematics as content. The content metaphor entails the notion that mathematics is placed in the container of the curriculum, which then serves as the primary vehicle for making mathematics accessible to students. In contrast, an analysis of the mathematical practices established by a classroom community characterizes what is typically called content in emergent terms. In the case of the 'Candy Shop' sequence, for example, a significant mathematical idea, that of the invariance of numerical quantities under certain transformations, emerged gradually as the collective practices of the classroom community evolved. It should be acknowledged that the shift from the *content metaphor* to the *emergence metaphor* involves a major change of paradigm. However, the emergent view has the merit of highlighting individual students' constructive efforts while treating mathematics as a socially and culturally situated human activity. This suggests that it is an approach that is worth pursuing.

The final more general point concerns the role of symbols and other tools in mathematical learning. It should be apparent from the sample analysis that ways of symbolizing do not stand apart from classroom mathematical practices but are instead integral aspects of both the practices and of the activity of the students who participate in them. Consider, for example, the third mathematical practice in which the teacher drew pictures to record alternative partitionings

Paul Cobb

of 43 candies. I do not have any direct information on the individual students' reasoning as they participated in this exchange. However, it seems reasonable to speculate that some of the students might have reasoned with the pictures as they generated alternative possibilities. For example, some of them might have imagined breaking one or more rolls in a pictured collection into ten individual candies, or they might have imagined packing ten pictured candies into a roll. The latter possibility is particularly plausible given the students' prior participation in the second mathematical practice, that of mentally grouping ten individual candies.

Given these considerations, it seems self-evident that the ways of symbolizing established in the teaching-experiment classroom profoundly influenced both the mathematical understandings the students developed and the process by which they developed them. It is in fact possible to trace the evolution of ways of symbolizing:

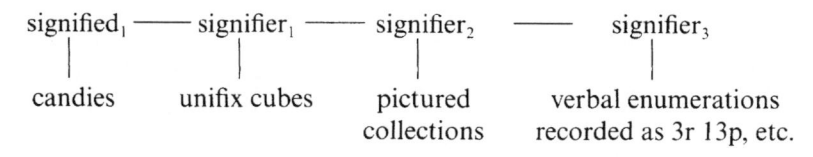

$$\text{signified}_1 \longrightarrow \text{signifier}_1 \longrightarrow \text{signifier}_2 \longrightarrow \text{signifier}_3$$

$$\text{candies} \quad \text{unifix cubes} \quad \text{pictured collections} \quad \substack{\text{verbal enumerations} \\ \text{recorded as 3r 13p, etc.}}$$

In Walkerdine's (1988) terms, one can speak of a chain of signification emerging as the mathematical practices evolved. Walkerdine notes that succeeding signifiers may initially be established as substitutes for preceding terms, with the assumption that the sense of those terms is preserved through the links of the chain. For example, pictured collections were initially introduced as substitutes for collections of candies/unifix cubes. However, Walkerdine goes on to argue that the original sign combination (i.e. candies/unifix cubes) is not merely concealed behind succeeding signifiers. Instead, the meaning of this sign combination evolves as the chain is constituted. Walkerdine's fundamental contention is that a sign combination that originates in a particular practice *slides under* succeeding signifiers that originate in other practices motivated by different concerns and interests. In the case of the 'Candy Shop' sequence, for example, the meaning of the candies/unifix cubes sign combination was initially constituted within a narrative about Mrs Wright's candy shop. The concerns and interests in this instance were those of a simulated buying and selling activity. Later, the concerns and interests were primarily mathematical and involved structuring collections of candies in different ways. When the students participated in the third mathematical practice, rolls of ten candies instantiated units of ten of some type, and the activity of packing candies by making bars of ten unifix cubes had been displaced by that of mentally creating and decomposing such units. In a very real sense, they were no longer the same candies that the students had acted with as when they participated in the first mathematical practice.

The process of signs sliding under succeeding signifiers can be schematized as follows by modifying the preceding diagram of signifiers:

Figure 11.4 Chain of signification for the sample instructional sequence

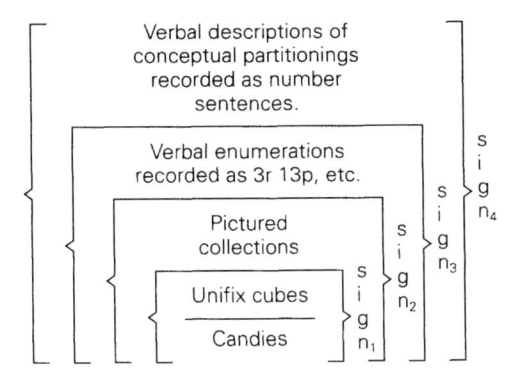

```
                    ┌─────────────────────┐
                    │ Verbal descriptions  │
                    │ of conceptual        │
                    │ partitionings        │
                    │ recorded as number   │
                    │ sentences.           │
                  ┌─┴─────────────────────┤
                  │ Verbal enumerations   │      s
                  │ recorded as 3r 13p,   │      i
                  │ etc.                  │  s   g
                ┌─┴───────────────────┐   i   n₄
                │ Pictured            │   g
                │ collections         │ s n₃
              ┌─┴─────────────────┐   i
              │ Unifix cubes      │ s g
              ├───────────────────┤ i n₂
              │ Candies           │ g
              └───────────────────┘ n₁
```

This, in sociolinguistic terms, is an account of the process of mathematization. It should of course be stressed that the symbols themselves do not, in and of themselves, have any particular magic. Instead, the focus of this account is on ways of symbolizing – on symbols as integral aspects of individual and collective activity. Viewed in broader terms, accounts of this type help move the debate beyond that of attempting to determine whether concepts or symbols are primary. Signification and the development of mathematical understanding are instead seen to be intimately related in that mathematical activity even at the most elementary level involves reasoning with symbols wherein one thing is taken to stand for another.

Conclusion

In this chapter, I have illustrated an analytical approach that locates students' mathematical development in social context while simultaneously treating learning as an active, constructive process. In contrast to theoretical approaches that give primacy to social processes, I have characterized the relation between individual students' mathematical activity and the communal classroom practices in which they participate as one of reflexivity. I would therefore question an account that spoke of classroom mathematical practices first being established, and then somehow causing students to reorganize their mathematical understandings. Similarly, I would question an account that spoke of students first reorganizing their understandings and then contributing to the establishment of new practices. The theoretical position inherent in the interpretive framework and in the sample analysis is one that focuses on both individual students' activity and on the social worlds in which they participate without attempting to derive one from the other. From this point of view, individual students are seen to contribute to the evolution of classroom mathematical practices as they reorganize their mathematical understandings. Conversely, their participation in those practices is seen to both enable and constrain the ways in which they reorganize their understandings.

In this analytical approach, the process of coordinating psychological and social analyses is not merely a matter of somehow pasting a psychological analysis on to a separate social analysis. Instead, when conducting a psychological analysis, one analyzes individual students' activity *as they participate in the practices of the classroom community*. Further, when conducting a social analysis, one focuses on communal practices *that are continually generated by and do not exist apart from the activities of the participating individuals*. The coordination at the heart of the interpretive framework is therefore not that between individuals and a community viewed as separate, sharply defined entities. Instead, the coordination is between different ways of looking at and making sense of what is going on in classrooms. What, from one perspective, is seen as a single classroom community is, from the other, seen as a number of interacting individuals actively interpreting each others' actions. Thus, the central coordination is between our own ways of interpreting classroom events. Whitson (1997) clarifies this point when he suggests that we think of ourselves as viewing human processes in the classroom, with the realization that these processes can be described in either social or psychological terms. Throughout this chapter, I have attempted to illustrate that both these perspectives are relevant to the concerns and interests of mathematics educators who engage in classroom-based developmental research. The interpretive framework I have outlined represents one way of coordinating perspectives that draws on Glasersfeld's foundational contributions to constructivism and on recent developments in interactionist theory.

Note

1 The general theoretical analysis reported in this paper was supported by the Office of Educational Research and Improvement under grant number R305A60007. The analysis of the sample instructional sequence was supported by the National Science Foundation under grant number RED-9353587. The opinions expressed do not necessarily reflect the views of either OERI or the Foundation.

References

BAUERSFELD, H. (1988) 'Interaction, construction, and knowledge: Alternative perspectives for mathematics education', in COONEY, T. and GROUWS, D. (eds), *Effective Mathematics Teaching*, Reston, VA: National Council of Teachers of Mathematics and Lawrence Erlbaum, pp. 29–46.

BAUERSFELD, H. (1993) *Teachers Pre- and In-Service Education for Mathematics Teaching*, Montréal: University of Québec, Cahier du CIRADE no 78 (March).

BAUERSFELD, H., KRUMMHEUER, G. and VOIGT, J. (1988) 'Interactional theory of learning and teaching mathematics and related microethnographical studies', in STEINER, H.G. and VERMANDEL, A. (eds), *Foundations and Methodology of the Discipline of Mathematics Education*, Antwerp: Proceedings of the TME Conference, pp. 174–88.

BERNSTEIN, R.J. (1983) *Beyond Objectivism and Relativism: Science, Hermeneutics, and Praxis*, Philadelphia: University of Pennsylvania Press.

BISHOP, A.J. (1988) *Mathematical Enculturation: A Cultural Perspective on Mathematics Education*, Dordrecht: Kluwer.

BLUMER, H. (1969) *Symbolic Interactionism: Perspectives and Method*, Englewood Cliffs, NJ: Prentice Hall.

COBB, P. (1989) 'Experiential, cognitive, and anthropological perspectives in mathematics education', *For the Learning of Mathematics*, **9**, 2, pp. 32–42.

COBB, P. (1994) 'Where is the mind? Constructivist and sociocultural perspectives on mathematical development', *Educational Researcher*, **23**, 7, pp. 13–20.

COBB, P. (in press) 'Conducting classroom teaching experiments in collaboration with teachers', in LESH, R. and KELLY, E. (eds), *New Methodologies in Mathematics and Science Education*, Mahwah, NJ: Lawrence Erlbaum.

COBB, P. and BAUERSFELD, H. (1995) 'Introduction: The coordination of psychological and sociological perspectives in mathematics education', in COBB, P. and BAUERSFELD, H. (eds), *Emergence of Mathematical Meanings: Interaction in Classroom Cultures*, Hillsdale, NJ: Lawrence Erlbaum, pp. 1–16.

COBB, P., GRAVEMEIJER, K., YACKEL, E., MCCLAIN, K. and WHITENACK, J. (1997) 'Mathematizing and symbolizing: The emergence of chains of signification in one first-grade classroom', in KIRSHNER, D. and WHITSON, J.A. (eds), *Situated Cognition Theory: Social, Semiotic, and Neurological Perspectives*, Mahwah, NJ: Lawrence Erlbaum, pp. 151–233.

COBB, P. and WHEATLEY, G. (1988) 'Children's initial understandings of ten', *Focus on Learning Problems in Mathematics*, **10**, 3, pp. 1–28.

COBB, P., WOOD, T. and YACKEL, E. (1992) 'Learning and interaction in classroom situations', *Educational Studies in Mathematics*, 23, pp. 99–122.

COBB, P. and YACKEL, E. (1996) 'Constructivist, emergent, and sociocultural perspectives in the context of developmental research', *Educational Psychologist*, 31, pp. 175–90.

CONFREY, J. (1990) 'A review of the research on student conceptions in mathematics, science, and programming', in CAZDEN, C.B. (ed.), *Review of Research in Education*, Washington, D.C.: American Educational Research Association, 16, pp. 3–55.

CONFREY, J. (1995) 'How compatible are radical constructivism, sociocultural approaches, and social constructivism?' in STEFFE, L.P. and GALE, J. (eds), *Constructivism in Education*, Hillsdale, NJ: Lawrence Erlbaum, pp. 185–225.

CONFREY, J. and LACHANCE, A. (in press) 'A research design model for conjecture-driven teaching experiments', in LESH, R. and KELLY, E. (eds), *New Methodologies in Mathematics and Science Education*, Mahwah, NJ: Lawrence Erlbaum.

CONFREY, J. and SMITH, E. (1995) 'Splitting, covariation, and their role in the development of exponential functions', *Journal for Research in Mathematics Education*, 26, pp. 66–86.

DEWEY, J. (1981) 'Experience and nature', in BOYDSTON, J.A. (ed.), *John Dewey: The Later Works, 1925–1953* (Vol. 1), Carbondale: Southern Illinois University Press.

ERICKSON, F. (1986) 'Qualitative methods in research on teaching', in WITTROCK, M.C. (ed.), *The Handbook of Research on Teaching* (3rd edn), New York: Macmillan, pp. 119–61.

FUSON, K.C. (1992) 'Research on whole number addition and subtraction', in GROUWS, D.A. (ed.), *Handbook of Research on Mathematics Teaching and Learning*, New York: Macmillan, pp. 243–75.

GLASERSFELD, E. VON (1978) 'Radical constructivism and Piaget's concept of knowledge', in MURRAY, F.B. (ed.), *Impact of Piagetian Theory*, Baltimore, MD: University Park Press, pp. 109–22.

GLASERSFELD, E. VON (1983) 'On the concept of interpretation', *Poetics*, 12, pp. 207–18.

GLASERSFELD, E. VON (1987) 'Learning as a constructive activity', in JANVIER, C. (ed.), *Problems of Representation in the Teaching and Learning of Mathematics*, Hillsdale, NJ: Lawrence Erlbaum, pp. 3–18.

GLASERSFELD, E. VON (1989) 'Constructivism', in HUSEN, T. and POSTLETHWAITE, T.N. (eds), *The International Encyclopedia of Education* (1st edn, supplement. Vol. 1), Oxford: Pergamon, pp. 162–3.

GLASERSFELD, E. VON (1991) 'Abstraction, re-presentation, and reflection: An interpretation of experience and Piaget's approach', in STEFFE, L.P. (ed.), *Epistemological Foundations of Mathematical Experience*, New York: Springer, pp. 45–67.

GLASERSFELD, E. VON (1992) 'Constructivism reconstructed: A reply to Suchting', *Science and Education*, 1, pp. 379–84.

GRAVEMEIJER, K.E.P. (1994) *Developing Realistic Mathematics Education*, Utrecht: CD-b Press.

GRAVEMEIJER, K., COBB, P., BOWERS, J. and WHITENACK, J. (in press) 'Symbolizing, modeling, and instructional design', in COBB, P., YACKEL, E. and MCCLAIN, K. (eds), *Symbolizing and Communicating in Mathematics Classrooms: Perspectives on Discourse, Tools, and Instructional Design*, Mahwah, NJ: Lawrence Erlbaum.

GREENO, J.G. (1991) 'Number sense as situated knowing in a conceptual domain', *Journal for Research in Mathematics Education*, 22, pp. 170–218.

KAPUT, J.J. (1991) 'Notations and representations as mediators of constructive processes', in GLASERSFELD, E. VON (ed.), *Constructivism in Mathematics Education*, Dordrecht: Kluwer, pp. 53–74.

LAMPERT, M. (1990) 'When the problem is not the question and the solution is not the answer: Mathematical knowing and teaching', *American Educational Research Journal*, 27, pp. 29–63.

LERMAN, S. (1996) 'Intersubjectivity in mathematics learning: A challenge to the radical constructivist paradigm'? *Journal for Research in Mathematics Education*, 27, pp. 133–50.

MCCLAIN, K.J. (1995) The teacher's proactive role in supporting students' mathematical growth', unpublished doctoral dissertation, Vanderbilt University, Nashville, TN.

MCCLAIN, K. and COBB, P. (in press) 'Patterning and partitioning: Early number concepts', in COPLEY, J. (ed.), *Mathematics in the Early Years (2000 Yearbook of the National Council of Teachers of Mathematics)*, Reston, VA: National Council of Teachers of Mathematics.

MCCLAIN, K., COBB, P., GRAVEMEIJER, K. and ESTES, B. (1999) 'Developing mathematical reasoning within the context of measurement', in STIFF, L. (ed.), *Developing Mathematical Reasoning (1999 Yearbook of the National Council of Teachers of Mathematics)*, Reston, VA: National Council of Teachers of Mathematics, pp. 93–106.

MEHAN, H. and WOOD, H. (1975) *The Reality of Ethnomethodology*, New York: John Wiley.

NICKSON, M. (1992) 'The culture of mathematics: An unknown quantity?', in GROUWS, D.A. (ed.), *Handbook of Research on Mathematics Teaching and Learning*, New York: Macmillan, pp. 101–15.

NUNES, T. (1992) 'Ethnomathematics and everyday cognition', in GROUWS, D.A. (ed.), *Handbook of Research on Mathematics Teaching and Learning*, New York: Macmillan, pp. 557–74.

PIRIE, S. and KIEREN, T. (1994) 'Growth in mathematical understanding: How can we characterise it and how can we represent it?', *Educational Studies in Mathematics*, 26, pp. 61–86.
PUTNAM, H. (1987) *The Many Faces of Realism*, LaSalle: Open Court.
RORTY, R. (1982) *Consequences of Pragmatism*, Minneapolis: University of Minnesota Press.
SFARD, A. (1994a) 'The Development of the Concept of Concept Development: From God's Eye View to What Can Be Seen With the Mind's Eye, paper presented at the Symposium on Trends and Perspectives in Mathematics Education, Klagenfurt, Austria (September).
SFARD, A. (1994b) 'Reification as a birth of a metaphor', *For the Learning of Mathematics*, 14, 1, pp. 44–55.
SIMON, M.A. (1995) 'Reconstructing mathematics pedagogy from a constructivist perspective', *Journal for Research in Mathematics Education*, 26, pp. 114–45.
SIMON, M.A. (in press) 'Research on mathematics teacher development: The teacher development experiment', in LESH, R. and KELLY, E. (eds), *New Methodologies in Mathematics and Science Education*, Mahwah, NJ: Lawrence Erlbaum.
STEFFE, L.P. (1996) 'Social-cultural approaches in early childhood mathematics education: A discussion', in MANSFIELD, H., PATEMAN, N. and BEDNARZ, N. (eds), *Mathematics for Tomorrow's Young Children*, Dordrecht: Kluwer, pp. 79–99.
STEFFE, L.P., COBB, P. and GLASERSFELD, E. VON (1988) *Construction of Arithmetical Meanings and Strategies*, New York: Springer.
STEFFE, L.P. and WIEGEL, H.P. (1994) 'Cognitive play and mathematical learning in computer microworlds', *Educational Studies in Mathematics*, 26, pp. 111–34.
STEPHAN, M. (1998) 'Supporting the development of one first-grade classroom's conceptions of measurement: Analyzing students' learning in social context', unpublished doctoral dissertation, Vanderbilt University, Nashville, TN.
STREEFLAND, L. (1991) *Fractions in Realistic Mathematics Education: A Paradigm of Developmental Research*, Dordrecht: Kluwer.
THOMPSON, P.W. (1994) 'Images of rate and operational understanding of the Fundamental Theorem of Calculus', *Educational Studies in Mathematics*, 26, pp. 229–74.
TREFFERS, A. (1987) *Three Dimensions: A Model of Goal and Theory Description in Mathematics Instruction – The Wiskobas Project*, Dordrecht: Reidel.
TREFFERS, A. (1990) 'Rekentot twintig met het rekenrek' ('Addition and subtraction up to twenty with the arithmetic rack') *Willem Bartjens*, 10, 1, pp. 35–45.
VOIGT, J. (1985) 'Patterns and routines in classroom interaction', *Recherches en Didactique des Mathématiques*, 6, pp. 69–118.
VOIGT, J. (1994) 'Negotiation of mathematical meaning and learning mathematics', *Educational Studies in Mathematics*, 26, 2–3, pp. 273–98.
VOIGT, J. (1995) 'Thematic patterns of interaction and sociomathematical norms', in COBB, P. and BAUERSFELD, H. (eds), *Emergence of Mathematical Meaning: Interaction in Classroom Cultures*, Hillsdale, NJ: Lawrence Erlbaum, pp. 163–201.
VOIGT, J. (1996) 'Negotiation of mathematical meaning in classroom processes', in STEFFE, L.P., NESHER, P., COBB, P., GOLDIN, G. and GREER, B. (eds), *Theories of Mathematical Learning*, Hillsdale, NJ: Lawrence Erlbaum, pp. 21–50.
WALKERDINE, V. (1988) *The Mastery of Reason*, London: Routledge.
WHITENACK, J.W. (1995) 'Modeling, mathematizing, and mathematical learning as it is situated in the classroom microculture', unpublished doctoral dissertation, Vanderbilt University, Nashville, TN.

Paul Cobb

WHITSON, J.A. (1997) 'Cognition as a semiotic process: Grounding, mediation, and critical reflective transcendence', in KIRSHNER, D. and WHITSON, J.A. (eds), *Situated Cognition Theory: Social, Semiotic, and Neurological Perspectives*, Mahwah, NJ: Lawrence Erlbaum, pp. 97–150.

YACKEL, E. (1995) 'The classroom teaching experiment', unpublished manuscript, Purdue University Calumet, Department of Mathematical Sciences.

YACKEL, E. and COBB, P. (1996) 'Sociomath norms, argumentation, and autonomy in mathematics', *Journal for Research in Mathematics Education*, 27, pp. 458–77.

12 Perspectives on Practice in Mathematics Education

Leslie P. Steffe

Although the decisions concerning the choice of goals prior to mathematics teaching cannot be made on purely rational grounds, the decision-maker does have choices concerning the course of action that he or she follows in developing rational grounds for those decisions. The mathematical choices can be made based on a mathematicians' view of mathematics. After making such a choice, two distinctly different paths can be followed. First, a curricular analysis of the mathematics under consideration can be undertaken and a logical sequencing of the mathematical topics for classroom instruction can be produced. This way of operating is traditional and leads to the notion of hard constraints and the paradox of happy agreement as explained by Lewin (Ch. 4). Second, an analysis of the mathematics under consideration can be undertaken for the purpose of orienting the curriculum developer. The second of these two paths is illustrated by Brink (this volume, Ch. 9). Rather than begin with the assumption that plane Euclidean geometry should be the mathematics of choice, Brink instead assumed the attitude that 'not only one geometry was taken as the holy truth. This opens up possibilities for multiple conceptions and it helps keep the student's ideas viable' (p. 123 above).

Using Multiple Mathematical Perspectives

Brink's choice of multiple geometries rather than just plane Euclidean geometry as suitable for classroom use has justification in the refutation of Kant's ideas of space and time as a priori forms of intuition by Einstein's special theory of relativity. Rather than posit a priori forms of geometric intuition, Brink instead agrees with Glasersfeld that whatever might constitute geometric intuition is a construction. By not being committed to any one system of geometry, Brink is able to demonstrate that all students' intuitive constructions and viewpoints do not fit into only one system of geometry. He even has the tolerance to ask the students for each others' point of view. These viewpoints are considered by Brink as states of development in students' geometries. That is the way in which Brink (Ch. 9) used his knowledge of several geometrical systems to understand students' constructions and productions: 'Spherical geometry, plane geometry, and solid geometry are formalized backgrounds

Leslie P. Steffe

that can be used to appreciate the differences between students' ideas (e.g. about what a great circle might be). To understand the meaning of a student's remarks, one has to know differences among various types of geometry' (p. 107). Domain specific knowledge is required.

Constructing Numerical Systems of Children

The way in which Brink used his knowledge of geometry to appreciate the differences between students' ideas is compatible with how the researchers in the project Interdisciplinary Research on Number (IRON), in which Wright (Ch. 10) and Cobb (Ch. 11) participated, used their knowledge of the system of cardinal numbers and the system of ordinal numbers in their work with young children. But, it is not identical because the researchers in IRON also based their work on the premise that the numerical knowledge of children can be understood as systems of knowledge distinctly different from the systems of cardinal and ordinal number. In this work, it was discovered that more than one system of numerical knowledge can be found among children of the same age in a way that is compatible with the differences Brink found in students' intuitive conceptions of geometry. In fact, each stage of the five-stage model Wright (Ch. 10) uses constitutes a system of numerical knowledge of children.[1] Each stage supersedes the stage immediately preceding in the sense that it solves all of the problems of the preceding stage but solves them better, and solves problems that were not solvable in the preceding stage. So, the rational basis of the mathematical choices of Wright's program of recovery education is not found in the systems of cardinal and ordinal number *per se*, but rather in children's numerical systems. The divergence between the rational bases of Wright's and Brink's choices has to do in part with the differing choices of goals in Didactic Realism and in IRON – in Didactic Realism the goal is to develop curricula for the schools by confronting the viewpoints of different students (as geometries in a state of development), and in IRON the goal is to explain children's construction of numerical systems as they engage in mathematical interactions. However, the intent of the researchers in IRON is that these numerical systems will in part serve as mathematical foundations in curriculum work of the kind exemplified in the chapters by Brink and Cobb in this volume.

Conceptual Analysis

Wright's choice, to use children's numerical systems as a rational basis, might seem more problematic than Brink's choice to use multiple systems of geometry. However, the claim that children's numerical systems are indeed rational finds partial justification in the idea of conceptual analysis as explained by Glasersfeld (1995). Conceptual analysis is analysis of mental operations. In developing this method of analysis, Glasersfeld drew from his experience with Silvio Ceccato's Italian Operational School, whose goal was to 'reduce all linguistic meaning, not to other words, but to "mental operations"' (1995, p. 6). The main goal of conceptual analysis is defined by a question from Ceccato's group: 'What mental operations must be carried out to see the presented situation in the particular way one is seeing it?' (ibid., p. 78). When the 'presented situation' is the mathematical language and actions of one or more children, conceptual analysis concerns the mental operations of children necessary to produce the children's observed mathematical activity.

Conceptual analysis can be only a partial justification for the claim that children's numerical systems are rational because the analysis is carried out *post hoc* – after the production of the experiential (presented) situations which serve as the subject of analysis. In that these 'presented situations' were language and actions of children which were brought forth by the researchers of IRON, the researchers' evolving conceptions of the children's mathematics are also a source of rationality. In these teaching sessions, the researchers' conceptions were built to account for the language and actions of the children and therefore were constrained by and constrained to them. So, to the extent that the researchers could establish internally consistent and viable working models of children's mathematical knowledge and its construction, these models could be regarded as rational. In this essential phase of the research preceding the conceptual analysis, the researchers were the teachers of the children as well as model builders. It is here that Brink's work and the work of the researchers in IRON find their closest compatibility.

To appreciate the nature of a numerical system of a particular stage, it is helpful to make a distinction between the living, experiencing child and an observer who is trying to understand how such a child can construct knowledge. In Piaget's words, 'one has to distinguish the individual subject, . . . and the epistemic subject or cognitive core that is common to all subjects at the same level' (1970, p. 120; quoted in Glasersfeld, 1995, p. 72). The cognitive core that is common to all subjects at the same level is an explanation of the mathematical thinking of an individual subject that has been compared and contrasted, and thus modified, with the mathematical thinking of other subjects whom the researcher imagines as operating in quite similar ways. The explanation constitutes what has been referred to as a numerical system within a particular stage. In the case of the IRON project, it is a product of conceptual analysis.

Recovery Education

In his program of recovery education, Wright (Ch. 10) notes that 'coping with a relatively wide range of ability levels is one of the most difficult challenges for classroom teachers. This is particularly so in classes of twenty-five to thirty or more students that are common in Australian schools and elsewhere' (p. 136 above). That is, it is not at all unusual to find children in each stage of Wright's

Leslie P. Steffe

five-stage model in the same first-grade classroom. Wright chose to focus on what he called 'at-risk' students – students in the first two stages – and developed a program in which these students were taught individually for a rather extensive period of time. The teaching program was not based on any extant mathematical curricula used in the schools. Instead, it was based on an understanding of those recursive operations that produce a metamorphosis in the numerical system of a stage, and of other operations that produce functional changes in that numerical system. An example of the former is a review of the items of a unitary structure produced in the immediate past. This operation, when sufficiently generalized, relieves the child from the necessity of always starting with 'one' when counting, because the child can take counting up to a given number word as given. An example of the latter operations is using available operations of composing or decomposing in the context of numerical patterns. It should be noted that Wright's choice to work with at-risk students was not grounded in completely rational considerations. Ethical matters were also involved in that it was based on the observational conjecture that what is a three-year difference in the lowest and highest stages in the first-grade becomes an even greater difference at the end of the elementary school years. Of course, this is unacceptable for a 'public educator' such as Wright, because it contravenes an ethics of social justice (Ernest, 1991).

Interestingly, Brink does not mention the possibility that the geometrical constructions and productions of the students with whom he worked might be forged into geometrical systems of students compatible with the numerical systems on which Wright based his recovery program. It is interesting, because in Brink's (Ch. 9) didactic constructivism, he 'tries to find conditions and means by which education develops in the sense of radical constructivism' (p. 122 above). That Brink, as well as Cobb, does not engage in the modeling activities necessary for the production of a mathematics of students can be explained by their goal to develop curricula for the schools which include methods the teacher uses in teaching.[2] The second reason is more subtle, and it has to do with the epistemological basis of Hans Freudenthal's (1983) didactic phenomenology.

Didactic Realism

According to Treffers (1987), Freudenthal set out his didactic phenomenology as follows:

> In opposition to concept attainment by concrete embodiments I have placed the constitution of mental objects based on phenomenology.... In order to teach groups, rather than starting from the group concept and looking around for material that concretise this concept, one shall look first for the phenomena that might compel the learner to constitute the mental object that is being mathematised by the group concept. (Treffers, 1987, p. 246)

Practice in Mathematics Education

Didactic realism, then, seems compatible with the Kantian position that the objects of perception are transformed by reason into concepts.

> He [Kant] takes it as self-evident that the objects of perception are the same for all individuals and that the concepts formed by reason are molded alike by all individuals. According to Kant, all knowledge refers to the phenomena but is not determined solely by experience (a posteriori) but also by the structure of our reason (a priori). (Born, 1968, p. 163)

Together, these comments imply that experience occurs within the a priori categories (reason) that might 'compel the learner to constitute the mental object'. But it is only compatible, because according to Brink, 'Freudenthal was interested in the "specific" phenomena of a concept, in the "local" and "particular" properties rather than in the "general" properties of a concept' (personal communication, 2 November 1968). In contrast to the Kantian position, E. Wright (Ch. 2) portrays perception as reading a sensory matrix, a choice which refutes the opinion 'that the sense perceptions of different individuals are identical and that the question is only to investigate this common world of phenomena' (Born, 1968, pp. 165–6). The assumption that the objects of perception are the same for all individuals, when coupled with the assumption of a priori categories, relieves one from the ethical responsibility of studying individuals in order to build abstract epistemic subjects. This heritage of phenomenology fits with assuming the position of a non-teaching observer, which is basic in the symbolic interactionism in which Cobb works (Cobb et al., 1996, p. 5). It fits because to construct mathematical systems of students, it is necessary actually to teach the children whose constructive activity serves in the experiential abstraction of the epistemic subject.[3] However, in that Cobb does not work within a phenomenological position, his work can be regarded as introducing modifications in the instructional theory of didactic realism.

Developmental Research

The modifications can be found in Cobb's (Ch. 11) idea of developmental research that he attributes to Gravemeijer (1994). Cobb would seemingly agree with a comment made by Treffers that 'it is essentially the pupils themselves who construct the courses, albeit guided by the teacher' (1987, p. 260), but would also emphasize that 'themselves' not be interpreted as 'autonomously'. Rather, Cobb's (Ch. 11) emphasis is on learning in social context: 'Although Glasersfeld (1989) defines learning as self-organization, he is careful to clarify that this constructive activity occurs as the cognizing individual interacts with other members of a community' (p. 154 above). From this and other comments made by Glasersfeld, Cobb (Ch. 11) concludes that 'learning is not merely social in the sense that interactions with others serve as a catalyst for otherwise autonomous

Leslie P. Steffe

development. Instead, the products of learning increasingly sophisticated ways of knowing, are also social through and through' (p. 154).

Intersubjective Construction of Knowledge

In his modification of didactic realism, a central place is thus accorded to the intersubjective construction of knowledge. This emphasis was already anticipated by the idea of interactive instruction in didactic realism: 'The pupil's own constructions and productions, as well as phenomenological exploration and modeling, can be efficient only if they are realised in interactive instruction, that is, instruction where there is the opportunity to consult, to participate, to negotiate, to cooperate, with review afterwards and where the teacher holds back from providing explanations' (Treffers, 1987, p. 261). The primary difference between the researchers' view of interactive instruction in didactic realism and in Cobb's developmental research paradigm resides in Cobb's agreement with Bauersfeld (1988) that 'learning is characterized by the subjective reconstruction of societal means and models through negotiation of meaning in social interaction' (p. 39). The shift in emphasis from phenomena which 'compel the learner to constitute the mental object that is being mathematised' to 'subjective reconstruction of societal means and models through negotiation of meaning in social interaction' is a very interesting shift and has its roots in Born's problem of how to free oneself from the subjective and to arrive at objective statements.

The emphasis on reconstruction in the characterization of learning rather than simply on construction has its origins in observer language. That is, it is from the point of view of the observer that the child reconstructs societal means and models. The observer sees what he takes as a social action or model, and later sees children acting as if they now participate meaningfully in those settings. From the observer's perspective, what existed on 'the social plane' now exists on the psychological plane of an individual. The further emphasis on *subjective* reconstruction is compatible with the way Glasersfeld regards the indeterminacy in linguistic communication explained by Schmidt (Ch. 3, p. 27). The meaning of a word or a combination of words refers to whatever aspects of a conceptual structure have been associated with the word or combination of words within the awareness of the individual. Thus, the meaning of societal means and models is not universal among the members of the society. Rather, within the frames of reference of the members of the society, they are irrefutably subjective.

Although Cobb does not explicitly mention it, he assumes that the social context for subjective reconstruction has an instrumental function; that is, he uses the construct of social interaction for a purpose. In this assumption, social interaction is an instrument or a tool for learning, which is the way Schmidt (Ch. 3) explained Glasersfeld's view of language: 'According to Glasersfeld, linguistic competence can be attributed to animals only in cases where the

Practice in Mathematics Education

organism is able to apply a learned sign under new conditions with respect to new, i.e. nonconventional, reactions of others or of the environment. Only then a sign becomes a symbol' (p. 30).

This involves accommodation, which is fundamental in understanding negotiation of meaning. Although the receiver of a piece of language has to build up its meaning out of conceptual elements which he or she already possesses, 'This meaning can fit into the meaning the speaker or writer had in mind only insofar as both have built up a consensual domain (in H.R. Maturana's sense), i.e. a domain in which both (together with other native speakers) have adapted their conceptualizations to those of others by a succession of interactive experiences' (Schmidt, Ch. 3, p. 28). But Brink (Ch. 9) demonstrated that instead of one consensual domain, several incompatible conceptual structures may arise in interaction that are resistant to change. The discussions about a mental object like a 'straight line' were based on different geometrical viewpoints (spherical geometry, plan geometry and solid geometry), and the students had to learn to tolerate the constructions and viewpoints of their neighbors.

Phenomena in Developmental Research

How Cobb (Ch. 11) understands 'phenomena' is implicit in his comment that: 'The first aspect of the developmental research cycle shown... involves the development of sequences of instructional activities for students as guided by a domain-specific instructional theory' (p. 157). What constitute 'phenomena' in didactic realism are 'instructional activities' in developmental research. This raises an issue concerning the sense in which such phenomena or instructional activities can be construed as societal means and models whose meaning is to be reconstructed and negotiated through social interaction. One way to resolve the issue is to refute the idea of naturally occurring and compelling phenomena and focus on affordances of reality from the observer's point of view[4] that might fit within the interactive constitution of meaning by students.

Cobb (Ch. 11) emphasizes that 'Gravemeijer (1994) clarifies that the designer initially conducts an anticipatory thought experiment. In doing so, he or she envisions how students' mathematical learning might proceed as an instructional sequence is enacted in the classroom' (p. 157). Although Cobb does not mention it, this involves making decisions concerning a choice of goals, and thus it involves establishing a second-order of viability of these goals (cf. Steffe, Ch. 8). Establishing these goals involves the designer using his or her know-ledge of mathematics in a way that Brink (Ch. 9) used his knowledge of geo-metry to investigate possible affordances of reality. At the very least, the designer must be able to justify the proposed instructional activities as mathematical situations and explicitly state his or her intentions concerning what might be learned by the students. This does not mean that the instructional activities need be a direct embodiment of the observer's mathematics. But the

185

Leslie P. Steffe

observer must be able to envision how any situation could be mathematized and what other situations might be needed to support the organizing activities of students.

Thought Experiments and Goal Structures

Although ethics is normally thought to lie outside of rational considerations and to concern intersubjective relations, the intrasubjective decisions of a designer that are made relative to his or her mathematical knowledge in a thought experiment also involve an ethics. There is no question that an ethics is involved in intrasubjective decisions when the designer uses his or her knowledge of mathematics to develop instructional activities *for* students. Ethics is involved because there is no simple transformation of the mathematical knowledge of the designer that explains what mathematical knowledge the students' might learn. Nevertheless, the decisions made in the thought experiment involve the designer establishing internal consistency among the components of the evolving goal structure, which is another way of saying that the goal structure must be viable within the frame of reference of the designer.

A priori goal structures are established as starting points and the expectation is that they will be transformed through their use in teaching as Cobb (Ch. 11) explains: 'The ways in which we look at communal classroom practices and at individual student's activity and learning profoundly influence the instructional decisions we make and thus the instructional design process' (p. 157 above). In this transformation, what is regarded as constituting instructional activities or phenomena is opened up to include the mathematical practices of children. Maturana (1980) reminds us that 'The individual is the center and motor of social phenomena; no society exists beyond the individuals that integrate it, and every society includes all the individuals that constitute it' (p. 24). In Maturana's framework, and apparently in Cobb's framework as well, a mathematical practice such as counting by tens and ones is a production of individual children that can be taken as shared among those children. It thus constitutes a property or a rule that defines a small and perhaps temporary mathematical social system in the classroom. But it is also a practice that is to be transformed into a practice which supersedes it by the children who belong to the social system.[5] Hence, the mathematical practice becomes the 'mental object' which is to be mathematized by, from the designers perspective, the superseding mathematical practice. However, even though what constitutes the superseding mathematical practice can be conjectured in thought experiments by the designer, and even though this conceptual construct does orient the designer in certain directions in the design of instructional activities, it is the children who must produce the superseding mathematical practice and this practice is usually a modification of what the designer envisioned.

Practice in Mathematics Education

The Classroom as a Social System

Cobb's (and Bauersfeld's) idea of 'societal means and models' is a 'soft' version of socio-cultural theory in that they regard the classroom microculture as the culture of primary interest in which 'individual students are seen actively to contribute to the evolution of the classroom mathematical practices that both enable and constrain their individual mathematical activities' (p. 155). This idea finds rational justification in Maturana's (1980) idea of a social system as a network of interactions of a collection of living systems. According to Maturana, a living system is a self-producing (autopoietic) system, and in a social system the network of interactions is a medium for the realization of the autopoiesis of the living systems that constitute it in the process of realizing their autopoiesis. This recursive property of social systems is the basis for Cobb's claim that a reflexive relationship does not mean that individual and collective mathematical actions are merely interdependent. Rather, the claim is that one literally does not exist without the other. It also accounts for the idea that children can take a mathematical practice they produced through modifications of their more basic ways and means of operating (realization of their autopoiesis) as input for further constructive activity.

Cobb's decision to focus on classrooms is in no small part based on school organization. When contrasted with Wright's (Ch. 10) recovery program, the question arises whether mathematical social systems that are subsystems of the classroom microculture might emerge if they were encouraged and brought forth by the teacher. Maturana (1980) sees an individual as potentially belonging to several social systems. '[A] human being can, in principle, operate without contradiction as a member of several societies in parallel or in succession, permanently or transitorily' (p. 17). Consequently, it is reasonable to believe that several mathematical social systems could operate in a classroom and that individual students could be members of more than one of these systems. As noted above, Cobb (Ch. 11) identifies three mathematical practices which could qualify as those 'certain rules' which are essential for membership in any social system (Maturana, 1980, p. 12). It also would seem that the children in the stages in Wright's (Ch. 10) five-stage model could establish mathematical social systems and mathematical practices as a property of those systems in the sense that Maturana explained social systems. Interestingly, this opens the question of whether the individualized teaching in Wright's recovery program couldn't be modified to include two or three children with equally good results. But it raises even more basic questions because a social system is necessarily conservative: 'every society operates as an homeostatic system that maintains invariant the relations that define it' (Maturana, 1980, p. 14). If we maintain, as does Maturana, that the interactions of the members of a social system are realized through the operations of their properties as individuals, then the mathematical practices of a group of children within a stage would be realized by the functioning and modification of the mathematical schemes of those children. In fact, the mathematical schemes of the children of the group would

187

be mechanisms of mathematical interaction. When the mathematical schemes of children are constituted as a mathematical practice which is taken as shared, then the children would have reached a plateau and would remain at that plateau until either the particular schemes of one or more children of the social system undergo structural change or else until an observer outside of the social system intervened with an intention to provoke changes in the mathematical practices. In either case, the mathematical practice would constitute those 'mental objects' to be further mathematized.

In sum, the contributions of Brink, Wright and Cobb present important problems and opportunities for mathematics education. Perhaps the most fundamental of these problems is to understand mathematical social interaction in terms of the mathematical systems of children in interaction with those of their teachers as influenced by the institutional setting of schools and communities. This involves the level of reflective abstraction at which these systems function. Although these numerical systems need not be constructed in spontaneous development, Glasersfeld's (Ch. 1) quotation from Piaget is most relevant:

> What has not been acquired through experience and personal reflection can only be superficially assimilated and does not modify any way of thinking. The child acculturates itself in spite of adult authority and not because of such an authority. (p. 7)

In Wright's first two stages, the mathematical schemes of the children are yet to be interiorized, which makes the possibility that they could assimilate the mathematical knowledge of other children remote. The sense in which intersubjective knowledge might be produced in such cases is a basic research problem in mathematics education. This basic problem can be generalized to investigating the sense in which intersubjective knowledge might be produced in those cases where the constitutive operations of the mathematical systems of two or more children differ in their organization, structure or material of application. The realization that emerges is that we cannot take intersubjectivity as a given explanatory concept in the construction of knowledge.[6] Rather, intersubjectivity must itself be explained in part in terms of the mechanisms of interaction of the individuals.[7] And, reciprocally, the contribution of intersubjectivity must be understood in the construction and modification of those mechanisms. This might seem to introduce a circularity, but I prefer to regard it as a recursivity.

Final Comments

Cobb would not say that children can take a mathematical practice as input for further constructive activity. Rather,

> It is the individual who must reconstitute a way of participating in the practice (not the practice *per se*). I take the individual's way of participating to be

equivalent to his or her mathematical reasoning when described in psychological rather than communal terms. I would want to stress that there are a variety of ways of participating in a practice. (Cobb; personal communication, 30 October 1998)

For Cobb, a mathematical practice is at the same level of analysis as 'taken-as-shared'. They are both communal notions that are attributed by an observer of a group to the group and do not involve any claims about individuals. The 'individuals play an active role as they contribute to the joint or collective constitution of what the observer claims is taken as shared. However, I would not want to talk of aspects of individuals' ways and means of operating because this slides taken-as-shared over from the group to the individual. For me, they are non-intersecting domains of description' (Cobb; personal communication, 4 November 1998).

Cobb's claim of non-intersecting domains of description finds justification in Maturana's (1978) idea of non-intersecting phenomenal domains of interaction – the domain of interactions of the components of a composite unity and the domain of interactions of the composite unity as a simple unity with other simple unities. However, by assuming only the frame of reference of an observer outside of the interaction, at first glance, his claims seem to be inconsistent with Maturana's idea of the recursive nature of these two types of interaction in which the interactions of the composite unities as simple unities serve as a medium (input) for the interactions of the components of the composite unity. Here, the frame of reference is that of an interacting participant.

The clarification in perspective is crucial to how one conceives of what one is doing. From the frame of reference of an interacting participant, for a particular mathematical practice to be 'out there', the individual would need to project his or her ways and means of operating into his or her own experiential reality as if it was an externalized mathematical activity that could be used to understand (and be compared with) the mathematical activity of others. At the very least, the individual would need to be able to reproduce the practice of others as if it were his or her own in order to consider it as taken-as-shared. This is certainly compatible with the non-participant observer's goal that, 'students will become able to participate in mathematical practices on their own' (Cobb; personal communication, 30 October 1998).

However, in the frame of reference of the non-participant observer, 'the students and the teacher jointly produce superseding mathematical practices, and even though the individual students actively contribute to this process, they do so while interacting with a teacher who is proactively (or planfully) attempting to support their learning' (Cobb; personal communication, 22 October 1998). So, in his frame of reference, Cobb can share with the teacher a mathematical practice that may not be apparent to the children and that the teacher uses as a guide when supporting the learning of the children, which is an important characteristic of didactic realism: 'we try to find a "perspective" (a pointer) for the teacher to find his/her way in the overwhelming creation of

Leslie P. Steffe

children's particular ideas. You may not stay in subjective reconstructions and reinventions. You, as teacher, have to guide children in a specific domain' (Brink; personal communication, 2 November 1998). In his focus on mathematical practice from the perspective of the teacher, Cobb's analysis of mathematical practice is quite different from that of Wright (Ch. 10) because Cobb's starting place is 'societal means and models' whereas Wright's starting place is the mathematics of children. In Wright's system (Ch. 10), mathematical practice is realized by the functioning and modification of the mathematics of children.

Being once removed from the teacher, a non-participant observer interprets the classroom events from the point of view of his interpretations of the teacher's goals and activities, which include abstracted mathematical practices. How members of the group might learn these practices constitutes a different level of analysis; that of the individual children.

> This focus on the experience of an individual is, for me, made from a different (and important) perspective – a psychological one. The trick for me is to coordinate an analysis of what the group is up to with analysis of the experience of the individuals who actively contribute to it and apart from whom it does not exist. (Cobb; personal communication, 30 October 1998)

In this, the experience of the individuals is interpreted from the point of view of what the group is up to. This understanding of coordination is crucial in interpreting Cobb's work. It brings to mind von Foerster's statement of the principle of relativity, which rejects a hypothesis when it does not hold for two instances together, although it holds for each instance separately. An issue Cobb's work raises is whether in principle, a non-participant observer is excluded from formulating and testing hypotheses concerning children's learning of a mathematical practice in the sense in which von Foerster's statement requires. Does formulating and testing such a hypothesis require the latitude and perspective of a participating observer, i.e. the latitude and perspective of a teacher with sufficient knowledge and expertise as Wright (Ch. 10) proposes in recovery education? A participating observer with sufficient knowledge and expertise can focus on the dynamics of the language and actions or interactions of children, and based on an interpretation of these dynamics, formulate and test hypotheses on the spot. Such latitude seems necessary to fulfill the requirements of von Foerster's statement of the principle of relativity if it is the goal of the teacher to explore the mathematical realities of students. The teacher would have the advantage of a history of interactions with the children, which contributes to interpretation and hypothesis generation and testing. For example, a teacher might make a conjecture about what a child can learn and present a situation of learning. How the teacher proactively (or planfully) attempts to support learning may itself be conjectural and open to testing rather than be predetermined. In this way, teaching may become a method for experimentation and scientific investigation.

The teacher's conceptions must certainly include mathematical practices in which the children are not currently engaged, and these practices must be used as a guide as Brink indicated. However, Kieren (Ch. 6) sees no reason why a teacher must a priori establish the nature of the conditions under which inquiry in his or her classroom will be regarded as valid. He sees the teacher's actions only as occasioning constructive action on the part of students, which, in turn, provides occasions for the teacher's and other students' knowing in action. In this conception of inquiry teaching, what is learned by the students is known only in retrospect, and what is learned provides occasions for further learning. So, in this frame of reference, which emphasizes the teacher as a participating observer, it is the students who reconstitute their own mathematical practice which is occasioned or brought forth by the teacher.

It is not simply a coincidence that Cobb's view of teaching is compatible with that of Kieren. The major factor in the differing points of view concerning children's mathematical practice comes from an explicit acknowledgment of the concept of viability made by Larochelle (Ch. 5) in her comment that

> Indeed, when the viability of a schema or a structure is established by a subject, this entails that the subject performs an operation of *reflexive monitoring* of his or her experiences and cognitive paths. By the same token, the action which results from reflexive monitoring is, at least in principle, consistent not only with this operation of coordination but also with the understanding that the subject has of the conditions of his or her action. In other words, it is plausible to think that the subject *has indeed good reasons* to do what he or she does or to believe what he or she believes, even if from the point of view of a particular community this belief is not valid. (p. 55)

But, it is insufficient to leave the role of the researcher by acknowledging that the researcher has indeed good reason to do what he or she does or to believe what he or she believes. The scientific and social consequences of the role that the researcher assumes must also be explicitly articulated and debated within the community of mathematics education because the images and conceptions of classroom practice the involved researchers create have far-reaching consequences for the practice of mathematics education.

Notes

1. Each stage is a stage in children's construction of their number sequences.
2. They write as if the teacher is an epistemic teacher who shares their worldview. This way of regarding the teacher is compatible with the role of the teacher in the constructivist teaching experiment (Steffe and Thompson, In Press). But it is not identical because in the latter kind of teaching experiment, the teacher is one of the researchers who participates in conceptual analysis (cf. Potari, Ch. 17).
3. This claim finds its justification not only in the necessity of experience in constructive activity, but also in the experimentation made possible by using teaching as a method of scientific investigation.

4 This can be the cultural as well as the physical reality of the observer.
5 Cobb would emphasize that the children contribute to this process of transformation while interacting with a teacher who is proactively or planfully attempting to support the children's learning.
6 Intersubjective knowledge is an observer's concept and can only make sense when we position it in the head of an observer who constructs it out of the observations of interaction. In this, the observer may be one or more of the individuals in the interaction.
7 I say 'in part' because intersubjectivity involves more than rationality. In involves ethics and preference as well.

References

BAUERSFELD, H. (1988) 'Interaction, construction, and knowledge, Alternative perspectives for mathematics education', in COONEY, T. and GROUWS, D. (eds), *Effective Mathematics Teaching*, Reston, VA: National Council of Teachers of Mathematics/ Lawrence Erlbaum, pp. 29–46.
BORN, M. (1968) *My Life and My Views*, New York: Scribner's.
COBB, P., JAWORSKI, B. and PRESMEG, N. (1996) 'Emergent and sociocultural views of mathematical activity', in STEFFE, L.P., NESHER, P., COBB, P., GOLDIN, G.A. and GREER, B. (eds), *Theories of Mathematical Learning*, Mahwah, NJ: Lawrence Erlbaum, pp. 3–19.
ERNEST, P. (1991) *The Philosophy of Mathematics Education*, London: Falmer Press.
FREUDENTHAL, H. (1983) *Didactical Phenomenology of Mathematical Structures*, Dordrecht: Reidel.
GLASERSFELD, E. VON (1995) *Radical Constructivism: A Way of Knowing and Learning*, London: Falmer Press.
GRAVEMEIJER, K.E.P. (1994) *Developing Realistic Mathematics Education*, Utrecht: EC-b Press.
MATURANA, H. (1978) 'Biology of language: The epistemology of reality', in MILLER, G.A. and LENNEBERG, E. (eds), *Psychology and Biology of Language and Thought: Essays in Honor of Eric Lenneberg*, New York: Academic Press, pp. 27–63.
MATURANA, H.R. (1980) 'Man and society', in BENSELER, F., HEJL, P.M. and KÖCK, W.K. (eds), *Autopoiesis, Communication, and Society: The Theory of Autopoietic System in the Social Sciences*, Frankfurt: Campus, pp. 11–31.
STEFFE, L.P. and THOMPSON, P. (in press) 'Teaching experiment methodology: Underlying principles and essential elements', in KELLY, A. and LESH, R. (eds), *Research Design in Mathematics and Science Education*, Hillsdale, NJ: Lawrence Erlbaum.
TREFFERS, A. (1987) *Three Dimensions: A Model of Goal and Theory Description in Mathematics Instruction – The Wiskobas Project*, Dordrecht: Reidel.

Section Four

Teacher Education in Mathematics and Science

For many years people associated radical constructivism with research on learning and teaching in school mathematics and science classrooms. More recently, constructivist theorists have given increased attention to matters surrounding the preparation of mathematics and science teachers. This was a natural move, as attempts to reform mathematics and science instruction in schools brought greater focus on teachers' roles in children's learning. In clarifying these issues it became essential to reconceptualize teachers and teaching from constructivist perspectives. The result is a more coherent image of teachers as humans who participate in the educational enterprise over their lifetimes – as students, as students preparing to teach, and as teachers of students.

You will find two recurrent themes among the chapters in this section. One theme is that we must understand teachers as we would learners in a school setting. This would entail a substantial understanding of their mathematical and scientific understandings, their motivations for becoming teachers, their images of what it means to teach something to someone, and their images of the social contexts of schooling. A second theme is that teachers are products of the systems in which they participate. Teachers were school students, and their lives as students have a substantial impact on their lives as teachers.

Désautels (Ch. 13) examines what he calls 'the re-production cycle', which is the regeneration of teaching genres over time and their resistance to change. He relates one intervention aimed at injecting a break in students' experiences through their participation in conversations that engender epistemic reflexivity. Simon (Ch. 14) considers teachers' epistemological perspectives and how they are entangled with the entirety of their conceptions of mathematics teaching. Simon proposes a normative 'mathematics teaching cycle' and its implications for teacher education programmes that are aimed at systematically influencing preservice teachers' perspectives. Hunting (Ch. 15) discusses the contexts in which teachers learn how to influence the learning of students and the important role that classroom culture plays in shaping students' attitudes, beliefs and actions. Potari (Ch. 16) relates the struggles of novice *researchers* as they simultaneously conceptualize constructivism and reconceptualize mathematics teaching and learning in the context of a constructivist teaching experiment.

A final theme common to these chapters is their observations of the enormous, thoughtful effort – and significant resources – required of persons intervening to make change, and the even greater effort required of teachers and researchers to actualize that change. This section has important implications for efforts to reform mathematics and science education.

13 Science Teacher Preparation: An Attempt at Breaking the Re-Production Cycle of the Traditional Model of Teaching[1]

Jacques Désautels

In the radical constructivism of Ernst von Glasersfeld (1995), it goes without saying that there can be no true interpretation of 'reality'. Indeed, within his inspiring theoretical framework on knowledge construction, the very concept of truth has been declared *persona non grata*. However, the dismantling of truth, when the latter is conceived of as a correspondence to or a mirror image of reality *per se* (Lawson and Appignanesi, 1989), has not had the perverse effect predicted by so many commentators in education: students have not adopted a solipsistic stance toward knowledge (Larochelle and Désautels, 1992). On the contrary, a radical constructivist outlook on the nature and development of knowledge has in fact made all of us aware of our ethical responsibility not only for the narratives and fictions we use to tell *our world* but also for the necessary epistemological choices we have at one time made – consciously or not – when adopting a particular perspective as part of constructing these stories (Foerster, 1992). Thus, radical constructivism has proven especially fertile, since by virtue of its very principles, it initiates an endless conversation in the community of educators about the ins and outs of knowledge development both individually and collectively. This conversation constitutes not only a safeguard against indoctrination, but it also represents the promise of a continuous renewal of our narratives about what it means to educate and to learn. In keeping with this outlook, I will first briefly present some aspects of the theoretical and practical background of an experiment in pedagogy during which my colleague Marie Larochelle and I attempted to create a number of conditions by which preservice science educators might be induced reflexively and critically to question their representations of scientific knowledge and the appropriation of this knowledge by students in a classroom context[2] (Désautels et al., 1994). Following this, I will discuss part of the results of this experiment, focusing more specifically on certain features of students' epistemological paths. A case study will be used to illustrate how the ontological commitments held by students can place limitations on this process of questioning and reflection. Finally, in my concluding remarks, I will suggest, following Cobern (1996), that in the case of preservice teachers, the task of understanding the constructivist thesis is more usefully conceived of as an opening into alternative worldviews than as an instance of conceptual change.

The Nature of the Re-Production Cycle

A review of teacher education literature does not give cause for much optimism about the transformation of preservice teachers' ideas of knowledge, learning and teaching during their education courses. In their thoroughgoing analysis of research on the socialization of preservice teachers, Zeichner and Gore (1990) conclude with the following: 'Studies of the influence of the formal curriculum of programs suggest that preservice programs are not very powerful interventions' (p. 338). In other words, although there are many reasons which may weigh against thinking of the socialization of preservice teachers as a deterministic and mechanistic process of reproduction, it seems that for most members of this group, little change will occur in the beliefs, predispositions or *habitus*[3] they have developed over the course of their own schooling prior to enrolling in education programs. In short, *chances are that they will go on teaching the way they themselves were taught*, as Bauersfeld (1998) has also emphasized. With respect to this particular problematic, science education also offers its share of illustrations.

Numerous studies in the field of science education have brought out a general consensus about the dominance of an empirico-realist representation of the production of scientific knowledge among science teachers (Cross, 1997; Haggerty, 1992; Palmquist and Finley, 1997). This will come as no great surprise when one considers the fact that teachers' initial preparation, whether in science or education, does not include any serious reflection on such representations (Gallagher, 1991). Moreover, it has been shown that their epistemological stance plays an important role in shaping their pedagogical practice (Geddis, 1988; Lemke, 1993), with the result that, consciously or not, a particular idea about science nevertheless ends up being promoted in the classroom. Thus a cycle originates in primary school, continues on into university, and returns once more to primary school. This cycle is at the heart of what Wagner (1994) has called folk sciences, and explains the long lease on life enjoyed by one particular representation of science in schools (Larochelle et al., 1995).

> It seems that a vicious circle is operating in the training of science teachers: The young person who would be a teacher of science is probably one who has had success at school science, i.e., success at mastering a static body of facts and ideas. The student enters an institution of higher education where the guild structure ensures that the student receives a larger dose of other factual knowledge and then leaves the science apprenticeship program before receiving any real understanding of how science operates. The student is likely to believe that the important part of science consists of the accumulated facts despite the mitigating influence of a science education course or two. The student becomes a teacher and teaches science in the same way it was taught to him or her. The whole cycle repeats itself. (Ryan, 1982, pp. 14–15)

During their school years, and in keeping with the largely dominant educational model (Gallagher, 1993), preservice teachers have also constructed an empiricistic representation of teaching and learning. Knowledge has become reified, turning into a commodity which can be transferred or communicated from the teacher or the book to the students through the presumably transparent medium of language. The following excerpt from a statement by a preservice teacher provides one such empiricistic, albeit sensuous, representation of the appropriation of knowledge by learners.

> I am visual, very visual. Science that is put into words – that's all fine and good. The same for books, too. But we have to have concepts, even a reality, so that something is shown to us. Now that I loved. I've had teachers who showed me – simple as that. I was in biology. Well, if there is something important to see, it is to try to conceptualize something, it is to get a hands-on kind of feeling for it, to put it in front of your eyes and simply be able to see.... That was something that really helped me.... What I like is to show how science is not something up there in the clouds, it is concrete, we can visualize it.... That is what I liked about the way I was taught science. It is putting it right before our eyes, so we could touch it, so that we could see it and look at it. That's good. (Ruel, 1994, p. 277)

It follows that when the time for teacher education arrives, these students have not yet really had their beliefs challenged. They have been successful in school. They have received a social sanction in the form of their official diploma in science. They think they know what science teaching and learning are all about. And if there are any problems remaining, these can only be technical or procedural in nature – i.e. how one develops the proper communication skills, works up a good lesson, creates motivation in children, or maintains discipline in the classroom. In other words, they appear to have interiorized what Tobin and McRobbie (1996) call the cultural myths that constrain the enacted science curriculum. It is a development that is all the more obvious in that preservice teachers have already become 'insiders' (Pajares, 1993). They simply recognize a familiar educational situation[4] and see no point in questioning their prior beliefs. It is a small wonder that repeated attempts at breaking the re-production cycle have proven less than a resounding success (Jungwirth and Zakhalaka, 1989; Trumbull and Johnston Slack, 1991). But under what conditions might the cycle be broken?

A Sketch of Our Educational Strategy

Breaking with experience, as with breaking the circle of re-production of the traditional model and practice of teaching, is a necessary condition for renewing science education from a constructivist perspective. Ever since Lortie's *Schoolteacher* (1975), this concern has been at the core of many attempts to renew teacher education programs. The following brief, almost elliptical paragraphs describe the constructivist-inspired theoretical orientation that guided Marie Larochelle and myself when designing a series of activities aimed at bringing about significant changes in the preparation of preservice high school science teachers at our university.

We think preservice teachers should be given the time and opportunity to develop their capacity to reflect on the content, instruments and habits of knowledge they rely on to construct their representations of the production of scientific knowledge and to develop notions of what it means to teach and learn science in a classroom context. One of the lessons to be drawn from other experiments is that if preservice teachers have never been required explicitly to consider these prior representations (Pajares, 1993), critically to examine the assumptions (epistemological, metaphysical, ideological, etc.) informing these representations, or overtly to grapple with other possibilities, we should not expect them to grasp the implications of our constructivist discourse or agree with the pedagogical inferences we have drawn from it, as Holt Reynolds (1992) has pointed out. In other words, we believe that it is necessary for preservice teachers to engage in an authentic exercise of epistemic reflexivity[5] in order to complexify the habits of cognition they have developed throughout their schooling. They have to create problems for themselves and by themselves, where initially no problems appeared to be present (Piaget and Garcia, 1983). It is by no means an easy task.

The radical constructivist perspective on learning cannot achieve credibility among preservice teachers simply by changing course contents. In fact, our own pedagogy has to serve as an example of what we intend, by means of taking the form of a discursive process, or a 'metalogue', which Bateson (1981) has defined as follows: 'A metalogue is a conversation about some problematic subject. This conversation should be such that not only do the participants discuss the problem but the structure of the conversation as a whole is also relevant to the same subject' (p. 1).

Participation in various activities meant first of all that preservice teachers (as learners) had to be able to gauge the usefulness of this new rhetoric for their own experience of cognition *in situ*, and second, that they had to generate problematic subjects which they were interested in discussing and exploring further. In other words, educational strategy had to become a recursive process in the sense that the products of the process were reintroduced into the process as elements necessary for maintaining and continuing it. This also meant that the educational strategies we enacted had to be not only consistent with a constructivist model of knowledge development, but also to be seen as transposable into high school science classrooms. The following are a number of activities that were explicitly associated with this particular aim.

- Students individually and collectively created metaphors which they thought were most appropriate for describing what they meant by teaching and learning. They were encouraged to identify the epistemological roots of these metaphors and to discuss their relevance in terms of what they thought the finalities of science education actually were.
- In groups of three or four, students were asked to elaborate upon their comprehension of fundamental concepts of science, such as the concept

of heat. This exercise was designed to help them become aware of their own conceptual difficulties in connection with producing clear-cut explanations of what initially seemed like simple phenomena, and take notice of how members of the group had produced a range of different explanations although all had taken university courses. They then reflected on the origins of these conceptions before they prepared and conducted interviews with two adolescents (12 and 16 years old) on the same subject. This activity was followed by an analysis of these adolescents' conceptions and a discussion of their cognitive status, which was a good way of introducing the theme of students' prior knowledge and its relation to learning.

- In small teams of 'researchers', students participated in the simulation of a number of conditions governing the production of scientific knowledge; as part of this process, they had to propose a solution to a riddle and organize a forum for debate over the value of the various solutions advocated. Throughout this activity, we acted as epistemological devil's advocates, asking students to give reasons justifying their decisions and their proposals.
- Students participated in a second simulation, which this time was related to the epistemological and social relevance of the sociobiological thesis. This was an opportunity to look into the epistemological viability of the ideas of biological determinism and reductionism, as well as to elucidate the social and ideological stakes involved in promoting these notions. For many students, this was no doubt a first in their intellectual career.
- One of the most important activities of this part of the pedagogical strategy consisted in having students keep a personal epistemological journal. Students were to write down their reflections on such problematic matters as the nature of scientific knowledge, the aims of science teaching (social, personal, etc.), how students learn, etc. We read these journals on a regular basis, asking their authors to clarify and justify their positions – an activity they were unaccustomed to – and occasionally suggesting other avenues of reflection.

Providing students the opportunity to reflect on, question and call into question their own representations is a necessary condition if they are to consider other possibilities and other ways of conceiving the ins and outs of science education. This does not mean we expect them to reinvent the wheel, however. Thus, they had to be given the opportunity of familiarizing themselves with and criticizing contemporary developments in science education. Activities such as the following were organized to promote this aim.

- A conference was given by Ernst Glasersfeld on constructivism. Prior to the conference, students had to read a text written by this author and frame questions they would ask him at the end of his talk.

- A video prepared by a group of researchers from Great Britain (Johnston, 1990) on a constructivist approach to teaching the particle model of matter was shown, thus serving as a springboard for reflection on what it means to teach science from within this perspective.
- A conference and a series of workshops given by Glen Aikenhead offered an excellent opportunity for discussing the relevance of a Science-Technology-Society approach to science education.
- An introduction to the social history of science was provided through a series of exercises such as analyzing textbooks in order to determine the type of history favoured by the authors.
- A conference followed by a period of questions was organized on the work done by Normand Lessard (1989) concerning the role of laboratory experiments in science education, and in particular the ritualization of this type of activity in school.

These activities were held during the fall semester over a period of twelve weeks during which we met students for six hours every week. This group of 26 preservice teachers,[6] each of whom held at least a bachelor's degree in science, also participated in two series of interviews which were designed to probe their initial and final viewpoints on the teaching of science (Ruel, 1994) and the role of the history of science in science teaching (Gagné, 1996).

Students' Epistemological Paths

We were deeply interested in learning about the possible complexification of students' epistemological viewpoints, since these particular beliefs appear to play a crucial role in the way teachers enact their pedagogical practice and promote a particular view of science in their classroom (Hashweh, 1996; Maor and Taylor, 1995). To that end, we used the 'Views on Science, Technology and Society' (VOSTS) questionnaire developed by Aikenhead (1987) and Aikenhead and Ryan (1992), which presents features that are different from those characterizing other research instruments of this type. The viewpoints presented in the questionnaire were constructed using students' statements on the subject rather than the official philosophy of science literature. Also, the various items referred not only to the traditional context of justification of science, but also to 'science-in-the-making' and the controversies which are constitutive of this social practice. The themes selected by the authors reflect this preoccupation, since one can find items ranging from the classical belief in the elegance and simplicity of scientific theories to the participation of scientists in *Big Science*, not to mention the social negotiation of scientific facts. In addition, the format of the questionnaire is such that the respondents can choose from a variety of viewpoints about a controversy rather than being confronted with a dichotomy on a particular subject. However, the VOSTS suffers from some of the same limitations affecting other questionnaires, since

Science Teacher Preparation

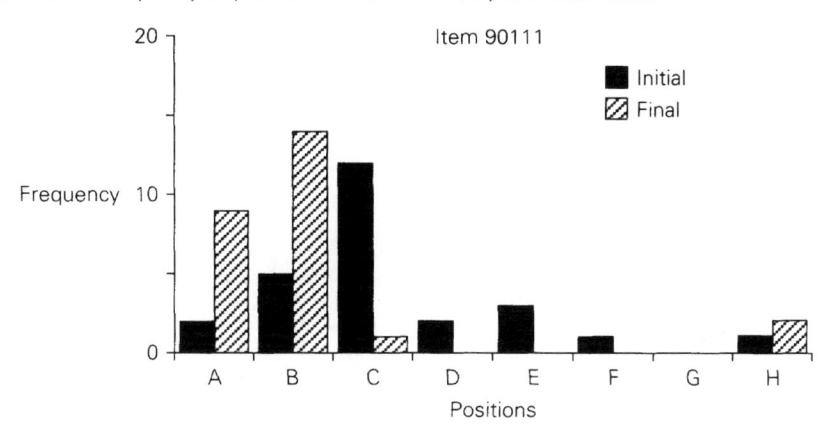

Figure 13.1 Frequency of positions: relation of theory and observation

Scientific observations made by competent scientists will usually be different if the scientists believe different theories.

Your position, basically:

A. Yes, because scientists will *experiment* in different ways and will notice different things.
B. Yes, because scientists will *think* differently and this will *alter their observations*.
C. Scientific observations will *not differ* very much even though scientists believe different theories. If the scientists are indeed *competent*, their observations will be similar.
D. No, because observations are as exact as possible. This is how science has been able to advance.
E. No, observations are exactly what we see and nothing more; they are the facts.
F. I do not understand.
G. I do not know enough about this subject to make a choice.
H. None of the choices fits my basic viewpoint.

it is actually impossible to know how the respondents interpret the viewpoints they choose from. For instance, is a student who chooses the statement 'Models change with time and with the state of knowledge, as theories do', expressing a relativistic or a realistic viewpoint? That is why we asked the students to justify their choices by writing a paragraph when they filled out this questionnaire at the beginning and at the end of the semester.

In the context of our experiment, the question arose whether students did significantly transform their epistemological posture. If we consider the choices they made at the beginning and at the end of the semester on questions typically related to classical epistemological themes, we can make out a general trend. For instance, as we have commented elsewhere (Larochelle et al., 1995), if we consider the histogram in Figure 13.1, it appears that a majority of students initially chose statements C, D and E, which describe observations as being more or less independent of the theoretical position held by a scientist. At the end of the experiment almost all of them chose statements A and B, which postulate that observations made by scientists are said to be dependent

Jacques Désautels

Figure 13.2 Frequency of positions: relation of classification and nature

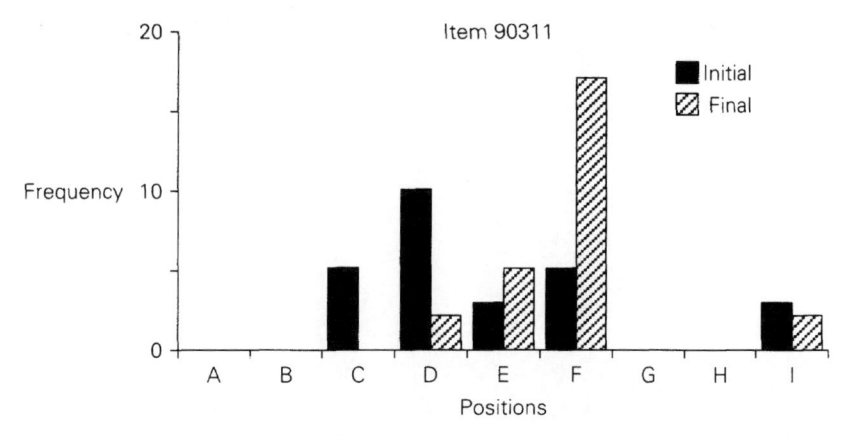

Item 90311

■ Initial
▨ Final

Frequency

Positions

When scientists classify something (e.g. a plant according to its species, an element according to the periodic table, energy according to its source, or a star according to its size), scientists are classifying nature according to *the way nature really is*: any other way would simply be wrong.

Your position, basically:

A. Classifications match the way nature really is, since scientists have proven them over many years of work.
B. Classifications match the way nature really is, since scientists use observable characteristics when they classify.
C. Scientists classify nature in the most simple and logical way, but their way is not necessarily the only way.
D. There are many ways to classify nature, but agreeing on one universal system allows scientists to avoid confusion in their work.
E. There could be other correct ways to classify nature, because science is liable to change and new discoveries may lead to different classifications.
F. Nobody knows the way nature really is. Scientists classify nature according to their perceptions or theories. Science is never exact, and nature is so diverse. Thus, scientists could correctly use more than one classification scheme.
G. I do not understand.
H. I do not know enough about this subject to make a choice.
I. None of these choices fits my basic viewpoint.

on the theoretical position they hold – a position which reintegrates the observer within the science-making process.

A similar trend can be observed when we look at the choices the students made when they were questioned about the epistemological status of classifications in science, since they opted for a more relativistic stance at the end of the semester (see Figure 13.2).

These results do indeed hold some interest for us, since they provide indications of some kind of change in students' epistemological posture. However, they offer little indication as to the meaning we can ascribe to the observed trend, and indeed say nothing about the process itself. But after analyzing the content of the paragraphs they wrote to justify their choices, we at least had a better idea of the meaning they attributed to the different statements. Performing this analysis enabled us to identify four orientations in their epistemological postures. The following excerpts from students' statements suggest the following synthesis.

Naïve realism. We considered that a student held such a position if, for instance, he or she referred to the concepts of replication or description to describe the relation between scientific knowledge and reality.

'Models are fabricated by drawing on what has been seen. What more is needed?' (S-10).

Asymptotic realism. This epistemological position integrates time and/or complexity in the scheme of naïve realism. For example, scientific knowledge constitutes a simplification or an approximation of reality, but over time it manages to get closer and closer to reproducing reality.

'So, even today, models are a simplified image of reality' (S-21).

'These models evolve, get better and better everyday until perhaps one day they become similar to this reality' (S-5).

Mitigated realism. This epistemological position differs from the two preceding views through the integration of the observer who is responsible for the production of scientific knowledge. Then, scientific knowledge is thought of in terms of conceptions or representations of reality that are useful for action. But, the subject–object dichotomy is maintained all the same, and there has to be a real and orderly world 'out there' – i.e. which exists independently of the observer.

'Models are conceptualizations of reality. We want to know, learn, communicate, and models are tools to express what we don't know' (S-12).

Relativism.[7] We held that students adopted this position if somehow they not only integrated the observer into the process of knowledge production but also did away with the subject–object dichotomy and, in some instances, alluded to the constructed and social character of scientific knowledge. Accordingly, conceptions, representations, models and theories were conceived of as representing contextualized and standardized sense-making instruments.

'Scientific models are used to facilitate the vision we want to have of things. These models are representative of the ideas that researchers invent according to the studies they perform' (S-23).

'The question of how we can have access to reality is not well-formulated. Our reality is constructed, in the sense that it is created by the people [living] in our societies' (S-2).

Given these four orientations, a variety of personal epistemological paths became possible (1 to 2 or 1 to 4, or 2 to 3, etc.). However, by the end of the experiment, most students expressed a viewpoint that could be associated with a form of mitigated realism. They claimed that reality *per se* is not accessible through scientific knowledge, since there is no way of comparing this knowledge with some ontological reality; thus, knowledge is indeed a construction. At the same time, however, they still believed that there is an organized, rule- or law-governed world which exists independently of the observer. Moreover, this belief was never pictured as representing a methodological postulate. Hence, a trend can be detected in the choices students made on the VOSTS that can be interpreted in terms of an evolution over a realistic continuum. In other words, as we concluded in the research report (Désautels et al., 1994), if most students did in fact *rehumanize* the production of scientific knowledge by reintegrating the observer and his or her personal characteristics or projects within the process, they did not, however, *resocialize* this endeavor by conceiving of it as a social practice. In the following section, the statements of one student will be analyzed with a view to grasping how a number of his ontological and ethical commitments guided him in adopting this type of epistemological posture.

An Active Subject of Science

The student whose statements I will comment on was a marine biologist who had some experience working at sea on a research boat. He was one of the more active subjects in the group. During the simulation portion of the experiment, he gave an outstanding performance endorsing a pro-sociobiological position, even though this thesis stood in deep contradiction with his own views, which gives an indication of his ability to deal with epistemological matters. He wrote extensively in his journal, noting at one point that he wanted to build a model of an 'active subject of science'. We can now take a look at the intellectual path he followed, beginning with the problem of the nature of scientific knowledge. Here is what he wrote at the beginning of the semester:

> Science is explaining and understanding the world in which we live in the most objective fashion possible. That is how I would sum up what science is. The explanatory character of science is very important for me. I believe that this is what has attracted me to studying science since when I was in high school. Different scientific disciplines study particular phenomena and try to put together plausible explanations. I think human beings have always attempted to understand their environment. Understanding the world gives human beings the possibility of using the forces and resources of nature. (pp. 2–3)

As is apparent from this first statement, he gives a rather traditional definition of science. The world (nature, environment, etc.) containing or being constituted by self-evident phenomena is an enigma for human beings who, at all times, have longed to understand it. The various scientific disciplines are defined as being the most plausible or objective explanations of particular phenomena, and it is these explanations which offer the possibility of using the forces or resources of nature. Such knowledge makes possible the development of modern technology, which, as he noted, paradoxically contributes to the environmental problems with which we are currently faced. At first glance, his epistemological posture appears fairly straightforward and common-sensical. The traditional subject–object dichotomy serves as a foundation for claiming that the explanations produced by disciplines tell something about the world as it is and create the possibility of harnessing its resources. But as he delved deeper into his subject, this somewhat simplistic picture became more complex. His practical, situated knowledge of science in the making clearly influenced the position he went on to develop. Reflecting on the production of scientific knowledge, he wrote:

> Research is what enables science 'to progress'. New knowledge is the result of research. If we do not search, if we do not question ourselves, we progress very slowly. Now, there are researchers, scientists and students who work for the advancement of scientific knowledge. They study and validate what is known. They develop new ideas, test models, experiment, interpret, analyze, develop and finally reject – or find no reason to reject – their hypotheses. Then they write their results in the form of technical reports or scientific articles. Those results are hypotheses, indexes, models, effects, formulas, relations and functions. (p. 4)

Although obviously nothing he now said stands in contradiction with my interpretation of the realist posture embodied in the first excerpt, his statements at this point cannot be qualified as indicative of a naïve epistemological position of the type whereby the knower would be some kind of passive spectator receiving messages from the world. Explanations are the result of a process designed to answer questions formulated by an intellectually active subject. Furthermore, even though this process is not conceived of as a social practice, it is nevertheless portrayed as involving communities of people dedicated to the advancement of scientific knowledge in the form of reports or articles. The different activities involved in that process are performed, as from within a quasi-Popperian perspective, for the purpose of conducting a test, that is: 'to reject – or find no reason to reject . . . hypotheses'. Finally, it is quite obvious that he did not imagine the product of the research (hypothesis, indexes, models, etc.) as a picture or a literal description of the world. If his epistemological posture had to be fitted within one of the categories suggested above, I think it might be classified as a form of refined mitigated realism. There is a given and organized world to be deciphered, for which scientists propose plausible answers or explanations via research or investigative process.

The question then arose as to how he would react to our request to reflect somewhat further on these problematic matters. A few weeks later, he made this interesting and insightful comment on the epistemological status of the concept of representation:

> I accept the notion that I can only know a representation of the world. However, I also believe that I am responsible for the effects that I as an individual

> and society in general have on the environment. It is difficult to find an answer to 'how to assume one's responsibilities toward a world that I do not know', all the more so since we live in a society where world views vary so greatly from one another as do each individual's interests. I think that it's a responsibility of government, but it is the people that must decide without being manipulated. Thus, it is the goal of education to enable people to become conscious, critical. But how is this to be achieved? Do I have a critical mind? How am I influenced by what I am and what I have done in my life? (p. 5)

In a way, he appears to have accepted one of the principles of constructivism, saying that he can only know a representation of the world. However, he maintained the subject–object dichotomy by conceiving of the environment as a distinct entity separate from the knower, who can produce an effect on that particular object. This dichotomy then led him into what he perceived as an ethical dilemma, which he put in the form of the question concerning the possibility of being responsible for what one does not know. In other words, if we do not have access to the essence of the world, but only to the representations we have constructed – which, for this student, amounts to something less than really knowing the world – on what basis are we to feel responsible for our actions in the world? Here we can see how the ontological beliefs and the ethical commitments of a student preoccupied by environmental problems are central to his epistemological reflection. As illustrated in the following excerpts, such concerns will remain present as he explores the ins and outs of the constructivist thesis of cognition in an analysis of Glasersfeld's position.

> One of the principles of constructivism is that 'experience is the only contact that the knowing subject can have with the world'. In addition 'there is no way of comparing the products of this experience with reality. . .'. I agree with these propositions but I think these propositions are located at a different level than the one I'm at when I'm sitting in a molecular biology class, for example, when I'm listening to explanations on cellular division, making diagrams, writing notes and trying to understand the logic of the explanations I'm being given. On one level of thought, this model is presented to me as a viable version of cellular division. On another level of thought, I admit that what is taught are only concepts, tools of thought that explain cellular division. Those tools are chosen because they are related to the experience of students so they can understand. You might say the danger at that point is that we begin to believe that the representations we are taught are images of reality. In fact, I think we do fall into this trap until we actually take time to switch to a second level of thought and say to ourselves: 'Let's not forget this is only a model, a way of understanding with all the limitations that go with it.' (pp. 6–7)

At first glance, this student showed a good understanding of one of the propositions of constructivism. He was well aware that it is quite easy to imbue representations with ontological attributes. That is why he reminded the reader that one has to be reflexively aware – on what he calls a second level of thought

– of the constructed character of representations. He nevertheless maintained his ontological commitments, if it is admitted that his statements about cellular division represent a form of reification. The concepts of cell and cellular division did not appear to be pictured as intellectual inventions that scientists construct in order to solve some riddle they had created. Such phenomena presumably had an existence of their own, and it was possible to develop a variety of models for them. Further on, he explicitly stated the problem while once again commenting on Glasersfeld's discourse.

> Glasersfeld goes on to contrast the following two points of view: 'a world which consists in objective facts' compared to a world 'which consists in invariants, in constants that we can estimate according to our personal experience'. I can see the difference between those two propositions, but as I already said, it seems to me that we are referring here to two levels of reflection.... You can always tell me that I am not taking a position by opting for such a compromise, but it's hard to exclude either one of the visions expressed on page 80 of Glasersfeld's text. I have the impression that there should be room for complementarity between these two visions. (pp. 7–8)

In this statement, the tension between a realist and a constructivist epistemological stance is quite apparent; the student was also well aware of the situation. Even though he claimed he understood the difference between both positions, he could not make a decision about what Foerster (1992) has shown to be undecidable propositions. This again is a good illustration of the weight his initial ontological or metaphysical commitments had on his reflection. Adopting a constructivist epistemology would imply a change in those commitments. In his case, it became a source of intellectual unease with pedagogical implications, as will become apparent from the following excerpt in which he describes the situation in the classroom.

> How are students going to feel if, according to their standards, they do not have the impression that they have learned much? How will students feel if they do not have the security of knowing they have the right answer? What is going to give students confidence in their ideas if they do not have rules by which to measure and evaluate their knowledge? ... These questions come to me in connection with the idea that people are rigid and preoccupied by security. (p. 9)

It is tempting to interpret his statement about the insecurity of students who do not know the right answer as a projection of his own feelings of insecurity. However, we can also view what he is saying as a comment on the impossibility of transposing the constructivist perspective within the science classroom. Now, this student is by no means an unreflective and uncommitted individual, as is indicated by the fact that he is now teaching in an Aboriginal community in northern Québec and has maintained a dialogue with us on these questions. When, in the final paragraphs of his journal, he tries to define what he means by human beings as 'active subjects in science' (sensory apparatus, intelligence, language, communication, etc.), he nevertheless falls back on his initial realist stance, as the following excerpt brings out.

> But I represent this information to myself, which is integrated by the brain, as though our environment were rebuilt by the mind using the information it receives from the senses. For example, I can represent a tree or a hockey game in my mind. I can also represent situations which are pleasant or unpleasant.... This capacity to reflect, to integrate the messages received by the senses, this cognitive capacity is what we call intelligence. (p. 13)

In this statement, it is easy to recognize his initial epistemological stance. A pre-organized world sends human beings messages that are integrated or encoded by them. The activity of the knower is limited to the processing of information, and each person has a different processing capacity, called intelligence. Likewise, the 'active subject of science' is conceived of as an individual, not a social actor. We have here an unmistakable portrait of what Glasersfeld has so often qualified as a trivial form of constructivism, which offers a family resemblance with the now-dominant cognitivist model of cognition in education.

Concluding Remarks

Many lessons can be drawn from the pedagogical experiment this chapter has described. For instance, one of our colleagues who acted as an independent observer (our blind spot guardian) during simulation of the production of scientific knowledge noticed that students strategically reproduced the *rapport* with knowledge (Charlot, 1997) and authority embedded in their school *habitus*, even though the didactic contract had changed significantly. In fact, throughout this simulation, the professors had constantly to initiate and sustain epistemological questioning, thus creating a certain degree of dissociation between the activity centering on knowledge production on the one hand, and epistemological reflection on the other. In other words, during the initial phase of our educational strategy, students seemed unable to give meaning to epistemological questioning and appeared incapable of creating problems for themselves and by themselves, where such problems seemed to be absent. Thus, very coolly and pragmatically, they acted in a way suggesting that they were saying to themselves that if the teachers wanted them to play this particular knowledge game, they would give them what they wanted. However, the constitution of problematic subjects was not restricted to the simulation exercise, and in the long run class interaction tended to become a little more like a metalogue. For example, when a good number of students realized that their explanations on the subject of the propagation of heat in a piece of metal were quite similar to those offered by high school students, they experienced something of a shock. What, then, might reasonably account for this situation? How was science being taught that made clear that something in this state of affairs needed changing? The sociobiological simulation, like other activities, triggered questions among all members of the class, and stimulated an investigation into the ins and outs of the production of scientific knowledge. As time went by, students developed new discursive resources to make sense of their role as science teachers. By their own account, they could picture how a constructivist perspective might help them think differently about such complex problems although, on the other hand, many of them saw the limitations of the school curriculum as insurmountable obstacles to a constructivist project. It is not possible to establish the true depth of their reflection, nor to determine how their participation in the experiment enabled them significantly to complexify their initial representations. While it is clear that the vast majority of students appreciated the experiment experience, there are serious reasons for not becoming overly optimistic about the impact of one course (Zeichner et al., 1996). After all, this experience challenged their worldview, or, the social representations which, in a particular society, determine that which is held as admissible and as reasonable beliefs (Wagner, 1995).

It is against this backdrop of worldviews that the marine biology student's statements should be interpreted. For indeed, how is one to explain that even though he showed a fairly good comprehension of the constructivist thesis, he remained committed to his core belief in realism. Or, as Cobern (1996) would frame the question, why is it that the central ideas did not acquire force and scope for this student? Adopting a constructivist perspective on cognition cannot be reduced to a conceptual transformation or a process of comprehension whereby logical or epistemological arguments, such as the impossibility of comparing a model with what is held to be modeled, prevail over other reasons for gaining someone's assent. Looking back at the intellectual and ethical struggle that this student experienced, one can understand why he continually maintained the metaphysical assumptions underlying his apprehension of what he called the world or the environment (i.e. the subject–object dichotomy, the organized character of the universe or the environment, etc.), for such assumptions are built into our society's prevailing forms of common-sense or worldview through which meaning is derived. Furthermore, we must not forget that these assumptions also constitute the tacit conceptual framework of the dominant representation of scientific knowledge in schools. Given these conditions, significant changes in preservice teachers' epistemological postures can only be hoped for in the long run. They will emerge only if we are able to provide the conditions for the enactment of meaningful conversations on problematic subjects. But as Ernst von Glasersfeld once said to me, we must be prepared to remain patient, since according to his own experience it took him forty years of hard work to become familiar with constructivism.

Notes

I wish to thank Donald Kellough, who, with vigilance and diligence, has provided me this translation.

1 In this text, by using re-production instead of reproduction, I wish to indicate that I am not referring to a mechanistic process whereby the actors in a situation are considered as cognitive or cultural puppets completely determined by external conditions. For instance, language in society is re-produced by actors while also being transformed by them. Thus, language can simultaneously be conceived as a constraint and a resource. Likewise, children learn a specific language, which is most definitely a constraint, but also develop the intellectual instruments and potential for action that can help them overcome the determinations constitutive of any social situation.
2 This work was made possible thanks to a grant from the Social Sciences and Humanities Research Council of Canada.
3 The concept of habitus can be understood as a set of dispositions, of schemes of perception, constructed in context by a historical agent that explain why he or she takes a certain situation for granted or finds it normal or natural. A habitus, as Bourdieu (in Bourdieu and Wacquant, 1993) has stated, tends to generate all the forms of conduct which are assumed to be reasonable or common-sensical. A good example of the constitution of an habitus is offered by Pajares (1992), who reported the description of van Fleet's 8-year-old niece teaching to her dolls: 'standing there [in front of the blackboard] with the chalk balanced perfectly in her fingers, and with the right tone of voice and facial expression, she was teaching: urging her doll students to pay close attention during this important lesson. She had "teacher" down pat' (p. 45).
4 An educational situation can be defined as a particular configuration (network) of interactions between actors (human and non-human) who have been mobilized in the pursuit of pedagogical or educational ends. The student, as an intentional actor, can mobilize other beings and things in the realization of his or her projects. The textbook or the curriculum, as representatives of their authors, surely mobilize other actors even though they are interpreted. The concept of actor has a long semantic history in sociology, but it is used here in the particular sense that Callon (1989) has defined it.
5 The concept of epistemic reflexivity as I use it in this chapter refers to the possibility of recursively becoming aware and reflecting on one's own epistemological posture. It does not mean that it is possible for someone to transcend the position she or he is speaking from, but rather that they are able to constitute it as an object of reflection while not forgetting that it is impossible to do away with the 'blind spot' of the observer who cannot simultaneously make observations and account for this action.
6 The details about the conduct of the experiment and the methodological orientations of the inquiry can be found in the published research report (Désautels et al., 1994).
7 I think that the distinction between relativism and relativization proposed by Fourez, Englebert-Lecompte and Mathy (1997, pp. 67–8) is particularly fertile. Relativism corresponds to a viewpoint that postulates the equivalence of all ways of knowing. Relativization expresses a viewpoint whereby models or theories are said to be context-dependent and their value relative to the use one can make of them in a given situation. From this perspective, all knowledge claims are not equivalent.

References

AIKENHEAD, G.S. (1987) 'High-school graduates' beliefs about science-technology-society. III. Characteristics and limitations of scientific knowledge', *Science Education*, **71**, 4, pp. 459–87.

AIKENHEAD, G.S. and RYAN, A.G. (1992) 'The development of a new instrument: "Views on Science-Technology-Society" (VOSTS)', *Science Education*, **76**, 5, pp. 477–91.

BATESON, G. (1981) *Steps to an Ecology of Mind*, 9th edn, New York: Ballantine Books.

BAUERSFELD, H. (1998) 'Remarks on the education of elementary teachers', in LAROCHELLE, M., BEDNARZ, N. and GARRISON, J. (eds), *Constructivism and Education*, New York: Cambridge University Press, pp. 213–32.

BOURDIEU, P. and WACQUANT, L.J.D. (1993) *Réponses*, Paris: Seuil.

CALLON, M. (ed.) (1989) *La Science et ses Réseaux*, Paris: La Découverte/Conseil de l'Europe/Unesco.

CHARLOT, B. (1997) *Du Rapport au Savoir*, Paris: Anthropos.

COBERN, W.W. (1996) 'Worldview theory and conceptual change in science education', *Science Education*, **80**, 5, pp. 579–610.

CROSS, R.T. (1997) 'Ideology and science teaching: Teachers' discourse', *International Journal of Science Education*, **19**, 5, pp. 607–16.

DÉSAUTELS, J., LAROCHELLE, M. and PÉPIN, Y. (1994) *Étude de la Pertinence et de la Viabilité d'une Stratégie de Formation à l'Enseignement des Sciences*, Ottawa: Social Sciences and Humanities Research Council of Canada, research report.

FOERSTER, H. VON (1992) 'Ethics and second-order cybernetics', *Cybernetics & Human Knowing*, **1**, 1, pp. 9–18.

FOUREZ, G., ENGLEBERT-LECOMPTE, V. and MATHY, P. (1997) *Nos Savoirs sur Nos Savoirs: Un Lexique d'Épistémologie pour l'Enseignement*, Brussels: DeBoeck University.

GAGNÉ, B. (1996) *Histoire des Sciences et Enseignement des Sciences: Points de Vue de Futurs Enseignants et Enseignantes de Sciences*, unpublished master's thesis, Québec: Université Laval.

GALLAGHER, J.J. (1991) 'Prospective and practicing secondary school science teachers' knowledge and beliefs about the philosophy of science', *Science Education*, **75**, 1, pp. 121–33.

GALLAGHER, J.J. (1993) 'Secondary science teachers and constructivist practice', in TOBIN, K. (ed.), *The Practice of Constructivism in Science Education*, Hillsdale, NJ: Lawrence Erlbaum, pp. 181–91.

GEDDIS, A.N. (1988) 'Using concepts from epistemology and sociology in teacher supervision', *Science Education*, **72**, 1, pp. 1–18.

GLASERSFELD, E. VON (1995) *Radical Constructivism: A Way of Knowing and Learning*, London: Falmer Press.

HAGGERTY, S. (1992) 'Student teachers' perceptions of science and science teaching', in HILL, S. (ed.), *The History and Philosophy of Science in Science Education*, Vol. I, Kingston: Queen's University, pp. 483–94.

HASHWEH, M.Z. (1996) 'Effects of science teachers' epistemological beliefs', *Journal of Research in Science Teaching*, **33**, 1, pp. 47–63.

HOLT REYNOLDS, D. (1992) 'Personal history-based beliefs as relevant prior knowledge in course work', *American Educational Research Journal*, **29**, 2, pp. 325–49.

JOHNSTON, K. (ed.) (1990) *Interactive Teaching in Science: Workshops for Training Courses*, University of Leeds: Centre for Studies in Science and Mathematics Education.

JUNGWIRTH, E. and ZAKHALAKA, M. (1989) 'The "back-to-square-one" phenomenon: Teacher-college students' and practicing teachers' changes in opinions and reactions', *International Journal of Science Education*, **11**, 3, pp. 337–45.

LAROCHELLE, M. and DÉSAUTELS, J. (1992) *Autour de l'Idée de Science. Itinéraires Cognitifs d'Étudiants et d'Étudiantes*, Québec/Brussels: Presses de l'Université Laval and De Boeck-Wesmaël.

LAROCHELLE, M., DÉSAUTELS, J. and RUEL, F. (1995) 'Les sciences à l'école: Portrait d'une fiction', *Recherches Sociographiques*, **36**, 3, pp. 527–55.
LAWSON, H. and APPIGNANESI, L. (eds) (1989) *Dismantling Truth. Reality in the Post-Modern World*, New York: St. Martin's Press.
LEMKE, J.L. (1993) *Talking Science. Language, Learning and Values*, Norwood: Ablex.
LESSARD, N. (1989) *Une Étude Ethnographique d'un Laboratoire de Chimie en Contexte Scolaire: Activités Expérimentales ou Activités Rituelles?* unpublished master's thesis, Québec, Université Laval.
LORTIE, D. (1975) *Schoolteacher: A Sociological Study*, Chicago: University of Chicago Press.
MAOR, D. and TAYLOR, P.C. (1995) 'Teacher epistemology and scientific inquiry in computerized classroom environments', *Journal of Research in Science Teaching*, **32**, 8, pp. 839–54.
PAJARES, F.M. (1992) 'Teachers' beliefs and educational research: Cleaning up a messy construct', *Review of Educational Research*, **62**, 3, pp. 307–32.
PAJARES, F.M. (1993) 'Preservice teachers' beliefs: A focus for teacher education', *Action in Teacher Education*, **15**, 2, pp. 45–54.
PALMQUIST, B.C. and FINLEY, F.N. (1997) 'Preservice teachers' views of the nature of science during a postbaccalaureate science teaching program', *Journal of Research in Science Teaching*, **34**, 2, pp. 595–615.
PIAGET, J. and GARCIA, R. (1983) *Psychogenèse et Histoire des Sciences*, Paris: Gallimard.
RUEL, F. (1994) *La Complexification Conceptuelle des Représentations Sociales Discursives à l'Égard de l'Enseignement et de l'Apprentissage Chez de Futurs Enseignants et Enseignantes de Sciences*, unpublished PhD thesis, Québec, Université Laval.
RYAN, A.G. (1982, November) 'Scientific literacy: Some thoughts on preparing teachers to teach it', a paper presented at the NSTA/SSTS/CASE Joint International Science Conference, Saskatoon.
TOBIN, K. and McROBBIE, C.J. (1996) 'Cultural myths as constraints to the enacted curriculum', *Science Education*, **80**, 2, pp. 223–41.
TRUMBULL, D. and JOHNSTON SLACK, M. (1991) 'Learning to ask, listen and analyze: Using structured interviewing assignments to develop reflection in preservice science teachers', *International Journal of Science Education*, **13**, 2, pp. 129–42.
WAGNER, W. (1994) 'Fields of research and socio-genesis of social representations: A discussion of criteria and diagnostics', *Social Science Information*, **33**, 2, pp. 199–228.
WAGNER, W. (1995) 'Représentations sociales en situation – commentaires à propos de politique quotidienne et théorie', *Les Cahiers Internationaux de Psychologie Sociale*, 28, pp. 55–66.
ZEICHNER, K.M. and GORE, J.M. (1990) 'Teacher socialization', in HOUSTON, R. (ed.), *Handbook of Research on Teacher Education*, New York/London: Macmillan, pp. 329–48.
ZEICHNER, K., MELNICK S. and GOMEZ, M.L. (1996) *Currents of Reform in Preservice Teacher Education*, New York/London: Teachers College Press.

14 Constructivism, Mathematics Teacher Education, and Research in Mathematics Teacher Development

Martin A. Simon

Radical constructivism has provided a major theoretical foundation for current efforts to transform the teaching of mathematics (National Council of Teachers of Mathematics, 1989, 1991). It has contributed to change in the perspectives of mathematics educators concerning the nature of mathematical knowledge and activity and the nature of mathematics learning. As a result, traditional tell-and-show approaches to mathematics teaching are being rejected in favor of ways of teaching that are considered to be more optimal based on evolving views of mathematics and mathematics learning. However, the possibility for widespread and long-term change in the teaching of mathematics is dependent on a concomitant change in the education of both prospective and practicing mathematics teachers. This chapter focuses on the impact and potential impact of constructivism on mathematics teacher education and on mathematics teacher development research.

The Impact of Constructivism on Mathematics Teacher Education

The potential impact of constructivism on mathematics teacher education is both direct and indirect. 'Indirect' indicates a chain of influence: constructivism influences the reform of mathematics teaching which in turn influences the reform of mathematics teacher education (see Figure 14.1). This section first deals with the direct effects and then the indirect effects.

Direct Impact of Constructivism on Mathematics Teacher Education

Constructivism represents a major theoretical shift in what knowledge is and how knowledge is developed.

> This view differs from the old one in that it deliberately discards the notion that knowledge could or should be a representation of an observer-independent world-in-itself and replaces it with the demand that the conceptual constructs we call knowledge be viable in the experiential world of the knowing subject. (Glasersfeld, 1989, p. 122)

Martin A. Simon

Figure 14.1 Influence of constructivism on mathematics teacher education

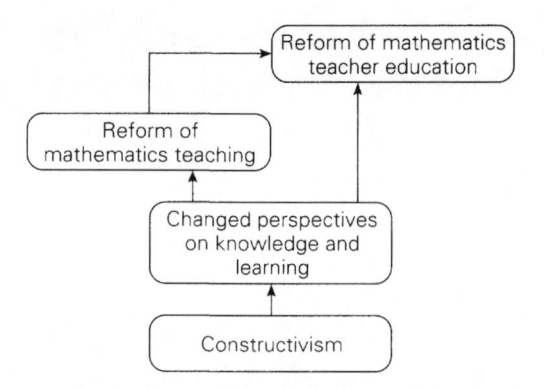

```
                              ┌─────────────────────┐
                         ┌───►│  Reform of mathematics│
                         │    │  teacher education    │
                         │    └─────────────────────┘
                         │                ▲
              ┌──────────────────┐        │
              │    Reform of     │        │
              │ mathematics teaching│     │
              └──────────────────┘        │
                         ▲                │
                         │                │
              ┌──────────────────┐        │
              │ Changed perspectives│     │
              │  on knowledge and  │──────┘
              │     learning       │
              └──────────────────┘
                         ▲
                         │
                 ┌──────────────┐
                 │ Constructivism│
                 └──────────────┘
```

Learning involves adaptive shifts in knowledge. The human learner is conceptualized as actively building up and modifying her[1] knowledge based on her extant knowledge in response to present experience. This conceptualization of the human learner demands rethinking educational processes in every field, including mathematics education and mathematics teacher education. What might it mean for mathematics teacher education to include a view of prospective and practicing mathematics teachers as active agents in the construction of their knowledge? The following are some implications of such a view:

- The knowledge and experience of teachers would be a specific focus of inquiry by mathematics teacher educators and researchers in mathematics teacher development. Because teacher knowledge is constantly changing, mathematics teacher education would need to involve ongoing assessment of that knowledge. A key here is that assessment would not be based on the question, 'Did they learn what I intended them to learn?' but rather on, 'How do they now conceive of the issues at hand?'
- It would be understood that all teacher education experiences are assimilated on the basis of prior knowledge and that it is the meaning that teachers give to these experiences that is important in their development. This is a recognition that teachers and the teacher educators who work with the teachers are likely to understand their interactions in different ways based on their differing knowledge and values (McNeal and Simon, 1994).
- Telling teachers the ideas of teacher educators and/or mathematics education researchers is at best a limited way of promoting understanding and is often ineffective. Although verbal exposition of ideas can result in learning, it often does not engage the processes needed for significant cognitive reorganization (i.e. particular activity and reflection on that activity).
- Teacher development experiences must be conceived of in ways that anticipate the potential processes of cognitive reorganization of the teachers involved.

These implications of a constructivist reconceptualization of the human learner can be seen as significant challenges for mathematics teacher education. In the section on the indirect impact of constructivism, I discuss how we might think about beginning to meet those challenges.

So far, I have indicated that reconceptualizing learning necessitates a reconceptualization of the *process* of mathematics teacher education. I now turn to the impact of constructivism on the *content* of mathematics teacher education. Because of the significant role that a constructivist perspective plays in the current mathematics education reform, it would seem important for participating teachers to understand the basic principles of constructivism. However, we must define this goal clearly. Currently, there is widespread use of the term 'constructivism' to describe perspectives on learning and teaching, and, in many cases, these perspectives differ considerably from the constructivism explicated by Glasersfeld (1989). Some distinctions are important here.

Cobb, Yackel and Wood (1992) articulated the difference between a radical constructivist perspective and what Putnam (1988) called a 'representational view of mind'. In the former, knowledge serves in an organization of one's experiential world, while in the latter, knowledge is seen as a mental representation of an ontological reality. Cobb, Yackel and Wood (1992) pointed out that this idea of direct access to a reality independent of human experience has significant impact on decisions made about teaching. They articulated how the label of constructivism often is assigned from this perspective.

> From the representational perspective, learning is a process of acquiring accurate mental representations of fixed mathematical structures, relationships, and the like that exist independently of individual and collective activity... If we accept these assumptions, our instructional options are relatively limited as we attempt to make the mathematical structures apprehensible to students. We can of course develop external representations to make the mathematical structures as transparent as possible. The only other obvious variable is the extent to which we might spell out the mathematical relationships that students are to apprehend. At one extreme, we might be as explicit as possible in a manner compatible with behaviorism, whereas at the other extreme we might be radically noninterventionist in a manner compatible with romanticism. Given that the only instructional options that come to mind are located somewhere on this continuum as long as we adhere rigidly to the representational view, it seems plausible to equate the noninterventionist extreme with constructivism. To construct then means to learn by spontaneously apprehending fixed mathematical relationships without the teacher's guidance. (Cobb et al., 1992, pp. 27–8)

Our recent empirical work (Simon et al., 1998; Tzur et al., 1998) has led us to the conclusion that many teachers participating in current reforms base their epistemological perspectives on the assumption of direct access to an ontological reality. They interpret the mathematics education reform as emphasizing the value of learners' first-hand experience 'seeing' mathematical relationships,

relationships which are taken to exist independent of human activity and to be perceivable by all in identical ways. We refer to this as a 'perception-based perspective', which we contrast with a 'conception-based perspective' such as a radical constructivist view of mathematical knowing (Simon et al., in press).

The distinction between perception- and conception-based perspectives is important for two reasons. First, it contributes to articulating further key aspects of a goal for mathematics teacher education, to foster a useful perspective on mathematical knowing. Second, it leads to consideration of the difficulty of accomplishing this goal. Let's unpack this second point a bit. Based on our research with limited numbers of teachers and prospective teachers and our informal observations of many other teachers and prospective teachers participating in various reform-based teacher education programs, we conclude that such programs have frequently fostered the development of a perception-based perspective, while infrequently promoting a conception-based perspective. As we take a hard look at the nature of the two perspectives and the underlying epistemological differences, we come to an understanding of why the challenge to promote a conception based perspective is so formidable.

We see these two perspectives as constituting different paradigms. We use the term 'paradigm' to focus attention on two internally coherent systems. The phrase 'perception-based perspective' refers to a comprehensive view of knowledge and learning that affects the teachers' views of mathematics, expectations about how it is learned, approaches to teaching, adaptations of new curricula and teaching tools, and interpretations of professional development experiences. That is, it has a tremendous capacity for assimilating new experiences, which makes changes from the perspective difficult to promote. Let me illustrate the assimilatory power of this perspective as it functions in the classroom and in professional development experiences. (The two examples that follow are composites derived from recent data.)

Mary is a fifth-grade teacher who is committed to students understanding the mathematics that they are doing. Her mathematics classes are generally organized as follows. Mary gives a task for students to do in pairs or individually. The students do the task using the materials available. Mary circulates through the classroom asking the students to articulate their understandings of their work.

In our observations, Mary often gets quite diverse responses from the students. However, rather than using these responses as indications of the conceptions of her students, conceptions to be built on, Mary uses the students' responses to assess whether they saw the relationships that she intended them to focus on. She then assigns further work based on which relationships they have not yet perceived. Mary assimilated the experience of listening to the students' explanations to her perception-based perspective.

Harvey is a first-grade teacher who, as part of a teacher education course, participated in a mathematics activity involving two-digit addition using a 'foreign' (base-five) number system and base five blocks. As a result of this activity, Harvey felt that he understood place-value and operations with place-value much more deeply. On the basis of this experience, he decided to have his students work with base-ten blocks 'so they will see place value'.

Harvey assimilated his experience into his perception-based perspective. He assumed that the blocks were a transparent representation of an independent mathematical reality accessible to all. This is in sharp contrast to the conception-based perspective represented by Cobb, Yackel and Wood:

> Mathematical meanings given to these representations are the product of students' interpretive activity. Consequently ... a pedagogical device ... becomes 'a "representation" only when a student uses it to express a conception'. (Confrey, 1990, p. 56; cited in Cobb et al., 1992)

These two examples were designed to demonstrate the assimilatory power of a perception-based perspective and thus the difficulty of provoking a change in that perspective, i.e. successfully incorporating the development of a constructivist or emergent perspective into the content of mathematics teacher education. It is a problem for developmental research (Gravemeijer, 1995) to explore how teacher education (broadly conceived) might promote this paradigm shift.

Indirect Impact of Constructivism on Mathematics Teacher Education

In the last section, I considered the direct impact of constructivism on mathematics teacher education. In this section, I focus on the indirect impact; constructivism affects mathematics teaching which in turn affects both the content and process of mathematics teacher education. As new models of mathematics teaching are developed, they serve to redefine the role of mathematics teacher and the knowledge and skills needed to teach effectively. Thus, the goals and content of mathematics teacher education are necessarily altered. New models of mathematics teaching can also affect the process of mathematics teacher education by providing useful principles of teaching, developed in the context of teaching mathematics, that can be adapted to foster the mathematical and pedagogical development of teachers. Then the process of teacher education efforts can increase teachers' insight into these new approaches by affording them opportunities to reflect on the roles of teacher and students in a situation structured by the particular model of teaching.

Constructivism and Mathematics Teaching

Constructivism offers a fundamentally different way to think about mathematical knowledge and its development. By redefining the human learner and furnishing a framework for understanding the complex processes of learning, it has caused a re-examination of mathematics teaching. However, whereas constructivism provides a foundation for reconceptualizing mathematics teaching, it does not provide a particular model of mathematics teaching.

Martin A. Simon

> Constructivism, as a general theory, is used to explain knowledge development in diverse situations (including teacherless situations). Mathematics teaching in schools is a particular situation in which *intentional interventions* are made to promote the construction of powerful mathematical ideas. These intentional interventions can be labeled 'pedagogy' and include the actions of teachers as well as the design of curriculum. However, constructivism does *not* describe the role of (nor the *potential* role of) pedagogy in knowledge development. (Simon, 1997, p. 58)

Models of mathematics teaching grounded in constructivism are likely to share some important features, e.g. attention to the students' mathematics (Steffe and D'Ambrosio, 1995). However, they may vary significantly in how they articulate the teacher's role. The generation of new models of teaching consistent with constructivism is in its early stages and much work remains to be done.

An Evolving Model of Teaching

In this section, I discuss a particular model of mathematics teaching in order to demonstrate the relationship between models of mathematics teaching and reform of mathematics teacher education. A more complete discussion of this model and its relationship to other work in the field can be found in Simon (1995). The section begins with a brief description of the epistemological framework (based in part on constructivism) on which the model of teaching is grounded. A description of the model is followed by an examination of its implications for the content and the process of mathematics teacher education.

An Epistemology Based on Constructivism

Besides its impact on mathematics teaching and mathematics teacher education, constructivism has contributed to the elaboration of a number of related epistemological perspectives, particularly those which include social perspectives on knowledge development.[2] The perspective on mathematics teaching discussed in this chapter is grounded in what Cobb and Yackel (1996) have called an emergent perspective. This perspective combines radical constructivism with symbolic interactionism (Blumer, 1969). The interactionist perspective, when combined with a constructivist perspective, affords the researcher (observer) a broad range of explanatory mechanisms. Whereas constructivism results in postulating individual learners and focuses on their individual experience, interactionism results in postulating various characteristics of activity in social groups, e.g. classroom social norms, interactive constitution of meanings, and taken-as-shared knowledge and practices. Use of the emergent perspective involves coordinating the results of psychological (constructivist) and social (interactionist) analyses.

Description of the Model

The emergent perspective (constructivism and symbolic interactionism) provides an overarching framework for thinking about mathematical knowledge development. From a cognitive perspective, perturbations and the mechanisms of assimilation, accommodation and reflective abstraction are key components in the development of knowledge. From a social perspective, participation in a classroom microculture that fosters acculturation into powerful mathematical practices and ways of knowing (thinking) are important features. Based on an understanding of these processes, what might mathematics teachers do to promote the development of powerful mathematics? I describe the role of mathematics teachers by identifying six overlapping, though not exhaustive, categories of interaction with students:

- Inquiry into students' mathematics is a key aspect of the teacher's role. Through problem posing, questioning, listening and observing, the teacher attempts to make sense of students' current mathematical thinking and understanding.
- Constraining and fostering students' construction of concepts involves teaching interventions designed to promote particular assimilatory and accommodative responses on the part of the students, through carefully chosen mathematical problems and materials. Ball (1993) referred to problems used in this way as 'representational contexts' and Tzur (1995) analyzed this as a 'task oriented approach'. 'Materials' is used broadly and encompasses manipulative aids, computer and calculator environments, availability and types of paper (e.g. graph paper), measuring devices, and available contextual or mathematical information.
- Encouraging and orienting reflection includes promoting what Cobb, Boufi, McClain, and Whitenack (1997) refer to as reflective discourse, 'characterized by repeated shifts such that what the students and teacher do in action subsequently becomes an explicit object of discussion' (p. 258). The teacher probes solution strategies, elicits justifications and invites comparison among diverse mathematical actions or ideas. The teacher also solicits written reflection on mathematical thinking and learning.
- Encouraging and organizing communication in the classroom includes determining who speaks to whom, encouraging and monitoring understanding and making decisions as to what ideas are followed up. Teachers encourage and organize communication in the classroom by working with the students to develop a level of safety for communication of ideas and feelings. Communication among class members serves to perturb current conceptions and promote reflection.
- Participating in negotiation of norms and practices for classroom mathematics involves the teacher interactively constituting (with the students) useful norms and practices for mathematical activity in the classroom.

Martin A. Simon

Figure 14.2 Mathematics teaching cycle

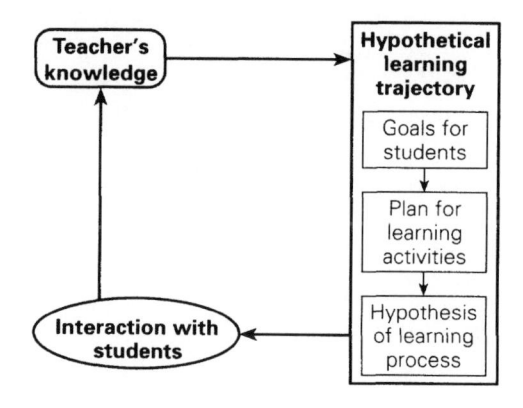

```
Teacher's knowledge  →  Hypothetical learning trajectory
                         ├─ Goals for students
                         ├─ Plan for learning activities
                         └─ Hypothesis of learning process
        ↑                        ↓
Interaction with students ←──────┘
```

This process of establishing new and modified norms and practices is referred to as a 'negotiation' because it is affected by the participation of both teacher and students, and because each party is involved in orienting to the other's actions while representing their own perspectives and motivations. Classroom norms include issues such as what constitutes justification of an idea, how mathematical correctness is determined, and what kinds of contributions to mathematical discussion are valued. Mathematical practices include content-specific ways of working with the mathematics (working with composite units of ten, drawing diagrams for fractions, and using congruent triangles to establish equivalence among angles and among sides of different geometric shapes).

- Facilitating the negotiation of shared meanings contributes to the mathematical growth of the classroom community. Shared meanings are usable by community members, without explanation or justification, in service of more sophisticated mathematical ideas. The teacher is often instrumental in promoting dialogue about various mathematical ideas and solutions in order to arrive at (taken-as) shared meanings.

So far, the description of teaching has focused on teachers' interactions with students. In the *mathematics teaching cycle* (Simon, 1995), the relationship between teacher–student interaction, teacher knowledge and teacher decision-making are described. The basic structure of the cycle is represented schematically in Figure 14.2.

According to this model, the mathematics teacher's actions are at all times guided by her current goals for student learning. 'Current' emphasizes that these goals are continually being modified based on the teacher's interactions with students. The teacher's goals for student learning provide direction for a *hypothetical learning trajectory*, which is the teacher's prediction of the path by which learning might proceed.

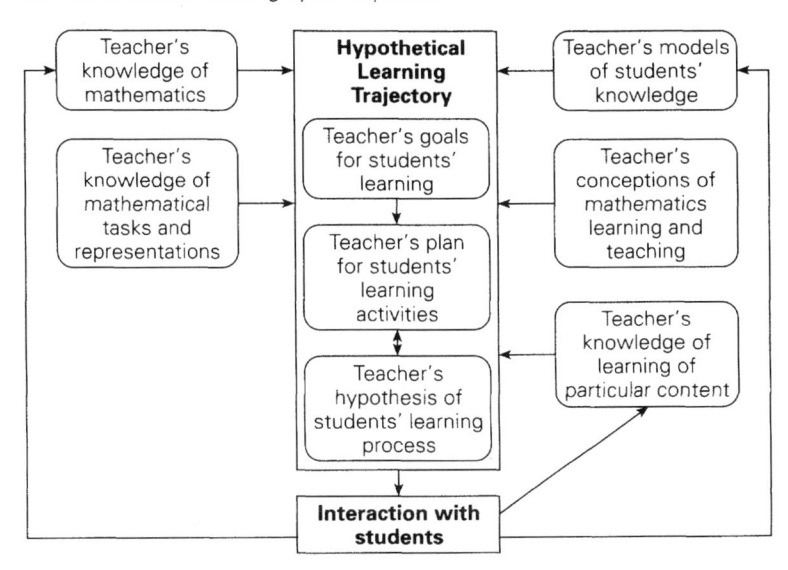

Figure 14.3 Mathematics teaching cycle: expanded

The hypothetical learning trajectory is made up of the learning goals, the learning activities and the hypothetical learning process – the teacher's conjecture of how the students' thinking/understanding will evolve in the context of anticipated learning activities. The bi-directional arrows in Figure 14.2 between the hypothetical learning process and the learning activities indicate a reflexive relationship; the generation of learning activities is based on the teacher's conjectures about the development of students' thinking, and the conjectures about the development of students' thinking depends on the nature of anticipated activities.

According to this model, the generation of a hypothetical learning trajectory prior to mathematics teaching is the process by which the teacher develops her plan for classroom activity. However, in the classroom, the teacher and students collectively constitute the mathematical activity, which, by its social nature, may be different from what the teacher anticipated. The teacher's interaction with and observation of the students' activity may lead to modifications in the teacher's knowledge of mathematics, teaching and learning, as well as in her ideas about these particular students (individually and collectively). The diagram of the mathematics teaching cycle (Figure 14.2) is meant to be interpreted to indicate that adaptations in the teacher's knowledge lead to a new or modified hypothetical learning trajectory.

Figure 14.3 gives a more detailed picture of the mathematics teaching cycle by identifying relevant aspects of the teacher's knowledge and describing the connections between that knowledge and the planning and interaction phases of the model. The teacher's determination of what can be learned is based on relating her own knowledge of the pertinent mathematics to her knowledge of the students' current understandings of that and related mathematics. The teacher's mathematical knowledge includes understandings of the pertinent mathematics and the ability to analyze the conceptual field in question, i.e. to consider the relationship among concepts for the learner. The teacher's observation of and communication with her students lead her to form models of her students' current mathematical knowledge. These two interacting sources of knowledge, teacher's mathematical knowledge and teacher's knowledge of students' mathematical knowledge, are the basis for the teacher's choice of learning goals for her students.

> [U]sing their own mathematical knowledge, mathematics teachers must interpret the language and actions of their students and then make decisions about possible mathematical knowledge their students might learn. (Steffe, 1990, p. 395)

Three other aspects of teacher knowledge contribute to the generation of the hypothetical learning trajectory. First is the teacher's sense of how students learn. (A constructivist or emergent perspective on knowledge development would be important for the teacher.) Second, her understanding of how particular mathematics is learned, derived both from research and from her reflection on her own work with students, informs her choice of intervention. Third, her vision of the role of the mathematics teacher contributes to defining her choice of actions with respect to her students. Thus, the teacher's model of teaching is a key factor in the model of teaching described here.

To summarize, this model of mathematics teaching emphasizes the teacher's involvement in model building and hypothesis generation (e.g. models of students' mathematical understanding, hypotheses of how students' learning might progress). Such teaching is *goal directed, yet constantly changing*. The teacher's relationship with the students is one of *both direction setting and following student initiative*; this tension between the teacher's current goals for student learning and commitment to respond to the mathematics of the student is inherent in teaching.

Implications for Mathematics Teacher Education

The current challenge facing mathematics teacher education is two-fold; to change the content of what is learned in order to reflect the knowledge and skills necessary for realizing current visions of mathematics teaching, and to improve the process of mathematics teacher education so that it has a substantial and lasting impact on the thinking and practice of teachers. Teacher education programs have often been unsuccessful in changing the views of inservice and preservice teachers, views which teachers began developing as students in traditional classrooms. Teachers often teach as they were taught, not as they were taught to teach. Mathematics teacher education must help teachers and prospective teachers 'break with experience' (Ball, 1990), that is, to change their relationship to mathematics, mathematics learning and mathematics teaching.

Competencies for Teaching

Using the model of teaching described above as the goal of mathematics teacher education, we can identify particular knowledge and competencies that are required:[3]

- understanding of relevant mathematics;
- ability to analyze relevant conceptual fields and knowledge of related research;
- personally meaningful theory of mathematics learning (an emergent perspective would be an appropriate goal);
- knowledge of students' development of particular mathematical ideas;
- ability to assess students' thinking and develop useful understandings of students' mathematical knowledge;
- ability to generate appropriate learning goals and useful hypotheses of how students might learn particular mathematical content;
- ability to plan instruction and generate appropriate problem contexts;
- ability to interact effectively with students (i.e. listening, questioning, monitoring, and facilitating classroom discourse);
- useful conceptualization of mathematics teaching (e.g. the model presented).

Adapting a Model of Mathematics Teaching

Viewing learning from a constructivist or emergent perspective (in this case the learning of teachers) calls into question traditional models of teacher education as it does traditional methods of mathematics education. As Ball observed:

> Rarely do [teacher educators] treat teacher education students as learners who actively construct understandings about specific subject matter and its pedagogy. Instead of taking what they know and believe into account, teacher educators tend to view prospective teachers as simply lacking particular knowledge and skills. (1988, p. 40)

Not only must the content of mathematics teacher education change, but so must its process. In this section, I explore the notion that new models of mathematics teaching can be used to generate parallel approaches to the teaching of mathematics pedagogy. As mentioned earlier, coherence between the approach to teaching promoted in mathematics teacher education and how mathematics teacher education is taught may provide additional support for teachers transforming their ideas about teaching and learning.

Drawing an analogy between mathematics teaching and mathematics teacher education can be defended based on the similarities among the objectives of each. Both aim toward the development of powerful thinkers and confident problem solvers (teaching is a series of non-routine problems), who possess conceptual understanding and who can bring these attributes along with intuition and creativity to the tasks that they face. Therefore, it seems reasonable that recent innovations in mathematics teaching might provide, by analogy, the rudiments of a model of mathematics teacher education. I will use the model of teaching described above as an example of how such analogical thinking might proceed.

The following implications follow from constructing a model of mathematics teacher education parallel to the model of mathematics teaching presented:

- Understanding the mathematical and pedagogical thinking of the teachers is central to providing effective educational opportunities. Educational interventions must interweave opportunities to inquire into teachers' thinking in order to update and improve the teacher educator's understanding of teachers' thinking.
- Clear goals for teachers and hypotheses of how their learning might proceed are needed to organize the design and sequence of opportunities for teacher development. This could potentially replace the 'smorgasbord' approach, common in teacher education, in which the teachers participate in a variety of experiences deemed beneficial. Such an approach lacks attention to the developmental processes of teachers.
- The teacher educator's interactions with students can be categorized in a similar manner to the mathematics teacher's interactions with her students: inquiry into teachers' thinking (discussed above); constraining and fostering teachers' construction of concepts and skills; encouraging and orienting reflection; negotiating norms, practices and shared meanings; and encouraging and organizing communication with other professionals.

Although thinking about mathematics teacher education as analogous to mathematics teaching may contribute to the development of useful models of teacher education, the inherent challenges are greater. Understanding pedagogical thinking and promoting its development is a far more difficult task for the following reasons. First, it encompasses many diverse areas of knowledge (including knowledge of and about mathematics). Second, the research base is less developed than it is with respect to many areas of mathematical understanding. Third, because this is an emerging model of practice, the aspects of pedagogical thinking that are important have neither been well articulated by the research community nor are they observable in most classrooms. Also, because of the interrelatedness and interdependency of teachers' mathematical and pedagogical understandings, it is often insufficient to focus on isolated areas of understanding. This makes the conceptualization of teachers' understanding extremely complex.

The Impact of Constructivism on Mathematics Teacher Development Research

The perspective taken in this chapter regarding reform of mathematics teacher education implies the need for two general areas of research, both of which are affected by a constructivist or emergent perspective: developing and elaborating new models of teaching and investigating mathematics teacher development. In this section, I characterize these areas of needed research and point to some recent work of that type that has begun to meet that need.

Developing and Elaborating New Models of Teaching

A first area of research involves the creation and further elaboration of empirically grounded, new visions (models) of mathematics teaching. It is only through clear understanding of the nature of the mathematics teaching that might be achieved that mathematics teacher education can be effectively directed.[4] Several research programs, informed by constructivist and related epistemologies, are contributing to this work. I call attention here to a few of these.

One of the more long-standing and better-developed efforts is that of Realistic Mathematics Education (RME) in The Netherlands. RME, which has a major emphasis on curriculum development and developmental research (Gravemeijer, 1995), has made significant progress in articulating a pedagogical approach. RME is based on a view of learning mathematics as 'proceeding from one's own informal mathematical constructions to what could be accepted as formal mathematics' (Streefland, 1990, p. 1). The RME pedagogy promotes 'guided reinvention' (Freudenthal, 1991), a process that is organized around five teaching/learning principles:

1. constructions stimulated by concreteness;
2. developing mathematical tools to move from concreteness to abstraction;
3. stimulating free productions and reflection;
4. stimulating the social activity of learning by interaction;
5. intertwining learning strands in order to get mathematical material structured (for students to develop a connected knowledge of related ideas and operations). (Streefland, 1990, p. 4)

RME provides a specific pedagogical approach that builds on constructivist and emergent perspectives on learning. The approach, particularly its use of principles 2 and 3 above, offers a unique way of navigating the tension between responding to children's mathematics and fostering the development of particular mathematical ideas.

Several other research programs are contributing an articulation of aspects of mathematics teaching. The work of French researchers (e.g. Brousseau, 1981; Cobb et al., 1993; Yackel and Cobb, 1996, and that of Bauersfeld,

Martin A. Simon

Krummheuer and Voigt (cf. Voigt, 1995) has developed empirically grounded theory with respect to the development of norms for mathematical activity in classrooms. Ball (1993) and Lampert (1990) used their own elementary school teaching practices as sites for theory development with respect to mathematics teaching. Their work has focused particularly on portraying the complexity of the task of teaching and the dilemmas inherent in the endeavor. Schifter (1996) has provided a set of different views of teaching by creating a context for teachers to articulate their experiences of changing their practices.

Although the work referred to above has been important in the creation of new models and images of mathematics teaching, much work remains to be done in order to establish comprehensive models on the basis of which mathematics teacher education can be organized.

Investigating Mathematics Teacher Development

A second key area of research is investigations to further understanding of the processes of mathematics teacher development in the context of efforts toward mathematics education reform. Particularly, how do traditionally reared teachers develop the knowledge, skills and dispositions needed for cutting-edge mathematics teaching? Constructivist and emergent theoretical frameworks can provide a foundation for new research methodologies designed for this purpose. In this section, I describe a research methodology that has emerged in the course of our recent research projects.

The seed crystal for the methodology that we have been developing is the constructivist teaching experiment (Steffe and Thompson, in press; Steffe, 1991; Cobb and Steffe, 1983). The purpose of the constructivist teaching experiment methodology is to develop useful models of learners' mathematics and its development. Earlier, I discussed how this is part of a teacher's inquiry, albeit at an informal level. The teaching experiment methodology and the model of teaching that I described represent a *rapprochement* between teaching and research. That is, teaching ideally involves the type of inquiry characteristic of constructivist teaching experiments and the teaching experiment methodology incorporates aspects of teaching as described in the model herein.

The key premise of the constructivist teaching experiment methodology is that researchers are better able to investigate mathematical conceptual development if they are engaged not only in observing and analyzing it, but also in fostering it. Simon (in press) has elaborated a methodology for studying mathematics teacher development that builds on the constructivist teaching experiment and the whole-class teaching experiment (Cobb, in press) by adapting the notion of fostering development as a context for studying development. The methodology combines whole-class teaching experiments in teacher education courses with a particular adaptation of case study methodology (Simon and Tzur, 1999). Both components serve the perspective on mathematics teacher education, described above, by contributing to the development of empirically based models of teachers' conceptions and activity (together this makes up what we refer to as their 'practice') at different points in their ongoing development.

The Struggle to Reform Mathematics Teaching: A Postscript

Constructivism represents a paradigm shift in our view of knowledge and learning. As such it has contributed to a dissatisfaction with traditional mathematics teaching and mathematics teacher education. Participation in and promotion of a major paradigm shift in mathematics education brings about a range of problems. The reform of mathematics teacher education, critical to the reform of mathematics teaching, is a daunting undertaking. How do we assist teachers in teaching mathematics based on a paradigm that is different from the one in which they were reared?

The struggle to meet this challenge is hampered in a number of ways by the inability of many to appreciate its enormity. In particular, the following issues arise:

- Because the proposed reforms are not well understood, particularly by policy-makers, the radical nature of the changes are not appreciated. This translates into unrealistic expectations about the length of time and level of intervention needed for teachers to change their practices. Thus, inadequate, and often trivial, levels of professional development are provided. Support for and patience with teachers who are taking the risks of and going through the awkward process of being a novice in a new paradigm are often insufficient. There is a lack of understanding that small changes (e.g. use of manipulatives or cooperative learning) do not add up to a profound change in mathematics instruction.
- There is a lack of awareness of the need to develop an infrastructure of adequately prepared teacher educators for making innovative teacher development opportunities available on a large scale. Educators who can teach mathematics in ways that are consistent with the evolving paradigm are needed for the effective mathematics teacher education of others. Although the infrastructure made up of such teachers/teacher educators can grow exponentially, the early part of the growth curve is necessarily modest. Thus the current infrastructure is insufficient for widespread interventions with teachers.
- Many fail to understand that being a good mathematics teacher, though necessary, is not sufficient to make one a good mathematics teacher educator. Teachers can understand well the mathematical development of children, yet have little insight into or conceptualization of the pedagogical development of teaching professionals. Thus, programs that assume that once teachers have learned to teach in new ways, they can teach others to do the same, are unlikely to be successful.

- Finally, the need for careful and extensive research into the development of mathematics teachers must be prioritized. Little is known about the developmental processes by which teachers come to participate in the emerging paradigm. Mathematics teacher education requires a knowledge base of this type. Such knowledge will not derive from large-scale interventions with teachers that incorporate a small research/evaluation component. Needed are theoretically sound, focused projects whose principal goal is the understanding of mathematics teacher development.

Notes

1 In order to avoid the awkwardness of he/she and him/her, I use the feminine pronouns for the generic third-person singular.
2 For an examination of the relationship of constructivism to other emerging epistemologies, see Steffe and Gale, 1995.
3 Some of these competencies overlap with those needed for other models of practice.
4 See Simon, 1997 for a more detailed discussion of this point.

References

BALL, D.L. (1988) 'Unlearning to teach mathematics', *For the Learning of Mathematics*, 8, pp. 40–8.
BALL, D.L. (1990) 'Breaking with experience in learning to teach mathematics: The role of a preservice methods course', *For the Learning of Mathematics*, 10, pp. 10–16.
BALL, D.L. (1993) 'Halves, pieces, and twoths: Constructing representational contexts in teaching fractions', in CARPENTER, T., FENNEMA, E. and ROMBERG, T. (eds), *Rational Numbers: An Integration of Research*, Hillsdale, NJ: Lawrence Erlbaum, pp. 157–96.
BLUMER, H. (1969) *Symbolic Interactionism: Perspectives and Method*, Englewood Cliffs, NJ: Prentice-Hall.
BROUSSEAU, G. (1981) 'Problemes de didactique des decimaux' (Problems in teaching decimals), *Recherches en Didactiques des Mathematiques*, 2.1, pp. 37–125.
COBB, P. (in press) 'Conducting teaching experiments in collaboration with teachers', in LESH, R. and KELLY, E. (eds), *Innovative Research Designs in Mathematics and Science Education*, Dordrecht: Kluwer.
COBB, P., BOUFI, A., McCLAIN, K. and WHITENACK, J. (1997) 'Reflective discourse and collective reflection', *Journal for Research in Mathematics Education*, 28, pp. 258–77.
COBB, P. and STEFFE, L.P. (1983) 'The constructivist researcher as teacher and model builder', *Journal for Research in Mathematics Education*, 14, pp. 83–94.
COBB, P. and YACKEL, E. (1996) 'Constructivist, emergent, and sociocultural perspectives in the context of developmental research', *Journal of Educational Psychology*, 31, pp. 175–90.
COBB, P., YACKEL, E. and WOOD, T. (1992) 'Interaction and learning in mathematics classroom situations', *Educational Studies in Mathematics*, 23, pp. 99–122.

COBB, P., YACKEL, E. and WOOD, T. (1993) 'Learning mathematics: Multiple perspectives, theoretical orientation', in WOOD, T., COBB, P., YACKEL, E. and DILLON, D. (eds), *Rethinking Elementary School Mathematics: Insights and Issues*, Journal for Research in Mathematics Education Monograph Series, 6, pp. 21–32.

CONFREY, J. (1990) 'Student conceptions, representations, and the design of software', in *Design for Learning*, Cupertino: Apple Computer, External Research, pp. 55–62.

FREUDENTHAL, H. (1991) *Revisiting Mathematics Education: China Lectures*, Dordrecht: Kluwer.

GLASERSFELD, E. VON (1989) 'Cognition, construction of knowledge, and teaching', *Synthese*, 80, pp. 121–40.

GRAVEMEIJER, K. (1995) 'Educational development and developmental research in mathematics education', *Journal for Research in Mathematics Education*, 25, pp. 443–71.

LAMPERT, M. (1990) 'When the problem is not the question and the solution is not the answer: Mathematical knowing and teaching', *American Educational Research Journal*, 27, pp. 29–63.

MCNEAL, B. and SIMON, M. (1994) 'Development of classroom social norms and mathematical practices with preservice teachers', *Proceedings of the Sixteenth Annual Meeting of the North American Chapter of the International Group for the Psychology of Mathematics Education*, Vol. II, Baton Rouge, LA, pp. 231–7.

NATIONAL COUNCIL OF TEACHERS OF MATHEMATICS (1989) *Curriculum and Evaluation Standards For School Mathematics*, Reston, Author.

NATIONAL COUNCIL OF TEACHERS OF MATHEMATICS (1991) *Professional Standards For Teaching Mathematics*, Reston, Author.

PUTNAM, H. (1988) *Representation and Reality*, Cambridge: Bradford Books.

SCHIFTER, D. (ed.) (1996) *What's Happening in Math Class?* Volume 1: *Envisioning New Practices Through Teacher Narratives*, New York: Teachers College Press.

SIMON, M. (1995) 'Reconstructing mathematics pedagogy from a constructivist perspective', *Journal for Research in Mathematics Education*, 26, 2, pp. 114–45.

SIMON, M. (1997) 'Developing new models of mathematics teaching: An imperative for research on mathematics teacher development', in FENNEMA, E. and NELSON, B. (eds), *Mathematics Teachers in Transition*, Hillsdale, NJ: Lawrence Erlbaum, pp. 55–86.

SIMON, M. (in press) 'Research on mathematics teacher development: The teacher development experiment', in KELLY, E. and LESH, R. (eds), *Handbook of Research Design in Mathematics and Science Education*, Hillsdale, NJ: Lawrence Erlbaum.

SIMON, M. and TZUR, R. (1999) 'Explicating the teacher's perspective from the researchers' perspectives: Generating accounts of mathematics teachers' practices', *Journal for Research in Mathematics Education*, 30, pp. 252–64.

SIMON, M., TZUR, R., HEINZ, K., KINZEL, M. and SMITH, M. (1998a) 'Characterizing a perspective on mathematics learning of teachers in transition', in BERENSON, S., DAWKINS, K., BLANTON, M., COULOMBE, W., KOLB, J., NORWOOD, K. and STIFF, L. (eds), *Proceedings of the Twentieth Annual Meeting North American Chapter of the International Group for the Psychology of Mathematics Education*, Vol. 2, Columbus, OH: ERIC, pp. 768–74.

SIMON, M., TZUR, R., HEINZ, K., KINZEL, M. and SMITH, M. (in press) 'Characterizing a perspective on mathematics learning of teachers in transition', *Journal for Research in Mathematics Education*.

STEFFE, L. (1990) 'Mathematics curriculum design: A constructivist perspective', in STEFFE, L. and WOOD, T. (eds), *Transforming Children's Mathematics Education: International Perspectives*, Hillsdale, NJ: Lawrence Erlbaum, pp. 389–98.

STEFFE, L. (1991) 'The constructivist teaching experiment: Illustrations and implications', in GLASERSFELD, E. VON (ed.), *Radical Constructivism in Mathematics Education*, Dordrecht: Kluwer, pp. 177–94.

STEFFE, L. and D'AMBROSIO, B. (1995) 'Toward a working model of constructivist teaching: A reaction to Simon', *Journal for Research in Mathematics Education*, 26, 2, pp. 146–59.

STEFFE, L. and GALE, J. (1995) *Constructivism in Education*, Hillsdale, NJ: Lawrence Erlbaum.

STEFFE, L. and THOMPSON, P. (in press) 'Teaching experiment methodology: Underlying principles and essential characteristics', in LESH, R. and KELLY, E. (eds), *Research Design in Mathematics and Science Education*. Hillsdale, NJ: Lawrence Erlbaum.

STREEFLAND, L. (1990) 'Realistic Mathematics Education (RME) What does it mean?', in GRAVEMEIJER, K., VAN DEN HEUVEL, M. and STREEFLAND, L. (eds), *Contexts Free Productions Tests and Geometry in Realistic Mathematics Education*, Utrecht: Research Group for Mathematics Education and Educational Computer Centre State University, pp. 1–9.

TZUR, R. (1995) 'Interaction and Children's Fraction Learning', unpublished PhD dissertation, Athens, University of Georgia.

TZUR, M., SIMON, M., HEINZ, K. and KINZEL, M. (1998) 'Meaningfully connecting mathematical pieces: An account of a teacher in transition', in OLIVIER, A. and NEWSTEAD, K. (eds), *Proceedings of the 22nd Annual Meeting of the International Group for the Psychology of Mathematics Education*, Vol. 4, Stellenbosch, South Africa, pp. 145–52.

VOIGT, J. (1995) 'Thematic patterns of interaction and sociomathematical norms', in COBB, P. and BAUERSFELD, H. (eds), *The Emergence of Mathematical Meaning: Interaction in Classroom Cultures*, Hillsdale, NJ: Lawrence Erlbaum, pp. 163–201.

YACKEL, E. and COBB, P. (1996) 'Sociomath norms, argumentation, and autonomy in mathematics', *Journal for Research in Mathematics Education*, 27, pp. 458–77.

15 Themes and Issues in Mathematics Teacher Education

Robert P. Hunting

Several themes will be explored in this chapter relevant to principles of a constructivist epistemology as it might be applied in mathematics teacher education. I take up the issues of understanding the nature of the mathematics teacher against the context of traditional mathematics instruction, the relation between learning and control, and the exhausting effect of the 'classroom press'. The implications of shifting control over one's learning from the teacher, to the students and teacher together, is discussed. The role of language in communications about mathematics is addressed with reference to the idea of a consensual domain, or culture of the classroom. The necessity to make explicit how language serves the learning process, and the need for opportunities to clarify meanings for terms, is illustrated by examples from teacher education classes I have taught recently. The significance of the unexpected response in communicating with students is discussed, highlighting the need for teachers to become engaged in ongoing networks of mathematics practice. Teachers need to be active mathematically. The importance of a program component which emphasizes the mathematical activity of teachers and opportunities to broaden and deepen personal networks of mathematical concepts is underlined. Finally, I return to the issue of classroom culture, and suggest that beginning teachers will be influenced positively by role models who are actively seeking better to understand their own practice. I propose a special experimental laboratory that would serve as a half-way house between the university campus and the school classroom where the education of mathematics teachers could be focused.

Understanding the Beginning Teacher

Teacher education students enter their programs with a range of backgrounds with respect to past achievement in mathematics, their feelings about and attitudes to mathematics and its teaching, preference for style of teaching they would like to experience at the university, as well as style of teaching they would use in teaching children. They also come with different levels of consciousness as to what teaching is about, as Calderhead suggested.

> Some students, for example, may have the appropriate attitudes, knowledge, and skills to analyze and appraise their entering conceptions of teaching, while

> others may need considerable and varied experience of classroom observation and teaching before they are able to identify their own preconceptions. (1992, p. 142)

Bauersfeld (1998) noted the need to change the teacher's habitus before old patterns and practices are reinforced by the overwhelming pressure of the school system to reproduce old solutions. Such pressure works to maximize smoothness of regular classroom processes with a minimum of effort on the part of the teacher. The regressive effect of school life as it is, feeds on the teacher's own socialization which has already occurred over the previous twelve to thirteen years. As Bauersfeld observed:

> Prescriptions and models for preservice education particularly underestimate – indeed ignore – the negative power and impact of student teachers' own classroom experiences as students over a dozen or more years of schooling. (1998, pp. 214–15)

A significant part of the teacher's socialization takes place outside the classroom, where the influence of parents, care givers, the wider family and community in general reinforces attitudes learned as a result of school experiences.

To compound these problems, conceptions of mathematics as a human activity, and the belief that mathematical meaning is constructed as a result of such activity, run counter to the teacher's personal experience of mathematics as a student. Not only do teachers as students experience mathematical rules and procedures as the core of mathematics, but as Byers suggested, they are also 'exposed to a formal, sanitized version of the subject', where 'over the years every hint of struggle and controversy has been wiped clean' (1983, p. 37).

Understanding the Practicing Teacher

Programs designed to help teachers reconstruct their ideas about mathematics and mathematics teaching need to take account of a, if not *the*, dominant paradigm in teacher education: the apprenticeship model, where learning how to teach is achieved by way of emulating working teachers and repeated practice (Britzman, 1986). According to Britzman, two implicit rules govern the hidden tensions of classroom life. '[U]nless the teacher establishes control there will be no learning, and, if the teacher does not control the students, the students will control the teacher' (1986, p. 447). Thus learning becomes equated with social control, and responsibility for establishing and maintaining control is considered to fall primarily to the individual teacher. Grossman argued that the idea of first establishing control, then turning one's attention to content and student learning is too simplistic. 'How teachers manage classrooms enables or constrains the possibilities of teaching, classroom discourse, and student learning' (1992, p. 174). Dewey (1965[1904]) realized that the apprenticeship model of teacher education, which has as its goal mastery of the procedural aspects of teaching, was likely only to perpetuate existing practices.

Another dimension of teaching, related to the notion of learning as social control, is the extent to which the teacher sees authority as emanating from within herself.

> Once a person or teacher begins to accept herself or himself as a legitimate authority, she or he begins to lay the groundwork for the acceptance of contextuality and relativism that fosters a sense of self and control. (Cooney, 1994, p. 628)

Cooney continued to argue that

> the ability to be reflective and adaptive requires that an individual have the capacity to see the world as contextual, that is, as a world in which one tries to understand how others (e.g., students) come to know and believe what they do. Such a constructivist orientation cannot be achieved when the world is seen in absolute terms. (ibid., p. 628)

How teachers respond to the complexities and demands of teaching may be explained by relationships – yet to be properly understood – among their beliefs about learning as social control, their orientation to sources of authority, and their disposition to learning new ideas and practices. It may be that personality factors such as willingness to take risks, or a desire for stability and predictability, are also crucial determiners of teacher effectiveness.

The reality of classroom life needs also to be taken into account. Fullan and Stiegelbauer described the subjective reality of teaching in the following way:

> teachers must deal with constant daily interruptions, within the classroom in managing discipline and interpersonal conflicts, and from outside the classroom in collecting money for school events, making announcements, dealing with the principal, parents, central office staff, etc.; they must get through the daily grind. (1991, p. 33)

Huberman (1983) and Crandall et al. (1982) have concluded that the 'classroom press' described by Fullan and Stiegelbauer has the effect of focusing teachers on day-to-day events, isolates them from other teachers, exhausts their energy, limits their opportunities for sustained reflection, and increases their dependency on experiential knowledge for coping to the exclusion of other sources of knowledge.

Fostering Autonomy and Self-Regulation

Constructivist approaches to teaching reject the learning-as-control paradigm identified by Britzman (1986) and others. Cobb and his associates (Cobb et al.,

1990) observed that as their project teacher reconceptualized her role away from the traditional overseer, making sure children stayed on task, to that of a facilitator of learning, her students simultaneously gained more autonomy. This reconceptualization was necessary to achieve an important goal of the research; that is, for the teacher to adopt a role similar to the constructivist researcher in a teaching experiment. A major concern in the constructivist teaching experiment is to construct models of children's mathematical understandings. Constructing such models requires a milieu where problematic tasks and social interactions between researcher and children, and between children and children, afford children an opportunity to express or provide clues about meanings underlying their responses. It was important to the project team that a classroom climate was created where children's thinking and explanations were publicly communicated and discussed. The authority, control and ownership of learning shifted away from the teacher to the classroom community. Not only could the teacher more effectively guide the curriculum and make strategic decisions, the students made contributions in establishing a community of mathematical practice. The goal of enabling students to take more responsibility for their work – student emancipation – is an indication of teacher emancipation, which Jaworski (1992) has linked to a process of developing critical reflective practice. Other indicators included the teacher's overt knowledge of mathematics and pedagogy, and confidence in personal ability to make appropriate choices and judgments.

There is a connection between self-regulation and autonomy of a group of learners, such as in a classroom, and that of the individual. Self-regulation for the group as a whole in the classroom is motivated by the teacher, and to a lesser extent, by the ethos of the school. Self-regulation in the individual is determined both by the social norms at play in the classroom, and processes of cognitive adaptation as individuals elaborate and reorganize their mental schemes. Paris and Byrnes (1989) identified three promising instructional strategies in the teaching of reading that seemed to promote self-regulated learning in children. First is a form of direct teaching in which greater emphasis is placed upon explanations of learning strategies. Second is teaching which emphasizes peer tutoring, dialogues between children, or Socratic discussions. The third involves cooperative learning involving group discussion, argument and co-construction of appropriate learning strategies. The critical questions in fostering autonomy and self-regulation are:

- How does one transpose the time-intensive constructivist research methodologies of clinical interview and small-group teaching experiment to classroom settings?
- How should schools be organized to allow such time-intensive practices to take place?
- What characterizes teachers who are able to create communities of mathematics practice?
- What does a teacher education program look like that will engender such teachings?

Some indication of an answer to the last question can be found in the work of the Educational Leaders in Mathematics (ELM) Project (Simon and Schifter, 1991) and the Construction of Elementary Mathematics (CEM) Project (Simon, 1994, 1995; Simon and Blume, 1994). It is likely that the most promising changes in the short term will come from projects targeted toward in-service teachers. One reason for targeting in-service teachers is that changes in teaching practice will most likely occur for those teachers who are already searching for alternatives to their teaching practice. A precondition for change in teaching practice is a feeling of dissatisfaction with one's current practice, and a feeling of dissatisfaction is likely to be found in teachers who have been immersed in traditional teaching practices but who understand mathematics relationally. However, projects like ELM are labor, cost and time intensive. They are built around the assumptions that autonomy and self-regulation need to be fostered in students, and that students' mathematical viewpoints need to be heard and heeded by teachers. More attention needs to be given to the development of visions of constructivist classroom teaching in which the mathematical thinking and reasoning of students can be experienced and studied (Maher and Alston, 1990). Skills, attitudes and stances for creating the necessary classroom cultures in which students' mathematical viewpoints and ideas will be expressed and valued need to be identified and more widely practiced. Finally, strategies for implementing change need to be developed that are sensitive to the difficulties involved in changing teaching practices which are embedded in traditional views of teaching and purposes of schooling as understood in a wider society.

Language and the Role of Communication

When discussing issues of learning and teaching mathematics with teachers it is important to be explicit about the part language plays in the communication process. As Glasersfeld (1991, 1995) has reminded us, a belief that language is the vehicle by which knowledge is transported from speaker to listener is an illusion. This illusion is very seductive, since at any given moment in a conversation, it often appears that the people in the conversation can be 'on the same wavelength' – that is, behave as if the meanings for the words somehow exist independently of the people conversing. Most of the discourse in mathematics classrooms seems compatible with this assumption.

In Maturana's (1988) account of communication, however, the participants are responsible for establishing, maintaining and modifying their own social system. A social system, according to Maturana (1980), is a network of interactions of a collection of individuals. A social system is constituted by a 'consensual domain of interactions' (Maturana, 1978), which is formed when, from the perspective of an observer, the interacting individuals act in accord, as if they have come to agreement regarding their underlying assumptions. Basic to the establishment of a consensual domain is the use of words in social action (Richards, 1991). Relative agreements are the material of consensual domains, where the subjective experiences of each of the parties are taken as shared.

Consciousness of the role of language in mathematics discourse is heightened by the precision in the use of language by the mathematical community. Precision in the use of language is a distinguishing feature which sets mathematics apart from other domains of knowledge and, in particular, ordinary discourse. In daily, non-technical, conversations it is usually possible to establish at least a modicum of understanding of the ideas and intentions of others. Among other things, the listener can anticipate, interpret, test and, above all, extend the speaker's utterances sufficiently to establish communication, especially in those cases where there is a history of shared experiences. In mathematical discourse, however, there is less ambiguity in the use of language than there is in everyday discourse, and conflicts can arise in discourse in mathematics classrooms as a result because students use their natural language not only to attribute meaning to the teacher's utterances, but also to carry on 'mathematical' conversations. As an example, in a pre-service teacher education course I taught, we had been considering number systems. At the start of a class I wrote the terms 'number' and 'numeral' on the board and asked the students what they thought these terms meant. As I expected, there was mostly silence, with a few desultory and uninspired responses. So I began to explain that the word 'number' referred to a concept, whereas the term 'numeral' referred to a symbol for the concept. One particular student asked an obvious (to her) question: 'Do you teach primary children this distinction?' Some discussion followed and the class agreed that while it is important for teachers to be aware of and use appropriately the meanings of technical terms, when communicating with children in the early years, a teacher can expect children to refer to numerals as 'numbers', since that is what they learn from their parents and that is how the term is used in the general community. Paradoxically, while it has been my experience that elementary teachers are themselves quite unsure of how to use mathematical terminology and of how this teminology relates to their teaching practice, secondary teachers often seem too formal in their use of language. As Bauersfeld said, 'many mathematics teachers are quite rigid in how they express themselves verbally and how they evaluate their own students' utterances. However they remain quite permissive with respect to the social organization of their class' (1998, p. 223). Bauersfeld went on to recommend that these teachers should accept and encourage students' mathematical utterances within very wide limits, but be more rigid in insisting on keeping social regulations such as turn-taking in speaking, listening to others' explanations and taking seriously others' contributions.

Incompatibility of meaning, and its resolution, was exemplified in a discussion that occurred in another class I taught recently. We were investigating prime numbers. The students were exploring rectangular shapes which could be made from different numbers of wooden cubes. The aim of the investigation was to show how certain numbers of cubes could only be made into rectangular shapes just one cube wide, leading to a classification of prime and composite numbers. The investigation seemed to be proceeding quite well until we together checked the arrangements the students had made, beginning with two cubes. When we discussed possible arrangements of four cubes, one student remarked that a 2 × 2 cube arrangement was not a rectangular shape but a square. So, I asked the class what their ideas of a rectangle were. After some discussion, we settled on a definition along the lines of a quadrilateral with opposite sides equal and all interior angles of 90 degrees. The question to be resolved was: 'Does a 2 × 2 cube arrangement fit the agreed upon definition?' We then discussed the general issue of class inclusion. One of the students, who had a 5-year-old child just beginning school, mentioned that her daughter had recently brought home a math activity sheet on which were pasted simple geometric shapes, such as a square, a rectangle, a circle, etc., along with their labels. She asked this question: 'Should a kindergarten teacher teach five-year-olds that a square is also a rectangle?' I stonewalled for a few seconds while I considered how I would respond and then took the less desirable option. Even though this is just the sort of issue that provokes spirited classroom discussion, I felt that the students were sufficiently interested so that my comments might make sense to them. So, rather than turn the question over to the class for consideration and comment, I chose to make the following observations:

- Five-year-olds in general haven't constructed the operation of class inclusion needed to produce an inclusion of squares in rectangles, so take care in what you ask the children to do.
- If you think there is a chance some children can produce an inclusion relation, then go for it, because the intuitive separation of squares and rectangles may persist in later times even when the children are in fact capable of producing the inclusion relation, and it may never seem intuitive that a square is also a rectangle.

Learning How to Deal with the Unexpected Response

An important issue to be addressed in mathematics teacher education programs is how to educate teachers in such a way that they realize the significance of children's unexpected responses. As Confrey observed, '[T]he most basic skill a constructivist educator must learn is to approach a foreign or unexpected response with a genuine interest in learning its character, its origins, its story, and its implications' (1990, p. 108).

Teachers generally believe that they are expected to be the fountain of all wisdom in the classroom. Schools and the community indeed have expectations that teachers will fulfill certain obligations in planning and directing the learning experiences of the children for whom they are responsible. Unfortunately, while curriculum statements (NCTM, 1989; Australian Education Council, 1990) are based on constructivist principles of learning, the statements are framed without due regard to the psychological boundaries that constrain students' learning of mathematics. And classroom teaching remains dominated by the textbook as the guide to selecting and implementing mathematical content. As a consequence, teachers are likely to interpret a student's response in terms of the mathematical content being taught rather than in terms of the interpretive constructs of the student.

Dealing with the Unexpected Response in the Living Flow of Classroom Life

Models, examples and interpretations of constructivist mathematics teaching are needed which illustrate the interactive nature of the teacher's goals and actions (Simon, 1994). Careful planning is critical for effective teaching, but the plan should be viewed as a point of departure. As Simon (Ch. 14) has observed, the actual experience of interaction between students and teacher, as perceived by the teacher, is usually different from that anticipated. The teacher's ideas and knowledge are used instrumentally in the sense-making processes in which she is involved. For a student's response to be classified as unexpected suggests that the teacher rests, probably uncomfortably, on the threshold of an adaptation as she experiences perturbation foreshadowing an accommodation in *her* knowledge structures. An impediment to the accommodation is the flow of classroom discourse and classroom pressures impinging at the moment. Such discourse and pressures may well act against, or even prevent, further interactions or reflection necessary for an adequate interpretation of the student's unexpected response. Implicit in Confrey's (1990) observation is the desirability of departing from the planned activities in order to explore, with the student and his/her peers, the meaning of the unexpected response. A common experience of many teachers is that the complexity of managing the classroom prevents them from exploration of the unexpected response. In that case, personal reflection and consultations with other teachers can leave the way open for a follow-up discussion in a subsequent class. Opportunities to discuss children's responses highlight the need for communication between peers and establishment of professional networks, as well as highlighting the importance of the role of communities of mathematics practice.

When Unanticipated Silence is the Unexpected Response

Through experience and appropriate education, a teacher can learn to anticipate a good proportion of students' responses to tasks or problems. What seems essential in this is for the teachers to engage in pedagogically relevant and specialized mathematical experiences and to use these experiences as a point of departure for bringing forth mathematical activity of their students. Recently I had my pre-service elementary teachers, who were in their senior

Figure 15.1 How would you find the area of this figure?

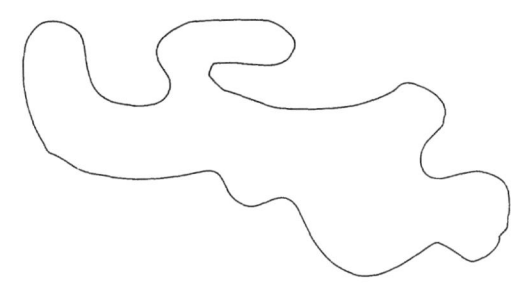

year just prior to the final semester of student teaching, consider the measurement of area, and in particular the relation between area and perimeter. I invited them to consider the 'blob' shown in Figure 15.1.

As directions, the teacher education students were told that a child was asked to find the area of an irregular region shaped like the 'blob' in Figure 15.1. They were then told that the child responded as follows: 'Wrap a string around the blob. Then use the string to form a rectangle. This area will be the same as the area of the blob.' They were then asked: 'Suppose you are the teacher, and you know that the child normally does good work. What would you do or say to the child?' I expected, from previous experience, that most of the teacher education students would consider the responses of the child as very creative. So I structured the session in the following way:

- I handed out the blob as in Figure 15.1 along with the directions. I also handed out a length of string for each teacher.
- I invited them individually to consider the blob along with the directions and, without discussion, write a response. I allowed about five minutes.
- The students were encouraged to share individual responses within their table groups. After about five minutes I directed them to draw a line under what they had first written, and write anything further thay would like to add as a result of the group discussion.
- We then had a whole-class discussion, where I invited opinions to be shared. At this point, the main thrust of the comments was that the child should be commended for the response, and that he (she) be encouraged to carry out the activity.
- I then passed out a sheet of 1 cm grid paper, and asked the teachers to trace around their foot or shoe. We spent some time – about 15–20 minutes – exploring issues of area of non-rectilinear regions including strategies for counting square units intersected by the shape boundary, the notion of a measure being an approximation, and how by superimposing a smaller scale grid it would be possible to trap the theoretical measure of the area of the foot-shaped region between bounds.

- I directed the teachers to draw another line under the most recent comment addendum, and invited them to record any further thoughts they had on the original task.

Almost uniformly, these students agreed that this was a *better* way to figure out the area of the blob. I then invited them to make rectangles with their pieces of string by tying the ends. There was no spontaneous 'aha' response, so I explained how the shape of a rectangle, and thus area enclosed, could be varied, by manipulating the string using their fingers. My hope was that at least one student would realize that the dimensions of the rectangle they had made were relatively arbitrary, but that the length of string was fixed, so perimeter and area could not then be directly related. Here was a situation in which I resorted to some explicit guidance. It was a professional decision, which I would have preferred not to initiate, except that the shadows on this lesson were growing fairly long, and nearly time for class to end. In this case, the unexpected response was in fact an unwelcome silence. As teachers we stumble often when our intended goals evaporate due to unanticipated or unproductive responses to our questions.

It is easy to underestimate the importance of the mathematical experience of the teachers in bringing forth, sustaining and modifying the mathematical activity of their students. It is also easy to underestimate the importance of the teachers understanding, then coming to own, the epistemological framework underpinning constructivist teaching. Owning it in a general sense – that is, deliberately and intentionally planning lessons with principles compatible with constructivist teaching to the fore – and consistently implementing it on each specific occasion, may be two different issues, as the previous example indicates. Only an epistemology that celebrates the reality of subjective meanings has any use for foreign or unexpected responses as significant indicators of student knowledge structures.

The Unexpected Response as an Occasion for Re-interpretation

A foreign or unexpected response is an indication that the teacher may need to revise or reorganize her existing knowledge structures in order to fit that response into them in a coherent way. At La Trobe University we established a professional development program called 'Clinical Approaches to Mathematics Assessment' to provide advanced training for practicing teachers in the theory and method of clinical assessment and teaching (Hunting, 1997; Hunting and Doig, 1992, 1997). Underpinning the workshop sessions was a rationale encompassing the key terms *observe, interpret* and *act*. We distinguished between observation and interpretation, since individuals may observe an event or behavior and 'see' different things. They may also attach more or less significance to the event or behavior, depending on their experience and knowledge base. Action is dependent on interpretation, and often it is through interpretation that meaning is imputed to observation. Although an observation is not regarded as independent of the observer, an interpretation of an observation can be distinguished from the observation if constructs are used in the interpretation that are not used in the observation.

There seem to be two kinds of teacher action. One kind is consequent upon interpretation. Having interpreted a set of responses to given tasks the teacher moves to design a teaching strategy that takes account of the students' current knowledge states. The second kind of action is a result of observation and unresolved effort to interpret the observation to one's satisfaction. In this case, steps would be taken to engage the students in further dialogue, possibly involving a new or modified problem, to clarify what the students know. Experiences of working with students may lead also to the teacher *re-interpreting* students' behavior. In this case, the teacher's interpretive framework is fluid and developing. Often a student's behavior will not fit existing expectations a teacher has for that student or of any other student with whom she has previously worked – not because that teacher has a limited experience base, but rather because that teacher's interpretive framework is not adequate to account for the possible behaviors that a student might exhibit. Even the most erudite mathematics educator should hold open the possibility of being surprised because it is the surprises that remind us that our understanding of others is just that – our understanding – and we should not make the mistake of believing that our interpretations are identical to the knowledge of the interpreted. It follows then, that sometimes as teachers we will be able to interpret what we see against the background of some interpretive principles or propositions. But often adaptations will have to be made in our ways and means of understanding children's mathematical learning to account for some behavior which cannot be otherwise interpreted adequately. Re-interpretation is perhaps the most crucial action of all, since teacher growth and effectiveness depends upon it.

Maximizing Problem Solving for Insight

'Improving mathematical education in the schools starts with improvements in the mathematical knowledge of teachers' (Steffe, 1990, p. 184). Teachers need to transform their conception of mathematics in such a way that they establish a network of mathematical concepts and operations that encompasses what can be pointed at in a textbook. For example, rather than take the axioms of equality as a starting place in teaching the solution of linear equations, teachers need to rely on the mental operation of subtracting as the inversion of adding that is available to most algebra students and then guide them in producing the axioms of equality in symbolic form. Mathematically active teachers are likely to understand what it means for their students to become mathematically active at their own level. Encouraging mathematics teachers to be mathematically active and to reorganize the mathematics that they teach is essential in a *constructivist teacher education*.

Robert P. Hunting

Pedagogical Knowledge

Mathematics teacher education programs need to provide opportunities for teachers to be pedagogically as well as mathematically active. Although these two activities are highly related, they involve different kinds of problem solving. In pedagogical problem solving, a mathematical problem from the classroom, such as finding the area of a blob (Figure 15.1), might be presented for solution. When selecting the mathematical problems to be solved, the teacher educator should bear in mind the school mathematics curriculum and the mathematical sophistication of the teachers. Sequences of problem situations can be developed which lead to important results that have general implications for reorganizing the mathematics curriculum. Pedagogical problem solving should serve to broaden and deepen the mathematical concepts of the teachers, and to encourage discussion and reflections on processes leading to insight. Written records of solutions of pedagogical problems provide material upon which students can reflect. A strategy that works well is to ask the students to record their personal solutions to a problem prior to sharing them within a small group setting. If they are then asked to revise their personal solutions after small-group discussion and after whole-class discussion, each student would then have a record of the development of his or her thinking as it has evolved through engagement with ideas and thinking of peers and teacher.

Mathematical Knowledge

To enhance teachers' personal network of inter-connected mathematical schemes is no easy task. For example, in my pre-service elementary mathematics methods course we considered the topic of two dimensional geometry as well as measurement (of which the blob task in Figure 1 is a particular example). In one investigation, I asked the students to investigate which of a collection of geometric shapes would tessellate the plane. Included were various triangles and quadrilaterals. In the next class meeting I posed this question: 'Can you measure area by using any tessellating shape'? We did not discuss it, but I hinted there would be a question on an upcoming mid-term test related to that issue. The relevant question for the mid-term was designed to encourage an integration of taught topics involving both geometry and area measurement (Figure 15.2).

While many teachers could remember a formula for calculating the area of a trapezoid, only two of forty-eight explicitly indicated their awareness of the fact that a trapezoidal shape will tessellate. So it was not surprising that no one discussed how the problem of comparing measures could be solved. However, a majority of students indicated that applying a square grid would be a better approach, especially in the case of the trapezoidal table. Many of the students said iterating the trapezoid unit would create gaps. It was not clear if they were referring to gaps only at the boundaries.

Figure 15.2 Question on an examination in an elementary mathematics methods course

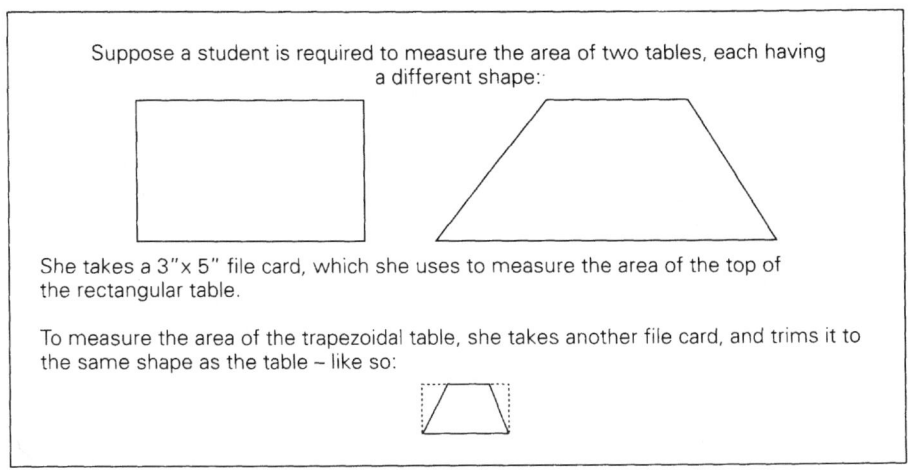

Suppose a student is required to measure the area of two tables, each having a different shape:

She takes a 3"x 5" file card, which she uses to measure the area of the top of the rectangular table.

To measure the area of the trapezoidal table, she takes another file card, and trims it to the same shape as the table – like so:

Comment on these responses, and outline several questions, tasks, or activities that you feel would be useful to assist this student in her understanding of area.

Classroom Culture

In general, the cultures of university classrooms and school classrooms are quite different. Efforts of teacher educators to communicate a vision for how mathematics learning and teaching might be practiced rapidly evaporate under the necessity for newcomers to teaching to move toward full participation in the sociocultural practices of a school community (Lave and Wenger, 1991). Generally, mathematics teacher education faculty working with pre-service elementary school teachers have almost no influence over the quality of the mathematics teacher with whom a student is placed for practice teaching. In most cases, the vision of an apprentice learning the craft of mathematics teaching from a master has quite a different meaning than what is intended by mathematics education faculty. If, however, classroom teachers with whom beginning teachers interact are themselves active participants in reflective teaching and learning, and if they are interacting with mathematics educators and reading the mathematics education literature on a regular basis, so that they in turn serve as 'teacher apprentices' at a higher level, then the powerful socializing influence of the classroom could have positive effects.

As it now stands, ways need to be found of educating mathematics teachers so that they may make intentional and informed decisions concerning their teaching practices. Both beginning teachers and practicing teachers would benefit from opportunities to consider and reflect on the mathematics teaching of others. Sarason et al. (1986, quoted in Fullan and Stiegelbauer, 1991) reported that a frequent criticism of psychology courses by students was lack of opportunity to observe in a live situation how the principles of psychology could be derived. It is valuable to video record classroom practice with the purpose of allowing different analyses of the same episode from different perspectives and theoretical orientations. Bringing the reality and complexity of classroom life on to the university campus via the video medium enhances the impact of the teaching of theoretical orientations as well as assists teachers to see how the explanations and constructs are manifested in practice. Supervising teachers who are willing to undertake programs of advanced training in mathematics teaching should be given incentives and university faculty should have regular involvement in some form of school classroom life. Establishment of experimental zones of best practice that are half-way houses between the university and the school, after the style of a laboratory or demonstration school, could help bridge the gap between the imperatives of school classrooms and theoretical perspectives, driving new ways of thinking about mathematics learning and teaching. In such zones, teachers and children would engage in practices illustrative of a mathematics learning community. Partners in carefully planned interventions and teaching experiments, in addition to in-house teaching faculty, would include university faculty, pre-service teachers, and teachers enrolled in graduate and other professional development programs. The in-house teachers would be appointed following a careful selection process. These would be leader teachers able to foster autonomy and self-regulation in their students, and aware of the critical role of language in mathematical discourse. The leader teachers would be expected to contribute to seminars and classes dealing with methods and curriculum issues, and their teaching loads would be adjusted accordingly. Some of the children might be long-term students – subjects of longitudinal studies of conceptual development. Other children may be invited to participate for an academic year; or visit for shorter periods from nearby schools. The university professors and leader teachers would spend significant time at the beginning of the school year establishing team approaches to teaching. It would be commonplace to see a professor teaching a whole class or a group of children, observed by his or her teacher education students, and recorded for later analysis and reflection. Whether or not the professor or the leader teacher taught the class, teachers would be able to observe the outcomes of hypothetical learning trajectories within mathematical teaching cycles (Simon, 1995), and later engage in dialogue about the intentions, outcomes and reasons for divergences.

Pre-service and in-service teachers would engage in practical projects related to their professional development, supervised directly by leader teachers and university faculty members. Such projects could embrace teaching experiments or clinical interventions to investigate children's knowledge and its development, implement and/or evaluate new curriculum materials, models of teaching, or assessment tools. Pre-service teachers would understudy a leader teacher for a time, as happens conventionally. The difference would be that the pre-service teachers would be immersed in a culture of reform that would permeate the experimental zone as envisaged. Mathematics teacher education would be integrated with living exemplifications of new models of mathematics teaching.

Conclusion

I have discussed the broad context in which teachers learn how to advance the mathematics knowledge of students, and subsequently practice what they have learned in the classroom. A dominant theme is classroom culture and how it shapes attitudes, beliefs and actions of pre-service teachers. The present classroom culture works against progress. Establishment of the classroom as a *community*, where a teacher accepts that he or she is also a learner, and where authority, control and ownership of learning is shared between students and teacher, warrants deeper study.

If the notion of teaching as imparting knowledge is rejected in favor of fostering powerful constructions, then the role of language needs careful consideration. Development of meanings for symbols, verbal and written, assumes priority. One must assume students' meanings associated with the utterances of a teacher are likely to be different from the teacher's meanings, rather than the other way around. Opportunities for better understanding the knowledge structures of students are in part afforded by instances of foreign or unexpected responses to mathematical tasks, problems and questions. The notion of curriculum as content to be delivered is no longer viable. Teaching is transformed into problem solving just as learning involves problem solving. An implication is achievement of a specific learning objective will be less likely to be completed in short half hour or 50 minute periods. Both teacher and students alike need time to reflect, revisit and to re-examine comments, assertions, solutions and propositions. There will be less pressure on the teacher to *tell*, so it is unlikely that closure will be reached neatly in a single class session.

A priority for mathematics teacher education is to improve teachers' personal networks of interconnected schemes. Improvement of such networks comes with experience, but as a profession we need to develop ways to provide richer environments that will stimulate and enhance scheme network development. One possibility is the establishment of experimental zones of learning and practice where practicing teachers and teachers-to-be can be immersed in a rich and reform-positive environment. Such zones would incorporate scholarly inquiry into important issues of mathematics pedagogy that are rooted in classroom life. Here significant contributions to this process would be sought and expected from practitioners.

Teaching is a complex multidimensional world, where progress in educational reform seems to follow the swing of a pendulum (Throne, 1994). We believe we have ideas about what constitutes quality teaching, but as Sullivan and Mousley suggest, 'attention needs to be focused on the practical and theoretical meanings of the constructs which comprise our understanding of the tasks of teaching and of educational research' (1994, p. 21).

References

AUSTRALIAN EDUCATION COUNCIL (1990) *National Statement on Mathematics for Australian schools*, Carlton: Curriculum Corporation.

BAUERSFELD, H. (1998) 'Remarks on the education of elementary teachers', in LAROCHELLE, M., BEDNARZ, N. and GARRISON, J. (eds), *Constructivism and Education*, New York: Cambridge University Press, pp. 213–32.

BRITZMAN, D.P. (1986) 'Cultural myths in the making of a teacher: Biography and social structure in teacher education', *Harvard Educational Review*, 56, pp. 442–55.

BYERS, B. (1983) 'Beyond structure: Some thoughts on the nature of mathematics', in BERGERON, J.C. and HERSCOVICS, N. (eds), *Proceedings of the Fifth Annual Meeting of PME-NA*, Volume 2, Montreal, pp. 31–40.

CALDERHEAD, J. (1992) 'The role of reflection in learning to teach', in VALLI, L. (ed.), *Reflective Teacher Education: Cases and Critiques*, Albany, NY: State University of New York Press, pp. 139–46.

COBB, P., WOOD, T. and YACKEL, E. (1990) 'Classrooms as learning environments for teachers and researchers', in DAVIS, R.B., MAHER, C.A. and NODDINGS, N. (eds), *Constructivist Views on the Teaching and Learning of Mathematics*, Reston: National Council of Teachers of Mathematics, pp. 125–46.

COBB, P., WOOD, T. and YACKEL, E. (1991) 'A constructivist approach to second grade mathematics', in GLASERSFELD, E. VON (ed.), *Radical Constructivism in Mathematics Education*, Dortrecht: Kluwer, pp. 157–76.

CONFREY, J. (1990) 'What constructivism implies for teaching', in DAVIS, R.B., MAHER, C.A. and NODDINGS, N. (eds), *Constructivist Views on the Teaching and Learning of Mathematics*, Reston: National Council of Teachers of Mathematics, pp. 107–24.

COONEY, T.J. (1994) 'Research and teacher education: In search of common ground', *Journal for Research in Mathematics Education*, 25, pp. 608–36.

CRANDALL, D. and ASSOCIATES. (1982) *People, Policies and Practice: Examining the Chain of School Improvement*, Andover: The Network, Vols 1–10.

DEWEY, J. (1965) 'The relation of theory to practice in education', in BORROWMAN, M. (ed.), *Teacher Education in America: A Documentary History*, New York: Teachers College Press. (Original work published 1904)

FULLAN, M.G. and STIEGELBAUER, S. (1991) *The New Meaning of Educational Change*, London: Cassell.

GLASERSFELD, E. VON (1991) 'Introduction', in GLASERSFELD, E. VON (ed.), *Radical Constructivism in Mathematics Education*, Dordrecht: Kluwer, pp. xii–xx.

GLASERSFELD, E. VON (1995) *Radical Constructivism: A Way of Knowing and Learning*, London: Falmer Press.

GROSSMAN, P.L. (1992) 'Why models matter: An alternative view on professional growth in teaching', *Review of Educational Research*, **62**, 2, pp. 171–9.

HUBERMAN, M. (1983) 'Recipes for busy kitchens', *Knowledge: Creation, Diffusion, Utilization*, 4, pp. 478–510.

HUNTING, R.P. (1997) 'Clinical interview methods in mathematics education research and practice', *Journal of Mathematical Behavior*, 16, pp. 145–65.

HUNTING, R.P. and DOIG, B.A. (1992) 'The development of a clinical tool for initial assessment of a student's mathematics learning', in STEPHENS, M. and IZARD, J. (eds), *Reshaping Assessment Practices: Assessment in the Mathematical Sciences Under Challenge*, Hawthorn: ACER, pp. 201–17.

HUNTING, R.P. and DOIG, B.A. (1997) 'Clinical assessment in mathematics: Learning the craft', *Focus on Learning Problems in Mathematics*, **19**, 3, pp. 29–48.

JAWORSKI, B. (1992) 'The emancipatory nature of reflective mathematics teaching', in GEESLIN, W. and GRAHAM, K. (eds), *Proceedings of the Sixteenth PME Conference*, Durham: University of New Hampshire, pp. 289–96.

LAVE, J. and WENGER, E. (1991) *Situated Learning: Legitimate Peripheral Participation*, Cambridge: Cambridge University Press.

MAHER, C.A. and ALSTON, A. (1990) 'Teacher development in mathematics in a constructivist framework', in DAVIS, R.B., MAHER, C.A. and NODDINGS, N. (eds), *Constructivist Views on the Teaching and Learning of Mathematics*, Reston: National Council of Teachers of Mathematics, pp. 147–66.

MATURANA, H. (1978) 'Biology of language: The epistemology of reality', in MILLER, G. A. and LENNEBERG, E. (eds), *Psychology and Biology of Language and Thought*, New York: Academic Press, pp. 27–64.

MATURANA, H.R. (1980) 'Man and society', in BENSELER, F., HEJL, P.M. and KÖCH, W.K. (eds), *Autopoiesis, Communication, and Society: The Theory of Autopoietic Systems in the Social Sciences*, New York: Campus, pp. 11–32.

MATURANA, H.R. (1988) 'Reality: The search for objectivity or the quest for a compelling argument', in KENNY, V. (ed.), *Radical Constructivism, Autopoiesis, and Psychotherapy, Irish Journal of Psychology*, 9, 1, pp. 25–82.

NATIONAL COUNCIL of TEACHERS of MATHEMATICS (1989) *Curriculum and Evaluation Standards for School Mathematics*, Reston, VA: Author.

PARIS, S.G. and BYRNES, J.P. (1989) 'The constructivist approach to self-regulation and learning in the classroom', in ZIMMERMAN, B.J. and SCHUNK, D.H. (eds), *Self-Regulated Learning and Academic Achievement*, New York: Springer, pp. 169–200.

RICHARDS, J. (1991) 'Mathematical discussions', in GLASERSFELD, E. VON (ed.), *Radical Constructivism in Mathematics Education*, Dordrecht: Kluwer, pp. 13–51.

SARASON, S.B., DAVIDSON, K.S. and BLATT, B. (1986) *The Preparation of Teachers: An Unstudied Problem in Education*, Cambridge, Mass.: Brookline Books.

SIMON, M.A. (1994) 'Learning mathematics and learning to teach: Learning cycles in mathematics teacher education', *Educational Studies in Mathematics*, 26, pp. 71–94.

SIMON, M.A. (1995) 'Reconstructing mathematics pedagogy from a constructivist perspective', *Journal for Research in Mathematics Education*, 26, pp. 114–45.

SIMON, M.A. and BLUME, G. (1994) 'Building and understanding multiplicative relationships: A study of prospective elementary teachers', *Journal for Research in Mathematics Education*, 25, pp. 472–94.

SIMON, M. and SCHIFTER, D. (1991) 'Towards a constructivist perspective: An intervention study of mathematics teacher development', *Educational Studies in Mathematics*, 22, pp. 309–31.

STEFFE, L.P. (1990) 'On the knowledge of mathematics teachers', in DAVIS, R.B., MAHER, C.A. and NODDINGS, N. (eds), *Constructivist Views on the Teaching and Learning of Mathematics*, Reston, VA: National Council of Teachers of Mathematics, pp. 167–86.

STEFFE, L.P. and D'AMBROSIO, B.S. (1995) 'Toward a working model of constructivist teaching: A reaction to Simon', *Journal for Research in Mathematics Education*, 26, pp. 146–59.

SULLIVAN, P. and MOUSLEY, J. (1994) 'Quality mathematics teaching: Describing some key components', *Mathematics Education Research Journal*, 6, pp. 4–22.

THRONE, J. (1994) 'Living with the pendulum: The complex world of teaching', *Harvard Educational Review*, 64, pp. 195–208.

WILDMAN, T.M., NILES, J.A., MAGLIARO, S.G. and MCLAUGHLIN, R.A. (1990) 'Promoting reflective practice among beginning and experienced teachers', in CLIFT, R.T., HOUSTON, W.R. and PUGACH, M.C. (eds), *Encouraging Reflective Practice in Education*, New York: Teachers College Press, pp. 139–62.

16 Becoming a Teacher-Researcher in a Constructivist Teaching Experiment

Despina Potari[1]

To understand the dynamics of teachers reforming their mathematical and instructional practices is widely recognized as a fundamental problem in mathematics education. Many efforts to bring about reforms are grounded in some form of constructivism. A number of studies have examined ways that teachers reconceptualize their role in a constuctivist perspective (Cobb et al., 1990; Maher and Alston, 1990; Simon and Schifter, 1991; Wood et al., 1995), while others have attempted to identify the attributes that are given to 'constructivist teaching' (Confrey, 1990; Simon, 1995a, 1995b; Steffe and D' Ambrosio, 1995, 1996; Glasersfeld, 1995). Some of those studies have explored teachers' development in a classroom learning environment (Cobb et al., 1990), while others have attempted to examine the effect of teacher education programs on this development (Maher and Alston, 1990; Simon and Schifter, 1991). However, there have been no studies of how budding researchers become constructivists and of the dilemmas they face while doing so.

In this study, I examine the attempts of five novice teacher-researchers to reconceptualize teaching as a method of scientific investigation in the context of a constructivist teaching experiment. In a constructivist teaching experiment, researchers act as teachers who interact with children in order to build models of their mathematical realities. Studying novice teacher-researchers' reconceptualization of teaching involves investigating the meanings they give to 'constructivist teaching' and the development of these meanings in the teaching experiment. It also involves closely examining their decisions and actions, motivations and interpretations in their attempts to investigate children's thinking.

Another aim of this investigation was to identify elements of the learning environment that encouraged the novice teacher-researchers to reconceptualize their roles as researchers.

The Constructivist Teaching Experiment as a Research Site

The constructivist teaching experiment is a research methodology used in formulating interpretations of children's behaviors. Cobb and Steffe (1983), Steffe (1991), and Steffe and Thompson (in press) described this methodology as a way of creating models of children's mathematics by interacting with children in a series of teaching episodes for an extended period of time. The researcher acts as a teacher who observes children's constructive processes and attempts to influence them. She formulates and tests hypotheses about children's mathematical knowledge. She also uses the models that she builds about children's learning as the basis for creating a possible mathematical environment for the students while creating learning situations that are designed to be in the children's zone of potential construction (Steffe, 1991). The teaching is 'a goal directed activity' where the goals, rather than being taken as given, continuously change according to children's actions.

The models that the teacher-researcher constructs about children's learning are also crucial when she makes on-the-spot decisions when building the actual mathematical environment in her interaction with the children. In this interaction, she actually learns about children's mathematics through the constraints which she faces. These constraints provide her the opportunity to reflect on what she has tried to achieve, on how she has tried to achieve it and on the environment in which she has tried to achieve it.

In constructivist teaching experiments, teaching as a method of scientific inquiry is predicated on an understanding of human beings as self-organizing and self-regulating organisms. In her attempt to teach the students, the teacher-researcher systematically creates situations and ways of interacting with the students that encourage them to modify their current thinking. But children, as self-organizing systems, become disequilibriated to the extent that their current thinking differs substantially from what the teacher is trying to engender. It is signs of disequilibrium that point the teacher-researcher to critical areas of her model that can be refined by tactful interaction with the children. Through these situations she generates and tests conjectures and local hypotheses concerning the mathematical learning of the children (Steffe and Thompson, in press; Cobb and Steffe, 1983).

The senior teacher-researchers (project directors) in this study's teaching experiment aimed to build models of children's conceptual operations that generate the rational numbers of arithmetic (Steffe and Tzur, 1994). The children, 9–12 years of age, worked with a computer microworld where they used a variety of actions in the microworld to construct fraction concepts and schemes (Biddlecomb, 1994). Five mathematics education graduate students worked with the project directors as novice teacher-researchers. Two male students (Robert and Brian) and the one female student (Anne) had not taught primary school children before, while the other two females (Helen and Diana) had been primary school teachers prior to their involvement in the project. At that time, almost all but one (Helen) had no experience of doing research in Mathematics Education. Helen was also working on her PhD thesis. The rest had virtually just begun the Mathematics Education doctoral program at the University of Georgia in which they had to attend courses and seminars in mathematics, education and psychology. They also participated in various academic activities parallel to their involvement in the project. All except Helen had not encountered constructivism or the constructivist teaching experiment.

Despina Potari

The project directors met regularly with the novice teacher-researchers to plan the teaching episodes. Members of the research team observed the actual teaching episodes. The project directors also intervened, at times, to suggest activities that the novice teacher-researchers might initiate (Cobb and Steffe, 1983). The research team discussed their initial reactions after each teaching episode, and most of them viewed their own videotaped sessions before planning the next one. The discussions about children's learning occasionally were made systematic either by viewing videotaped episodes or after the actual teaching episodes. In these discussions, the researchers made inferences about children's learning and discussed aspects of the models that each of them was building.

While the main purpose of a teaching experiment is to provide a way for researchers to experience the constraints imposed on them by children's mathematics, in this study I use it as a site to experience the constraints imposed on us while trying to understand novice teacher-researchers' constructions of their knowledge about children's mathematics and of constructivist pedagogy.

Method

The data came from the videotaped teaching episodes of the five graduate students from October 1992 to February 1993. The main work in these episodes was on unit fractions and proper and improper fractions. By observing these episodes, I tried to identify moments that were typical of the interactions between the teacher-researchers and the children. Moreover, I tried to identify in these interactions situations of 'learning', situations where the researchers 'imposed' their mathematics on the children, situations that caused conflict which the novice teacher-researchers could not resolve. Generally speaking, I attempted to build my own models of the teaching for those teacher-researchers and see how the teaching developed during this period for each individual. To verify my models, to relate more closely to the research side of the teaching experiment and to look more closely at the teacher-researchers' reflections and motivations I planned two two-hour sessions with each novice teacher-researcher. These sessions (interviews) took place during the winter semester of the academic year 1993–4 (a year after their actual teaching). In these meetings they reflected on their actions and decisions while viewing two of their videotaped teaching episodes. One of these episodes was from early in the teaching experiment and another was from late in the teaching experiment. In these sessions, I also asked them to talk about the children's learning, viz.:

- their selection of tasks;
- constraints that children posed in their initial planning and in their actions;
- their conceptualization of their role as teachers in the project;
- things they learned from their interaction with the children;

- their experience in participating in the project and in what ways this experience influenced their professional life as teachers and researchers.

Another source of data was the discussion with the project directors especially with one of them who also read and commented on this chapter.

Results

Throughout the teaching episodes both the experienced and the novice teacher-researchers questioned the children about their methods. They looked for explanations of and justifications for children's actions and they tried to encourage children's interaction and participation. Their main goal was to help children construct powerful fraction concepts and schemes by acting on situations of learning in the microworld which they had planned. They were trying to facilitate children's learning by inducing perturbations in the children and by helping the children to eliminate them. They were attempting to base their decisions on the models which they had created of what the children were able to do and to help the children move toward an explicit awareness of their fraction concepts and schemes. This was the framework in which all the novice teacher-researchers were encouraged to work during the actual teaching experiment. In this framework they were also encouraged by the project directors to analyze the episodes and construct models of children's mathematics. It was expected that each novice teacher-researcher would provide his or her own interpretation of what it might mean to construe teaching as a method of scientific investigation. All the novice teacher-researchers wanted the children to interact mathematically with their partners, with them and with the microworld. The ways they tried to achieve these three goals varied from person to person. It depended on their prior images of teaching and learning and it was influenced by the nature of their interactions with the children, with the project directors and with the other novice teacher-researchers.

My analysis focuses on the novice teacher-researchers' actions while they interacted with the children in critical moments in the two selected teaching episodes and on how these interactions developed. They discussed some of their actions and decisions during their sessions with me, in which they reflected on their videotaped sessions. I took into consideration what they said in the interview with questions such as, 'What is good teaching?', 'What is constructivist teaching?', 'What is learning?', 'What did you learn from the children?', 'What did the children learn?', and 'What were the conflicts or perturbations you had because of your participation in the project?' These interviews contributed to my understanding of how they regarded teaching as a method of scientific investigation.

I present below an analysis of each novice teacher-researcher. Initially I summarize the key features that characterize the teaching of each novice teacher-researcher, then I indicate these characteristics through analyzing specific

Despina Potari

interactions with the children and I try to show the development of the novice teacher-researchers in the constructivist teaching experiment. In this analysis, I consider their reflections as a way to interpret their actions and to understand what was their overall experience in the project.

The Case of Robert

Robert was an experienced teacher in his country (Israel) who had worked mainly with adolescents and only rarely with primary school children. His main concern was the cognitive and affective development of the children. He wanted children to interact mathematically, to work cooperatively, to have an emotional balance, to be successful, to negotiate meaning, to construct schemes, and to make connections. Early in the teaching experiment Robert tried to affect the children through his own admonitions and explanations. For example, he tried to encourage children's participation and cooperation by stating 'I want you to talk to each other – I want you to communicate.' These admonitions fell short of achieving his goals. He was the one who actually verified the children's responses, and explained what the children should have done. As a result, the children did not feel a need to communicate. His goal was to give voice to the children, but he did not monitor his teaching actions and modify them to fit with what the children were doing.

The First Teaching Episode

In the first teaching episode the children built a 'staircase' of sticks up to a 10-stick and then up to the 12 and the 15-stick by using a unit stick, as shown in Figure 16.1.

Robert tried to make the children reflect on their actions by asking them to describe how they constructed the sticks and what was the quickest way. He wanted the children to reason multiplicatively by using previously constructed sticks to make new ones, and often he said so explicitly. In Protocol 1,

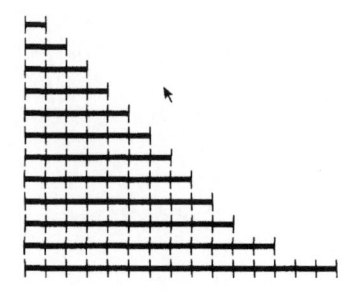

Figure 16.1 A staircase of sticks

A Constructivist Teaching Experiment

Robert described what the children did instead of allowing them to express these connections themselves. He was eager to create a cause–effect relationship between his actions and the children's learning. Sometimes, this eagerness led him to engage in direct teaching, what Bauersfeld described as the 'funnel pattern of interaction' (Bauersfeld, 1988).

In Protocol 1, the children had made a 30-stick by repeating a 15-stick twice. The teacher, Robert, asked, 'What is the 15 stick of the 30 stick?'

Protocol 1 (J refers to Jordan, L to Linda, and R to Robert.)

J: *A half.*
R: *A half. This is what we had last time. What makes it half? Why is it half? What did you do to build the 30 stick?*
L: *Repeat ...*
R: *Repeat the 15-stick twice. We need to take the 15 twice. If you need to repeat it twice, it makes a half. Out of the 30 stick, the part that it was made twice is the half [the children are listening].*

By presenting this extract, I want to emphasize the difficulty that Robert had in allowing children to act without his authority and to explain their actions. Here, he had learned from others in the project about the iteration of composite units, and this became a part of his knowledge of children's mathematics. He had a hypotheses to test for this group of children, whether they relate the fraction ($\frac{1}{2}$) to the iteration of two composite units but, in Protocol 1, he tried to impose iteration on the children rather than attempt to support them in creating it. He seemed unaware of how ineffective it was to tell children the multiplicative relationship between the iterated unit and the result of iterating it. He attempted to 'see' the children's mathematics, but his anticipations were driven by his own mathematics. He faced a dilemma that Ackermann (1995) identified as the teacher's dilemma. 'At the core of the teacher's dilemma resides the question: How can a teacher give reason to a student by appreciating the uniqueness and consistency of her thinking while, at the same time, giving right to the expert whose views coincide with more advanced ideas in a field' (1995, p. 351). Robert needed first to experience what children do and build first-order models of them to anticipate their actions and reactions. He then needed to build second order models (Steffe and Sprangler, 1993) to explain how he knew what he knew. That is, Robert had to build his own learning theory about the children.

Throughout the discussion about this teaching episode, during the interviews, Robert had an awareness that children think differently from adults. He said of Protocol 1 that

> Now I will first try to see what they can say and if they can try to show it to me, to do other halves on the screen. Let their actions show that they have understood instead of me saying what I think it is right, but it has nothing to do with their thinking.

Moreover, in the interviews he came to realize differences between the two children. For example Linda tried to check whether the 5-stick, the 6-stick, or the 7-stick is the $\frac{1}{4}$ of the 30-stick. She tried to do visual estimations while Jordan works mentally. Robert commented further that

> This is one of the times that I started to consider that really I am doing things that are wrong, because it is not in the mode of thinking of the child. You can see Linda: she is doing things very differently than Jordan. She is basically much more visual than he is.

He also commented that he learned from the perturbations which the children generated in him. For example, he asked the children to make a stick half of the 24-stick. Linda repeated the 2-stick 12 times to make the 24-stick. The children had already done tasks of finding unit fractions so Robert expected that she would use the 12-stick.

> It was obvious that she must come up with the 12 stick, what else could she do and she comes with 2 ... you see a teacher who is doing things not according to the children but according to what is obvious in mathematics for him.

During this interview, it became clear that Robert had constructed a case history of each child (Confrey, 1990). He knew in what ways the children differed: Jordan is competitive, Linda is quiet; Linda works mainly visually, Jordan mentally; Jordan does not want to face his mistakes; Linda is more willing to accept that something is 'wrong'. He spoke about their schemes, their learning; he stated that his main research goal was to make hypotheses and design situations to test them. He was aware that his mathematics and their mathematics were different and his teaching decisions were not only intuitive. He was ready to construct cognitive models of the children and was becoming aware that the goals in teaching are occasioned and constrained by what the children do.

The Second Teaching Episode

Robert's reflections during the first interview indicated that his views had changed during his involvement with the teaching experiment. The change was also evident in his later teaching episodes. Robert and I viewed a videotaped teaching episode that took place four months after the one presented in Protocol 1. The children were presented a stick in TIMA, and they posed their own problems of finding a fractional part of that stick. Robert's interactions with the children are more open than before. In this episode, the children interacted with each other, not because Robert demanded it but because he encouraged it by the type of task he chose and by the tactfulness of his interventions. The children needed to clarify their meanings in order to assimilate the learning situation presented. Interactions among themselves were essential for successful

A Constructivist Teaching Experiment

assimilation. Robert was much more aware of his role as facilitator: 'This is what I like in these interactions, these are the good ones, they serve the learning of both better than anything I can do.' He was more confident of where to go next, and he looked for generalizing assimilations (Steffe and Sprangler, 1993). For example, he changed the context to a sharing context, which in turn led Linda to speak of sharing a birthday cake. For Linda, the stick could take the place of other items to share, and her partitioning scheme was not restricted to the context of the microworld. Robert encouraged children to imagine items other than TIMA sticks to be shared, by asking them to share a birthday cake among the twenty-four people in their class. He was willing to change his initial decisions in order to maintain a balance between the children being challenged and motivated. For example the goal arose to make a piece of the cake that three people out of twenty-four would get. The children made it by iterating $\frac{1}{24}$ three times and they named it $\frac{3}{24}$. Robert wanted to see if they could explore its equivalence with $\frac{1}{8}$, but he chose not to proceed further because he decided that it was not appropriate for the children. It was not in the children's zone of potential construction:

> That would probably had led them beyond their range of resolving a perturbation and they had worked so beautifully, this was not part of their thinking yet.

The above statement suggests that Robert differentiated between what he wanted the children to do and the sense they made of what he said and why he said it. By comparing his teaching in the two teaching episodes, Robert commented that in the last episode,

> the children dominate what mathematics is done, who is providing the context, who is providing the questions, they have more voice and I am in the background intervening, whenever the situation asks me to intervene. At the beginning they were sometimes intervening in my talk [meaning that he was the one who was mainly talking].

Although in the last extract Robert seemed to undervalue the importance of his interventions both in the actual teaching and in his planning of the tasks, in the following extract it appears that Robert appreciated the interaction between teaching and children's learning. It also seems that his goals at the time of the latter episode and interview were more research oriented. Robert noticed this as well.

> I guess that being a teacher as at the beginning I would have missed the whole episode, the parts and the whole and the context. I was much more open to accept their mathematics [in the second episode], to use my knowledge as an experimenter. While at the beginning I was teaching, I did not facilitate learning. It is not only the quantity of talking but also the quality of what I was speaking and how I was intervening in the interactions.

255

Robert became aware of a number of things during the teaching experiment. He became aware of his teaching actions:

- the difference between his mathematics and children's mathematics;
- the need to monitor his goals and the children's goals;
- the need to consider both affective and cognitive aspects; and
- the need to create models of the children's thinking.

It is difficult to say, at this time, what helped Robert become aware of them. It seems that this change occurred through his interactions with the other researchers and especially with the project directors, and through his own reflections prompted by watching his videotaped teaching sessions. It was not only the children who constrained his decisions and made him aware of what actions to take to help them construct meanings. It was the feedback that he was getting from actually teaching the children in interaction with the development of his theory through reading and discussions with the others. As he stated:

> Working in the project, includes so many interactions with other people and the second quarter I worked with Steffe writing papers and reading papers about teaching and learning and trying to find my theoretical perspectives [for his doctoral thesis]. It was time for me, and I very fast grew up to change myself and modify myself with the constraints of the children and the reflections of my moves as a teacher and the strategies that I used in the planning sessions. All together were accumulated and made me a very different person.

Robert actively constructed his own conceptualization of constructivist teaching:

> The teacher's role is to facilitate learning by providing things that the children would not have done without the teaching. The teacher's interventions, the neutralizing of perturbations – all is directed by a general question: what can they do now more than they would have done by themselves in the specific domain?

It is not just this statement that indicates the constructivist framework within which Robert eventually worked. His actual interaction with the children indicates it even more clearly. My observations of Robert's latest teaching sessions found him sensitive to what children actually do – he designed his tasks according to where the children were and where he believed they could go. He tried to consider both the social interaction and individuals' constructions. Robert had started to learn from the children.

The Case of Helen

Both the observation of the two videotaped teaching episodes and the discussion on them during the interviews gave Helen the opportunity to confront again some of the difficulties she had experienced during her previous year's participation in the project. I summarize in the next two paragraphs what came out mainly from the discussion with Helen about her experience as a teacher-researcher in the teaching experiment. Later on in this section I focus on her actual teaching actions in the two chosen teaching episodes. For Helen, an experienced elementary school teacher in her country (Germany), the most important thing was for children to be inspired and be fascinated by mathematics. This value came from her own learning and education and it led her to pose challenging tasks to children and then to observe what they do. She had previously examined children's counting models in her doctoral study which she had completed when the interviews took place. In her study, she had focused on the role of group cooperation, but she was yet to construct her theory of children's understanding of fractions.

Helen was frustrated by her teaching in the project. She faced a conflict between what she wanted to do with the children and what she perceived as her role as a member of the research team. She had to reconsider her own knowledge of children and it was not easy for her to take the theories of others and use them in teaching. Her frustration appeared to keep her from reflecting on what she was doing with the children, and it seemed to prevent her from building her own models of the children's thinking. Through watching the videotaped episodes, it became evident that the way Helen interacted with the children varied. Sometimes she was 'staying back' and was being fascinated by what the children were doing when following their own goals. However, it was difficult for her to build on what the children had shown. In other cases, she was goal directed. Nevertheless, she did not monitor her goals and modify them to be harmonious with the children's goals. These different approaches were the result of her trying to establish an image of her teaching role in the project.

The First Teaching Episode

The following example shows her belief about encouraging children's cooperation in practice. Helen asked the children to share a stick into equal shares. Melissa started to act immediately but Helen stopped her and asked her to verbalize what she was going to do. This is one of her typical strategies, asking children to anticipate before they act. Rebecca said that she did not understand the task. Melissa tried to make it clear: 'It means each of us get equal shares.' Rebecca still did not understand. Rather than explain herself to Rebecca, Helen asked Melissa to explain it once more. This gave Melissa an opportunity to create a familiar context for Rebecca:

> *Let's say you go to a candy store and you get candy sticks and your brother and sister say, 'Let's divide it to equal parts and share it.' Then you try to make them the same size so that each one can get the same share.*

Helen gave Melissa the authority to make an explanation, and this led Melissa to reformulate the problem by making reference to other contexts. It also allowed Rebecca to assimilate the problem and to appreciate the difficulty of the task: 'This is hard.' Helen's decision to stand back and wait was critical in promoting communication between the children, which was one of the primary goals of the project.

Helen's teaching was partly compatible with teaching as a method of scientific investigation. The reason it is not wholly compatible is that her orientation left important parts out. Helen intended to create the conditions for children to have insight, but she did not imagine actions that she might take other than establishing these conditions.

The Second Teaching Episode

The following episode, which occurred three months later than the example above, illustrates Helen's difficulty in building on children's knowledge and in viewing teaching as co-construction. The task is to share a stick among three people. Rebecca visually estimated $\frac{1}{3}$ of the stick and drew it. She then copied the stick twice and joined the three pieces. However, the joined pieces were longer than the original. Rebecca's next move was to take the extra part (the difference between the stick she made and the given) and remove it from her estimate for $\frac{1}{3}$ of the original stick. She copied again and joined the three pieces, but this time the three together made a stick shorter than the original. Rebecca was surprised, because her result was not what she expected. She compensated for the extra part, but she could not see that she needed to distribute the extra among the three pieces. Helen asked Melissa to 'get it closer', but Melissa also had not developed a workable strategy and simply cut the extra part from the longer stick. In Rebecca's next attempt, she again compensated for the extra part. Helen observed what Rebecca did, but she did not intervene. She did not help Rebecca to reflect on her actions and possibly resolve the perturbation which she experienced.

In our discussion of this teaching episode, Helen admitted that she could have intervened by asking them, 'What is going to happen if you use that piece?' She added, 'That would also have helped to put Melissa back in . . . this could have made the conflict more obvious.' In this case, seeing only what the children were doing was not enough to help them past their impasse. To use teaching as a scientific method, Helen needed to use her observation of what Rebecca did as a basis for hypothesis formulation and testing. In other words, she needed to use her observation as a basis for further interaction. The interaction she had with the children was 'responsive and intuitive' (Steffe and Thompson, in press) in that she 'lost' herself in her interactions and made no intentional distinction between her mathematics and the students' mathematics. But the children's actions were clearly an occasion for Helen to imagine an action she could take that would make sense to the children yet lead them to a modification that would solve their problem.

Helen was not oriented toward fostering functional accommodations in children's ways and means of operating that do not involve major reorganizations. She did not take into account her possible contributions to the children's thinking, focusing instead on what the children contributed to the situations. As she stated in the discussion,

> I like when I teach once in a while to make jumps, to pose a task which is ... [pause] he [one of the project directors] tells me that I am always going for an insight and he goes for schemes of actions and operations. He is right to a certain extent. I want this flash of insight coming out and I like to challenge them with tasks which are outside their possibilities right now. I do not mind sending them away frustrated.

Data generated by the interviews explain Helen's tendency to look for big steps in children's constructions, and to leave them in a perturbed state. Her image of a good teacher is of someone who inspires the children. This image comes from her personal experience teaching elementary school children and from her educational experiences while preparing to be a teacher. She sees perturbation as a way of motivating children for further action. Her decisions were influenced, perhaps, by the way that she learns and does mathematics herself. During her interview, Helen talked generally about her experience as a teacher:

> Sometimes the mathematics takes over, they ask me an innocent question and I take off, which goes over their capacity of understanding. I forget the teaching, then I am one of the three.

However, during the interviews Helen has became aware that children are different from her. She admitted that she probably needed to reformulate her image of a good teacher.

> As a constructivist teacher you need to take what the kids do more seriously, you need to formulate your goals differently. When I said before that the mathematics takes over, this should not happen for a constructivist teacher.

From her reflections during our interview, it appeared Helen's participation in the project had created a perturbation for her – she was not satisfied by her teaching, and this helped her to make more explicit how she intended to make a transition.

> I would like to consolidate good methods I was using in the past in my teaching with the kids' own ways. I am going from being very structured and goal directed to the other end and saying 'this is fascinating, this is so fascinating' but I do not necessarily say what does it mean and what I am going to do with it and how I can use this to share my goals and their goals. So I still have this work to do.

Despina Potari

She needs some time and experience to reconceptualize her role as a constructivist teacher-researcher in the teaching experiment: 'Without building my own theory, without adapting it to the way I am thinking, without filling it with life, I will not be successful with the kids, no matter what.' This is an important point about learning in general and it is relevant for both children and the researchers of children's thinking. Just as we need to build on what children have and try to help them reconstruct their knowledge, we need to build on what the researchers have and try to help them reconstruct their own beliefs and theories.

The Case of Diana

Diana taught elementary school children for one year and prospective elementary teachers for three years before her involvement in the project. The most important thing for her was for the children to understand and to strengthen their understanding in different contexts. She wanted the children to see the relationship between the fractions they were doing in school and in the project. In the teaching episodes, Diana easily got children to collaborate toward her goals.

The First Teaching Episode

When analyzing the teaching episodes, especially the initial ones, I observed that Diana rarely changed her line of inquiry when the children could not resolve a perturbation. I asked Diana about this. For her, 'perturbation' was a means of helping children 'to figure out where the fault was'. As she admitted, she was not looking for examining how the children's constructions were affected by the perturbation; she wanted children to modify their constructions. In her view, a modification did not entail a construction. This belief prevented her from anticipating children's constructions and then taking appropriate actions like changing the context, reformulating the problem, or abandoning the current task to help them modify these constructions.

Diana's anxiety not to leave children in a perturbed state led her frequently to 'tell the answer' by asking questions that were too leading. This is illustrated below in her attempt to help children to see $\frac{1}{4}, \frac{1}{6}$ and $\frac{1}{12}$ of a 12-stick. The task was to share a 12-stick among four persons by using some given sticks, and it aimed to encourage the use of iteration and part of a whole in a sharing context. The children had constructed the 12-stick by using a 3-stick, a 2-stick, and a unit stick.

Protocol 2 (A *refers to Adam,* J *to Jerry,* D *to Diana*):

D: *What number is the $\frac{1}{4}$ of 12?*
A: *A 4-stick.*

A Constructivist Teaching Experiment

D: *Is the 4-stick $\frac{1}{4}$ of the 12?*
A: *Yes.*
D: *So, if I repeat it 4 times you get the 12-stick.*
A: *No. It is the 3-stick.*
D: *In how many pieces is this one split up?* [The one divided in 6 pieces].
J: *12.*
D: *In how many pieces?*
A: *6.*
D: *So, one piece is what fraction?*
J: $\frac{1}{12}, \frac{1}{6}.$
D: *Good! $\frac{1}{6}$. So, what will be $\frac{1}{6}$ of 12?*
J: *2.*
D: *Very good.*

The questioning continued in the same way for $\frac{1}{12}$. Here, Diana wanted to hear the right answer, and she achieved it by narrowing the scope of the questions. Her questions were also poorly worded. For example, 'So, one piece is what fraction?' and she also moved from the context of the sticks to the number context without allowing the children to make their own connections. In this, there was no awareness of using teaching as a method of scientific investigation. Moreover, the children's success did not imply that they understood fractions in the way intended by the project directors. The children's lack of understanding was verified later in this episode. In most teaching episodes, even in the cases where children were perturbed, Diana did not build on their perturbation. She saw the perturbation as social in origin and as a discrepancy between the child's answer and her expected answer. She used the discrepancy as a way to establish the answer in the children, but she did not explore how they arrived at it.

The Second Teaching Episode

Diana's questioning in the first episode can be contrasted with her questioning two months later. In the later episode, the children's task was to find what fraction one stick was of another stick. Diana expected children to choose one of the auxiliary sticks that existed on the screen, iterate it, and then use the results of iteration to compare the two given sticks.

Adam said, 'It is a unit stick without the $\frac{1}{4}$'. By this, he meant that the smaller of the two sticks was equal to a stick that the children had agreed would be one, and that the difference in the two sticks would be about $\frac{1}{4}$ of one. Adam's comment provoked Jerry to find what fraction the missing part is of the unit stick. This time, Diana maintained a balance between her goals and expectations, the comparison of the two sticks by the use of the auxiliary sticks, and what the children did. Her questions were not leading. Rather, they were more open and anticipatory. 'What can it not be?' 'Can it be $\frac{1}{5}$?' Instead of simply verifying their answers, as she had done earlier, Diana encouraged the

261

children to reflect on each other's actions. For example, when Jerry constructed two $\frac{1}{6}$ sticks to cover the difference, she asked Adam, 'What did Jerry do?'

In this episode, the children's difficulty in answering her questions made her anxious. However, this time Diana's questions 'How many 1/6ths did you add?' 'How many 1/6ths are in the unit stick?' had meaning for the children because they had been involved in activity to which the questions were directed.

At one point, Adam extended his part-whole understanding of fractions to see the relationship of the complementary part to the whole in exclaiming, 'It is $\frac{4}{6}$ and then you add 2 more'. I cannot claim that, prior to the teaching episode, Diana was aware that Adam might extend his part-whole understanding in this way. However, Diana adapted her questions to the activity in which the children were engaged, which led the children to create mathematics that was meaningful to them. Her mathematical image in the second teaching episode seemed to include children's actions, and she was becoming aware that the children had a mathematics independently of hers. But she was yet to form an understanding of what that mathematics might be, nor did she form a goal to construct such an understanding.

Given her orientation to teaching and to mathematics, Diana experienced conflict in her participation in the project. She said that it arose from the fact that she could not combine her role as a teacher and as a researcher.

> I think that part of my problem with the project was that I did not see myself as a researcher. I think I saw myself as a teacher. I do not think that I ever saw the big picture of the 12 kids, their schemes and how they were progressing. I understood it and I saw it as something up there, but I did not apply it to my teaching.

In my discussion with Diana it emerged that she could not make the project's vision her vision. She could not stand back from her actual teaching and reflect on how she could understand mathematics teaching in the context of the interaction of self-regulating systems. As she admitted in the interview, Diana viewed teaching as a means to make children learn. She did not view teaching as a means to investigate what children know or what they might be able to learn.

> I think that the project directors were looking on what impact the perturbation had in their construction, as opposed . . . I did not want the kids to take whatever constructions they had and [then I] blow it completely and ignore it. I wanted them to modify their constructions. I had a preconceived notion on how I wanted them to respond to the perturbation. I wanted them to modify their construction so that this perturbation makes sense, so it was not a perturbation any more. The project directors wanted to see how it affected their thinking.

One reason for Diana's difficulties was that her theories concerning children's learning differed from the project directors' theories. This may have precluded her construal of teaching as a scientific enterprise. My analyses of the videotaped episodes, and of Protocol 2 of her first teaching episode, suggest that Diana expected the children to learn quickly; she did not see learning as a long process evolving from within the children. As Diana stated in our discussion, she felt that the aim of the project was to pose tasks to see what the kids were thinking, but she wanted them to 'learn' something. Her view about learning was more local to each particular episode and she considered herself responsible for making this learning happen. Diana attempted to make the mathematical structures, in this case fractions, comprehensible to students by developing helpful external representations. Her view of learning and teaching is closer to a 'representational perspective' (Cobb et al., 1992) than to a constructivist perspective. Later in the teaching experiment, Diana started to consider children's mathematical reality in that she came to believe that 'kids make what we call faulty constructions, but they are very logical to them'. She conceived of interaction with the children mainly as a one-way relation, wherein she helped children to adjust to the teacher's mathematical reality. As she mentioned in the second interview, she believed that she learned about children's thinking. She spoke about the way that they learn and about their social and cognitive development.

> I think that I became better in listening to what kids say. I think that I am more aware of what a barrier language is for kids. They have things in their heads that they cannot explain. Jerry's actions in this episode, the typical classroom teacher would never see and would never have any idea of the strength of his understanding. You actually need to see actions that they employ in their problems.

Diana also developed some alternatives as a teacher to deal with children's wrong answers.

> Now I would try to create a perturbation and try to help the child to strengthen her constructions instead of me trying to hand them a solution to fix up their problem.

It is interesting that, even in retrospect, Diana's remarks are about her aims as a teacher who employs teaching to affect what children learn. She had not advanced to the level of viewing teaching both as a means to affect children's understandings and as a means to gain insight into what those understandings are.

The Case of Anne

Upon entering the teaching experiment, Anne's teaching experience was mainly with adult students. It was the first time that she had worked with elementary school children. The videotaped episodes of her teaching, which she and I analyzed, showed her teaching one child, Joe. From this analysis, I identified some typical characteristics of her teaching. Anne wanted children to construct knowledge, but the affective factor was also very essential to her. She tried to achieve it by playing the role of a partner. She encouraged Joe to pose problems for her to solve and moved to a new line of inquiry if the problematic was too distant from Joe's current understanding for him to resolve. In most cases she could balance her goals implied through the planned tasks with the child's mathematics by encouraging him to show what he was doing and tie this to her goals. Anne succeeded in creating and maintaining this balance especially when she was playing the role of the partner, by pretending that she was making mistakes similar to those which Joe made. However, at the same time she purposely made mistakes and openly reflected on her strategies with the aim of helping Joe reflect similarly.

The First Teaching Episode

Joe tended to change the length of his unit stick whenever his estimates led to conflicts. This was problematic for Anne. This issue arose once when Joe intended to share a stick equally among four people. Joe estimated the length of one share and repeated it four times. The result was too long. Consequently, he added a piece to the original stick to adjust his estimate of the four shares. Anne tried unsuccessfully to get him to reflect on his actions. She said, 'Is that good? You are cheating, you are supposed to work with that one [the original stick].' At the end, Anne cleared the screen and posed the same problem, but this time emphasized that Joe could not add or take away anything.

Joe changed his strategy, and tried to mark four equal shares on the stick. He compared the shares by breaking the stick at each mark[2] and placing each share under the other. He then iterated the biggest piece four times, but the result was longer than the original stick. Anne encouraged Joe to make a closer estimate, but he did not develop a strategy for doing this. She then gave a hint for how Joe might make a better estimate. 'I liked the way that you had it before,' referring to Joe's original approach wherein his first action was to produce an initial estimate.

Anne's next move was to ask Joe to make his thinking explicit, but Joe ignored her and did not do that. She then reformulated the initial situation (share a stick among four people), but Joe still had no systematic way of making estimations. Anne then recognized that even the new context could not encourage an actual learning environment, so she simplified the situation by asking Joe to share the stick among two persons. Joe marked and compared the pieces, but again added a piece to make them equal. His actions were not influenced by Anne, who tried to create a conflict in Joe by saying, 'You are cheating' as he joined the two pieces together. Anne asked him to compare the stick he made with the original in an attempt to create a conflict. The way Joe resolved this conflict was again to add a piece to the original when he saw that

A Constructivist Teaching Experiment

the one he produced was longer. Anne accepted Joe's approach by saying, 'That's good.' At that moment, Anne regarded Joe's emotions as being more important than his understanding.

Anne returned to the original situation, but this time asked Joe to share the stick that he had already made. Her expectation was that Joe would halve the half of the stick,[3] which he did. Joe still was not interested in the equality of the pieces, so Anne tried to create a personal conflict: 'If I give you that share [pointing to the smallest one] will you be happy?' This led Joe to see the necessity that the sticks be equally long, and he ranked the four pieces one under the other to verify that they were not the same. Anne then asked him, 'How can we make them equal without adding anything?' Joe then took away the extra pieces. Anne accepted it and closed the session.

When discussing Anne's actions in this episode with her I could see she was aware that Joe did not progress toward the particular mathematics learning goal she had in mind. The significance for this study is that Anne became willing to modify her initial task, to make the problem more familiar or simpler. Pirie and Kieren (1992) describe this willingness as one of the qualities that can support a teacher's efforts to encourage children's mathematical learning and understanding.

Although Anne's flexibility in changing her planned interventions did not have an immediate effect on Joe's way of operating, it did help him move closer to a strategy for estimating equal shares after a few teaching episodes. At the same time, Anne did not adjust her conception of what she wanted Joe to do. She wanted Joe to solve the problem – end up with equal shares. The project directors wanted Joe to conceive the task differently – as one entailing a proportional relationship between excess or deficit in aggregate and excess or deficit in unit.[4]

In this session, Anne's teaching can be characterized mainly as hopeful; she intervened, but she waited and, as she mentioned in the interview, struggled to keep from telling Joe to compare the pieces by ranking one under the other. How far a teacher can go or how far she can wait depends on her knowledge of the child and on the way that she interprets his actions. Anne decided that Joe was not ready to move toward her initial plans and expectations, and she wanted to see where he could go. At the same time she did not want Joe to be overly perturbed, so, in line with her concern about Joe's emotions, she accepted Joe's tendency to alter the whole.

Joe's tendency to alter the whole instead of alter the estimate appears in most of the episodes. But the way that she balances her mathematics with Joe's mathematics is usually different from how it appears in the previous episode. In Protocol 3, Joe has divided a stick in to eleven equal pieces and Anne asks him to pull one piece out.

Protocol 3 (J stands for Joe, A stands for Anne)

    A: *What fraction is this?*
    J: *Eleventh.*

Despina Potari

> A: One eleventh. Can you make me a stick that is five times as long as 1/11th? *[He draws a stick underneath the stick which is divided into eleven pieces and then he takes the 1/11th which he has pulled out by using the mouse and iterates it five times.]*
> A: Which one is right? *[Joe shows the iterated one]*
> A: What fraction is the one you have drawn? *[underneath the initial stick]*
> J: This *[pointing to the entire stick]* is 11, this *[pointing at his 5-iteration of $\frac{1}{11}$]* is 5, 5/6ths, no 1/5th.
> A: Why do you say that?
> J: Wait! I don't know. If you use it six more times you get 11.
> A: This one is 1/11th *[she pulls 1/11th out]*.
> J: No, it is 5/11th *[referring to the stick which is the 5-iteration of 1/11th]*.
> A: Why?
> J: It is five parts of the 11th.

Anne's goal is for Joe to use his unit iteration to generate proper fractions. Her decision to act and intervene by pulling 1/11th out of the stick leads Joe to develop a language ('five elevenths') based on his actions. In the episode, she does not accept Joe's answers of 5/6ths or 1/5th. She does not lead him directly to the 'right answer' but she anticipated that he could build on what he had already constructed, and her intervention was appropriate.

Anne started to meet the ideas of constructivism by working on the project and she easily incorporated them into her theories about teaching and learning. One reason for her adaptability could be that she did not already have solid theories about teaching young children in school. Not being committed to any particular point of view, it was easy for her to be adaptive in her new experience as a teacher and as a member of the research team. This interpretation is countermanded by her work in doctoral seminars with one of the project directors. She had a deep understanding of constructivism and this understanding permeated her interactions with Joe.

Her adaptability was also driven by her own view of mathematics. For her, processes and problem solving were an essential part of mathematics. Through her struggle to give meaning to what constructivist teaching is in the context of working with Joe, she developed a model of a teacher who took into consideration what the children were doing and she could make her model work in practice. She found a way of monitoring her goals over the children's goals, and of building her decisions on what she had learned from her interaction with Joe. Moreover, she made and tested hypotheses about Joe's mathematical learning. She found a balance between waiting and intervening. In this, intervening was the result of her curiosity to see what Joe was doing and to find what Joe could learn. Although Anne did not have an overall model of what Joe could possibly do, by working with him she learned what children at that age are like. I cannot say that the dialectic relationship between Joe's learning and her learning about Joe was clear for her from the beginning of her participation in the project. Initially, it was probably her intuitions that were leading her actions. The fact that she did not have a theory of fraction understanding

A Constructivist Teaching Experiment

that entailed multiplicative reasoning prevented her from recognizing that Joe was conceiving the tasks additively. From the interview, it seemed that she had developed an awareness of the importance of this knowledge. In describing the things that she would change in her interaction with Joe, she commented:

> If I knew about children's ways of thinking about rational numbers, and if I knew what I know today, I would go back. If I was more prepared for the kind of constructions, the kind of constructions that he could possibly make, I am sure that I would have changed some of the tasks that I had designed. Or I would have controlled my curiosity in terms of one way or another.

This illustrates the development of an awareness of the importance of experience in her teaching. But this experience is toward what the child does and thinks. As Glasersfeld (1995) states, 'unless the teacher can elicit an explanation or generate an hypothesis as to how the student has arrived at the answer, the chance of modifying the student's conceptual structures are minimal'.

In the interview, Anne stated that her interpretation of her role working under the constructivist perspective was to

> be a partner in the session, to learn as much as your students, not the same things but you are an active participant in the learning process.

This belief was projected in her teaching with Joe; she was a partner who contributed her conceptual operations to her interactions just as Joe contributed his operations and basic structure of a logic-mathematical nature to his interaction (Steffe and Tzur, 1994).

The Case of Brian

Upon entering the teaching experiment, Brian had taught mathematics and physics to college students. Brian held a transmission model of teaching at the beginning of his involvement and moved eventually to one where children are engaged in mathematical activity and his role was to influence their actions. He was fascinated by the theoretical framework of constructivism and by scheme theory as a way of interpreting children's knowledge as it fit to his scientific background:

> When I came here I had very little knowledge of Piaget, none of constructivism, nothing like that but I had a lot of knowledge on self-organising systems but from a different viewpoint than they take in constructivism. So when I started reading, it made a lot of sense to me. I am not sure that I agree with radical constructivism, but I do not have problems with social constructivism. So, I had a significant amount of development in this direction. I am coming from a hard science background and that gave me a social background. My academic background was in hard science and my hobbies were philosophy, psychology. But nowadays it is gone the other way around. My academic training is about

267

philosophy and psychology whereas my outside interest is hard science. That is how my participation in this project has influenced me. A lot of the things have spoken to me because they seem valid.

Brian was trying to make sense of consructivism and how he could reconceptualize his teaching within this framework. He was interested in making inferences about children's learning and, through his interaction with his fellow researchers, he was building models of children's fraction knowledge.

The influence of his knowledge about constructivism and children's fraction knowledge appeared first when he had to choose tasks for the children. In his actual interaction with the children, the influence of this knowledge was more ambiguous. In the observed teaching episodes, and also as he stated in the interviews, a tendency to stay back and let the children's goals overcome his goals was apparent particularly during his first interactions with the children. This was the result of his own personality and of how he translated his developing theories into practice.

His struggle not to impose his mathematics on the children led him a number of times to the point where he was following what the children were doing without building on it. In the interviews, he conceived of teaching as a goal directed activity, one in which he looked for children 'to develop stronger schemes, more general schemes, integrated schemes'. The way that he tried to keep a balance between his goals and decisions and their goals is described by the following metaphor:

> You are trying to see where the child goes and you try to move towards that direction but you also try to change that direction towards your goals. In a sense it is more like martial arts as opposed to staying back and going by the child. You take your opponent's natural direction of motion and alter it slightly from you to the ground.

The time period in which I observed Brian's teaching was rather short to explain the change I observed. There were cases where the way that he balanced his goals with respect to the children's goals were close to the 'martial arts' that he described. The following example exemplifies this balancing.

The initial task was for the children to make sticks $\frac{1}{2}, \frac{1}{3}, \ldots, \frac{1}{8}$ as long as the length of a 24-stick. The children used their whole number knowledge to find $\frac{1}{2}, \frac{1}{3}$, and $\frac{1}{4}$ of this stick by saying, for example, that $\frac{1}{3}$ of the 24-stick is the 8-stick because 3 times 8 is 24. The problem started when they tried to find 1/5th of the 24-stick. They needed to move from using composite units to produce the fraction to making equal parts of the 24-stick by partitioning the stick. In this, the children needed to move from the discrete mode where 24 was an integral multiple of the fraction to the continuous mode where 24 was not an integral multiple of the fraction.

The children first looked for integral solutions. They tried the 4-stick but Drew found that this is $\frac{1}{6}$, not $\frac{1}{5}$, of the 24-stick. The children asked for a piece of paper to work out their calculations. They added 4 five times, and 5

A Constructivist Teaching Experiment

five times and they see that they do not get the 24. The first reaction of Chabwera was that it was impossible. Then Drew moved to the continuous mode by adding $4\frac{1}{2}$ five times and found that it produced a result less than 24.

Up to this point Brian had only posed the task; he was giving the children freedom to experiment. He intervened after Drew's attempt, and asked them, 'Will it [$\frac{1}{5}$ of 24] be closer to 4 or to 5?' and summarized that they had found that '4 is too small, 5 is too big.' Brian then asked the children to make a stick that would work by using the microworld. His reason, as he stated in the interview, was that he wanted the children to move from the pencil and paper actions that were too abstract and too algorithmic. Moreover, they had exhausted their guesses in the context of the paper and pencil environment.

Chabwera made the 5-stick and seemed to be restricted to his previous ways used in the paper and pencil. So, Brian reposes the task and this leads Drew to make the 4-stick and the 5-stick on the screen and repeat each of them five times. He then said that the stick which he made by using the 5-stick was one unit longer than the 24-stick. The teacher asks him, 'Can you make it closer?' They cannot see any other way and Chabwera suggests cutting the extra piece. Brian's intervention now is to ask them to draw a stick that works. Although this intervention was direct and suggested a way to approach the problem, the children were not able to act on the suggestion. Drew drew on the screen a whole stick underneath (parallel to) the 24-stick. The teacher reposed the problem again but the children had not developed their own way to make an appropriate stick. Drew says that it is too hard and suggests skipping this problem to go on to the next one. Brian chose to follow Drew's suggestion.

The children understood that the solution was not going to have a whole number of composite units. Brian was searching for a way in which he could encourage the children to modify the fractional schemes they used when 24 was a multiple of the fractional part, and in his search to find a way, I see goal directed teaching which left room for the children to act. I also see teaching in which the teacher's goals were influenced by the children's actions. I cannot say if his decision to skip the $\frac{1}{5}$ was a good decision, but I would not be able to evaluate the decision until consequences of the decision are considered in future teaching episodes. During his reflection on the episode, Brian criticized his decision to skip $\frac{1}{7}$ of 24 later in the teaching session. He appreciated that Chabwera had not realized how to make $\frac{1}{5}$ or $\frac{1}{7}$ of the 24-stick, and Brian still needed to experience how he might help the children make these unit fractions without forcing them to perform according to his initial goals.

The interviews revealed that Brian had developed a theoretical framework regarding constructivism and children's learning of fractions and that he saw how it could influence his practice. He began to make conjectures about children's mathematical realities and about what an instructional experience, from his perspective, might be like from the children's point of view.

> I think that the biggest thing I learned is that there are not significant mistakes from their point of view. There are minor mistakes and they can recognize

269

those but I think that they have a reason why they answer this way and it is important to see what the reason is.

He saw that his interpretation of constructivist teaching as being diagnostic was not enough to help children construct knowledge and make accommodations: 'You need to build on what you see.' Brian had seen a relation between his framework and his teaching, but he was in the process of building this relation. He still needed the experience of working with children to explore further how he could translate his theories into practice.

Reflections

Steffe and Thompson (in press) describe abilities and characteristics of a teacher-researcher in a teaching experiment in order to form models of children's mathematics. As it emerged from this study, the process of becoming a teacher-researcher depends on the strengths of the person's prior beliefs about teaching and learning and also on their commitment to developing insight into children's knowledge and reasoning. Those with the strongest beliefs in their ability to work mathematically with children and those who had in fact taught children seemed the least adaptable. They departed from the teaching experiment's goals of acquiring greater insight into children's mathematics in favor of trying to get the children to do what they would do, or simply to solve the task that was presented them. Those who were not committed to a particular style of teaching or to the goal of enabling children to solve problems presented to them were the most sensitive to the teaching experiment's goals. Their development into teacher-researchers came from their interaction with the children and their interactions with the project directors and other co-researchers. The nature of the interactions was important. They interacted with the aim of developing theoretical insights into what children knew and how they reasoned. Their focus was not on what they could do to make teaching successful.

Orientations to the Role of a Teacher-Researcher

Throughout their involvement in the project, the five novice teacher-researchers were building their own model of a constructivist teacher-researcher. Their teaching was learner-focused, but the way in which the children were taken into consideration by each of them was different. Helen and Diana looked for children's understanding, but in different ways. Helen expected to see children's understanding by posing challenging tasks and observing their actions. She was looking for major modifications of the children's schemes without intentionally intervening in the children's activity with the goal of bringing forth modifications in that activity. In this, she sometimes let the children's goals dominate her goals. On the other hand, Diana's attempts to reach understanding were more a step by step approach towards her goals.

Robert regarded children's mathematical communication as an important aspect of teaching. He moved from asking for it from the children to encouraging it by his actions. He became aware that by imposing his mathematics on the children, he essentially excluded the possibility that they would bring their mathematical knowledge forth in the context of their communicative interactions. He was able to reflect on what he was doing and to modify it a great deal.

Brian conceived of himself mainly as a researcher who was interested in creating theories about children's learning. In this, he initially attempted to observe learning by standing back, as it were, and waiting to see this learning take place without being occasioned by his actions. He became aware of the need to act in such a way that learning was influenced in his actual interaction with the children, their goals still dominated his goals. Brian's difficulties came from his belief that he understood constructivism and the abstracted model of children's mathematics. So, he could not easily acknowledge to himself that he had to learn how to interact mathematically with children. He started to become aware that knowing constructivist theory is not sufficient for posing appropriate situations of learning nor for communicating with children.

Anne's teaching was characterized by her attempts to balance affective and cognitive development of the children by balancing her goals with the children's goals. Anne could build on the models that she was constructing as a researcher about the children's mathematical learning by using these models in her teaching.

The models that I built about the teacher-researchers were the result of my own observations of their actual teaching. However, the discussion with the novice teacher-researchers supported my models. Another way to compare my interpretations with the teacher-researchers' image of themselves was through their comments on my first written report about them. All of them except Diana recognized themselves in my interpretation. Diana found my descriptions accurate but she regarded my claims as context dependent, something which I do not deny. She mentioned that the role of children's characteristics and her struggle to help them to be successful had to be considered in explaining her actions. She admitted that my model of her teaching is probably close to what happened, but it is not the way that she would like to be.

Prior Experience: Its Role in the Teacher-Researchers' Development

The way that the teacher-researchers conceived their role as constructivist teachers in the project was influenced by their previous teaching experience, by their beliefs about teaching and by their respective personalities.

Helen and Diana had experience with elementary school children and they had already established theories about teaching and learning which they were trying to integrate with the project's constructivist perspective. Both had a difficult time conceiving of teaching as a method for scientific investigation.

Helen had already worked under this perspective as a part of her dissertation and she had already started to reflect on the interaction between the ideas of constructivism and her teaching. She was trying to combine her role as a teacher and researcher by building her theory from her practice. She was struggling to help children understand and at the same time to gather data about children's learning. She was driven by her own ways of learning and she wanted to see their understanding without intervening. She saw her teaching in the project mainly as a bottom-up approach but she has started to become aware of the need of a more interactive approach. Helen's commitment in the project was more to the best interests of the children than to the research project.

Diana has been working under this framework for the first time in the project and she was mainly driven by her classroom practices. She was probably in the transition of reconstructing her theories from her practice. Her difficulty in conceiving the 'theories of others' as her theories, led her, at least at the beginning, to be more concentrated in the practice without probably being informed by the theory in an interactive way. Her worldview also constrained her a great deal to go along with the aims of the project. On the other hand, Anne and Brian were inexperienced in teaching elementary children, so they did not have preconceived notions about children's learning. As a result, they seemed more open to discover ways that they could facilitate children's learning. Moreover, they accepted working under a constructivist framework as it was close to their worldview, so they found themselves very compatible with the project's epistemology. Brian's initial interpretation was that he could facilitate this learning by posing tasks and observing children's actions. He started to build the interaction between theory and practice by giving meaning to the theory first and seeing how he could apply in to the practice. He has become aware that he needs to move from being an observer of children's constructions to a participant who helps these constructions to happen, and he is in the transition to achieve this goal. Anne started to give meaning to constructivist teaching by actually interacting between theory and practice. Her understanding of being a constructivist teacher was of a partner who was learning as much as a student and this learning was influencing her actions and decisions. However, Anne had to develop a theory of 'understanding fractions' to guide her interventions.

Robert did not have much experience with elementary school teaching before but he was confident in his teaching with adolescents. Initially, his attempt to take the children's actions into consideration was driven by his previous teaching experience but he had not developed his theories about children's learning and on how to integrate these theories in his teaching. Robert developed a balance between theory and practice, but perturbations in his interaction with the children led him to question his actions. Robert's development of a theoretical framework made him more aware of how to take into account the children's knowledge in his interactions with them.

Learning from Experience

Steffe and D'Ambrosio (1996) believe that it is a combination of the beliefs of the teacher about the learning process, the consistency of the teaching actions with her beliefs, and the continuous learning by the teacher throughout the teaching process that constitutes a profile of a constructivist teacher. The whole participation of the teachers in the project, their interaction with the project directors and the children, their own reading and reflection was a learning environment for them. Their attempts to resolve the perturbations they had led them to reflect on their teaching and provided opportunities to learn. What they learned depended on their prior knowledge and beliefs. Although I have already discussed the teacher-researchers' development earlier in this chapter, I find it important to summarize some of the things which I think they learned.

All the teacher-researchers became aware of the children's mathematical power and of the difference between children's mathematics and their mathematics. They also appreciated the need to negotiate this different meaning. Moreover, they started to form models about children's mathematics and discuss their hypotheses with the other members of the team. This modeling influenced their practice in different degrees while some of them moved towards a 'dialectic between modeling and practice' that Cobb and Steffe (1983) describe as a basic feature of constructivist teaching.

They also learned about the difficulty of keeping a balance between emotions and cognitions and they started to consider the children's different characteristics. The way that they attempted to relate the children's motivation and the resolution of cognitive conflict that the children experienced was different. This was expressed by the teacher's decisions to change the current task, to move on to another kind of inquiry or to help them arrive at the solution by more direct questioning.

Concluding Remarks

The different ways that the novice teacher-researchers conceived their role in the project, the difficulties which they faced, and their development support my view that becoming a teacher-researcher in a constructivist teaching experiment is not the result of a transmission of knowledge from the experienced researchers to the novice teacher-researchers. It is also not a matter of applying 'constructivism' or 'the abstracted models of children's constructions' in practice. The construction of meaning of this new role involves the teacher-researchers' regarding children's mathematics as legitimate mathematics. It also involves novice teacher-researchers learning how to interact with children to support children's construction of it. However, more is involved because novice teacher-researchers must construct ways of seeing the children that have their roots in genetic epistemology as well as mathematics. Constructs like scheme, accommodation, operations, interiorization and self-regulation are necessary but insufficient for building understanding of children's mathematics. These conceptual constructs provide orientation, but they do not provide the creativity and insight necessary to establish children's mathematical schemes nor for an understanding of how the children might modify these schemes. An appeal to mathematics is also orienting but not explanatory. Becoming a teacher-researcher can be facilitated through the novice teacher-researchers actual participation in a teaching experiment. In this project, the novice teacher-researchers' discussions with the other members of the project about children's mathematical knowledge and about possible tasks that would initiate mathematical constructions, helped the teacher-researchers to reconceptualize their role in a dialectic between their prior beliefs and their current experience. Nevertheless, their abilities to interpret children's actions developed to varying degrees and some of them combined their role as researchers and teachers in achieving what Cobb and Steffe (1983) describe as 'a dialectic between modeling and practice'. Others could not build themselves as researchers and remained as teachers.

It is difficult to combine theory and practice in action. It demands the creation of a possible environment where 'the teachers will need to attend to their own conceptual change at least as much as they attend to this process in their students' (Prawat, 1992). I felt that participating in the teaching experiment contributed to that development in the sense that it was an occasion for development. But intensive study of constructivist epistemology and children's mathematical development also proved to be critical.

Notes

1 This work was done during the author's sabbatical leave at the University of Georgia.
2 Marking a stick and breaking it at marks is a feature of the software.
3 'Halve the stick' is an operation within TIMA.
4 That is, the project directors hoped Joe would understand that however much excess there was in four copies of Joe's estimate, $\frac{1}{4}$ of that excess needed to be detached from each copy.

References

ACKERMANN, E. (1995) 'Construction and transference of meaning through form', in STEFFE, L.P. and GALE, J. (eds), *Constructivism in Education*, Hillsdale, NJ: Lawrence Erlbaum, pp. 341–54.

BAUERSFELD, H. (1988) 'Interaction, construction and knowledge: Alternative perspectives for mathematics education', in COONEY, T. and GROUWS, D. (eds), *Effective Mathematics Teaching*, Reston. VA: National Council of Teachers of Mathematics, pp. 27–46.

BIDDLECOMB, B.D. (1994) 'Theory-based development of computer microworlds', *Journal of Research in Childhood Education*, **8**, 2, pp. 87–98.

COBB, P. (1991) 'Reconstructing elementary school mathematics', *Focus on Learning Problems in Mathematics*, **13**, 2, pp. 3–32.

COBB, P. and STEFFE, L.P. (1983) 'The constructivist researcher as teacher and model builder', *Journal for Research in Mathematics Education*, **14**, pp. 83–94.

COBB, P., WOOD, T. and YACKEL, E. (1990) 'Classrooms as learning environments for teachers and researchers', in DAVIS, R.B., MAYER, C.A. and NODDINGS, N. (eds), *Constructivist Views on the Teaching and Learning of Mathematics*, Journal for Research in Mathematics Education, Monograph No. 4, Reston, VA: National Council of Teachers of Mathematics, pp. 125–46.

COBB, P., YACKEL, E. and WOOD, T. (1992) 'A constructivist alternative to the representational view of mind in mathematics education', *Journal for Research in Mathematics Education*, **23**, 1, pp. 2–33.

CONFREY, J. (1990) 'What constructivism implies for teaching', in DAVIS, R.B., MAYER C.A. and NODDINGS, N. (eds), *Constructivist Views on the Teaching and Learning of Mathematics*, Journal for Research in Mathematics Education, Monograph No. 4, Reston, VA: National Council of Teachers of Mathematics, pp. 107–22.

GLASERSFELD, E. VON (1995) 'A constructivist approach to teaching', in STEFFE, L.P. and GALE, J. (eds), *Constructivism in Education*, Hillsdale, NJ: Lawrence Erlbaum, pp. 3–15.

MAHER, C.A. and ALSTON, A. (1990) 'Building representations of children's meanings', in DAVIS, R.B., MAYER, C.A. and NODDINGS, N. (eds), *Constructivist Views on the Teaching and Learning of Mathematics*, Journal for Research in Mathematics Education, Monograph No. 4, Reston, VA: National Council of Teachers of Mathematics, pp. 79–90.

PIRIE, S. and KIEREN, T.E. (1992) 'Creating constructivist environment and constructing creative mathematics', *Educational Studies in Mathematics*, **23**, 5, pp. 505–28.

PRAWAT, R.S. (1992) 'Teachers' beliefs about teaching and learning: A constructivist perspective', *American Journal of Education*, **100**, 43, pp. 355–95.

SIMON, M. (1995a) 'Reconstructing mathematics pedagogy from a constructivist perspective', *Journal for Research in Mathematics Education*, **26**, 2, pp. 114–45.

SIMON, M.A. (1995b) 'Elaborating models of mathematics teaching: A response to Steffe and D' Ambrosio', *Journal for Research in Mathematics Education*, **26**, 2, pp. 160–2.

SIMON, M. and SCHIFTER, D. (1991) 'Towards a constructivist perspective: An intervention study of mathematics teacher development', *Educational Studies in Mathematics*, 22, pp. 309–31.

STEFFE, L.P. (1991) 'The constructivist teaching experiment: Illustrations and implications', in GLASERSFELD, E. VON (ed.), *Radical Constructivism in Mathematics Education*. Boston, Mass.: Kluwer Academic, pp. 177–94.

STEFFE, L.P. and D' AMBROSIO, B.S. (1995) 'Toward a working model of constructivist teaching: A reaction to Simon (1995)', *Journal for Research in Mathematics Education*, **26**, 2, pp. 146–59.

STEFFE, L.P. and D' AMBROSIO, B.S. (1996) 'Using teaching experiments to enhance understanding of students' mathematics', in TREAGUST, D.F., DUIT, R. and FRASER, B.J. (eds), *Improving Teaching and Learning in Science and Mathematics*, New York: Teachers College, Columbia University, pp. 65–76.

STEFFE, L.P. and SPRANGLER, D. (1993, March) 'Children's construction of iterative fraction schemes', paper presented at the 71st Annual Meeting of the National Council of Teachers of Mathematics, Seattle, Washington.

STEFFE, L.P. and THOMPSON, P. (in press) 'Teaching experiment methodology: Underlying principles and essential characteristics', in KELLY, E. and LESH, R. (eds), *Research Design in Mathematics and Science Education*, Hillsdale, NJ: Lawrence Erlbaum.

STEFFE, L.P. and TZUR, R. (1994) 'Interaction and children's mathematics', *Journal of Research in Childhood Education*, **8**, 2, pp. 99–116.

WOOD, T., COBB, P. and YACKEL, E. (1995) 'Reflections on learning and teaching mathematics in elementary school', in STEFFE, L.P. and GALE, J. (eds), *Constructivism in Education*, Hillsdale, NJ: Lawrence Erlbaum, pp. 401–22.

Acknowledgments

I would like to thank Leslie P. Steffe for his helpful discussions during the conduct of this study. I thank him, Pat Thompson and Heide Weigel for their thoughtful comments on earlier drafts of this chapter. I also thank all the teacher-researchers who participated.

17 Perspectives on Constructivism in Teacher Education

Leslie P. Steffe

In a period of time marked by Glasersfeld's presentation of radical constructivism to the Jean Piaget Society in Philadelphia in 1977 (Glasersfeld, 1987/1977) and by the publication of the *Curriculum and Evaluation Standards* by the National Council of Teachers of Mathematics in 1989, radical constructivism became a major force for reform in the teaching and learning of mathematics and science in the schools (Steffe and Kieren, 1994). The focus of this reform, which continues today, was different from the focus of the reform movement of the 'golden age of reason' of the 1960s. In the earlier reform, the old mathematics and science curricula were replaced by modern curricula, and institutes were held to prepare mathematics and science teachers to teach them. In spite of being the proposed view of learning and teaching in the modern mathematics curricula, discovery learning (Hendrix, 1961) and discovery teaching (Davis, 1966) had little impact on the practice of mathematics education. Teachers became experts in the concepts and principles of the subjects they taught, but most of them knew little about the psychological or epistemological foundations of mathematics education. As a consequence, in the main teachers simply taught the modern curricula in the same traditional way they had taught the old.

The modern curricula were based on Cartesian epistemology. In these curricula, the classical dualism of Cartesian epistemology – an endogenic (mind-centered) view vs. an exogenic (world-centered) view (Konold and Johnson, 1991) – provided the foundation for discovery learning and discovery teaching. In this dualism, mathematical structures were regarded as having a mind-independent existence, and the function of rationality was to come to know these fundamental structures, structures which were regarded as 'being there' to be discovered. In science education, knowledge was taken to be achieved when the inner states of the individual represented states of the external world – when mind served as a mirror of nature – and scientific objectivity was reified. In the current reform, the classical dualism of Cartesian epistemology is avoided. Rather than serve in the discovery of an objective, ontological reality, the function of cognition is regarded as adaptive, and as serving in the organization of the experiential world (Glasersfeld, 1995, p. 51). This principle has far reaching implications not only for how mathematics and science are regarded, but also for the education of teachers and teacher educators.

Leslie P. Steffe

Reforming Teacher Education

Why Cartesian epistemology still underpins many teacher education programs can be understood in part by Désautels' (Ch. 13) notion of the reproduction cycle – teachers go on teaching the way they themselves were taught in spite of attempts to change their beliefs, predispositions, or habitus developed over the course of their own schooling prior to enrolling in teacher education programs. Hunting (Ch. 15) also notes this 'regressive effect of school life', but he sees it as only a part of the reason why teachers go on teaching in the way that they were taught. He also questions the dominant paradigm used in teacher education for learning how to teach – the apprenticeship model. In this model, 'learning how to teach is achieved by way of emulating working teachers and repeated practice' (p. 232). The resiliency of the apprenticeship model is demonstrated by Hunting's (Ch. 15) comment that as early as 1904 'Dewey (1904/1965) realized that the apprenticeship model of teacher education, which has as its goal mastery of the procedural aspects of teaching, was likely only to perpetuate existing practices' (pp. 232–3). Of this traditional model of teacher education, Wideen, Mayer-Smith and Moon commented: 'Although critics ... have not been kind in their assessment of this traditional institutional model of teacher education, it persists, despite calls for reform' (1988, p. 133). The perpetuation of the traditional model of teaching is the basic fallacy in the apprenticeship model and it serves as a major deterrent to progress in teacher education.

The Traditional Model of Teaching

The traditional model of teaching has been made explicit by Griffin and Case (1998). Although they explained the model in the case of mathematics teachers, they would apparently agree with Désautels (Ch. 13) that, in addition to teachers' teaching the way they themselves were taught, their epistemological stance also plays an important role in shaping their pedagogical practice. Griffin and Case (1998, p. 26) hypothesize that a core set of conceptions operates at the center of the pedagogical knowledge of teachers. These conceptions concern the teachers' epistemological views of the particular subject being taught, the optimal way to learn this subject matter, and the role the teacher should play as a teacher of this subject. This core set of conceptions is regarded by Griffin and Case as broadly influencing teachers' pedagogical practices and as being formed very early on in the life of teachers. In traditional teaching, teachers regard the subject matter as an a priori and fixed body of knowledge, learning as accruing information, and teaching as transferring information (Griffin and Case, 1998, p. 27).

This image of traditional teaching is compatible with what Désautels (Ch. 13) takes as the dominant representation of scientific knowledge in the schools – conveying a strong sense of scientific statements as being accurate descriptions of reality. In his investigation of the possibility of pre-service science teachers 'complexifying' their worldviews, Désautels (Ch. 13) commented that

> Looking back at the intellectual struggle and ethical struggle that this student[1] experienced, one can understand why he continually maintained the metaphysical assumptions underlying his apprehension of what he called the world or the environment (i.e. the subject–object dichotomy, the organized character of the universe or the environment, etc.), for such assumptions are built into our society's prevailing forms of common sense or worldview through which meaning is derived. Furthermore, we must not forget that these assumptions also constitute the tacit conceptual framework of the dominant representation of scientific knowledge in the schools. (p. 209)

Simon's work (Ch. 14) also indicates that it is difficult to change pre-service teachers' views of representation to be more aligned with Glasersfeld's view of the function of cognition: 'As we take a hard look at the nature of the two perspectives and the underlying epistemological differences, we come to an understanding why the challenge to move to a conception based perspective is so formidable' (p. 216).

The Dynamic Notion of Living

Glasersfeld (1995) made a distinction between classical empiricism and constructivist rationalism that is basic to an understanding of why the challenge to move to a conception-based perspective is formidable.

> The difference, therefore could be characterized by saying that classical empiricism accepts without question the static notion of being, whereas constructivist rationalism accepts without question the dynamic notion of living. (p. 111)

Rather than view mathematics and science as having a mind-independent existence in themselves, radical constructivists understand them as a part of the dynamic notion of living. Désautels (this volume, Ch. 13) believes that 'in the case of preservice teachers, the task of understanding the constructivist thesis is more usefully conceived of as an opening into alternative worldviews' (p. 195). This implies a reflective attitude along with an ability to make decisions concerning one's own worldview without manipulation or coercion. However, a reflective attitude alone is insufficient to understand the difference that Glasersfeld pointed to because it is easy to conflate thinking of mathematics or science in the context of the dynamic notion of living and considering an individual as an active subject of mathematics or science while maintaining a correspondence theory of representation. Désautels (Ch. 13) characterized the latter position as 'mitigated realism'.

> This epistemological position differs from the two preceding views through the integration of the observer who is responsible for the production of scientific knowledge. Then, scientific knowledge is thought of in terms of conceptions or representations of reality that are useful for action. But, the subject–object dichotomy is maintained all the same, and there has to be a real and orderly world 'out there' – i.e. which exists independently of the observer. (p. 203)

Ernest commented that Glasersfeld's view of the function of cognition does not have 'any new practical implications for education and psychology, beyond those of [the active construction of knowledge]' (Ernest, 1991, p. 5). In mitigated realism, Ernest's comment would not be countermanded, because the mathematical and scientific knowledge produced by the subject's organization of experiential reality would be of little interest to the observer. That is, the knower's mathematical or scientific knowledge would be regarded primarily as invalid unless it could be demonstrated that it corresponded to a real and orderly world 'out there'. In the case such a correspondence could not be demonstrated, then the observer would be likely to classify the knower's knowledge as a misconception rather than to seek a way of understanding it that would portray it as an internally consistent system that is perhaps qualitatively distinct from the observer's knowledge.

In mitigated realism, '[T]he "active subject of science" is conceived of as an individual, not a social actor. We have here an unmistakable portrait of what Glasersfeld has so often qualified as a trivial form of constructivism, which offers a family resemblance with the now-dominant cognitivist model of cognition in education' (Désautels, Ch. 13, p. 208). Mathematics teaching that is consistent with trivial constructivism is caught by Simon's (Ch. 14) comment that

> Our recent empirical work . . . has led us to the conclusion that many teachers participating in current reforms base their epistemological perspectives on the assumption of direct access to an ontological reality. They interpret the mathematics education reform as emphasizing the value of learners' first-hand experience 'seeing' mathematical relationships. (p. 215)

The emphasis on first-hand experience is consistent with the premise that any epistemological position that claims to be a constructivism shares in the metaphor of construction. According to Ernest, what the 'metaphor of *construction* does not mean in constructivism is that understanding is built up from received pieces of knowledge' (1996, p. 461). Rather, the process is recursive so 'the "building blocks" of understanding are the product of previous acts of understanding' (ibid.). This is the case in any constructivism, according to Ernest. Trivial constructivism 'recognizes that knowing is active, that it is individual and personal, and that it is based on previously constructed knowledge. Just getting student teachers to realize this, by reflecting on "child methods" in mathematics or alternative conceptions in science, represents a significant step forward from the naive transmission view of teaching and the passive-receptive view of learning many arrive with' (ibid., p. 462).

Ernest's observation raises two crucial issues in mathematics and science teacher education today in which constructivist reforms are being attempted. The first concerns the design of programs in which the significant step forward from the naive transmission view of teaching and the passive-receptive view of learning is taken by the students without retreat, and the second concerns the sufficiency of this step in mathematics and science education. What does the significant step forward leave out if the next step implied by Glasersfeld's idea of the function of cognition is not taken, and what are the consequences of leaving these things out?

Trivial Constructivism in Teacher Education: What is Left Out?

The Intersubjective Construction of Knowledge

Any consideration of Born's problem of how to free oneself from subjective knowledge to arrive at objective statements (Born, 1968, p. 162) is left out for the simple reason that valid subjective knowledge is regarded as corresponding to a priori objective knowledge. In radical constructivism, the necessity of including the intersubjective construction of knowledge to arrive at knowledge that we would want to trust as though it were objective is clearly made by Glasersfeld (1995, p. 119). Constructing such knowledge involves a second-order of viability:

> It is obvious that this second-order viability, of which we can say with some justification that it reaches beyond the field of our individual experience into that of others, must play an important part in the stabilization and solidification of our experiential reality. It helps create that intersubjective level on which one is led to believe that concepts, schemes of action, goals, and ultimately feelings and emotions are shared by others and, therefore, are more *real* than anything experienced only by oneself. (ibid., p. 203)

The consequence of leaving out the roles that intersubjectivity plays in the construction of knowledge in a teacher education program in which trivial constructivism is the dominant paradigm is unacceptable, for intersubjectivity leads to the realization that there are experiential realities other than our own; that is, the experiential realities of others (Foerster, 1984). This realization is one of the most important aspects of radical constructivism in mathematics and science education *because it opens the way to formulating models of the mathematical or scientific realities of others*. It is here that mathematics and science as well as teaching and learning mathematics and science are reconstituted in the context of living. A passage from Glasersfeld (1989) quoted by Simon (Ch. 14) speaks to this point:

> This view differs from the old one in that it deliberately discards the notion that knowledge could or should be a representation of an observer-independent world-in-itself and replaces it with the demand that the conceptual constructs we call knowledge be viable in the experiential world of the knowing subject. (Glasersfeld, 1989, p. 122)

The Knower as a Self-Reflexive Social Agent

Interpreters of radical constructivism often read such passages from Glasersfeld as implying that radical constructivism is a solipsistic position. However, Simon

Leslie P. Steffe

(Ch. 14), in answering the question 'What might it mean for mathematics teacher education to include a view of prospective and practicing teachers as active agents in the construction of their knowledge?' (p. 214), interprets active agents as social agents, which is sufficient to countermand the solipsistic interpretation. Perhaps even more importantly, Simon interprets the *teacher educator* as a social agent in his crucial realization that teacher educators must apply the principles of radical constructivism first and foremost to themselves, a principle of radical constructivism called 'self-reflexivity' (Steffe and Wiegel, 1995, pp. 479–83). Self-reflexivity is quite similar to the concept of 'epistemic reflexivity' used in this volume by both Larochelle (Ch. 5) and Désautels (Ch. 13) in that self-reflexivity includes reflection on one's own epistemological stance. But it involves more as exemplified by part of Simon's (Ch. 14) answer to the question of what should be included in understanding the teacher education student as an active social agent:

> The knowledge and experience of the teachers would be a specific focus of inquiry by mathematics teacher educators and researchers in mathematics teacher development. (p. 214)

One way that is open for mathematics and science teacher educators or researchers to construct their own knowledge of their students' constructive processes is through the kind of scientific teaching that is embedded in teaching experiments. Scientific teaching opens out teacher education in mathematics and science into an exciting arena for productive and creative activity that is seriously curtailed in trivial constructivism. In trivial constructivism, mathematics and science are viewed as a priori and fixed bodies of knowledge. In this case, the teacher or researcher would interpret what students learn in terms of mathematical or scientific givens rather than attempt to formulate an explanation of it that may not fit with such givens. Although such explanations may seem to open up mathematics or science education to an 'anything goes' mentality, it instead opens the possibility of mathematics and science teacher education becoming legitimate fields of scientific inquiry. Teacher educators or researchers in mathematics and science are concerned, however, with more than the mathematical or scientific knowledge of their students. They are also concerned with their students learning pedagogical knowledge, which includes models of teaching.

The Inquiry Model of Teaching

Simon's assertion that inquiry teaching is based on radical constructivism and symbolic interactionism (Ch. 14) is compatible with Glasersfeld's emphasis on intersubjectivity in knowledge construction. In fact, Leslie Smith (1995), in a review of Glasersfeld's (1995) latest book on radical constructivism, commented that 'A central claim of RC is that social construction is as essential as abstraction and that both have a basis in Piaget's work' (Smith, 1995, p. 509). Smith's comment was made quite independently of the comment made by Glasersfeld (Ch. 1) concerning social interaction: 'This topic [social interaction] certainly requires investigation and its investigation should not be hampered by the unwarranted fabrication that there is a conceptual contradiction between the principle of subjective cognitive construction and the experiential reality of the phenomena that are called social' (p. 6).

Inquiry into students' knowledge is a key aspect of inquiry teaching. There are two aspects of students' knowledge of concern to the teacher – knowledge *of* students and knowledge *for* students. Knowledge of students refers to conceptual models which the teacher constructs to explain his or her experience of the students, and knowledge for students refers to possibilities which the teacher has reason to believe the students can construct. Both knowledge of and for students are constructs of the teacher, so any description of students' knowledge in inquiry teaching is a statement made by a teacher. These statements are what Simon (Ch. 14) envisions teachers placing in hypothetical learning trajectories and subsequently modifying both in and as a result of the teacher's interactions with students.

Inquiry teaching, rather than being thought of as transferring information, emphasizes the interactive communication between the teacher and students and among the students themselves.

> Such teaching is *goal directed, yet constantly changing.* The teacher's relationship with the students is one of both direction setting and following student initiatives; this tension between the teacher's current goals for student learning and commitment to respond to the mathematics of the student is inherent in teaching. (p. 222)

The tension to which Simon alludes is between the mathematics for students the teacher has constructed and what the students actually learn. I refer to this tension as an experienced provocation and it is a major factor that drives learning on the part of the teacher. An even more fundamental factor is the necessity of teachers to construct the mathematics of students as well as for students. The latter is especially challenging because mathematics for students is not necessarily explained in terms of standard curricular content. Rather, it is more appropriately understood as the mathematics other students have learned whose mathematics can be judged to be like the mathematics of the current students. Some notion of inquiry teaching is supported in trivial constructivism, but it would not include the major goal of teacher learning in the way Simon envisions. Rather, the major goal of the teacher would be found in Lewin's (Ch. 4) paradox of happy agreement, and that would be to 'hold forth for a correctness of response that is essentially univocal. . . . All the work of specification will have been done by the teacher drawing from the reigning tradition in establishing the conditions for inquiry while the student/knower is conceptualized as creative and inventive' (p. 43). Although the teacher might learn the creations or inventions of

Leslie P. Steffe

the students, these things would not be considered as legitimate candidates to be included in the mathematical or scientific education of students.

The Use of Language as a Communicatory Tool

As early as 1976, Glasersfeld (1987/1976) provided an account of the possible evolutionary advantages of cooperation and its role in the development of communicatory behavior. In this account, he explained that the incentive to communicate is based on the principle that communicatory behavior is *purposeful behavior*. It (communicatory behavior) is 'a *mode of action*, its function is to link concerted activity, and it is indispensable because without these links there could be *no unified social action*. Thus it is an *instrument*, which is to say, a *tool*' (Glasersfeld, 1987/1976, p. 47; quoted in Schmidt, this volume, Ch. 3, p. 27). Although communicatory behavior is more general than the use of language as a communicatory tool, language does serve as a primary means of communication in inquiry teaching. Glasersfeld regards the most important feature of language as 'its symbolic capacity to evoke ideas of things, actions, and situations in the speaker apart from actually experiencing them' (Schmidt, Ch. 3, p. 27).

Of symbolicity, Glasersfeld (1987/1976) explained that 'the semanticity of a linguistic sign is constituted, not by a tie that links it to a "thing", but by one that links it to a re-presentation or concept' (p. 54). Regarding semanticity in this way introduces a certain indeterminacy into the use of language which Hunting (this volume, Ch. 15) sees as basic in mathematics teaching. If the teacher's words and phrases are interpreted by students, it is clear that the students' interpretations are unlikely to coincide with the meaning the teacher intends to convey. '[L]anguage is not a means of transporting conceptual structures from teacher to student, but rather a means of interacting that allows the teacher here and there to constrain and thus to guide the cognitive constructions of the student' (Glasersfeld, 1990, p. 37).

If we interpret 'to constrain' as 'constrained to' as well as 'constrained by', this opens up the notion of 'to guide' in a positive as well as a negative sense. To appreciate this, it might help to consider what Glasersfeld (1995) considers to be the most important consequence of his model of knowing: 'our knowledge of clashes with what we have categorized as "environment" or "real world" can be articulated and re-presented only in terms of viable conceptual structures, i.e., structures which, themselves, have not come into contact with obstacles' (1995, p. 73). These viable conceptual structures are the positive aspect of the model of knowing, and they complement the negative aspect. It is the students' viable conceptual structures which the teacher attempts to bring forth and it is these conceptual structures which are modified by the knower in response to the clashes with reality.

Brink (Ch. 8) and Wright (Ch. 10) both emphasize that it may not be possible for students to reach compatibility among their conceptual structures in any immediate future. In such cases, not only should the teacher tolerate the students' knowledge as suggested by Brink (Ch. 8), the teacher also should expect to adjust his or her own knowledge in such a way that it contains a legitimate understanding of the students' knowledge. In this context, Hunting (Ch. 15) discusses how teachers might learn to deal with unexpected responses from students. Crucial in his discussion is the idea that 'A foreign or unexpected response is an indication that the teacher may need to revise or reorganize her existing knowledge structures in order to fit the response into them in a coherent way' (p. 240). Further, 'Even the most erudite mathematics educator should hold open the possibility of being surprised because it is the surprises that remind us that our understanding of others is just that – our understanding – and not make the mistake of believing that our interpretations are identical to the knowledge interpreted' (p. 241).

The above considerations indicate how Glasersfeld's insight concerning the semanticity of a linguistic sign orients mathematics or science teacher educators in a way that is quite different from considering such semanticity as constituted by a link to a 'thing' in an observer-independent world-in-itself. Glasersfeld's insight is especially important when considering that students' knowledge and constructive activity are formulated in terms of teacher knowledge, because it brings to the fore the necessity of considering the mathematics and science teacher as well as teacher educator or researcher as deeply competent professionals.

Learning Inquiry Teaching in Graduate Education

Both Hunting (Ch. 15) and Simon (Ch. 14) compare the role of a mathematics teacher to the teacher in a constructivist teaching experiment. A teacher in a constructivist teaching experiment must know how to interact mathematically with students and how to engage them in purposeful mathematical interactions. Moreover, such a teacher must be able to imagine how students think mathematically, and produce conceptual mechanisms to account for that thinking. On that basis, the teacher must be able to posit zones of potential construction (hypothetical learning trajectories) for students along with possible educational situations (Désautels, Ch. 13, p. 210) which might occasion changes in the students' thinking. That is, the teacher must be able to produce a local goal structure along with a possible local curriculum. And, as a result of actual mathematical interactions with the students, the teacher must be able to revise the local goal structure and posit another that includes the revised goal structure. All of this is included in Simon's (Ch. 14) notion of inquiry teaching.

Clearly, the inquiry model of teaching implies major reforms in mathematics teacher education, reforms that Simon (Ch. 14) referred to as a 'daunting undertaking'. That Simon's assessment is not exaggerated can be seen in Potari's (Ch. 16) discussion of the struggles of five graduate students in mathematics education as they tried to come to grips with inquiry teaching in a teaching experiment. She demonstrated that the epistemological beliefs of even advanced graduate students are fundamental in orienting their teaching practice. This finding not only confirms the hypothesis of Griffin and Case (1998) that a core set of conceptions operates at the center of the pedagogical knowledge of teachers, but it extends it as well. In the hypothesis of Griffin and Case (1998), the epistemological views concerned the subject being taught. The work of Potari (Ch. 16) indicates that more general and perhaps implicit models of knowing of a teacher operate at the center of his or her pedagogical knowledge. Her work also indicates that those core conceptions formed very early on in the life of teachers can be modified in the context of interacting with mentors concerning the experience of interacting with students. But these interactions were insufficient if the involved graduate students weren't themselves opening into an alternative worldview. That is, it was necessary for the graduate students to form the goal of understanding what mathematical teaching might consist of in a constructivist teaching experiment and that they be deeply engaged in their own self-study of constructivism outside of the context of the teaching experiment.

An unmistakable pattern emerges when contrasting the work of Potari with the work of Désautels, Simon and Hunting. A comment by Hunting (Ch. 15) highlights an essential precondition for a teacher changing from the traditional to the inquiry model of teaching:

> One reason for targeting in-service teachers is that changes in teaching practice will most likely occur for those teachers who are already searching for alternatives to their teaching practice. A precondition for change in teaching practice is a feeling of dissatisfaction with one's current practice, and a feeling of dissatisfaction is likely to be found in teachers who have been immersed in traditional teaching practices but who understand mathematics relationally. (p. 235)

Along with the finding of Désautels (Ch. 13) that even the most advanced science education student with whom he worked maintained the metaphysical assumptions underlying his apprehension of what he called the world, and the finding of Simon (Ch. 14) that the challenge to move to a conception-based perspective is formidable, the difficulty of educating pre-service teachers of mathematics and science capable of engaging in inquiry teaching emerges.

To engage in inquiry teaching, entering pre-service teachers need to move from their models of teaching, which are more or less captured by traditional teaching, to models of reform teaching. This involves major transformations of their belief structures concerning mathematics or science, learning, teaching, and the role of a teacher. These students simply cannot be told to make these transformations, as that would imply that a traditional model of teaching could be used in teacher education to teach a reform model of teaching. This presents us with the very deep problem in teacher education of learning to educate prospective teachers in such a way that they might transform their belief structures and use them as psychological tools in organizing their educational practices.

Final Comments

Perhaps the most basic realization emerging from the chapters in this section is that the education of teachers capable of engaging in inquiry teaching should be a *professional education*. The hallmark of a professional teacher comes to the fore when we consider the attempts of the chapter authors to reform their practice of teacher education. In essence, they are learning how to educate teachers in the context of educating them. That is, they are learning how to organize their curricula, how to reorganize their teaching, how to reconstitute principles from models of knowing so as to be useful to them, how to make structural changes in their programs, etc. It is even more difficult for teacher educators or researchers to learn how to educate their students than it is for pre-college teachers to learn to educate their students because the former have to learn on their own – there is no one else in institutions of education higher than the university whose goal it is to help them reform their practices (one might consider the social groups to which teacher educators belong as serving this educative function). *Their only recourse is to accept reforming their own educational practices as their professional responsibility.* The competence to carry out this responsibility for me is the defining hallmark of a professional teacher at any institutional level. How a professional teacher of mathematics and science might be educated is perhaps the most important problem that is opened by radical constructivism in mathematics and science education.

Note

1 'This student' was characterized in a way that one could expect him to be at least as reflective as a majority of students studying to be science teachers in pre-baccalaureate programs.

References

Born, M. (1968) *My Life and My Views*, New York: Scribner's.
Davis, R. (1966) 'Discovery in the teaching of mathematics', in Shulman, L.S. and Keislar, E.R. (eds), *Learning by Discovery: A Critical Appraisal*, Chicago: University of Chicago Press, pp. 114–28.
Ernest, P. (1991) *The Philosophy of Mathematics Education*, London: Falmer Press.
Ernest, P. (1996) 'The one and the many', in Steffe, L.P. and Gale, J. (eds), *Constructivism in Education*, Hillsdale, NJ: Lawrence Erlbaum, pp. 459–86.
Foerster, H. von (1984) 'On constructing a reality', in Watzlawick, P. (ed.), *The Invented Reality*, New York: W.W. Norton, pp. 95–116.

GLASERSFELD, E. VON (1987/1976) 'The development of language as purposive behavior', in GLASERSFELD, E. VON (ed.), *The Construction of Knowledge: Contributions to Conceptual Semantics*, Seaside, Calif.: Intersystems Publications, pp. 37–64.

GLASERSFELD, E. VON (1987/1977) 'The concepts of adaptation and viability in a radical constructivist theory of knowledge', in GLASERSFELD, E. VON (ed.), *The Construction of Knowledge: Contributions to Conceptual Semantics*, Seaside, Calif.: Intersystems Publications, pp. 135–43.

GLASERSFELD, E. VON (1989) 'Cognition, the construction of knowledge, and teaching', *Syntheses*, 80, pp. 121–40.

GLASERSFELD, E. VON (1990) 'Environment and communication', in STEFFE, L.P. and WOOD, T. (eds), *Transforming Children's Mathematics Education*, Hillsdale, NJ: Lawrence Erlbaum, pp. 30–8.

GLASERSFELD, E. VON (1995) *Radical Constructivism: A Way of Knowing and Learning*, Washington, DC: Falmer Press.

GRIFFIN, S. and CASE, R. (1997) 'Re-thinking the primary school math curriculum: An approach based on cognitive science', *Issues in Education*, 3, 1, pp. 1–49.

HENDRIX, G. (1961) 'Learning by discovery', *Mathematics Teacher*, 54, pp. 290–9.

KONOLD, C. and JOHNSON, D.K. (1991) 'Philosophical and psychological aspects of constructivism', in STEFFE, L.P. (ed.), *Epistemological Foundations of Mathematical Experience*, New York: Springer, pp. 1–13.

NATIONAL COUNCIL OF TEACHERS OF MATHEMATICS (1989) *Curriculum and Evaluation Standards for School Mathematics*, Reston, VA: Author.

OLIVE, J. (1995) 'Building a new model of mathematics learning', *Journal of Research in Childhood Education*, 8, 2, pp. 162–73.

SMITH, L. (1995) 'Radical constructivism: A way of knowing and learning. By Ernst von Glasersfeld', *British Journal of Behavioural Research*, 65, 4, pp. 508–9.

STEFFE, L.P. (1992) 'Schemes of action and operation involving composite units', *Learning and Individual Differences*, 4, 3, pp. 259–309.

STEFFE, L.P. and KIEREN, T. (1994) 'Radical constructivism and mathematics education', *Journal for Research in Mathematics Education*, 25, 6, pp. 711–33.

STEFFE, L.P. and WIEGEL, H. (1995) 'Cognitive play and mathematical learning in a computer microworld', *Journal of Research in Childhood Education*, 8, 2, pp. 117–31.

WIDEEN, M., MAYER-SMITH, J. and MOON, B. (1998) 'A critical analysis of the research on learning to teach: Making the case for an ecological perspective on inquiry', *RER*, 68, pp. 130–78.

Section Five

Reflections and Directions

18 Radical Constructivism: Reflections and Directions[†]

Patrick W. Thompson

I would like to bring the book full circle, returning to two points raised by Ernst von Glasersfeld in his opening chapter. These are the fact that radical constructivism is misinterpreted so persistently by its critics, and the need for radical constructivism to provide a clear model of social interaction. I return to these points not only to give the book a particular rhetorical structure, but because they penetrate many of the controversies both internal to mathematics and science education and at the boundaries of radical constructivism. At the same time, I will point out the importance of conceptual analysis in Glasersfeld's method and urge more people to use it in mathematics and science education.

Misinterpretations of Constructivism

Glasersfeld (Ch. 1, p. 5) noted that some misinterpretations of radical constructivism may be inevitable by-products of readers' conceptual operations.

> Insofar as these misunderstandings are honest, they seem to be caused by conceptual blinders the traditional epistemology has placed on the readers. As with panicky horses, the blinders shut out perturbing sights and insights.

Statements like this might seem a bit defensive to non-constructivists. Who are constructivists to be speaking of others' blinders? However, if you know Glasersfeld personally, you know his remark emanates from frustration at a persistent lack of communication rather than from his attempts to defend radical constructivism or from arrogance. As he points out, critics of radical constructivism often base their criticisms on assumptions that are not made by radical constructivists.

Lerman's (1994, 1996) criticisms of radical constructivism are a case in point. Lerman criticized radical constructivism for taking an incoherent stance in regard to the idea of intersubjectivity:

> Taking constructivism's view of the autonomy of the individual in the construction of her or his knowing, given her or his particular conceptual system and its particular filter, leads to a consistent, albeit very restricted, view. To

argue for an integrated view is to argue that sometimes the filter has very large holes and what is occurring beyond the individual can somehow enter without constraint. I argue, then, that it makes no sense to strengthen the functioning of the 'social' into a social constructivism. (Lerman, 1996, p. 140)

A close look at Lerman's criticism reveals some of the conceptual blinders Glasersfeld noted. The constructivism he criticizes deserves criticism. But it is not the constructivism I know.

Lerman said:	*My comment*:
Taking constructivism's view of the autonomy of the individual in the construction of her or his knowing ...	Constructivists evidently believe that people have explicit control over what knowledge they end up constructing.
given her or his particular conceptual system and its particular filter, ...	Conceptual systems act as filters, meaning that there are 'things to filter' and that what is not filtered is registered as such within the person's conceptual system
To argue for an integrated view is to argue that sometimes the filter has very large holes and what is occurring beyond the individual can somehow enter without constraint.	Lerman has set up constructivism for his criticisms by portraying it as taking stances to which few constructivists would agree.

In Piaget's genetic epistemology, assimilation is *constitutive* – a scheme's activation *constitutes* the subject's experience of the 'things' assimilated to it. It makes no sense when explaining persons' experiences to speak of their schemes acting as filters. It is only when we speak as observers of someone living his or her experiences, when we have identified that part of *our* experience that is not the observed person, that the idea of something outside the person passing through a filter becomes intelligible. However, this account describes *our* conception of what we have observed. It does not describe the observed person's experience. This is an epistemological stance. It is not an ontological stance. As observers of living organisms that have no metaphysical access to (what we see as) their environments, whose 'sensing' and 'knowing' entail nothing more than the chemical and electrical activity generated by their nervous systems, we understand that all knowledge boils down to a dynamic autoregulation of nervous functioning.[1] As Glasersfeld (Ch. 1) notes, 'I consider metaphysical assumptions vacuous as long as they do not specify a functional model of how ontology might determine the experiences from which we generate our knowledge. To say that something exists does not explain how we come to know it' (p. 6).

Reflections and Directions

Lerman's criticism reflects what I suspect is a major source of miscommunication between constructivists and non-constructivists. Lerman seems to have in mind a standard observer, one who watches all that happens, and for whom he can speak unproblematically. This image of a standard observer for whom anyone can speak suggests, to those having it, that human experience is *caused* by something penetrating a boundary between environment and individual. If this is the conceptual background within which we frame discussions of human experience, then our discussions of 'knowledge' will point to experience of those things that somehow penetrate the imagined boundary. Hence, discussions of 'construction' from this perspective will be about experiencers' constructions of those things that penetrate. This, indeed, is an incoherent model of knowing, and anyone who understands constructivism this way *should* question it. One strategy by which constructivists could counter objections that emanate from a 'standard observer' frame is to acknowledge the objections' legitimacy, within that frame, and then point out that this is not the model we have in mind.

(Mis)Interpretations Are Sometimes Well Founded

Not all misinterpretations of constructivism are due to others' conceptual blinders. Some, in fact, originate in honest attempts to apply constructivism directly to mathematics education. For example, Funderstanding defines constructivism as follows:

> Constructivism is a philosophy of learning founded on the premise that, by reflecting on our experiences, we construct our own understanding of the world we live in. Each of us generates our own 'rules' and 'mental models,' which we use to make sense of our experiences. Learning, therefore, is simply the process of adjusting our mental models to accommodate new experiences. (Funderstanding, 1999)

They state four principles of constructivism: learning is a search for meaning; learning processes must focus on primary concepts; we must understand students' mental models if we are to teach them well; and the purpose of learning is for each individual to 'construct personal meaning instead of regurgitating others' meanings'. From this they derive several conclusions, which include:

> Constructivism calls for the elimination of a standardized curriculum. Instead, it promotes using curricula customized to the students' prior knowledge. Also, it emphasizes hands-on problem solving. Under the theory of constructivism, educators focus on making connections between facts and fostering new understanding in students. Instructors tailor their teaching strategies to student responses and encourage students to analyze, interpret, and predict information. Teachers also rely heavily on open-ended questions and promote extensive dialogue among students.

> Constructivism calls for the elimination of grades and standardized testing. Instead, assessment becomes part of the learning process so that students play a larger role in judging their own progress. (Funderstanding, 1999)

Funderstanding's definition of constructivism and its principles and the conclusions they derive therefrom are not incompatible with the constructivism of Glasersfeld and Piaget. However, they are not implied by it either. First, constructivism is not a philosophy of learning. It is a model of knowing. Piaget's genetic epistemology addresses, to some extent, the learning of scientific concepts broadly, but it does not address learning *per se*. Theories of learning based on constructivism (e.g. Steffe et al., 1983), which claim to characterize knowledge people come to have and ways they might come to have it, might support such conclusions. But constructivism *per se* does not. Second, as an intellectual position, constructivism does not call for eliminating anything. The authors may have derived their position from other considerations, but tenets of constructivism, by themselves, do not warrant it.

Nevertheless, when non-constructivists see constructivism presented this way they are not positioned to understand that it is a mischaracterization. It would be interesting to know what percent of people's contacts with constructivism are with such ideological portrayals. I suspect the rate is high enough to support a popular understanding of constructivism as being about discovery learning, cooperation and a ban on lecturing.

One might think that the above applies only to 'popularized' constructivism. But even well-known constructivists sometimes write as if applying constructivism directly to mathematics education. For example, Dubinsky and Schwingendorf appeal directly to constructivism in justifying their student-centered approaches to instruction and curriculum development:

> The emphasis of the C^4L program [calculus, concepts, computers and cooperative learning] is a pedagogical approach based on a constructivist theoretical perspective of how mathematics is learned. According to this emerging theory, students need to construct their own understanding of each mathematical concept. Hence, we believe that the primary role of teaching is not to lecture, explain, or otherwise attempt to 'transfer' mathematical knowledge, but to create situations for students that will foster their making the necessary mental constructions. (Dubinsky and Schwingendorf, 1997)

Constructivism, by itself, cannot sanction any particular pedagogical approach. Though Dubinsky and Schwingendorf do not say *not* to lecture, many people interpret them to say so, and it seems clear that they do not value lecturing highly. However, it may be that lecturing is an appropriate pedagogical approach when used with learners who are in a position to listen actively to a speaker and engage in a private debate with the points they understand the speaker to make. It could also be that, at a particular moment in a student's conceptualization of a particular idea, it is counterproductive to have him or her remain focused on concrete activity. This is not to say that lecturing is

Reflections and Directions

always appropriate or that to focus on concrete activity is always inappropriate. Rather, our pedagogical decisions must be sensitive to context and goals and must be informed by theories that tie directly into issues of mathematics learning and teaching. As Simon (Ch. 14) notes, 'Whereas constructivism provides a foundation for reconceptualizing mathematics teaching, it does not provide a particular model of mathematics teaching' (p. 217). Our audiences often understand that constructivism does not imply a particular model of teaching, so when they hear statements to the effect that it does, they rightly wonder whether constructivism is just ideology or dogma. It may be, to quote Walt Kelly's Pogo, that 'We have met the enemy and he is us.'

Non-constructivists correctly see hypocrisy in someone saying, on the one hand, that *all* knowers' knowledge is constructed because it has proven viable within their experience, and on the other hand saying that realism and empiricism are untenable positions. Are realists and empiricists not knowers? Do they, in fact, not know what they claim to know? Perhaps it is productive to qualify our comments on realism or empiricism by saying that they are not useful if, as Glasersfeld (Ch. 1) notes, we require our models of learning to suggest how someone comes to know whatever they know and when we disallow metaphysical accounts of learning.

While I point out the need for constructivists to show signs of humility and to avoid projecting a sense of self-righteousness, I also am compelled to give a warning. It is that some people will employ others' attitudes of openness, humility and tolerance to the others' disadvantage. Chomsky and Fodor did this in their debate with Piaget on whether language is largely innate or emerges through an interaction between sensori-motor intelligence and the general semiotic function (Piattelli-Palmarini, 1980). Piaget was polite and open to criticisms of his position; they were not. They expressed an attitude similar to, 'You are uncertain, we are certain, therefore we are right.'

Similar stances have been adopted in the 'math wars'. Bishop (1999) gives one of the more blatant admissions that his group's goal is power, not insight. O'Brien (1999) observed that such public posturing can be as much a personality trait as an academic position.

- Parrot math reflects a deep-seated longing to control children through external rewards and punishments, rather than to harness children's urge to make sense of things. We've all seen controlling parents at poolside: 'Jonathan, get out of the pool. You're grounded for five minutes.' 'Gee, Dad, what did I do?' 'Out! Now you're grounded for 10 minutes!' (O'Brien, 1999, p. 435)

O'Brien also considered the motives of people advocating procedure- and memorization-oriented approaches to mathematics teaching. He observed that advocates of 'basic' mathematics (what he called 'parrot math') are more interested in garnering power to decide children's fates and seem more interested in controlling school instruction and curriculum than in children's education.

- [The debate over child-centered approaches to mathematics education] is a useful battering ram for advancing political candidates at the expense of teachers and educational leaders. Ironically, the critics' arguments seem to have a special appeal to parents and editors who themselves learned to hate and fear math because of the same parrot math approaches that are being recommended today.
- Publishers who specialize in back-to-basics approaches stand to gain from the rejection of other methods. For example, in December 1997 California's politically appointed state board rejected middle-of-the-road, 'balanced' mathematics standards that had been developed by a state-mandated academic standards commission and replaced them with a set of parrot math standards that were developed under highly controversial circumstances, a process and a result that were greeted by nationwide protests from mathematicians, math educators, teachers, and parents. In papers shared via the Internet, some from as far away as Hungary, [ostensive] leaders in math education reached the consensus view that the new standards were 'a disaster'. Several months later,
- California Gov[ernor] Pete Wilson called for some $250 million to be earmarked for new math textbooks that would be tied to the standards. (O'Brien, 1999, p. 435)

To put it sharply, O'Brien illustrates the practical knowledge that one cannot argue from a position of tolerance and openness with someone who is bent on achieving his own agenda by hanging you with your own words.

The Role of Radical Constructivism in Theories of Mathematics Education

Radical constructivism can be thought of as a background theory, or, as Noddings (1990) said, a post-epistemological stance. Background theories cannot be used to explain phenomena or to prescribe particular actions. Rather, their function is to constrain the types of explanation we give and to frame our descriptions of what needs explaining. The primary importance, to me, of radical constructivism is that it provides a continual reminder that humans are biological organisms whose only way to exert mutual influence, aside from physical harm or pleasure, is through mutual interpretation. This constraint on how we think of human knowing is always present – regardless of where we cast our net for theoretical problems. It is present when we consider how individual students come to understand a mathematical idea and it is present when we consider how newcomers are initiated into what we take as cultural practices.

As a background theory, constructivism orients us to formulate descriptions, problems, explanations and theories in specific ways. First, constructivism orients us to matters of what people know and how they might have come to know it.[2] It forces us to speak in the active voice. The passive voice is a strong ally of people speaking for the universal observer. By speaking in the passive voice, by writing subject-less sentences, a writer can proffer universal truths when actually expressing one viewpoint. However, within a constructivist framework, knowledge is knowledge because someone knows it, and when writers speak in subject-less sentences they should be criticized for being vague. You should insist that they say for whom they speak – for themselves, their subjects, or, perhaps, for a universal observer. To be specific, statements like

> Signs are incomplete, fundamentally context-dependent and possess imminently multiple meanings. Context, or what is brought to the communicational situation, inumbrates the sign, and is shaped by equivocality and ambiguity in messages (Cullum-Swan and Manning, 1995)

are very problematic from a constructivist view. Within constructivism, it makes no sense for anyone to talk about a sign possessing a meaning if he or she intends anything other than that people customarily bring to mind a particular meaning when observing what the speaker thinks is a sign. It also makes no sense, within constructivism, to speak of context being shaped by properties of messages if he or she intends anything other than that how a person contextualizes some event is influenced by the meanings he or she attributes to what a speaker has identified as worthy of discussion.[3]

Second, constructivism orients us to look for explanations and descriptions of interaction that are grounded in some equivalent of information theory (MacKay, 1951, 1955, 1964) and symbolic interactionism. More accurately, it orients us toward looking at social interaction as would someone from the school of symbolic interactionism that highlights the interplay of pragmatics and semantics instead of reifying symbols and interactions.

In summary, to pronounce constructivism as a background theory is not to announce a commitment to a particular theory of learning or pedagogy. Instead, it is to announce a set of commitments and constraints on the kinds of explanations we may accept and on the ways we frame problems and describe phenomena. A commitment to constructivism may have ramifications for the instructional actions we anticipate will be effective regarding students with certain characteristics coming to have particular understandings in the context of certain environments, but it does not, of itself, prescribe or exclude any particular action as possibly being effective.

A Conundrum

Having already said that constructivism cannot be applied prescriptively, I must confess that constructivism *does* seem to compel openness to alternative conceptualizations and tolerance of competing perspectives. It says that we cannot claim that any one perspective is 'right' – in the sense that all others are somehow 'wrong'. Thus, on the one hand constructivism seems to suggest a pedagogy based on openness, empathy and tolerance. On the other hand, it suggests that even this suggestion cannot be proffered or accepted dogmatically. These are ethical issues, in a sense, because they address matters of 'right' behavior in specific contexts and a system of beliefs that is more acceptable than are others. On the one hand, constructivism implies a correct behavior. On the other hand, it cannot do this. This is the issue Larochelle (Ch. 5) raises when she warns against the siren song of ethics. 'If constructivism is indeed a reflexive theory (i.e. one that practices what it preaches) it cannot then present itself as a meta-perspective dictating what ethics should be without simultaneously running the risk of lapsing into the very thing it denounces' (p. 62). Hence, it seems, on the surface, counter to constructivism that Lewin (Ch. 4) urges us to develop a constructivist ethics.

In addressing this conundrum I have found it useful to think of constructivism operating at different levels for different types of observer. The first is as if we are Martians, orbiting the earth, watching animals called humans scurrying about and apparently interacting by mutual influence and adaptation. We do not attribute any special sensory powers to them except that they each seem to send signals into and register signals from (what we see as) their environments. They also seem predisposed to attribute the same sensory and interpretive powers they experience to what we see as things in their environment, to the extent that this attribution proves viable within their experience. As Martians, it never occurs to us that any one or group of humans has 'correct' knowledge of their environment. It is a non-issue. It seems evident that none of them does. We do notice, however, that patterns of interaction and interpretation seem to stabilize over time for some groups, and the groups in fact seem to be defined reflexively by these patterns. That is, it seems that patterns of 'right' interaction emerge among various groups as members of them engage over time in mutual adaptation. But, as Martians, the idea that any group develops *the* correct pattern of interaction (i.e. ethics) never occurs to us. Rather, we conclude that ethical issues emerge within groups as patterns of interaction stabilize, and we observe that there are a great variety of stable patterns of interaction.

A second type of observer is one who empathizes with the observed. The earth-orbiter is an earthling like us, who can imagine being a member of the groups being observed. The observer can imagine experiencing what the observed experiences because of having been a member of one or several groups. This observer's observations are similar to the Martians', but are colored by the projection of personal experience into the process of interpreting the interactions. That is, this observer also sees that there is no 'right' pattern of interactions, but instead sees that any stable pattern provides its own constraints on the kinds of interaction that will allow the pattern to persist.[4] But this observer also feels a sense of identification with one of the groups. As such, he or she must act according to the constraints that come with having a set of values that support his or her participation in that particular pattern of interaction. However, this observer must also act according to the added constraint that comes with the knowledge that these constraints are not the only possible ones.

A model of ethics consistent with constructivism would explain, in principle, how *any* ethics comes about. However, our model of ethics would also have to allow the possibility of competing, incompatible ethics. It is a fact that the ethics of New Guinea headhunters differs from the ethics of Polynesian traders. As neutral observers interested in the emergence of ethical systems, our model of ethics must encompass both.

In short, constructivism, as an epistemological or post-epistemological stance, predicts that ethical considerations will emerge as groups of people exert mutual influence among themselves and come to value certain effects of having interacted in particular ways. It neither predicts nor dictates what any group's ethics will or should be. However, *if* one adopts a constructivist stance, *and* one considers ethical systems *consistent with having adopted a constructivist stance*, then these ethical systems will require its adherents to be open to competing viewpoints, tolerant of differences and tentative in the claims they make. This is not to say that adherents of constructivism may never act as if their knowledge is certain. Rather, it says they must be willing to reflect on their certainties – they must be ready to call into question anything they know.

This seems to resolve the conundrum. Constructivism does not dictate that anyone have a particular ethics. Rather, it predicts that ethical considerations will emerge as humans interact and form expectations about others' actions. At the same time, constructivism does impose constraints on anyone who consciously adopts it and who realizes, as Larochelle (Ch. 5) puts it, that people who adopt constructivism must practice what they preach.

It is important that adherents do not convey constructivism as dogma. The fact that many people do think of it as dogma is, I believe, a result of having heard others who claim to be constructivists but at the same time seem to argue that constructivism is correct (and that other viewpoints are incorrect). Glasersfeld never implies that constructivism is correct. Rather, he says only that constructivism is *useful*. At the risk of sounding amoral, I think we are wise to remove ethics from our educational decision-making and replace it with matters of practical reason. For example, it is commonplace for educators to state that students should feel a sense of responsibility for their own learning and decision-making. How might we justify this to teachers and parents?[5] On the one hand, we could make it an ethical argument about why it is the right thing to do. On the other hand, we could make it a practical issue by comparing the ramifications of students by and large *not* doing this with the ramifications of them doing it routinely.

In closing, I should point out that being open to competing viewpoints does not mean that all viewpoints are necessarily equal. If, in a particular area of inquiry, one model of knowing solves the problems a second model solves, and also solves problems the second problem does not solve, then the first model is more useful than the second. It is in this sense that I believe constructivism is more useful in education than is realism or empiricism. It supports insight into miscommunication as well as successful communication, whereas the others only support accounts of successful communication.

Patrick W. Thompson

A Disinterested View of Miscommunication

We must wonder about the extent to which it is unreasonable for us to expect others to understand questions of knowing in the sense that radical constructivists understand issues of knowing. After all, from our point of view, their knowledge that knowledge is a direct copy of reality must be viable in their experience – it must somehow work for them. My questions, then, are, 'What is the work that a representational view of mind does for the person having it?' 'What is the work that a radical constructivist view of knowledge does for the person having it?' I suspect that in answering these questions we might find ways to communicate more effectively across worldviews.[6]

A representational view of mind, the understanding that the representations people form of their worlds somehow mirror reality, seems to work for those holding it in the same way that Platonism works for practicing mathematicians and scientists. Platonism allows mathematicians and scientists to deal with their mental worlds with the same metaphors as when dealing with the physical world. They can take their constructs as objects of study unproblematically, so that their understandings of those constructs can be refined and tested in much the same way that they refine and test their understandings of physical phenomena. They can deal with the task at hand – 'discovering' connections between ideas – without having constantly to question the existence of the ideas they are connecting. They can believe that there *is* a solution to their problem if only they are clever enough to discover it.

A representational view of mind in educational research is like Platonism in mathematics and science. It relieves researchers of the need to take into account that subjects' perspectives on events of interest may not coincide at all with theirs. I am reminded of a public conversation I had in 1990 with a psychologist who is well known for his stance that all cognition is situated. The group was discussing young children's surprising answers to questions in another researcher's study of their thinking about ratios. I observed that it would be very helpful if we knew what questions the children had answered. The psychologist's response was immediate – the children had answered the questions that were asked. To him, the question was what the researcher said, or what was written on paper. To me, the question varied among children; the question any child answered was what he or she formulated *from* what the researcher said. In other words, what was unproblematic to the psychologist (the question children answered was the question the researcher asked) was problematic to me (the question children answered was what they formulated from what the researcher asked, and their surprising answers suggested their formulations were quite different from ours). Though this psychologist was convinced that all cognition is situated, it was he, in that case, who determined what the situation was in which the children's cognition happened. It is in this way that a representational view of mind simplifies theoretical life – researchers do not have to wonder about the experience of their studies' subjects. From my point of view, this omits from study the very thing that we hope to influence – our students' mathematical and scientific experiences.

The work that radical constructivism does for me is that it serves as a constant reminder that I must question my interpretations of how others understand what I take as a common setting. This is important to me because of what I do. I try to affect others' understandings of situations in ways that support the emergence of mathematical reasoning. I sometimes do this at close proximity to others (e.g. as a teacher or tutor) and I sometimes do this at great distance (e.g. as a policy maker or instructional designer). At close proximity, I try to think of ways my students might be thinking and adjust my actions accordingly. At greater distances I imagine groups of people interacting and try to think about ways in which we might intrude on those interactions to perturb them in productive ways. But at all times I am reminded that my point of view is not privileged, and I must constantly keep in mind that other people will act and interact in consonance with the inertia of their personal histories as solidified in their current conceptual operations. So, constructivism works for me. It does not guarantee success, but it reminds me that there are potential problems to avoid.

There are times when constructivists must suspend their constructivism. When designing instruction or working with students, at some point we must *act with certainty* that what we suspect is the case is actually the case. We must *act with certainty* that students actually understand an idea the way in which we suspect they do; we must *act with certainty* that they interpret a diagram or a computer screen in the way we have predicted. In order to *act*, we must believe, to some extent, that we are right and the students are as they see them.[7]

In acting with certainty, we become actors rather than observers. By an actor, I do not mean a theatrical performer. Rather, I mean that one becomes fused with the situation as he or she has constituted it (MacKay, 1969). Constructivists must function, at their moment of acting, as actors who take their experiential and conceptual worlds as real, just as any living organism becomes one with their constructed reality. To remain constructivists, they must interrupt their experiential realism to consider the consequences of their presumed certainty. Here I should point out once again the reflexivity of constructivism. Theoreticians, including us, are among those beings to whom constructivism applies, so theoreticians' knowledge, too, is a functional adaptation to experience.

We should take care not to convey the impression that we want mathematics and science students to become epistemologists. We want them to construct a coherent and powerful mathematics, but we want that mathematics to be real for them. We want them to *see* structure, to *see* relationships, to *see* quantity. It is unnecessary to consider epistemological questions while doing mathematics or science. Constructivism is better suited to addressing questions of what people might *know* as they have a mathematical or scientific idea, what they might know as they participate in a mathematical or scientific discussion, or what they might know as their thinking crystallizes while solving a complex problem. However, it is imperative that mathematics and science educators be aware of the epistemological claims inherent in any stance they take. It is imperative that mathematics and science teachers be sensitive to conceptions of situations that differ fundamentally from theirs, as if being seen from a completely different worldview.

In using constructivism we sometimes are pushed to act as if we are non-constructivists. To communicate with students we must at times say things that point to a reality of ideas that we would, if speaking as epistemologists, deny. For example, I was working with high school math students on the idea of sampling distributions. We were discussing opinion polling, and they were having difficulty distinguishing between the ideas of population parameter and sample statistic, and I began to suspect that their main problem was that they were unable to conceive a population parameter. I found myself saying this:

> Suppose we were like Mork[8] and could stop time for everyone but ourselves. Imagine freezing everyone in our target population. At that moment, each person in the population has an answer (yes, no, or no opinion) to the question we will ask, even if we happen not to ask him or her the question. So, the population as a whole, at that moment in time, has a percent of it who *would* say 'yes' to our question were they asked.

In other words, in order to talk about population parameters, students needed to think of populations as having characteristics whose measures have specific values at each moment in time. This is not to say that this example's population *really* had a characteristic whose measure had specific values at each moment in time. For the purpose of building a concept of sampling distribution, it is merely useful to think that it does. However, this was my realization – that it was merely *useful* to think of a population having a particular measurable characteristic. Students needed to *believe* that populations *can* have measurable characteristics, or else they would have been unable to conceive of sampling distributions as arising from repeatedly drawing samples of a given size from that population. They also would have been unable to consider how the set of sample statistics clusters around the population parameter. To coordinate all these aspects of sampling distributions, population parameters needed to be real for them.

The preceding example illustrated that the principles of constructivism, by themselves, do not provide guidance for acting in specific contexts – that one cannot simply turn responsibility to understand important ideas over to students. It does illustrate how one can employ constructivism in conjunction with an image of mathematical understanding to produce a model of knowing that *is* pedagogically useful.

I find distinctions between first- and second-order observers and between first- and second-order models of knowing (Steffe, 1995; Steffe et al., 1983; Steffe and Thompson, in press) very useful in explicating conditions that enable people to employ constructivism in pedagogically powerful ways. To understand these distinctions, one must first understand Maturana's famous position that 'Everything said is said by an observer' (Maturana, 1987) who in fact may be the observed. Maturana meant that any description of affairs must be done at a level of monitoring that is above what is being described. We can think of this monitoring happening in different ways. The person saying, 'I feel great' is not just feeling great. She is also monitoring how she feels. The researcher who says about children with whom she interacts, 'It seems they think of fractions as an additive part-whole relationship' is not just acting from an image of how students think. She is monitoring how she understands their thinking, and she has connected it with ways of thinking about whole numbers. It is also helpful to keep in mind that when Steffe et al. (1983) distinguished between levels of observers and levels of models they imagined *themselves* observing someone else in interaction with a third person (e.g. a student).

Observers act within the reality of their experience. As actors, they impute significance reflectively or unreflectively to aspects of what they take to be a situation of interaction. If they are interacting with another person, they are immediately aware of many aspects of that person. If they interact unreflectively, they are essentially actors in interaction. If they act reflectively as they interact with the other person, they are acting as an observer. To reflect allows one to 'step out of the stream of direct experience, to re-present chunks of it, and to look at it as though it were direct experience, while remaining aware of the fact that it is not' (Glasersfeld, 1991, p. 47). If teachers do not reflect on aspects of an interaction that are contributed by students, if they are fused with the situation as they have constituted it, then they are actors in the interaction, not observers. To be an observer of another while involved in interaction one necessarily moves to a level of reflection. When this happens it adds a dimension to the social interaction – the observer is now acting purposefully and thoughtfully, *using* the social interaction instrumentally. Reflection also opens the possibility that the teacher or researcher learns a mathematics consistent with the mathematical knowledge of those with whom he or she interacts.

The distinction between a first- and second-order observer is that first-order observers address what someone understands, while second-order observers address what *they* understand about what the other person *could* understand. As a first-order observer, a teacher would be oriented to understand that students might think differently than he or she and be oriented to formulate a particular image of the students' current thinking. As a second-order observer, the teacher would be oriented also to think about ramifications of positing alternative ways of thinking that might prove more profitable were students to think in those ways.[9] But the teacher could not draw directly on constructivism's principles to generate either those images of the students' current ways of thinking or images of alternative ways of thinking. Rather, those images would emerge by teachers conjoining a theory of mathematical understanding, which addresses explicitly the composition of individuals' understandings, and constructivism, which constrains and orients the descriptions they could formulate.

The ideas of first- and second-order models are even more important in their implications for mathematics education than the ideas of first- and second-order observer. First-order models are 'models the observed subject constructs to order, comprehend, and control his or her experience (i.e., the subject's knowledge)' (Steffe et al., 1983, p. xvi). Second-order models are 'models observers may construct of the subject's knowledge in order to explain their observations (i.e., their experience) of the subject's states and activities' (ibid.).

The distinctions between first- and second-order models and first- and second-order observers point to reasons why constructivism is so easily misused in teaching, curricula development and research. As necessary as they are, second-order models of knowing made by a first-order observer provide only weak guidance to a teacher, developer or researcher. The only thing they can draw from them is that what students end up knowing comes out of the sense they make of teaching and bears no necessary relationship to what the teacher, developer or researcher intended. Second-order models of knowing made by a second-order observer, however, can provide strong guidance for the teacher, developer or researcher who has developed a vocabulary and system of constructs to describe students' conceptual schemes together with transformations, reorganization or other modifications in them. Thus, we should not be overly optimistic about the ease with which constructivism can be used appropriately in teaching or research. I shall discuss this again in the section on conceptual analysis.

The Elusive Social Dimension

Another perceived shortcoming of research conducted within a radical constructivist perspective is that it ignores the social dimension of human cognition. However, it is worth noting that von Glasersfeld's elaboration of Piaget's genetic epistemology into what he eventually called radical constructivism (Glasersfeld, 1978) grew in large part out of his keen interest in understanding human communication and language (Glasersfeld, 1970, 1975, 1977, 1990; Foerster, 1979). So, from its very beginning, the core problems of radical constructivism begged the question of how physically disconnected self-regulating organisms could influence each other to end in a state where each presumes there is essential common agreement on what is their shared environment (Maturana, 1978; Richards, 1991). That is, from its very outset an image of cognizing individual's in social contexts was central to radical constructivism. This is one reason for its early appeal within mathematics education (Steffe and Kieren, 1994).

There is an essential difference between radical constructivism and social constructivism. It is that the former takes social interaction as a phenomenon needing explanation, whereas the latter takes it as a constitutive element of human activity. This difference expresses itself most vividly in the types of explanation emanating from radical constructivists and social constructivists.

Reflections and Directions

The former tend to focus on human discourse as emanating from interactions among self-organizing, autonomous individuals. The latter tend to focus on the collective activity in which individuals participate. That is, from a radical constructivist perspective, what we take as collective activity is constituted by interactions among individuals each having schemes by which they generate their activity and by which they make sense of others' actions. From a social constructivist perspective, collective activity and social interaction are given, predating any individual's participation in them. The individual accommodates to social meaning and practice.

Characteristics of group activity, from a radical constructivist perspective, emerge by way of individuals' mutual interpretation of what each perceives as other-oriented action. Collective activity is constituted by these interactions. If we also assume that individuals reflect on their actions, then it follows that each individual's participation changes as she becomes aware of, elaborates and interiorizes[10] her activity and her understanding of its repercussions. A radical constructivist perspective on the constitution of collective activity is similar to points of view originating in complexity theory and chaos (Mainzer, 1994; Sandefur, 1993). In complexity theory, the intention is to model complex phenomena by attempting to identify elementary processes that, through large numbers of interactions over sufficient amounts of time, regenerate the phenomena. The elementary processes, from a radical constructivist perspective, to account for collective activity are intersubjective operations within individuals[11] and interactions among overlapping groups of individuals. This, combined with the facts that people have memories and use them, and that interactions often produce artifacts that people use both informationally and practically, engenders social activity from a complexity theory point of view.

The elementary processes of social interaction in radical constructivism are similar in many respects to ideas from symbolic interactionism (Cobb et al., 1996; Miller, et al., 1997; Prus, 1996), at least that part that treats the fact of communication problematically. From this symbolic interactionist perspective, people do not communicate meanings *per se*. Rather, the phenomenon of one person 'communicating a meaning' to another is accomplished by listeners attributing meanings to the utterances they hear that are compatible with their own understandings and that are compatible with the image they've built of, or impute to, a speaker (see Figure 18.1).

Figure 18.1 portrays a symbolic interactionist understanding of two people interacting socially. We see the two of them interacting, but we understand both to be predicating their actions on an image they have of the other and implications that image has for their actions. Each person acts self-reflexively, and yet acts with consideration of others, much as Baursfeld (1980) has described. Figure 18.1 makes this point a bit too strongly, in that it portrays interactors as thinking this all through carefully, when that is not my intention at all. Instead, I mean that each person imagines and acts, sometimes reflectively but always through imagery built from past interactions. This is precisely the model of communication that allowed us to locate and describe the reasons

Patrick W. Thompson

Figure 18.1 A symbolic interactionist view of one moment in human communication

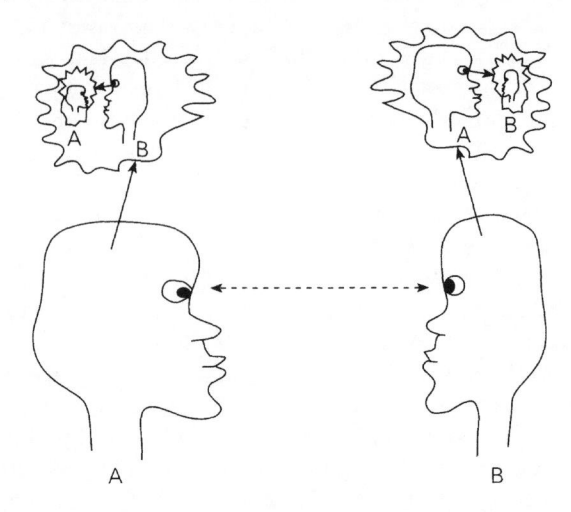

for severely dysfunctional communication between a teacher and his student (Thompson and Thompson, 1994) and to hypothesize a principled course of action that successfully remediated that miscommunication (Thompson and Thompson, 1996).

As Glasersfeld (1995) notes, to say two people communicate successfully means no more than that they have arrived at a point where their mutual interpretations, each expressed in action interpretable by the other, are compatible – they work for the time being. Intersubjectivity is the state where each participant in a socially ongoing interaction feels assured that others involved in the interaction think pretty much as does he or she. That is, intersubjectivity is *not* a claim of identical thinking. Rather, it is a claim that no one sees a reason to believe others think differently.

The importance of these considerations for educational research from a radical constructivist perspective is threefold. First, they point to some of the tacit assumptions behind the observation that individual's cognitions are, at once, psychological and social (Cobb, 1994; Ch. 11 above). Individual cognitions are simultaneously psychological and social *in the eyes of an observer who sees cognition happening in typical settings over prolonged periods.* From an observer's perspective, cognitions become *other-oriented*.[12]

Second, the processes by which we imagine conceptual development happening will be reflected in the theories we develop. If we imagine children becoming more mathematically developed by internalizing collective activity in which they participate ever more centrally (Forman, 1996; Lave, 1991), then that is what we will try to describe, explain and affect. If we see children becoming more scientifically literate by participating in discussions in which participants contribute and take away what is consistent with their individual schemes, then that is what we will try to describe, explain and affect.

Third, if educational research from a constructivist perspective is to carry weight with interpreters of it, then methodologies must be grounded in an epistemology that is compatible with the notion of intervention. 'Teaching' as the attempt to affect what children know is an oxymoron without a coherent base for thinking about intervention. Any epistemology that is solipsistic – in the sense that personal reality can be made without constraints and can be conjured independently of surroundings – cannot support the idea of intervention. While radical constructivism does not entail ontology, it does not deny a reality. It says only that it is essentially unknowable in any way that can be labeled 'correct'.[13] People can affect others' cognitions intentionally by placing themselves in a position to be interpreted by the persons they intend to affect. An 'informed' intervention is one in which the interventionist is guided by a model of those whom he wishes to affect. The effect may be circuitous, in that they (as teachers) might start by saying something they know will be interpreted by students in ways that differ predictably from what they intend students to understand, but which will provide springboards for moving the discussions in directions not possible without the initial (mis)interpretations. This is the model of teaching in radical constructivism – informed interventionists (i.e. folk with models of what they hope learners will learn) place themselves in positions to be interpreted in ways they intend by the persons they wish to affect.

Glasersfeld's Method of Conceptual Analysis

Most discussions of radical constructivism are about what it is and what it implies. However, radical constructivism is not just a set of principles. It is also an instrument for thinking about knowing. As such, when *doing* radical constructivism – as an earthling educator, not as a Martian observer – it is useful to describe ways of knowing that operationalize what it is students might understand when they know a particular idea in various ways. Glasersfeld (1995) calls his method for doing this *conceptual analysis*. As Steffe (1996) notes, the main goal of conceptual analysis is to propose answers to the question: 'What mental operations must be carried out to see the presented situation in the particular way one is seeing it?' (Glasersfeld, 1995, p. 78).

Glasersfeld first introduced me to conceptual analysis when he wondered how to convey the concept of triangle to a person who is congenitally blind and does not know the word already. His example went like this (if you are sighted, close your eyes).

Imagine that you:

- are in some location, facing in some direction;
- walk, straight, for some distance.
- Stop. Turn some amount.
- Walk straight for another distance.

Patrick W. Thompson

- Stop. Turn to face your starting position.
- Walk straight to it. (Glasersfeld and Czerny, 1979)

Your path is a triangle.[14]

Glasersfeld employed conceptual analysis in two ways. The first was to generate models of knowing that help us think about how others might know particular ideas. Glasersfeld's meaning of model is very much like Maturana's (1978) notion of scientific explanation:

> As scientists, we want to provide explanations for the phenomena we observe. That is, we want to propose conceptual or concrete systems that can be deemed intentionally isomorphic to the systems that generate the observed phenomena. (p. 29)

Glasersfeld's operationalization of 'triangle' was more than a way to define it to a blind person. It was also an attempt to develop one hypothesis about the operational aspects of imagining a triangle. I find this approach especially powerful for research on mathematics learning. For example, in research on students' emerging concepts of rate it has been extremely useful to think of students' early understanding of speed as, to them, speed is a distance and time is a ratio (Thompson, 1994; Thompson and Thompson, 1992, 1994). That is, speed is a distance you must travel to endure one time unit; the time required to travel some distance at some speed is the number of speed-lengths that compose that distance. Upper-elementary school children bound to this way of thinking about speed will often use division to determine how much time it will take to travel a given distance at a given speed, but use guess-and-test to determine the speed required to travel a given distance in a given amount of time. Their employment of guess-and-test is not a change of strategy. Rather, it is an attempt to assimilate the new situation into their way of thinking about speed – that it is a distance. Guess-and-test is their search for a speed-length that will produce the desired amount of time when the given distance is actually traveled.

There is a second way to employ Glasersfeld's method of conceptual analysis. It is to devise ways of understanding an idea that, if students had them, might be propitious for building more powerful ways to deal mathematically with their environments than they would build otherwise. Steffe and Tzur (Steffe, 1993; Tzur, in press) have employed this use of conceptual analysis to guide their instruction in teaching experiments on rational numbers of arithmetic. Confrey and her colleagues have employed conceptual analysis in similar ways to convey how one might think about multiplication so that it will simultaneously support thinking about exponential growth (Confrey, 1994; Confrey and Smith, 1994, 1995). Thompson (1998) employed conceptual analysis to show how a person's understandings of multiplication, division, measurement and fraction could each be expressions of a core scheme of conceptual operations, all entailed by multiplicative reasoning. As Steffe (1996) has noted,

Reflections and Directions

conceptual analysis (the conjoining of radical constructivism as an epistemology and a theory of mathematical understanding) emphasizes the positive aspect of radical constuctivism – that knowledge persists because it has proved viable in the experience of the knower. Knowledge persists because it *works*.

Conceptual analysis can also provide a technique for making operational hypotheses about why students have difficulties understanding specific situations as presented in specific ways. For example, standard fractions instruction often proposes fractions as 'so many out of so many' (e.g., $\frac{3}{5}$ of 10 apples is 'three parts out of five equal-sized parts of the 10 apples'). When students understand fractions, in principle, as 'so many out of so many', they understand fractions as an additive part-whole relationship. Fractional relationships like '$\frac{7}{5}$ of 10' apples make no sense whatsoever to students who understand fractions additively, because they would have to understand it as specifying 'seven parts out of five equally sized parts of 10 apples'.[15] Another example of the utility of conceptual analysis: It has been known for a long time that children have greater difficulty understanding quantitative comparisons specified as 'less' than comparisons specified as 'more'. Conceptual analysis can reveal possible reasons for it, and specify them in ways understandable in terms of the conceptual operations involved in understanding actual statements.

Figure 18.2 depicts an unfolding image of person X comprehending the statement, 'Joe has $15 more than Fred'. It shows X as first understanding that this story is about Joe having $15, then that the phrase 'more than' brings to mind that the $15 they originally imagined as being what Joe had is actually an excess in comparison to some other amount of money (which happens to belong to someone named Fred). Figure 18.3, on the other hand, shows an unfolding image of person X comprehending the statement 'Fred has $15 less than Joe'. It shows X as first understanding that Fred has $15, as before, but then person X had to backtrack when he realized that the $15 he imagined is *not* in Fred's possession. It actually belongs in another amount of money, and is the excess of that amount in comparison to whatever amount of money Fred has. Also, the fact that Fred actually has an amount of money must be imagined independently of the text, and in opposition to the realization that he did not have the $15 person X originally imagined him as having.

In summary, conceptual analysis can be used in three ways:

1   in building models of what students actually know at some specific time and what they comprehend in specific situations;
2   in describing ways of knowing that might be propitious for students' mathematical empowerment; and
3   in describing ways of knowing that might be deleterious to students' understanding of important ideas or their understandings that might be problematic in specific situations.

I find that conceptual analysis, as exemplified here and practiced by Glasersfeld, provides mathematics educators an extremely powerful tool. It

Patrick W. Thompson

Figure 18.2 Joe has $15 more than Fred

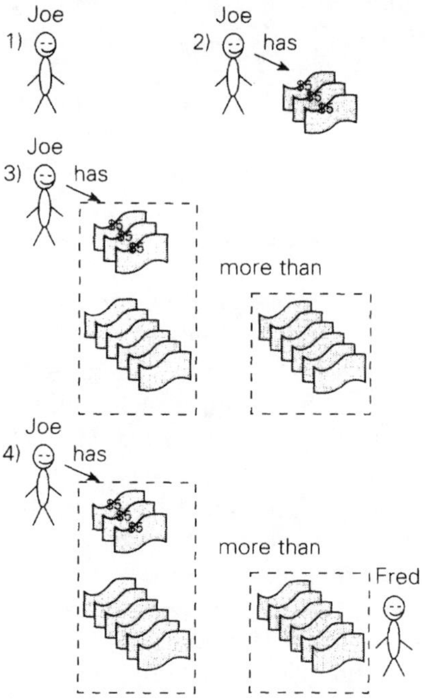

Figure 18.3 Fred has $15 less than Joe

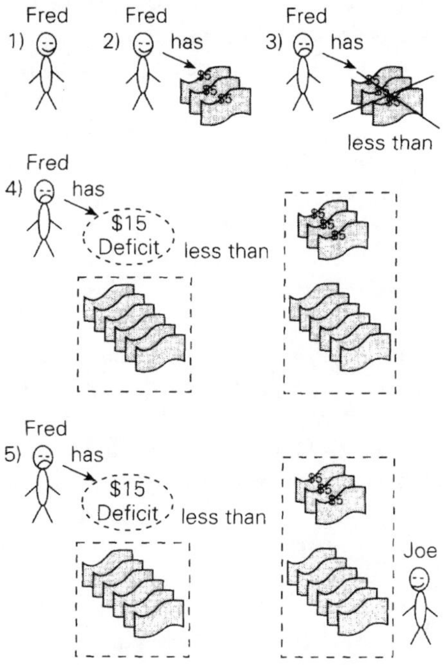

orients us to providing imagistically grounded descriptions of mathematical cognition that capture the dynamic aspects of knowing and comprehending without committing us to the epistemological quagmire that comes with low-level information processing models of cognition (Cobb, 1987; Thompson, 1989). Conceptual analysis provides a technique for making concrete examples, potentially understandable by teachers, of the learning trajectories that Simon (1995) calls for in his re-conceptualization of teaching from a constructivist perspective, and which Cobb (Ch. 11) and his colleagues (Gravemeijer, 1994; Gravemeijer et al., in press) employ in their studies of emerging classroom mathematical practices. In addition, when conceptual analysis is employed by a teacher who is skilled at it, we obtain important examples of how mathematically substantive, conceptually grounded conversations can be held with students (Bowers and Nickerson, in press). Teachers in the U.S. rarely experience these kinds of conversation, and hence they have no personal image of them. Having positive examples of such conversations will be very important for mathematics teacher education.

Coming Full Circle

Ernst von Glasersfeld opened his chapter by thanking the conference organizers and the people who wrote chapters for this book, noting the large debt he owed them for contributing to his point of view. I believe I speak for all those who were present at the conference, and for the mathematics and science education communities at large, when I say to Ernst, 'Thank *you* for contributing so much to *our* points of view.'

Allow me to end on a personal note. I have grown immensely through the inspiration of Ernst's work. However, I have grown even more by having had the pleasure and honor of seeing Ernst make radical constructivism real through his living example.

Notes

† I thank Les Steffe for his helpful comments on earlier drafts of this chapter. Preparation of this chapter was supported by National Science Foundation Grant No. REC-9811879. Any conclusions or recommendations stated here are those of the author and do not necessarily reflect official positions of the NSF.

1 It is through Glasersfeld's and von Foerster's contributions that we are aware that such statements must apply to the observer as well as the observed. That is, you must read every passage in this book as the authors' best attempts at finding coherence in their respective physical, intellectual and social experiences, even as they propose theories to account for others' social, intellectual and physical experiences.

2 I am using 'know' synonymously with 'understand' and 'comprehend'. So, 'to know a concept' does not point to a binary relationship between a person's knowledge and a concept of which they have knowledge. Rather, 'to know a concept', in my usage, is slightly redundant. It would be better expressed as, 'What this person knows can be called a concept.'

3 This itself may be problematic if the observed person does not make distinctions compatible with the speaker's distinctions.

4 We must be careful to remember that patterns are stable in our observation because of the interplay of interpretations made by actors within the group, so 'provides its own constraints' does not imbue properties to the pattern, rather it speaks about the interpretations people make in interacting.

5 Assuming we can explain what we mean by 'take responsibility for his or her learning' well enough to distinguish between when a student is doing it and when not.

6 See Bickard (1991), Cobb (Cobb et al., 1992), and Steffe (1991) for discussions of the deep issues involved in thinking of the mind as somehow repesenting reality and how constructivism offers a non-representational view of mind.

7 This was my point (Thompson, 1995) when I spoke of the need to act as a realist or a trivial constructivist when engaging in mathematics education research. In order to act, we must presume that what we think is the case actually is the case, and then after having acted, and sometimes while acting, we again put on the hat of the radical constructivist.

8 Of *Mork and Mindy*, a television program of the 1970s about an alien living on earth, starring Robin Williams. I know from other conversations that many of them had watched this program.

9 These alternative ways of thinking must be such that they are in the range of possibility for students as modifications of their current ways of thinking.

10 I use *interiorize* in a Piagetian sense. For an individual to interiorize actions means that they construct schemes of mental operations they may carry out in thought and by which they may anticipate outcomes of particular courses of action.
11 I address a constructivist meaning of intersubjectivity in later paragraphs.
12 This, in essence, was Piaget's opinion when he emphasized the importance of socialization for the development of semiotic and formal operations (Piaget, 1950, 1977, 1995).
13 This is not to say that there *cannot* be a 'correct' knowledge of reality. Even if there were such a thing, however, we could not know whether anyone has it.
14 For readers who recall 'Logo', the similarity between Glasersfeld's operationalization of a triangle and a turtle-procedure for drawing one is striking. However, his example predates the general availability of 'Logo', and neither of us had heard of it anyway.
15 This is not to say students couldn't give *some* meaning to '$\frac{7}{5}$ of 10 apples'. Children often change the meaning from the intended fractional relationship to a procedure for determining some number of apples, such as '$\frac{5}{5}$ is 10, $\frac{2}{5}$ is 4, so the answer is 14.' But that is not the same as understanding $\frac{7}{5}$ of 10 as the multiplicative structure that indicates a number that is 7 times as large as $\frac{1}{5}$ of 10, where $\frac{1}{5}$ of 10 refers to a number to which 10 is 5 times as large. This latter understanding of $\frac{7}{5}$ of 10 generalizes easily to $\frac{7}{5}$ of 9 apples. The former reasoning does not generalize so easily.

References

BAUERSFELD, H. (1980) 'Hidden dimensions in the so-called reality of a mathematics classroom', *Educational Studies in Mathematics*, **11**, 1, pp. 23–42.
BICKHARD, M.H. (1991) 'The import of Fodor's anti-constructivist argument', in STEFFE, L.P. (ed.), *Epistemological Foundations of Mathematical Experience*, New York: Springer pp. 14–25.
BISHOP, W. (1999) 'The California Mathematics Standards: They're not only right; they're the law', *Phi Delta Kappan*, **80**, 6, pp. 439–40.
BOWERS, J. and NICKERSON, S. (in press) 'Development of a collective conceptual orientation in a college-level mathematics course', *Journal of Research in Mathematics Education*.
COBB, P. (1987) 'Information-processing psychology and mathematics education: A constructivist perspective', *Journal of Mathematical Behavior*, 6, pp. 3–40.
COBB, P. (1994) 'Constructivism in mathematics and science education', *Educational Researcher*, **23**, 7, p. 4.
COBB, P., JAWORSKI, B. and PRESMEG, N. (1996) 'Emergent and socicultural views of mathematical activity', in STEFFE, L.P., NESHER, P., COBB, P., GOLDIN, G.A. and GREER, B. (eds), *Theories of Mathematical Learning*, Mahwah, NJ: Lawrence Erlbaum, pp. 131–47.
COBB, P., YACKEL, E. and WOOD, T. (1992) 'A constructivist alternative to the representational view of mind in mathematics education', *Journal for Research in Mathematics Education*, **23**, 1, pp. 2–33.
CONFREY, J. (1994) 'Splitting, similarity, and rate of change: A new approach to multiplication and exponential functions', in HAREL, G. and CONFREY, J. (eds), *The*

Development of Multiplicative Reasoning in the Learning of Mathematics, Albany, NY: SUNY Press, pp. 293–300.

CONFREY, J. and SMITH, E. (1994) 'Exponential functions, rates of change, and the multiplicative unit', *Educational Studies in Mathematics*, **26**, 2–3, pp. 135–64.

CONFREY, J. and SMITH, E. (1995) 'Splitting, covariation and their role in the development of exponential function', *Journal for Research in Mathematics Education*, **26**, 1, pp. 66–86.

CULLUM-SWAN, B. and MANNING, P.K. (1995; 21 September). *Codes, Chronotypes and Everyday Objects* (Web page), Society for the Study of Symbolic Interaction. Available: http://sun.soci.niu.edu/~sssi/papers/pkm1.txt [1999; 7 April].

DUBINSKY, E. and SCHWINGENDORF, K. (1997; 1 June). *Calculus, Concepts, Computers, and Cooperative Learning*, C4L. Available: http://www.math.purdue.edu/~ccc/ [1999; 10 March].

FOERSTER, H. VON (1979) 'Cybernetics of cybernetics', in KRIPPENDORF, K. (ed.), *Communication and Control in Society*, New York: Gordon & Breach, pp. 5–8.

FORMAN, E.A. (1996) 'Learning mathematics as participation in classroom practice: Implications of sociocultural theory for educational reform', in STEFFE, L.P., NESHER, P., COBB, P., GOLDIN, G.A. and GREER, B. (eds), *Theories of Mathematical Learning*, Mahwah, NJ: Lawrence Erlbaum, pp. 115–30.

FUNDERSTANDING (1999; 20 January). *About learning/Theories. Funderstanding*. Available: http://www.funderstanding.com/theories.htm [1999; 20 March].

GLASERSFELD, E. VON (1970) 'The problem of syntactic complexity in reading and readability', *Journal of Reading Behavior*, **3**, 2, pp. 1–14.

GLASERSFELD, E. VON (1975) 'The development of language as purposive behavior', in *Proceedings of the Conference on Origins and Evolution of Speech and Language*, Annals of the New York Academy of Sciences, New York: New York Academy of Sciences.

GLASERSFELD, E. VON (1977) 'Linguistic communication: Theory and definition', in RUMBAUGH, D. (ed.), *Language Learning by a Chimpanzee*, New York: Academic Press, pp. 55–71.

GLASERSFELD, E. VON (1978) 'Radical constructivism and Piaget's concept of knowledge', in MURRAY, F.B. (ed.), *Impact of Piagetian Theory*, Baltimore, MD: University Park Press, pp. 109–22.

GLASERSFELD, E. VON (1990) 'Environment and communication', in STEFFE, L.P. and WOOD, T. (eds), *Transforming Children's Mathematics Education*, Hillsdale, NJ: Lawrence Erlbaum, pp. 30–8.

GLASERSFELD, E. VON (1991) 'Abstraction, re-presentation, and reflection: An interpretation of experience and Piaget's approach', in STEFFE, L.P. (ed.), *Epistemological Foundations of Mathematical Experience*, New York: Springer, pp. 45–65.

GLASERSFELD, E. VON (1995) *Radical Constructivism: A Way of Knowing and Learning*, London: Falmer Press.

GLASERSFELD, E. VON and CZERNY, P. (1979) 'A dynamic approach to the recognition of triangularity', unpublished paper, Department of Psychology: University of Georgia.

GRAVEMEIJER, K.P.E. (1994) *Developing Realistic Mathematics Education*, Utrecht: Freudenthal Institute.

GRAVEMEIJER, K.P.E., COBB, P., BOWERS, J. and WHITENACK, J. (in press) 'Symbolizing, modeling, and instructional design', in COBB, P., YACKEL, E. and MCCLAIN, K. (eds), *Communicating and Symbolizing in Mathematics Classrooms: Perspectives on Discourse Tools, and Instructional Design*, Mahwah, NJ: Lawrence Erlbaum.

LAVE, J. (1991) 'Situating learning in communities of practice', in RESNICK, L.B., LEVINE, J.M. and TEASLEY, S.D. (eds), *Perspectives on Socially Shared Cognition*, Washington, DC: American Psychological Association, pp. 63–82.

LERMAN, S. (1994) 'Articulating theories of mathematics learning', in ERNEST, P. (ed.), *Constructing Mathematical Knowledge: Epistemology and Mathematics Education*, Washington, DC: Falmer Press, pp. 41–9.

LERMAN, S. (1996) 'Intersubjectivity in mathematics learning: A challenge to the radical constructivist paradigm', *Journal for Research in Mathematics Education*, **27**, 2, pp. 133–50.

MACKAY, D.M. (1951) 'The nomenclature of information theory', in FOERSTER, H. VON (ed.), *Proceedings of the Eighth Conference on Cybernetics*, Josiah Macy, Jr. Foundation, pp. 156–96.

MACKAY, D.M. (1955) 'The place of "meaning" in the theory of information', in CHERRY, E.C. (ed.), *Information Theory*, London: Butterworth, pp. 215–25.

MACKAY, D.M. (1964) 'Linguistic and non-linguistic "understanding" of linguistic tokens', in *Proceedings of the Conference on Computers and Comprehension*, Santa Monica, CA: The Rand Corporation, pp. 120–55.

MACKAY, D.M. (1969) *Information, Mechanism and Meaning*, Cambridge, Mass.: MIT Press.

MAINZER, K. (1994) *Thinking in Complexity*, New York: Springer.

MATURANA, H. (1978) 'Biology of language: The epistemology of reality', in MILLER, G.A. and LENNEBERG, E. (eds), *Psychology and Biology of Language and Thought*, New York: Academic Press, pp. 27–63.

MATURANA, H. (1987) 'Everything is said by an observer', in THOMPSON, W.I. (ed.), *Gaia: A Way of Knowing*, Great Barrington, MA: Lindisfarne Press.

MILLER, D.E., KATOVICH, M.A., SAXTON, S. L. and COUCH, C.J. (eds) (1997) *Constructing Complexity: Symbolic Interactionsim and Social Forms*, Greenwich, CT: JAI Press.

NODDINGS, N. (1990) 'Constructivism in mathematics education', in DAVIS, R.B., MAHER, C.A. and NODDINGS, N. (eds), 'Constructivist views on the learning and teaching of mathematics', *Journal for Research in Mathematics Education*, Monograph No. 4, pp. 7–18.

O'BRIEN, T.C. (1999) 'Parrot math', *Phi Delta Kappan*, **80**, 6, pp. 434–8.

PIAGET, J. (1950) *The Psychology of Intelligence*, London: Kegan Paul, Treuch Trübner.

PIAGET, J. (1977) *Psychology and Epistemology: Towards a Theory of Knowledge*, New York: Penguin.

PIAGET, J. (1995) *Sociological Studies*, New York: Routledge.

PIATTELLI-PALMARINI, M. (ed.) (1980) *Language and Learning: The Debate between Jean Piaget and Noam Chomsky*, Cambridge, Mass.: Harvard University Press.

PRUS, R.C. (1996) *Symbolic Interaction and Ethnographic Research: Intersubjectivity and the Study of Human Lived Experience*, Albany, NY: SUNY Press.

RICHARDS, J. (1991) 'Mathematical discussions', in GLASERSFELD, E. VON (ed.), *Radical Constructivism in Mathematics Education*, Dordrecht: Kluwer, pp. 13–51.

SANDEFUR, J. (1993) *Discrete Dynamical Modeling*, Oxford: Oxford University Press.

SIMON, M.A. (1995) 'Reconstructing mathematics pedagogy from a constructivist perspective', *Journal for Research in Mathematics Education*, **26**, 2, pp. 114–45.

STEFFE, L.P. (1991) 'The learning paradox', in STEFFE, L.P. (ed.), *Epistemological Foundations of Mathematical Experience*, New York: Springer, pp. 26–44.

STEFFE, L.P. (1993, February) 'Learning an iterative fraction scheme', paper presented at the Conference on Learning and Teaching Fractions, Athens, GA.

STEFFE, L.P. (1995) 'Alternative epistemologies: An educator's perspective', in STEFFE, L.P. and GALE, J. (eds), *Constructivism in Education*, Hillsdale, NJ: Lawrence Erlbaum, pp. 489–523.

STEFFE, L.P. (1996) 'Radical constructivism: A way of knowing and learning' (Review of the same title, by Ernst von Glasersfeld). *Zentralblatt für Didaktik der Mathematik (International Reviews on Mathematical Education)*, **96**, 6, pp. 202–4.

STEFFE, L.P., GLASERSFELD, E. VON, RICHARDS, J. and COBB, P. (1983) *Children's Counting Types: Philosophy, Theory, and Application*, New York: Praeger Scientific.

STEFFE, L.P. and KIEREN, T. (1994) 'Radical constructivism and mathematics education', *Journal for Research in Mathematics Education*, **25**, 6, pp. 711–33.

STEFFE, L.P. and THOMPSON, P.W. (in press) 'Interaction or intersubjectivity? A reply to Lerman', *Journal for Research in Mathematics Education*.

THOMPSON, A.G. and THOMPSON, P.W. (1996) 'Talking about rates conceptually, Part II: Mathematical knowledge for teaching', *Journal for Research in Mathematics Education*, **27**, 1, pp. 2–24.

THOMPSON, P.W. (1989) 'Artificial intelligence, advanced technology, and learning and teaching algebra', in KIERAN, C. and WAGNER, S. (eds), *Research Issues in the Learning and Teaching of Algebra*, Hillsdale, NJ: Lawrence Erlbaum, pp. 135–61.

THOMPSON, P.W. (1994) 'The development of the concept of speed and its relationship to concepts of rate', in HAREL, G. and CONFREY, J. (eds), *The Development of Multiplicative Reasoning in the Learning of Mathematics*, Albany, NY: SUNY Press, pp. 179–234.

THOMPSON, P.W. (1995) 'Constructivism, cybernetics, and information processing: Implications for research on mathematical learning', in STEFFE, L.P. and GALE, J. (eds), *Constructivism in Education*, Hillsdale, NJ: Lawrence Erlbaum, pp. 123–34.

THOMPSON, P.W. (1998; 30 March) *Multiplicative Relationships among Fraction, Measurement, Multiplication, and Division*, Patrick W. Thompson. Available: http://peabody.vanderbilt.edu//depts/tandl/mted/thompson/www.2250/MultReasoning/ [1999; 17 March].

THOMPSON, P.W. and THOMPSON, A.G. (1992, April) 'Images of rate', paper presented at the Annual Meeting of the American Educational Research Association, San Francisco, CA.

THOMPSON, P.W. and THOMPSON, A.G. (1994). 'Talking about rates conceptually, Part I: A teacher's struggle', *Journal for Research in Mathematics Education*, **25**, 3, pp. 279–303.

TZUR, R. (1999) 'An integrated study of children's construction of improper fractions and the teacher's role in promoting that learning', *Journal for Research in Mathematics Education*, **30**, 3, pp. 390–416.

Notes on Contributors

Jan van den Brink is a senior researcher and developer in the Freudenthal institute of mathematics education at the University of Utrecht (The Netherlands). He received a Master's degree in pure mathematics and his PhD in mathematics education. His research has centred on processes of acquiring mathematical objects and operations in children (4 to 18 year olds). He developed different settings for instruction based on these processes in order to facilitate mathematical education. Musical acoustic counting, arithmetic play acting, pupils as arithmetic book authors, geometrical debates, a geometrical reading book on the Internet, etc. were instructional formats for constructing mathematics by pupils themselves in interaction. His work and publications have pointed out the radical constructivist view in mathematics education.

Paul Cobb gained his doctorate from the University of Georgia in 1983 and is currently professor of mathematics education at Vanderbilt University. Until recently, his research focused on students' development of core quantitative concepts, K-3. The issues addressed in the course of this work include students' mathematical learning in instructional settings, the classroom social environment and discourse, the design of instructional sequences, and the teachers' proactive role in supporting students' learning. His current work focuses on statistical data analysis at the middle school level and involves designing a series of computer minitools as integral components of coherent instructional sequences.

Jacques Désautels is professor at the Faculty of Educational Science of Université Laval (Québec) and regular researcher at the Centre interdisciplinaire de recherches sur l'apprentissage et le développement en éducation (CIRADE) of the Université du Québec à Montréal. For more than 25 years now, Mr. Désautels has been examining the didactic and ideological dimensions of science teaching. He has authored or co-authored numerous books and articles in the field of science education from a socio-constructivist perspective. His current research interest centers on the type of power/knowledge relationships which are embedded in the 'spontaneous sociology of science' among both high school students and science teachers.

Heinz von Foerster was born in 1911 in Vienna, Austria, and after completion of his studies (PhD in physics) he worked in various industrial research laboratories in Germany and Austria. In 1949 he moved with his family to the United States and joined the staff of the Department of Electrical Engineering at the University of Illinois at Urbana, Illinois, and, at the same time, became secretary of the Cybernetics Conference Program of the Josiah Macy Jr. Foundation in New York. In this connection he edited five volumes of the proceedings of these conferences: *Cybernetics: Circular Causal and Feedback Mechanisms in Biological and Social Systems*. There are more than 180 papers published by Heinz von Foerster who is now Professor Emeritus of the Departments of Electrical and Computer Engineering, and of Biophysics and Physiology of the University of Illinois in Urbana, Illinois. He now lives with his wife in California.

Hugh Gash received his Ph.D. in Educational Psychology from the State University of New York at Buffalo. Following two years as a postdoctoral fellow in the Psychology Department at the University of Georgia, he returned to Dublin (Ireland) where he works in St Patrick's College, a College of Dublin City University. During the past decade his research was concerned with tolerance of difference. Part of this work consists of classroom intervention studies in a number of domains including gender stereotyping, and children's ideas about children with a mental handicap or about children from another country. Another part of this work consists of consideration of the ethical consequences of radical constructivism.

Ernst von Glasersfeld was born in Munich, 1917, of Austrian parents, and grew up in Northern Italy and Switzerland. Briefly studied mathematics in Zürich and Vienna and survived the 2nd World War as farmer in Ireland. Returned to Italy in 1946, worked as journalist, and collaborated until 1961 in Ceccato's Scuola Operativa Italiana (language analysis and machine translation). From 1962 director of US-sponsored research project in computational linguistics. After 1970 he designed the symbolic language for the chimpanzee communication experiments at the Yerkes Center in Atlanta and taught cognitive psychology at the University of Georgia. Professor Emeritus, 1987. Dr.phil.h.c., University of Klagenfurt, 1997. At present Research Associate at Scientific Reasoning Research Institute, University of Massachusetts, Amherst. Research Interests: Conceptual Analysis, Cognition, Epistemology.

Robert P. Hunting received his Ed.D. in mathematics education from the University of Georgia in 1980. He is currently Professor of Mathematics Education at East Carolina University, Greenville, North Carolina. His research work has been focused on studies of fraction learning by children aged 3 to 8 years. He has also published in the areas of clinical assessment methods, early mathematics learning, teacher-focused curriculum change, constructivist research methodologies, language aspects of mathematics learning, curriculum and teacher education issues, and ethnomathematics of Australian aborigines. He is currently leading a project to develop Internet-based mathematics materials for preschool children and their caregivers.

Thomas E. Kieren is Professor Emeritus of Mathematics Education at the University of Alberta. He received his PhD in mathematics education with a minor

Notes on Contributors

in mathematics from the University of Minnesota. He has engaged in well known research on rational number knowing for the past 25 years and has published widely in this area. With Susan Pirie from the University of British Columbia he also has been studying mathematical understanding as a dynamical process over the last 11 years. His further current research interests find him studying mathematical knowing in action and inter-action.

Marie Larochelle is professor at the Faculty of Educational Science of Université Laval (Québec) and regular researcher at the Centre interdisciplinaire de recherches sur l'apprentissage et le développement en éducation (CIRADE) of the Université du Québec à Montréal. For the last several years now, Ms. Larochelle has devoted much of her research to the socio-epistemological issues surrounding the teaching and learning of scientific knowledge, and has published primarily in the areas of science education and constructivism. Her current research interest centers on how students and preservice science teachers view the tensions, disagreements and socioethical stakes that inform the way technoscience is conducted and enacted.

Philip Lewin is an independent scholar living in Eugene, Oregon. His main academic interests are in the relationships between epistemology, narrative, and personhood.

Despina Potari received her PhD in mathematics education in 1987 from the University of Edinburgh, U.K. She is an assistant professor of Mathematics Education in the Education Department of the University of Patras. She has worked and published on curriculum development, on exploring children's conceptions on the area of geometry and on the development of mathematics teaching. Her current interest is on development in the mathematics teacher and on the cooperation between researcher and teacher.

S.J. Schmidt has been professor of text theory (since 1971), and professor of the theory of literature (since 1973) at the University of Bielefeld. Since 1979 he has been professor of German literature and theory of literature at the University of Siegen. Currently he holds a chair of communication theory and media culture at the University of Münster. He has published books and articles on philosophy of language, text theory, aesthetics, theory of literature, empirical science of literature, concrete and conceptual poetry. His current research interest is in communication and media theory and history of media.

Martin A. Simon is Associate Professor of Mathematics Education at Penn State University. He is PI of the NSF-supported Mathematics Teacher Development Project, a four-and-a-half-year research project inquiring into the development of prospective and practicing mathematics teachers. He is a former classroom teacher and former director of the SummerMath for Teachers Program at Mt. Holyoke College. Simon's research focuses on understanding mathematics teacher development in the context of current reform objectives, articulating a conceptual framework with respect to mathematics teaching, and developing new and adapted research methodologies for studying mathematics teacher development.

Leslie P. Steffe is a research professor in the Department of Mathematics Education at the University of Georgia, USA. His primary research interest has centered on specifying the mental operations, concepts, and schemes that constitute mathematical thought in childhood and how children use these mental constructs as mechanisms of interaction and change. He has also worked extensively to constitute mathematics education as an indisciplinary field of study. His work and publications have contributed to the development of the constructivist field and to ensure not only the quality of discourse on this subject, but also to constantly question the new ways of speaking about constructivism and the social.

Patrick W. Thompson received his Ed.D. in mathematics education from the University of Georgia in 1982. He is currently Professor of Mathematics Education at Vanderbilt University. His interests center around development of mathematical ideas, publishing in the areas of cognition, concept development, and artificial intelligence. His current research focuses on students' statistical reasoning and ways it can be influenced by drawing on their capacities to reason multiplicatively.

Edmond Wright is a poet and freelance philosopher, and a sometime Researcher at the Swedish Collegium for Advanced Study of the Social Sciences at Uppsala. He has published regularly in the philosophical journals on language, perception, and epistemology, being particularly interested in the structure of the intersubjective correction of percept and concept. He has written *The Horwich Hennets* (1976) and *The Jester Hennets* (1981), and he is the editor of *New Representationalisms: Essays in the Philosophy of Perception* (Avebury, 1993) and co-editor of *The Žižek Reader* (Blackwell, 1999).

Robert J. Wright holds a Master's degree in mathematics and received his Ed. D. in mathematics education from the University of Georgia. He is currently professor in mathematics education at Southern Cross University in Australia. His research interests are in the area of assessing young children's numerical knowledge and strategies. He has published many articles in this area and is coauthor of a recently published book on this topic. His work in the last ten years has included the development of the Mathematics Recovery Program which focuses on providing specialist professional development for teachers to advance the numeracy levels of young children assessed as low-attainers. The program has been implemented in school systems in several countries and has been applied extensively to classroom teaching.

Index

accommodation 28, 98, 122, 154, 185, 238
Ackermann, E. 253
adaptability 266
adaptation 40-1, 98, 122
ahistoricity 43
Aikenhead, G.S. 200
Alston, A. 235, 248
animals, language 29-30
antipoles 106-7
Appignanesi, L. 195
apprenticeship model 232-3, 278
areas 239-40
Aristotle 39, 52-3
assimilation 154
Association for Research in Nervous and Mental Disease xii-xiii
asymptotic realism 203
Atkinson, C. 11, 12, 18
attentional pulses 10, 11
Aubrey, C. 135
Audet, M. 65
Austin, J.L. 15, 16
authority 233
autonomy 233-5
autopoesis 187

back-to-basics approaches 296
Ball, D.L. 219, 223, 226
basic skills testing 136, 137-8
Bateson, G. xii, 47, 63, 85, 87, 198
Bauersfeld, H. 120, 153, 155, 158, 187, 196; funnel pattern of interaction 253; habitus 232; language 236; learning 184; self-reflexivity 305
Bednarz, N. 57, 63
bees, language 29, 30
Bent Stick Illusion 16
Bernstein, R.J. 154
Bickhard, M. 75
Biddlecomb, B.D. 249

biological context 40-1, 45, 46
Bishop, A.J. 153
Bishop, W. 295
Blume, G. 235
Blumer, H. 154, 218
Bobis, J. 134, 147
Bogdanov, A. 4
Born, M. 96-7, 99, 183, 184, 281
Boudon, R. 58
Boufi, A. 219
boundaries 44, 95
Bourdieu, P. 47, 60
Bowers, J. 310
Boxer, P. 88
Boyle, R. 13
Brink, J. van den 103, 105-33, 179-80, 181, 182, 183, 185, 188, 190-1, 284-5
Britzman, D.P. 232, 233
Brousseau, G. 62, 225
Byers, B. 232
Byrnes, J.P. 234

Calderhead, J. 231-2
Callon, M. 62
'Candy Shop' 163-70, 171-2
Carpenter, T.P. 138
Cartesian epistemology 277, 278
Case, R. 278, 286
Castoriadis, C. 47
Ceccato, S. 3, 181
chain of signification 172-3
chaos theory 305
character 39, 46
Charlot, B. 208
Cherry, C. 24, 27
child-centered approaches 296
chimps language 29, 30
Chomsky, N. xiii, 27, 295
Chuang Tsu xiv
class inclusion 237
classroom culture 235, 243-4

Index

classroom press 231, 233
Clay, M.M. 135, 146
'Clinical Approaches to Mathematics Assessment' 240
closed tasks 71, 73
Cobb, P. 3, 103, 122, 138, 139, 186-7, 188-91, 225, 226, 249; autonomy 233-4; cognition 306; conception-based perspective 217; contradictory experiences 107; developmental research 184; fixed entities 119; information processing models 310; interactionism 305; IRON 180; learning 183-4; phenomena 185; reconceptualization 248; recovery education 134, 141, 142, 154; reflective discourse 219; representational perspective 215, 263; shared meaning 120; social context 152-78; teacher-researcher 250, 273, 274; videotaping 144
Cobern, W.W. 195, 209
Cockcroft, W.H. 136
coercion 7
cognition 5, 31, 72, 206, 277, 280, 300, 306, 310
cognitive context 40-1
cognitive core 181
communication 23, 219, 235-7, 284-5, 305-6
communities 245
communities of practice paradigm 153-4
complexity theory 305
conception-based perspective 216-17, 279, 286
conceptual analysis 180-1, 307-10
conceptual situation 25
conflict 130
Confrey, J. 59, 153, 154, 157, 217, 248; case-histories 254; conceptual analysis 308; unexpected responses 237, 238
constraints 35, 39-49, 70-9, 102, 122, 284; hard 39-45, 82-4, 94-6; *paideia* 94-9; soft 45-9, 82-4, 96
Construction of Elementary Mathematics (CEM) 235
constructs 25, 26
content metaphor 171
contextual specification 87

continuity 5-6, 92
control 232-3
Conway, P. 86, 87
Cooney, T.J. 233
cooperation 7, 284
correctness 83
correlational grammar 26
'Count Me In Too' 146-7
counter-examples 86
Cowper, M. 144
Crandall, D. 233
critical realism 12
Cross, R.T. 196
Cullum-Swan, B. 297
cultural context 152
cultural myths 197
culture 31, 45, 47, 83, 235, 243-4

D'Ambrosio, B.S. 218, 248, 273
Davis, B. 75, 78
Davis, R. 277
decidability 83-4, 96-9
DeFord, D.E. 135
Désautels, J. 59, 60, 61, 193, 195-212, 278-9, 282, 285, 286
Descartes, R. 15
deutero-learning 47, 49, 85-8
developmental metaphor 86
developmental research 156-8, 171, 183-4, 185-6, 217
Dewey, J. 16, 154, 232-3, 278
didactic constructivism 122-9
didactic phenomenology 182
didactic realism 103, 105-33, 180, 182-3, 184, 185, 189
direct teaching 253
disappearance xi-xii
discovery learning 277
discovery teaching 277
disequilibrium 249
Doig, B. 136
Doig, B.A. 240
Dombey, H. 135
dreams 15
Dubinsky, E. 294
Dyson, R. 144

ecosystem 64-5
Edelman, G.M. 16

321

Index

Educational Leaders in Mathematics (ELM) 235
Einstein, A. 97
embeddedness 88–9
emergence xiv
emergence metaphor 171
emergent perspective 218–19
endogenic view 277
entity 10–22
environment 75
epistemic reflexivity 198, 282
epistemological context 40–1
epistemological democracy 59
Erickson, F. 160
Ernest, P. 182, 280
errors 83
essence xii–xiv
ethics 35, 45–53, 62–5, 91, 99–102, 162, 186, 298–9; epistemology 80–90; recovery education 182
evolutionary aspects 26–7
existence 6
exogenic view 277
experience, prior 271–2
experiential environment 122
experiential reality 5, 37, 46, 51, 281
experiential self 91, 92–3, 94
experiential sequence 6

false self 47
falsifiability 43
feedback 17, 27
Fennema, E. 138
Fermat's theorem 84
Feuerbach, L. 16
field-determinate description 13
Finley, F.N. 196
first-order observers/models 302–4
fixed entities 119
Fleck, L. 17
flux 17, 18
Fodor 295
Foerster, H. von xi–xv, 53, 56, 63, 190, 195, 207; decidability 83–4, 99, 207; ethics 80, 89; intersubjectivity 281; language 304; multiplication of potentialities 61; relativity 97, 100; self 87
formalization 130

Forman, E.A. 306
Foucault, M. 58
Fourez, G. 62, 63
Freudenthal, H. 103, 117, 182, 225
Freud, S. 47
Fullan, M.G. 233, 243
Funderstanding 293–4
funnel pattern of interaction 253
Fuson, K.C. 138, 166

Gagné, B. 200
Gallagher, J.J. 196
Garcia, R. 198
Gash, H. 35, 80–90, 96, 100, 102
Geddis, A.N. 58, 62, 196
genetic epistemology 4, 44, 292, 294, 304
geometry 103, 105–33, 179–80
Gibson, J.J. 15, 16, 42
Giddens, A. 56, 58, 60, 65
Glasersfeld, E. von 10–11, 37–54, 188, 248, 310–11; accommodation 122; capabilities 71; cognition 206, 277, 280; cognitive core 181; cognitive structures 77; communication 306; conception-based perspective 279; conceptual analysis 180–1, 307–10; conceptual structures 267; conference 199–200; constraints 72; contradictory experiences 107; direct experience 303; dogma 299; entity 10–22; ethics 99, 100; fixed entities 119; genetic epistemology 304; intersubjectivity 281, 282; knowledge 98, 139, 154, 213; language 23–33, 184–5, 235; learning 183; misinterpretations 291–2; models of learning 295; patience 209; problems with constructivism 3–9; reality 81–2, 195; rightness 89; self 87, 91–2, 93; semanticity 284, 285; students' constructions 105; theory of world 55; tolerance 80; viability 99; videotaping 144
gnomic map 107
goal directed teaching 249, 268, 270
goals 185, 186, 222, 224, 259, 266, 271
Gödel's Proof 19–20
Gore, J.M. 196
Gould, P. 134, 147

Index

Gould, S.J. 40
Gravemeijer, K. 142, 156, 157, 163, 183, 185, 217, 225, 310
great circles 105–6, 109–19, 120–30
Greeno, J.G. 163
Grice, H.P. 14
Griffin, S. 278, 286
Grossman, P.L. 232
group identity 87
Gutierrez, K. 58, 62

habitus 47, 59–60, 208, 232
Haggerty, S. 196
Hamlyn, D.W. 10
Hashweh, M.Z. 200
Heidegger, M. 6, 37–8
Hendrix, G. 277
Hermelin, B. 14
hero/heroine concept 87
Hewstone, M. 56
Hiele, P.M. van 117
Hockett, C. 24
Hodson, D. 59
Hofstadter, A. 24
Holt Reynolds, D. 198
Huberman, M. 233
Hunting, R.P. 193, 231–47, 278, 285, 286
hypothetical learning trajectories 220–1, 285

identity 56
inclusion 237
indeterminacy 27–9
indirect learning 155
information processing models 310
Inhelder, B. 57
inquiry teaching 282–3, 285–7
insecurity 207
insiders 197
insight 241–2
instrumentalism 5, 154
intelligence 38, 39, 52, 122
interaction 130, 184
interactionism 218, 305
Interdisciplinary Research on Number (IRON) project 103, 180, 181
interpretation 241
interpretive framework 158–70

intersubjectivity 16, 31, 184–5, 281, 282, 291–2
isomorphisms 13

Jaworski, B. 234
Johnson, D.K. 277
Johnston, K. 200
Johnston Slack, M. 197
Jungwirth, E. 197

Kant, I. 17, 50, 52, 101, 183
Kaput, J.J. 161
Katz, S. 11
Kelly, G. 47, 80
Kenny, V. 85, 88
Kieren, T. 35, 69–79, 93, 94–6, 101, 153, 191, 265, 277, 304
Kitchener, R.F. 16, 18, 19
Konold, C. 277

Lachance, A. 157
Lampert, M. 160, 226
Lana Project 29, 30
Langer, S. 23–4
language 23–33, 231, 235–7, 256, 284–5, 295
Larochelle, M. 35, 55–68, 95, 96, 195, 196, 197–8, 201; epistemic reflexivity 282; ethics 101–2, 298, 299; self 92, 93; viability 191
Latour, B. 62
Lave, J. 243, 306
Lawson 195
learning-as-control paradigm 233
learning problems 134–51
learning to learn 47, 85–8
Lemke, J.L. 59, 196
Lenart, I. 108, 121
Lerman, S. 154, 291–2, 293
Lessard, N. 200
levels of experience 92–4
Lévi-Strauss, C. 41
Levin, H.M. 134
Lewin, P. 5, 35–54, 298; accommodation 122; Gash's response 80–90; Kieren's response 69–79; Larochelle's response 55–68; paradox of happy agreement 120, 179, 283; sedimentation 56; self 55; Steffe's response 91–102

323

Index

Lewontin, R. 40
Lortie, D. 197
love 48-9, 84
loxodromes 127
Lyons, C.A. 135

McClain, K. 159, 162, 163, 219
McGinn, M.K. 60
Mackay, D.M. 297, 301
McNeal, B. 214
McRobbie, C.J. 197
Maher, C.A. 235, 248
Mainzer, K. 305
Malcolm, N. 15
Malinowski, B. 27
Manning, P.K. 297
Maor, D. 200
map projections 107
Masters, G. 136
math wars 295
Mathy, P. 63
Matthews, M.R. 5
Maturana, H. 28, 30, 80, 84, 88, 186, 189; autopoesis 40; communication 235; consensual domain 185; errors 83; love 48-9; observers 99, 303; scientific explanation 308; shared environment 304; social system 187; structural dance 75, 78
Maund, J.B. 12, 13
Mayer-Smith, J. 278
Mead, G.H. 16
meaning 7, 25, 28-9, 30, 120, 184, 185, 220, 236-7, 245
Mecca 108-11, 114, 115-16
Mehan, H. 154
Meisels, S.J. 135
Mercator projection 107
metalogue 198
metaphor of construction 280
metaphysics 83-4
Michelson xii-xiii
Miller, D.E. 305
misinterpretation 4-6
mitigated realism 203, 204, 279, 280
Moon, B. 278
Morf, A. 55, 57, 61
Morgan, M. 86
Morley xii-xiii

Moscovici, S. 56
motion-picture paradigm 153
Mousley, J. 245
Movitype screen 12-13, 14, 16
Muller, J. 60
multiple-frame paradigm 153

naive realism 203
nature nurture debate 137-8
negotiation 120, 155, 219, 220
network of properties 120-2
Nickerson, S. 310
Nickson, M. 153
nihilism 46, 47, 88
Noddings, N. 296
Noumenon 17, 18
number concept 5, 19-20
Nunes, T. 153

object-determinate description 13
objectivity 12
O'Brien, T.C. 295, 296
observation 241
observers 303
occasioning 75-8
ontological reality 37
ontology xii, 5-6, 15
operating stage/structure 56
owning 240

paideia 35, 37-54, 69-79, 91, 94-9, 101, 121, 122
paidia 121, 122
Pajares, F.M. 197, 198
Palmquist, B.C. 196
Panglossian World 40
paradigm change 43
paradox of happy agreement 43, 45, 48, 120, 121, 179, 283
parallelism 121
Paris, S.G. 234
pedagogical knowledge 242
perception 12, 16-18, 216-17
personal constructs 47, 78
personality 233, 295
perturbation 259, 260, 261
phenomena 185-6
phenomenology 183
Phenomenon 17, 18

phronesis 39, 52
Piaget, J. 3, 6–8, 92, 93, 139, 154, 188; adaptation 122; cognitive core 181; contexts 40; debate xiii; epistemological reflection 59; genetic epistemology 4, 44, 292, 294, 304; intelligence 38; language 295; operating stage/structure 56; problem creation 198; reflection 59; reflective abstraction 5; social aspect 11; students' knowledge 57
Piattelli-Palmarini, M. xiii, 295
Pinnell, G.S. 135, 138
Pirie, S. 77, 153, 265
Pirsig, M.R. 82
place-value 216–17
plane geometry 107, 121, 124, 127, 130
Platonism 300
Plomin, R. 138
polar maps 107, 125
poles 106–7
Popper, K. 43, 45
population parameters 302
poststructuralism 47
Potari, D. 193, 248–76, 285–6
potentialities, multiplication 61
powerlessness 85
Prawat, R.S. 274
preformation 7
professional development 134–51
Prus, R.C. 305
psyche 39, 47
psychological perspective 158
Putnam, H. 154, 215

re-interpretation 241
re-production cycle 193, 195–212, 278
realism 17, 203, 204, 279, 280
Realistic Mathematics Education (RME) 157, 225
reality xii, 81–2, 84–5, 195, 233, 281; experiential 5, 37, 46, 51, 281; ontological 37
reconceptualization 214, 215, 234, 248, 260
recovery education 134–51, 181–2, 187
recursive theory 153
reflection 303
reflective abstraction 5

reflective discourse 219
reflective practice 234
reflexive monitoring 58, 65
reflexive theories 298
reflexivity 155, 156, 173, 187, 193, 198, 282, 301
reform-based teacher education 216
relativism 203
relativity 97, 100
remedial education 135
remediation 136–7
representation 26–7
representational contexts 219
representational perspective 263
representational view 215, 300
Resnick, L. 138
respect 82
revolving door 113–15, 128
Richards, J. 3, 44, 236, 304
rightness 89
Rommetveit, R. 12, 17
Rorty, R. 58, 154
Rosch, E. 72
Roth, W.-M. 60
Ruel, F. 197, 200
Ryan, A.G. 196, 200

Sandefur, J. 305
Sarason, S.B. 243
Schaafsma, W. 107–8, 110, 112, 113, 115, 123–8
schema of docility 58
Schifter, D. 226, 235, 248
Schmidt, S.J. 23–33, 184, 185
Schommer, M. 86
Schubauer-Léoni, M.L. 62
Schutz, A. 6, 12, 17
Schwingendorf, K. 294
second-order observers/models 302–4
sedimentation 56, 75
Segal, L. 56, 63
selection pressure 75
self 14, 35, 38, 46, 47, 52, 55–6, 87, 88, 91–4
self-reflexivity 281–2, 305
self-regulation 233–5
Sellars, R.W. 12, 15
semantic analysis 25–6, 27
semanticity 284, 285

Index

Sense-Datum theory 11
Sfard, A. 152–3
Shannon, C. 24, 28
shared meanings 120, 220
Shonkoff, J.P. 135
signs 23–4, 27, 30, 172, 284–5, 297
silence 238–40
Simmel, G. 17
Simon, M.A. 157, 193, 213–30, 238, 279, 280, 281–2, 283, 295; conception-based perspective 286; inquiry teaching 285; reconceptualization 248; teaching cycles 244
simplification 265
single-frame paradigm 152–3
situatedness 37, 38, 45, 48, 300
slavery 49
Slavin, R.E. 135
Smith, E. 153, 308
Smith, J. 135
Smith, L. 282–3
'smorgasbord' approach 224
Smythies, J.R. 16
social constructivism 304–5
social context 35, 152–78, 183, 184
social dimension 304–7
social interaction 6–8
social norms 160
social perspective 158
social support 88
social systems 187, 235
social theory 41–2
socialization 7
sociomathematical norms 161–3
Socrates 139
solid geometry 107
solipsism 10, 11, 14, 15, 281, 307
spherical geometry 105–33
spontaneous development 93–4
Sprangler, D. 253, 255
Stanger, G. 144
Steffe, L.P. 3, 91–102, 139, 154, 185, 226, 248, 249, 258; attention to students 218; conceptual analysis 307, 308–9; early learning 138; first and second-order models 302–4; goals 185, 222; motion-picture paradigm 153; number concept 5, 164; perspectives on practice 179–92; recovery education 134, 141, 142; self-reflexivity 282; social context 154; teacher education 277–88; teacher-researcher 250, 253, 255, 267, 270, 273, 274; teachers' knowledge 241; videotaping 144
Stengers, I. 64
Stephan, M. 171
stereotypes 83, 85, 86
Stewart, R. 134, 147
Stiegelbauer, S. 233, 243
Streefland, L. 157, 225
subject–object dichotomy 205, 206, 209, 279
subjective awareness 91
subjective environment 107
subjective reconstruction 155, 184
subjectivity 28–9
Sullivan, P. 245
Sumara, D. 75
superego 47
Support Teacher Learning Difficulties (STLD) 137
Sutton, C. 63
symbolic interactionism 305
symbols 24, 27, 30
symmetry 58, 60

task oriented approach 219
Taylor, N. 60
Taylor, P.C. 200
teacher-researchers 248–76
teachers: development 134–51, 213–30; education 193–288; mathematical knowledge 242; pedagogical knowledge 242; preparation 195–212
teacher's dilemma 253
teaching cycle 141, 193, 220, 221–2, 244
Terhart, E. 59
Thompson, A.G. 306, 308
Thompson, E. 72
Thompson, P.W. 3, 153, 226, 248, 249, 258, 270, 291–315
thought experiments 186
Throne, J. 245
thrownness 6, 38
Tobin, K. 197
tolerance 80, 81, 121–2, 297
Toulmin, S. 10
traditional model 278–9

Treffers, A. 157, 160, 182, 183, 184
trivial constructivism 280, 281–5
Trumbull, D. 197
truth xii, 195
Tzur, M. 215
Tzur, R. 219, 226, 249, 267, 308

undecidability 96–7, 207
unexpected responses 237–41, 285
units 19–20

validity 88
Varela, F. 40, 72, 75, 78
viability 35, 57–62, 72–5, 81, 122, 154, 191; decidability 99; *paideia* 37, 39–49, 51; second order 281
Vico 48
Views on Science, Technology and Society (VOSTS) questionnaire 200–1, 204
Voigt, J. 58, 62, 153, 155, 162, 226
Vygotsky, L. 141

Wagner, W. 196, 209
Walkerdine, V. 172
Wasik, B.A. 135
Watzlawick, P. 99

Wenger, E. 243
Wheatley, G. 139, 166
Whitenack, J. 219
Whitenack, J.W. 163
Whitson, J.A. 174
whole-class teaching 226
Wideen, M. 278
Wiegel, H. 153, 282
Wiener, N. 24
Wilcox, S. 11
Wiles, A. 84
Wilson, P. 296
Winnicott 47
Wittgenstein, L. 11–12, 16–17, 18, 89
Wood, H. 154
Wood, T. 215, 217, 248
Wright, E. 10–22, 183
Wright, R.J. 103, 134–51, 180, 181–2, 187, 188, 190, 284–5

Yackel, E. 138, 155, 157, 158, 161, 162, 215, 217, 225
Young-Loveridge, J. 135

Zakhalaka, M. 197
Zeichner, K. 209
Zeichner, K.M. 196